The Resilience of Democracy

The Resilience of Democracy

Learnings from Stability Theory of Complex Systems

Joseph Livni

• HART •

OXFORD • LONDON • NEW YORK • NEW DELHI • SYDNEY

HART PUBLISHING
Bloomsbury Publishing Plc
Kemp House, Chawley Park, Cumnor Hill, Oxford, OX2 9PH, UK
1359 Broadway, New York, NY 10018, USA
Bloomsbury Publishing Ireland Limited, 29 Earlsfort Terrace, Dublin 2, D02 AY28, Ireland

First published in the United States of America 2026

Cover design by Jason Enterline
Cover image by Joseph Livni

A catalogue record for this book is available from the British Library.

Library of Congress Cataloging-in-Publication Data

Names: Livni, Joseph author
Title: The resilience of democracy: learnings from stability theory of complex systems / Joseph Livni.
Description: Oxford ; New York: Bloomsbury Academic, 2026. | Includes bibliographical references and index.
Identifiers: LCCN 2025032982 (print) | LCCN 2025032983 (ebook) | ISBN 9781666965216 hardback | ISBN 9781666965230 paperback | ISBN 9781978760097 epub | ISBN 9798216264453 pdf | ISBN 9781978747098
Subjects: LCSH: Constitutional law | Constitutional law—North America | Democracy | Stability | Equilibrium (Economics)
Classification: LCC K3165 .L59 2026 (print) | LCC K3165 (ebook) | DDC 342—dc23/eng/20250729
LC record available at https://lccn.loc.gov/2025032982
LC ebook record available at https://lccn.loc.gov/2025032983

ISBN: HB: 978-1-6669-6521-6
ePDF: 979-8-2162-6445-3
eBook: 978-1-9787-6009-7

Typeset by Deanta Global Publishing Services, Chennai, India

Contents

Introduction

History provides examples of vibrant civilizations, including powerful empires, wealthy kingdoms, and strong leagues of city-states that collapsed. The Western Roman Empire is probably the most studied example. It disintegrated in small little county-size political entities. Pharaonic Egypt ceased to exist. Later, the end of the First World War heralded the collapse of three grand empires: the Austro-Hungarian, the Ottoman, and the Czarist Empire. The Second World War not only terminated the Third Reich but also brought to an end the worldwide colonial rule of France and Britain.

Scholars studied the reasons of these and similar events. The multitude of theories explaining the causes of each collapse indicates that deducing the past is not a safe endeavor. Moreover, other scholars engage in a more risky business: foretelling the future collapse of current sociopolitical regimes in general and democracies in particular.

The reader has heard and read many doomsday warnings predicting the end of democracy. Generally speaking these warnings reflect intuitive negativity of politicians, journalists, and scholars.[1] One should distinguish between instinctual predicting collapse in association with political players with *bad intentions* and quantitative examination pinpointing at side effects of *well-intentioned* government directives.

The topic of resilience of democracies has been studied by scholars. For example, seven chapters of an edited book and seventeen contributors, mostly political scientists, treat the subject.[2] Not surprisingly, contributors invoke political factors of toughening resilience of democracies, for example: *strong legislature*,[3] judicial review working as a "brake against autocratization,"[4] accountability,[5] depolarization,[6] and civic education.[7] This book offers another angle. It starts with the notion that sociopolitical entities are multifunctional organizations; each function is administered according to determined objectives and policies; the government specifies the functions; branches of the executive monitor specific functions. The functions are not independent. The chapters of this book explain how governmental responsibilities and actions are intertwined; as a consequence, monitoring one function generates unintended responses of other functions. This type of system of multifunctional entanglement is not news. The chapters of this book discuss that nature and technology consist of exactly that type of system. Nature and technology also combine extinction and evolution. Studies of such resilience are known as investigations of equilibrium and stability. These studies show that in spite of different disciplines, the stability of all systems is a question of adequate negative feedback control loops (see Chapter 3 and Figure 3.4); on the other hand instability is caused by positive feedback loops. Not surprisingly, sociopolitical systems follow the same laws; identical mathematical relationships represent the coupling of factors determining equilibrium and stability.[8]

Consequently, this book looks at a quantitative approach examining factors of societal resilience. It is multidisciplinary. After all, translating the interdependence of societal functions of a state to algebraic expressions of dependence of one variable on many others requires linking algebra with various other disciplines like law, political science, and economics. Algebra solves equations. Understanding the relationship between factors requires exploring social, legal, economic, and other knowledge; this understanding is necessary to formulate the equations.

A sensible examination of resilience of democracy requires a unique interpretation of the term *societal resilience*. There are several interpretations of the terms *societal resilience*[9] or *democratic resilience*.[10] For our purpose, *resilience* is the capability of a social system to return to its equilibrium after a shock. This interpretation originates from studies of nature and technology. Nevertheless, it is often found in social studies as well.[11]

Chapter 1 answers a question related to the point of departure of this book: Can exact science contribute anything to understanding the equilibrium and stability of sociopolitical systems? On one hand *Equilibrium and Stability* of natural systems is a discipline widely utilized in science and technology (Chapter 1 lists examples). Establishing conditions of equilibrium and examining the stability the equilibria are problems solvable by "the application of rules and principles in an established way."[12] Moreover the mathematical expressions utilized in such problems are identical across all the disciplines studying equilibrium and stability. This is typical to many distinct applications that can be solved by a common algebraic expression (see, for example, Table 0.1).

The chapter makes the case for using the expressions studying equilibrium and stability in various fields of engineering and science in studying *resilience of democracies*. This book is multidisciplinary, bridging science of equilibrium and stability in nature and technology with equilibrium and stability in society in general and democratic societies in particular. Consequently, Chapter 1 explains the terms, scientific method, and scientific knowledge; subsequently, the chapter describes tools of determining conditions of equilibrium and criteria of stability of equilibrium. These tools comply with requirements of the rigorous scientific method.

The chapter discusses the analogy of equilibrium of a physical system (aircraft) and a sociopolitical system. An aircraft at constant speed and level flight is in equilibrium. A society with steady socioeconomic parameters (political establishment, prices, demographics, GDP, crime, power centralization, etc.) is also in equilibrium. The quantitative determination of the parameters requires the same algebraic routine.

Table 0.1 The Mathematics Consists of the Same Equation; It Is Applied in Several Applications with Different Meaning

Application	a	x	y	Expression
Mechanics	Speed [Miles/hour]	Time [hours]	Distance [miles]	
Economy	Price [$/lbs.]	Wheat [lbs.]	Cost [$]	$y = ax$
Fluids	Density [lbs./gallon]	Liquid [gallons]	Weight	

The chapter continues to discuss the stability of systems. Both in nature and in society one evaluates the response of the system at equilibrium to a small disturbance. If the parameters return to their values at the previous equilibrium, the system is stable. The mathematical procedure determining whether the parameters return to their previous values in systems in nature, technology, and society is the same. Once stability is determined, different applications have separate conclusions. In aircraft, stability assures flight safety. In sociopolitical systems, stability analysis results indicate whether certain interventions have stabilizing or destabilizing effects.

Unlike all the others, Chapter 2 is heavy in mathematical jargon, equations, derivations, and demonstrations. If that is bad news, then the good news is that readers may skip the chapter. It provides the algebraic foundations of the logic of the thesis that a growing multitude of interrelated government-controlled undertakings, strong centralization, and slow economic growth bring to societal instability and often to sudden disintegration. The following chapters substantiate the thesis in commonsense terms. The chapter has been inserted because the case for the message of the book is incomplete without the algebraic evidence. Moreover, I met scholars in social studies who are fluent in mathematical jargon. For these two reasons, Chapter 2 presents and mathematically discusses the equilibrium and stability model proving the case. It explains that interrelated acts and consequences of acts of governmental systems are mathematically represented by a system of algebraic equations; the algebraic expressions of these relations are the same as the system of equations of any set of controlled interdependent magnitudes of complex systems in nature, physics, or technological process. Therefore, following consensual procedures it arrives at the conclusion that growing the number of governmental branches of activities has under certain conditions destabilizing effect. The chapter extracts the conditions that accelerate the progression of the system toward the brink of instability or collapse.

Chapter 3 returns to intelligible language. It starts with an everyday mechanical example consisting of the temperature control of hot water in a tank; it explains in commonsense sentences how the desired temperature is maintained; the explanation is helpful because of the analogy to societal control: both consist of determining a policy, detecting deviations and initiating corrective actions. Subsequently the chapter illustrates the analogy by comparing temperature control with capital control of a business. Both the temperature and capital control monitor one single magnitude. The chapter then slightly increases the complexity by elevating the number of controlled elements to two. The analogy of prey and predator populations to criminal population size and police size allows illustrating why the algebraic expressions of the population size dynamics are identical in both domains of study. The example introduces the term *state variables,* which in this case consist of the studied population sizes. This analogy opens the door to the concept that the same algebra may express similar dynamics in nature and society.

The chapter then turns to treat a complex society with many interrelated *state variables.* The examination of equilibrium and stability examination is exemplified by a factual sociopolitical system that grew in complexity and collapsed: the Roman Empire. The example helps explaining what government state variables are, why and how are they interrelated, how governmental acts controlling one *state variable* affects another, and how an intended correction can create unintended effects not only on other state variables but also on the *state variable* the corrective action was initiated. This occurs when the chain of state variable creates a closed loop. Such a loop is called *positive feedback loop.* The term *feedback loop* signifies that the unintended side effect affects the very state variable for which the intended corrective action has been activated. The attribute *positive* suggests that the unintended effect *increases* the deviation opposing the intended corrective action which decreases the deviation.

A positive feedback loops harms the controllability of a *state variable.* The chapter continues to explain why adding more *state variables* by increasing the number of governmental spheres of action the controllability of the system is reduced. The chapter refers to the mathematical demonstration of Chapter 2 showing that one can reach a critical number of state variables; if a system possessing more than such a critical number of state variables is at equilibrium, then any small nudge on the system will disallow the return to its previous equilibrium. Such a system is technically *instable.* Archaeologists use the term *collapse* for reaching societal instability.[13]

Chapter 4 examines the resilience of constitutional democracies without equations. It justifies the association of the term *social complexity* with the number of *state variables* a government controls. It discusses that the term *stratification* is well defined when discussing aristocratic systems with practically impenetrable borders between classes. However, enlightenment, democracy, and industrialization replaced *aristocracy* with *meritocracy* in the sense of opportunities to climb social ladders, or in Heywood's words:

> Meritocracy: Literally, rule by those with merit, merit being intelligence plus effort; a meritocratic society is one in which social position is determined exclusively by ability and hard work.[14]

The chapter shows that socio-physical examination of democratic societies sheds light on stabilizing factors such as separation of powers, decentralization of the government system, control of unelected administrators by elected officials, political participation, and strict checks and balances.

Chapter 5 deals with crime control. Theoretically, crime control is one of two most essential functions of the state; if crime control or defense fail, the system fails regardless how well other functions work. About defense we have plenty of evidence: Babylon's defeat to the Achaemenid Empire in 539 BCE marked the end of the a remarkable civilization, Pharaonic Egypt became a province of the Roman Empire in 30 BCE; in 1572 the Inca Empire fell to Spanish conquerors and ceased to exist. There are theories directly relating crime to "the collapse of the state authority."[15] Researchers of emerging democracies associate hazards with "crime and the resulting civil insecurity that endangers the nascent democratic government."[16] Crime is one of many uncontrollable state variables in current unbalanced governmental system of Haiti characterized by a gang violence–induced "insecurity crisis and a lack of State legitimacy."[17] The World Bank report[18] points at a likely vicious circle destabilizing a governmental system (see also Figure 0.1).

Chapter 5 makes the case for the argument that crime occurs because crime pays. The chapter mentions and disputes competing theories. It returns to the model of crime control of Chapter 3 in order to discuss the two factors controlling criminality at equilibrium: deterrence and recidivism. The chapter discusses the causes, the effects, and the treatment of recidivism. The chapter focuses on two controversial treatments: education and stigma.

Chapter 6 tackles the topic of *resilience* of democracy from the angle of a failed democracy. The Weimar Republic was a democracy with a Constitution; the Weimar Republic failed. The chapter claims that the Weimar Republic failed not because of mistakes in its Constitution, but because of the absence of constitutionalism. Therefore, the chapter starts off by explaining the difference between Constitution and *constitutionalism*.

The consensus is that the Weimar Constitution was flawed. For example checks and balances were weak. The chapter agrees with the opinion; for example, it stresses the weakness of judicial review. Nevertheless, the chapter explains why the judicial review of the Weimar Constitution was anemic. It compares the cultural legacies of the Weimar Republic with the United States of 1776: namely, Imperial Germany with Colonial America. It explains that Puritans and their reverence for a covenant carved into the civic culture a concept of forcing the government to act within contractual boundaries. The legacy of the Weimar Republic came from an Imperial government that was limited only by a self-imposed willingness to address concerns of the governed.

Usually scholars spotted Article 48 as the principle fault of the Weimar Constitution. The article indeed played a role in the demise of the Republic. It was invoked by the enactment of the infamous Fire Decree suspending most civil liberties under

Figure 0.1 Crime's destabilizing effect. Author's work.

the pretense of preventing violence; Article 48 authorized the President to sign the decree. The Constitution was problematic; nevertheless, it had a remedy. It prescribed overruling such a presidential decree by the Reichstag. The elected Reichstag did not act. Nonexistent constitutionalism and imperial traditions set off the extinction of the Weimar democracy. American framers of the constitution had a preliminary model as a starting point. It consisted of written and unwritten constitutions controlling the day-to-day governmental practice. In Europe constitutions could not reflect a pre-constitutional democratic practice because Europe's constitutions launched the transition from autocracy to democracy. In Europe framers of constitutions had to rely on inspiration and on a pool of visionary thinkers known as the Enlightenment. Chapter 6 compares the typical effects of the Enlightenment in general and in Germany in particular. The general case is illustrated using France as an example. In the particular case of Germany the ideas of the Enlightenment were applied not to mark a transition toward democracy but toward an enlightened despotism. In Germany both before and during the Weimar Republic, education realized great achievements. However, neither the enlightened despotism nor democratic Weimar achieved anything in educating toward democratic values. The chapter looks through researches proving the contrary.

The chapter questions what impact education has on acquiring democratic values in other democracies. Studies indicate that in spite of expectations, *culturati* do not possess stronger affinity toward democracy than anyone else.

Chapter 7 describes several current democracies from the point of view of constitutionalism and stability. The chapter is not aspiring to cover the constitutional stability of the world. Such an endeavor would be as pretentious as unfeasible. The aim is to illustrate the relationship between constitutionalism and stability of the constitutional democracy. Therefore, the examples are not according to common political categories like New World and Old World, or First, Second, and Third World.

Asian democracies are not discussed in this book. Chapter 7 provides an explanation why not. One of the most populous democracies in the world is India. India is one of the most ancient civilizations; India evolved along the history accumulating a diversity of political constructions with a large variation in time and space. I propose to read the following statement regarding the state of Andhra Pradesh in order to underline the theoretical complexity of the political fragmentation of this vast and ancient subcontinent:

> The rich peasantry of the Reddy, Kamma and Kapu castes, which were the main beneficiaries of the above reforms, thus constituted the core support base of the Congress Party in the countryside.[19]

The quote refers to the land reform of the Andhra Pradesh government transferring land ownership from landlords to tenants. The quote opens the window to a variety of factors in play in terms of public state of mind; the socialism of Congress Party coexists with ancient caste classifications; we detect enthusiasm for legislating property confiscation which probably encountered ancient values opposing such acts. The land reform in Andhra Pradesh was carried out differently than in other states, for example, in West Bengal.[20] Land confiscation is incompatible with constitutionalism. According to Article 39 (b) of the Indian Constitution, "ownership and control of material resources should be distributed to serve the common good." This affirmation sounds more like a political election platform than a legal decree. It is not enforceable; it does not authorize anyone to distribute or redistribute property; nevertheless, in terms of state of mind it rules out constitutionalism. Hopefully the reader will understand why the stability of Indian democracy cannot be related to constitutionalism or analyzed using classical models of government stability. India is the most populous democracy; however, it is also the most diversified in its constituent roots. Consequently the stability of Indian democracy is out of scope.

Chapter 7 lumps together democracies according to similarities in their history of constitutionalism: Latin America, Europe, and constitutional democracies of the British Parliamentary system. The constitutional democracy of the United States deserves a special chapter, and it is portrayed in Chapter 8.

Chapter 8 is dedicated to the United States. Constitutionalism came to existence in the United States; the US Constitution served as model for the rest of the world. Therefor the United States deserves a chapter comparing it with other democracies as far as its system's equilibrium and stability are concerned. The chapter starts off by revisiting the relationship between constitutionalism and constitution. It shows that in the United States constitutionalism preceded the Constitution; constitutionalism made the Constitution both necessary and possible. The chapter subsequently substantiates why three government functions play key roles in keeping the US democracy in equilibrium and determining the stability of the equilibrium. The chapter identifies the three central functions as judicial review, government structure, and academia. The two first functions are described as typical American; they stemmed from colonial roots and have been captured by the framers in the Constitution. Academia with its education and research function is an integral part of the global academic establishment with two contradictory impacts on the constitutional democratic system:

a. The US academia is the locomotive of American scientific progress and economic growth; both have stabilizing effects on the democratic system.
b. Academic staff on US campuses is engaged also in destabilizing endeavors both in its education branch and in some of its research activities.

Chapter 8 closes by determining that after all, the United States has been the most resilient democracy from its inception.

Chapter 9 illustrates by example the hidden stability perils involved in grand-scale projects initiated, encouraged, timetabled, protected, and funded by government. The example is the electric vehicle project. The chapter envisages a great future for the electric vehicle. As long as the pace of the conversion from fossil fuels is dictated by market-driven supply and demand, the project does not endanger the governmental system. The chapter scans problems related to supply of electric power, battery prices, battery end-of-life disposal means, power lines' reliability, and health hazards. The role of government is not to hasten the project but to insist on determining risks and regulating their mitigation.

The role of private enterprise is to plan, test, and prove the safety and reliability of the vehicle and of its energy demands. The increase in demand dictates the rate of progress; consequently, the private sector is motivated to fund and constantly improve the product and its infrastructure. Stability concerns require that the government detect deviations from public safety regulations and initiate corrective actions.

Inverting the roles, namely, government promoting the project and the private sector regulating itself to meet risk mitigation requirements, is destabilizing.

Notes

1 e.g. Miguel Goede, "The Future of Democracy: The End of Democracy as We Know It," *Kybernetes* 48, no. 10 (2019): 2235–65.

2 Anna Lührmann and Wolfgang Merkel, *Resilience of Democracy: Responses to Illiberal and Authoritarian Challenges* (Milton Park and Abingdon: Routledge, 2023).

3 Ibid., 7.

4 Vanessa A. Boese et al., "How Democracies Prevail: Democratic Resilience as a Two-Stage Process," in *Resilience of Democracy: Responses to Illiberal and Authoritarian Challenges*, ed. Anna Lührmann and Wolfgang Merkel (Milton Park and Abingdon: Routledge, 2023), 17–39.

5 Melis G. Laebens and Anna Lührmann, "What Halts Democratic Erosion? The Changing Role of Accountability," ibid, 40–60.

6 Murat Somer, Jennifer L. McCoy, and Russell E. Luke, "Pernicious Polarization, Autocratization and Opposition Strategies," ibid, 61–80.

7 Steven E. Finkel and Junghyun Lim, "The Supply and Demand Model of Civic Education: Evidence from a Field Experiment in the Democratic Republic of Congo," ibid, 102–23.

8 See also Joseph Livni, "Investigation of Collapse of Complex Socio-Political Systems Using Classical Stability Theory," *Physica A: Statistical Mechanics and Its Applications* 524 (2019): 553–62.

9 For example "we argue that the current "undefinition" of resilience is not entirely undesirable for social studies," Rosanne Anholt et al., "Understanding Societal Resilience: The Case for Engaged Scholarship," in *Multisystemic Resilience: Adaptation and Transformation in Contexts of Change*, ed. Michael Ungar (New York: Oxford University Press, 2021), 555.

10 Lührmann and Merkel, *Resilience of Democracy: Responses to Illiberal and Authoritarian Challenges.*

11 See Rosanne Anholt et al. "Understanding Societal Resilience: The Case for Engaged Scholarship," 552; Peter J. Burnell and Peter Calvert, *The Resilience of Democracy: Persistent Practice, Durable Idea* (London and Portland: F. Cass, 1999), 19; Lührmann and Merkel, *Resilience of Democracy: Responses to Illiberal and Authoritarian Challenges*, 872. "the ability to withstand [internal and external challenges] without (major) changes.

12 Beth-Anne Schuelke-Leech, "The Place of Wicked Problems in Engineering Problem Solving: A Proposed Taxonomy" (paper presented at the 2020 IEEE International Symposium on Technology and Society (ISTAS), 2020).

13 Bernardo Mingarelli, "Collapse of the Hunnic Empire: Jordanes, Ardaric and the Battle of Nedao" (Ottawa: Université d'Ottawa/University of Ottawa, 2018); C. Bottari, M. Coltelli, and C. Monaco, "Evidence of Late Roman Collapse at Catania (Sicily, Southern Italy): An Earthquake in the 4th Century AD?," *Quaternary International* 357 (2015): 336–46; Brandon L. Drake, "The Influence of Climatic Change on the Late Bronze Age Collapse and the Greek Dark Ages," *Journal of Archaeological Science* 39, no. 6 (2012): 1862–70; Eric H. Cline, *1177 B.C.: The Year Civilization Collapsed*, Kindle edition (Princeton: Princeton University Press, 2015); Joseph A. Tainter, *The Collapse of Complex Societies* (Cambridge: Cambridge University Press, 1990).

14 Andrew Heywood, "Conservatism—A Defence for the Privileged and Prosperous?," *Politics Review* 25, issue 1 (2015).

15 Vladimir Popov, "The State in the New Russia (1992–2004): From Collapse to Gradual Revival?," *PONARS Policy Memos* 324 (2004).

16 Orlando J. Pérez, "Democratic Legitimacy and Public Insecurity: Crime and Democracy in El Salvador and Guatemala," *Political Science Quarterly* 118 (2003): 627.

17 Thomas Cantens et al., "Haiti: Strengthening Customs Administration in an Insecure Environment" (Washington, DC: World Bank Publications, 2024).

18 Ibid.

19 Karli Srinivasulu, "Caste, Class and Social Articulation in Andhra Pradesh: Mapping Differential Regional Trajectories" (Hyderabad: Osmania University, 2002).

20 Tim Hanstad and Jennifer Brown, "Land Reform Law and Implementation in West Bengal: Lessons and Recommendations" (Seattle: Landesa, Rural Development Institute, 2001).

1

Equilibrium and Stability Studies in Nature, Technology, and Society

Primer

The theme of this book is resilience of democracies. This chapter seems to deviate from this theme; bear with me, the relevance will soon be substantiated. The chapter takes off by discussing a series of catastrophic events in aviation related to instability of flight control systems. The first reassuring argument in favor of relevance is that *stability* in physics is equivalent to *resilience* in social studies.[1] Analyzing stability of aircraft is a requirement of compliance with airworthiness regulations.[2] Scientific methods assuring safety of flight and compliance with regulations had to be utilized and validated. Not surprisingly, the mathematical expressions for *equilibrium and stability* of aircraft is the same as in other technical fields like electrical engineering,[3] mechanical engineering,[4] civil engineering,[5] transportation dynamics,[6] population dynamics,[7] and biomathematics.[8] Consequently it is safe to address this standard methodology as *classical equilibrium and stability analysis.*

After reviewing the meaning of the term *scientific methods*, the chapter turns to shed light on the applicability of the *classical equilibrium and stability analysis* in the study of resilience of social systems. The practical outcome of social system stability studies is differentiating between stabilizing and destabilizing governmental lines of action.

Aircraft Accident of Flight UA585 of March 1991

On March 3, 1991, United Airlines Flight UA585 crashed. The aircraft accident investigation of case UA585 was not conclusive. The NTSB report[9] submitted two theories that could explain the accident (Table 1.1).

By 1994, three very similar airline accidents had been investigated. All three involved Boeing 737 aircraft (Table 1.2)

The NTSB accident report of flight US427 analyzed all three cases of Table 1.2 and examined four probable causes for the accident.[10] The examination involved flight simulations and physical tests. The physical examination of the equipment showed

Table 1.1 Probable Causes Identified for UA585

#	Probable Cause - NTSB report
1	A malfunction of the airplane's lateral [roll] or directional control system
2	An encounter with an unusually severe atmospheric disturbance

Table 1.2 Three Similar Boeing 737 Fatal Accidents

Date	Flight	Aircraft Model	Designation in This Chapter
March 3, 1991	United Airlines Flight 585	Boeing 737-291	UA585
June 9, 1996	Eastwind Flight 517	Boeing 737-200	W9517
September 8, 1994	US Airways Flight 427	Boeing 737-300	US427

Table 1.3 Investigation of Probable Causes (1999)

#	Theory	Page	
		Considered	Ruled Out
1	Dual slam jam	100	273
2	Secondary slide jam	100	
3	Physical jam in the rudder system input linkage	100	273
4	Crewcommanded, sustained left-rudder input	100	272

no evidence for theories 1, 2, and 3 of Table 1.3; the flight data examination ruled out theory 4 of Table 1.3 and theory 2 of Table 1.1. Theories 1, 2, and 3 of Table 1.3 are particular variants of theory 1 of Table 1.1.

The NTSB report of 1999 did conclude that the cause of the accidents is theory 2 of Table 1.3 in spite of "no physical evidence" of secondary slide jam. Dedicated tests showed that dual slam jam and input linkage jam must leave evidence, while secondary slide jam does not necessarily leave evidence. The principle "absence of evidence is not evidence of absence"[11] implies that:

1. If an event occurs and it must leave evidence then the absence of evidence proves that the event did not occur.
2. If an event may occur without leaving evidence, or there is no way to find the evidence due to circumstances of time, location, or means of detection then the absence of evidence proves nothing.

Consequently, the report scientifically proved that the accident occurred because of loss of control of the directional control system of the aircraft. The pilots properly deflected the rudder to correct a wrong direction of the airplane; however, the airplane flew at an excessive speed producing sufficient aerodynamic pressure to reverse the rudder action; this created a so-called *secondary slide jam*. In human language, this means that the more the pilot tried to correct the direction of the airplane, the more the airplane continued to turn in all three possible directions (Figure 1.3) conflicting with pilot's command. The airplane was uncontrollable, and it crashed. *Equilibrium and Stability* scholars call an uncontrollable system *unstable*.

The results of the NTSB investigation (1999) meet the criteria of *scientific conclusions*. The Introduction also mentioned the notion of stability. The next section focuses on the term *scientific conclusions*.

Science

Scientia (Science) is a Latin word for *knowledge*.[12] Nevertheless confusing knowledge with science is risky. Galilei, the scientist, distinguishes between two types of knowledge:

1. Opinions in a discussion in which neither true nor false applies, for example Hobbes claims that human nature is bad, i.e., every man is enemy to every man; Rousseau claims that human nature is good, i.e., man "breathes only peace and freedom."[13]
2. Conclusions of an analysis demonstrating that the knowledge is true. For example observing the free fall of bodies, Aristotle claimed "that the speed v of fall is proportional to the weight W of the body and inversely proportional to the density ρ of the medium."[14] Indeed a leaf falls faster than a branch. Scholars call this type of knowledge *inductive reasoning*.[15] Galilei proved that this intuition is false; Galilei carried out free fall tests dropping various bodies from the leaning tower of Pisa.[16] Comparing the time it takes for the bodies to reach the ground he proved that the speed is not proportional with weight. Both Aristotle's and Galilei's hypotheses are *scientific theories* because "their truth or falsity can be tested."[17] Aristotle's *inductive reasoning* was false, and Galilei's *scientific* results are true. *Scientific knowledge is a true scientific theory.*

The good news is that this interpretation of the term *scientific knowledge* is concise, clear, and easy to remember. The bad news is that the demarcation is not in consensus. I encountered an editor of a scientific publication who considers scientific knowledge to be *exclusively* pertinent to formal, natural, or applied sciences.

Some scientists consider that identifying scientific knowledge with true scientific theory is *old school*. The *new school* views science as researching "questions with ends opening in all directions."[18] My understanding of this interpretation is that according to the *new school* the Hobbs–Rousseau dialogue is also science. The new school challenges the old school, claiming that its education gives "students no opportunity to develop their powers of criticism and judgment."[19]

This book is not intended to disregard either open-ended question or educating for criticism and judgment. However, for the sake of clarity this book distinguishes between research looking for the true answer to a question that has only one true answer and many false answers and research that opens questions in various directions.

Accordingly, this work calls *scientific knowledge* analyses proving that their findings are *true*. Any other reasonable knowledge is a *scientific theory*.

It is worthwhile mentioning that scientific knowledge is not necessarily related to certain disciplines. Social sciences and even art[20] can also pose questions with one correct answer and many wrong answers. "Modern physics-based models of social, economic and political behaviour invoke idealizations of human behaviour that might make sociologists blanch."[21] This book deals with the resilience of constitutional democracies. Scholars of constitutional democracy need not be proficient in formal, natural, or applied sciences. This book uses classical scientifically proven procedures of *equilibrium and stability* and identifies which features of the discussed society are stabilizing and which are destabilizing. Such knowledge is scientific knowledge. According to Prof. Eugene Stanley[22] this type of knowledge belongs to socio-physics.

An investigation produces scientific knowledge if it complies with the requirements of the scientific method; the scientific method consists of three compulsory steps of knowledge: observation, theory, and proof.

Observation

> That all our knowledge begins with experience there can be no doubt.
>
> Immanuel Kant[23]

Little children do not fight with bigger children. They *know* better. This is knowledge; however, no one calls it science. Children do not touch burning flames; adults do not touch live electric wires. Adults know that milk can go bad, that meat should be cooked not too little and not too much, that smoking is bad for you, and that if one caught a cold, chicken soup alleviates one's misery. These examples of *knowledge* are typical observations.

Scientific Hypothesis

I will illustrate by example how the chicken soup observation progressed into a scientific hypothesis.

A dietician's research[24] of the composition of chicken soup identified some ingredients increasing appetite and decreasing inflammation in the airways. Inflammations are responsible for "stuffy or runny nose, sneezing, coughing and thickened mucus."[25] The research established that the *umami* taste of the soup increases appetite. This sounds scientific; however, when the report translates *umami* taste to *meaty* taste, one is still in the realm of observation. The knowledge steps into *hypothesis* when it connects the *umami* taste to *amino acid glutamate*. The hypothesis accumulates credibility with six *scientifically established facts* (see later what that means):

1. Amino acids are the building blocks of proteins.[26]
2. Some proteins heal inflammation.[27]

3. Inflammation causes stuffy or runny nose, sneezing, coughing, and thickened mucus.[28]
4. Chicken soup can, in fact, lower the number of white blood cells traveling to inflamed tissues.[29]
5. Lower white blood cell activity in the nasal passages can reduce inflammation.[30]

Not only Teeman the dietician recommends chicken soup, but also Maimonides a physician[31] and Sagan the physicist mentioned that "chicken soup is widely known to be good for life."[32] The hypothesis is a scientific hypothesis not because several scientists endorse it, but because it may be either true or false. The researches mentioned by Teeman[33] are proven to be true. However, what confidence can one have that the ingredients tested in vitro sufficiently act in vivo? How much soup, how often shall one repeat the treatment? What is the rate of inflammation reduction of someone who consumes 15 oz, of chicken soup compared to someone who does not consume any chicken soup at all? These questions are not meant to find fault with the hypothesis; they are meant to distinguish between a scientific hypothesis that has merit and scientific knowledge. The *chicken soup is good for life* hypothesis has merit; however, it is not scientific knowledge.

Proof

There are three fundamental approaches to validate a hypothesis: experimental tests, mathematical models, and statistic inference.

Experimental Tests

Tests are the most commonly accepted way to prove a hypothesis. This chapter already mentioned that Galilei proved by dropping objects that the gravity on Earth is constant. All sciences utilize tests. Tests have shortcomings:

a) Inadequate Instrumentation
b) Environmental effects (temperature, humidity, motion, wind, light, atmospheric pressure, etc.)
c) Signal Noise
d) Transducer defects
e) Human errors
f) Undocumented or poorly documented setup

Mathematical Models

A hypothesis can be mathematically tested. For example consider the following hypothesis:

Hypothesis 1—in pre-industrial era the fertility of women should be at least four births per generation in order to bring the population size to equilibrium (i.e., constant).

Table 1.4 Verification of Hypohesis Using a Mathematical Model of Population Growth

#	Hypothesis	Symbols
1	Population size at equilibrium	$N(t+1)=N(t)$
2	If Fertility = 4/generation	$f=4$
3	And If Infant mortality is according to pre-industrial records	$\mu=0.5$

The population will add $\frac{N}{2}f$ children because there are $\frac{N}{2}$ mothers and each mother gives birth f times. However, $\frac{N}{2}f\mu$ children will not survive the generation because they will die before reaching maturity. At the end of generation $t+1$ all $N(t)$ parents will die. The population growth is:

$$N(t+1)-N(t)=\frac{N}{2}f-\frac{N}{2}f\mu-N(t)$$

Left-hand side	Right-hand side
By hypothesis 1 the population is at zero growth; consequently the left-hand side is 0	$\mu=0.5$ and $f=4$ by hypothesis (2) and (3) respectively.
$N(t+1)-N(t)=0$	Inserting in the equation the right-hand side $\frac{N}{2}4-\frac{N}{2}f\times 0.5-N=2N-N-N=0$
Population is in equilibrium	If fertility is 4/generation and infant mortality ratio is 0.5
Conclusion	Hypothesis 1 is true

The population growth is equal to the difference between birth rate and death rate. In pre-industrial times child mortality was about 50%.[34] Denoting f = fertility; μ = child mortality ratio; $N(t)$ =population size in generation *t*, then one arrives at the following model:

$$\text{Model } N(t+1)=N(t)+\frac{N}{2}f-\frac{N}{2}f\mu-N(t)$$

The equation $N(t+1)-N(t)=\frac{N}{2}f-\frac{N}{2}f\mu-N(t)$ is a mathematical model of population growth. It is a numeric expression representing a reality of a population of N individuals in generation *t*, an average fertility of four births per mother per generation and an infant mortality ratio of μ deaths per born infants. Table 1.4 verifies Hypothesis 1 using this model.

The model confirms that if the average fertility is 4/generation then the population size is at equilibrium; no doubt, a lower fertility predicts extinction and a higher fertility predicts population growth. A fertility value that keeps the population constant is often called *replacement-level* fertility.[35]

Is this model reality? Not really:

1. Not all mothers are born the same year.
2. Not all mothers give birth at the same age—generations may overlap.

3. Fertility varies with age of the mother—only the age interval 12–52 needs to be considered.
4. The fertility can vary from generation to generation.
5. The number of daughters is not necessarily equal to the number of sons.
6. Child mortality fluctuates around 0.5; however, it may go higher or lower.
7. Not all people die simultaneously.

This mathematical model represents a problem that is different than reality. However, in this case for many practical purposes the fertility value of four births/generation for pre-industrial societies and two births/generations in current societies is an adequate estimate. A more precise estimate for the United States is of 2.1 births per generation; the value is not 2.0 mostly due to the sex ratio of offspring being slightly in favor of sons.[36]

As a matter of fact, every mathematical model represents a problem that is only similar to reality. Engineering school teaches how to solve idealized problems. For example they teach how to determine the deflection of a cantilevered beam under load (Figure 1.1). However, reality might look like a bridge under construction (Figure 1.2).

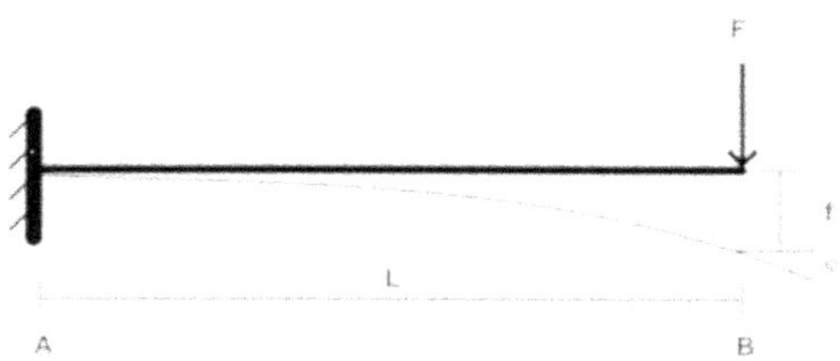

Figure 1.1 Deflections of a cantilevered beam under load. Public Domain. Created by Pekaje.

Figure 1.2 Cantilevered bridge: The Pierre Pflimlin bridge being constructed over the river Rhine between Germany and France. Public Domain. Credit: Leonard G.

Junior engineers learn from senior specialists how to idealize reality into a model and how to test if the model is good enough. I personally owe my initiation into model building and testing to the books and lectures of Dave Steinberg.[37] Engineering school imparts tools which determine if a mathematical model is good enough. These tools consist of mathematical and experimental methods. The most common mathematical method is sensitivity analysis.

Is a mathematical model less credible than a test? In my experience I heard several times the maxim: *Nobody trusts mathematical model results except the people who carried out the analysis. Everybody trusts test results except the staff that carried out the test.*

In cases when the validity of results are subject to questions of life and death (e.g., flight safety and nuclear reactor security), the model is tested experimentally. If the tests disprove the model, then either the model or the test is adjusted; this may be reiterated until the model and the test are mutually validating each other. Therefore, the most credible results are extracted from a combination of mathematical models and experimental tests.

Statistical Inference

One of the methods of evaluating a hypothesis is by statistical inference. Some hypotheses are formulated in likelihood terms. For example, let us return to the chicken soup theory. Even if chicken soup were good for life, some patients would not react to the treatment. That is not a reason to dismiss the hypothesis. If out of 100 patients 95 will benefit, the treatment should be recommended. Statistics is the branch of mathematics using data from a sample to draw inferences about a larger population.

In engineering, statistical inference answers questions like what is the mean time between failures of a product. This information helps to determine warranty cost. In healthcare statistical inference methods are widely used to evaluate the efficacy of a treatment (chicken soup, vaccine, surgery, radiation, etc.). The risk involved in exposure to environmental hazards is also determined using statistical inference methods. Table 1.5 lists various applications of statistical inference methods; the table lists for each method the results of interest, the type of test, the result, and the expression evaluating the certainty in the results. *Statistical inference does not eliminate uncertainty; it evaluates it.*

Is a result of statistical inference scientific knowledge? For example the efficacy of the Moderna–NIH mRNA-1273 vaccine was calculated according to procedure i) of Table 1.5 and found to be 94%.[38] This means that an unvaccinated person's chance to be infected is 17 times higher than the chances of a vaccinated person. Not only the vaccine does not provide immunity with certainty, but the results were harvested from one single set of clinical tests.

In Table 1.5 the column *Certainty Expression* evaluates the confidence the results provide. The column specifies a confidence level, and a confidence interval. In the case of the discussed *Moderna* vaccine, the confidence level is 95% and the interval is 84–95%.

Table 1.5 Examples of Statistical Inference Methods

Description	Result of Interest	Type	Result	Certainty Expression
Clinical Trials	Efficacy = Relative Risk Reduction	Case[e] – control[f]	RRR[j]	C%[n]., CI[o].,
Epidemiological Studies	Incidence[a]	Sub-population[g]	SIR[k]	C%, CI
	Exposure threat[b]	Case – control[h]	OR[l]	
	Exposure risk[c]	Exposed-Non-Exposed[i]	RR[m]	
Surveys	Opinions[d]	Percentages.	CI, Margin of error.	

[a] For example number of sleep disorder cases among teachers/number of cases in the general population.
[b] For example the cancer ratio among smokers is 60%; the ratio in the population is 2%; the incidence is 60/2=30.
[c] For example a sample (cohort) of smokers and a sample of nonsmokers is healthy; a year later 10% of the smoker cohort and 0.5% of the nonsmokers is diagnosed with cancer; the exposure risk is 10/0.5=20.
[d] For example: agree, disagree, do not know.
[e] Case group consists of treated participants.
[f] Control group consists of untreated participants/participants treated with a placebo.
[g] For example population living in a certain area, or people of a certain occupation (e.g., electricians, teachers).
[h] Case group consists of exposed participants; control group consists of unexposed participants.
[i] Exposed: for example smokers, occupation with high exposure to radiation, noise, etc.
[j] RRR = Relative Risk Reduction.

Example:

	Case	Control
Tested	50	50
Infected	1	25

$$RRR = 1 - \frac{\left(\dfrac{Number\ of\ infected}{Number\ of\ tested}\right)_{case}}{\left(\dfrac{Number\ of\ infected}{Number\ of\ tested}\right)_{control}} = 1 - \frac{1}{25} = .96$$

[k] SIR = Standardized Incidence Ratio.

$$SIR = \frac{Percentage\ of\ cases\ in\ the\ subpopulation}{Percentage\ of\ cases\ in\ the\ general\ population}$$

[l] OR = Odd Ratio.

Example:

	Case (exposed)	Control (not exposed)
Tested	50	50
Infected	25	5

(*Continued*)

Table 1.5 (Continued)

$$OR = \frac{\left(\dfrac{\text{Number of infected}}{\text{Number of not infected}}\right)_{case}}{\left(\dfrac{\text{Number of infected}}{\text{Number of not infected}}\right)_{control}} = \frac{\frac{25}{50}}{\frac{5}{50}} = 5$$

[m] RR = Risk Ratio.

$$RR = \frac{\left(\dfrac{\text{Number of infected}}{\text{Number of tested}}\right)_{case}}{\left(\dfrac{\text{Number of infected}}{\text{Number of tested}}\right)_{control}} = \frac{\frac{1}{50}}{\frac{25}{50}} = 1/25$$

[n] C% = Confidence Level.
[o] CI = Confidence Interval.

Therefore, a statistical inference is *scientific knowledge*. The question is: is a vaccinated person immune to infection? True or false? The statistical inference confirms that with a 95% confidence the risk is between seven times and twenty times lower than the unvaccinated person. That is true; consequently statistical inference is *scientific knowledge*. The chicken soup example provided the information that the soup has reducing inflammation ingredients. Does consumption of chicken soup reduce infection? The answer so far is neither affirmative nor negative. The theory is supported by scientific researches; however, the affirmation that "chicken soup is good for life" is a scientific theory waiting for proof.

Let me bring you another statistical inference illustrating the difference between scientific knowledge and theory.

The results of an analysis of clinical data "suggest that intercessory prayer to the Judeo-Christian God has a beneficial therapeutic effect in patients admitted to a [*Coronary Care Unit*], CCU."[39] Of 393 patients, 192 practiced prayer in addition to medical care; the rest did not.

Table 1.6 reproduces data from the published investigation[40] showing that the treatment (i.e., prayer) benefited 163, partially improved 2, and had no effect on 27 patients.

The investigation followed the following steps:[41]

a. It assumed that the prayer is not beneficial (null hypothesis).
b. It carried out a chi-square analysis resulting in a decision to reject the null hypothesis. (In statistical jargon the chi-squared statistics exceeded the critical chi-squared value with a *p*-value was less than 0.01.)
c. Consequently it favored the alternate hypothesis, i.e., that prayer helps.

The investigation did not provide an estimate for the efficacy of prayer. Using the formula of point *i*) of Table 1.5 one arrives at an RRR=0.401. Table lists various efficacy

Table 1.6 Example of Evaluating Treatment in Clinical Test

Effect / Group	Beneficial	Partial	No Effect	Total
Treated	163	2	27	192
Untreated	147	10	44	201
Number of patients in trial				393

Source: Table 3 of published research: Randolph C Byrd, "Positive therapeutic effects of intercessory prayer in a coronary care unit population," *Southern Medical Journal* 81 No 7 (1988).

results. Efficacy compares beneficial results with bad results; therefore, the calculation of Table 1.6 considered half of the partial improvements beneficial and half-bad outcomes

The 95% confidence level figures for this RRR are CI [lower bound-upper bound] =[0.02-0.61]. In English one concludes with a confidence of 95% that prayer increases the chances of a patient at least 1.02 times and at most 2.5 times (see row *Benefit* in Table 1.6). In practical terms a benefit of 1.02 times means no benefit; therefore, the 95% confidence interval indicates that in the worst case prayer does not benefit; in the best case, it promises a 2.5-fold increase in chances of recovery.

The original investigation answers "may be" to the question: Does prayer help healing? Table 1.7 provides true estimates to the question: How much does prayer help for healing? Confidence intervals increase the scientific value of the information. Statistical inference methods in most cases provide clear answers regarding the truth of a hypothesis. Unfortunately, wide confidence intervals make decision-making harder. As mentioned earlier, statistical inference quantifies uncertainty. The chicken-soup investigation generated a reasonable hypothesis. The prayer investigation tested the hypothesis and provided answers; the answers can quantify expected benefits and confidence intervals.

Equilibrium in Nature and Society

The demographic model of the previous section represents equilibrium in population size. A variable is at equilibrium if it is constant. Both in nature and in society variables are not independent. For example in the demographic model of the previous section, child mortality is affected by crop yield, and crop yield varies according to worker availability and skill, technical equipment efficiency, annual precipitation rate, soil fertility, and on incidence of parasites.[42] Therefore, models studying the equilibrium of interrelated variables should describe all significant factors and take into account the effects in one variable on all the others. The scientific term for such a collection of multivariable relationships is *system*, or *dynamic system*. The term *system* is justified because the mathematical model consists of a system of equations. The term *dynamic* signifies an interest in changes of the system variables in time. The values of the variables at a given time define the state of the system. Consequently, in most equilibrium studies

Table 1.7 Efficacy of Prayer according to Results of Table 1.6

	Efficacy	95% CI	
		Low	High
RRR	0.40	0.02	0.61
RR	0.60	0.98	0.39
Benefit	1.67	1.02	2.54
ARR	0.098	0.02	0.17

the variables are called *state variables.* If one *state variable* is constant over time, then different variables still change, the values of other state variables. For example, if the *equipment efficiency* is constant over several years the crop yield will still vary according to annual precipitation rates, annual soil fertility, and so on. Equilibrium is achieved if all state variables are constant. Consequently, models of equilibrium express the rate of variation of every state variable as a function of other variables. The condition for equilibrium is that the rate of change of every *state variable* is zero.

The variables do not necessarily consist of natural factors. For example, the crop yields depend on a combination of natural factors (soil, rain, etc.) and societal factors (workers, education, prices, government incentives, justice, and peace). There are equilibrium models exclusively consisting of societal factors; others exclusively consist of natural state variables or a combination of both. The method of determining the values of the state variables at equilibrium is the same for all applications; as explained earlier, it consists of setting the condition that all rates of change are zero. The principal advantage of mathematical models for equilibrium studies consists of this fact. Sometimes the same model can be used for two applications from different disciplines. For example, Chapter 2 substantiates how a prey and predator model serves to study the dynamics of police and criminals. After all, cats chase mice and law enforcement pursues criminals.

Very rarely systems meet the rigorous definition of no change of their state variables. That is true both in nature and in society. In many cases one uses the term *steady state* instead of *equilibrium* in order to stress that the *state variables* are not constant; however, either their average is constant, or for the practical time interval in question, changes in the values of the *state variables* are negligible.

Stability

Let us return to the example of flight UA585 on March 3, 1991. A flying aircraft is considered a system in steady state. The airplane was in level flight at constant altitude and speed; the trajectory was a straight line, and the aircraft flight angles were constant. The pilots deflected the rudder in order to change the yaw attitude of the aircraft (Figure 1.3). The rudder angle deflected more than intended due to excessive aerodynamic load; as a consequence, the ruder jammed. The aircraft was not in equilibrium anymore, and the pilots could not trim

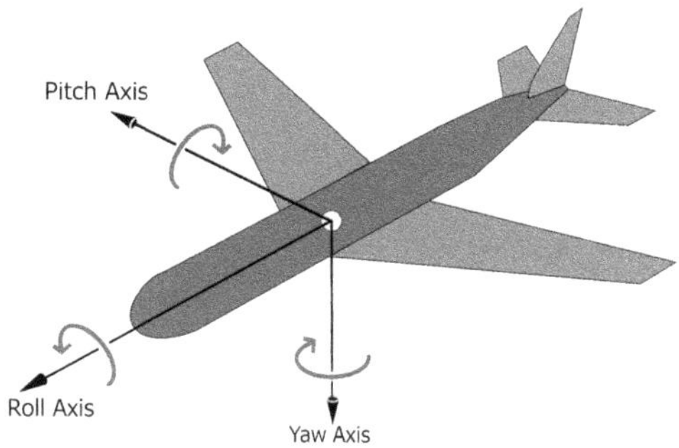

Figure 1.3 Aircraft flight angles. Public Domain. Credit: Auawise.

down the excessive yawing of the aircraft. Possibly all three flight angles went out of control because in flight one angle change affects the other. The aircraft became uncontrollable, and it crashed. Obviously, the event describes a typical loss of stability.

In general if a system is in equilibrium any small disturbance can affect one or more *state variables*. If after the disturbance the system returns to its previous equilibrium, then the equilibrium is stable. In cases were social *state variables* are present (crime, law enforcement, public health, monetary intervention, etc.) the system also may or may not return to the previous equilibrium. Both in nature and in society, the new equilibrium may be comparable or dissimilar to the previous equilibrium. In the case of an aircraft crash, there is no doubt that one deals with system collapse. In society, there are also cases where total collapse is obvious. For example in the Bronze Age the whole East-Mediterranean civilization collapsed in 1177 BCE.[43] The collapses of the Roman Empire, of the Austro-Hungarian and the Ottoman Empire, and the Soviet Empire are also events that transformed the course of history. The fall of the Weimar Republic consisted also of a dramatic transition from a democracy to totalitarianism. The chapters of this book focus on the stability of democratic systems, asking if such a malfunction can happen again.

Conclusion

1. Equilibrium and stability analysis of complex technological systems rely on safe methodologies and are utilized to prove compliance with safety regulations of the equipment.
2. The methodologies follow the path of scientific method: observation, theory, and proof.
3. Methodologies of equilibrium and stability analysis of systems in nature are applicable to systems in society.
4. The chapter distinguishes between proven scientific knowledge and theories derived by inductive reasoning, extrapolation of observations, or intuitive logic.

5. Equilibrium and stability methods in nature have been validated by scientific proof.
6. The method involves formulating mathematical relationships representing the interdependence of the *state variables* in play; the result is a mathematical model. The confidence in the predictions of regarding equilibrium and stability depends on the trustworthiness of the model.

Notes

1 "Resiliency is the ability of a system to adjust its configuration and function under disturbance," Joseph A. Tainter, "Social Complexity and Sustainability," *Ecological Complexity* 3, no. 2 (2006): 91-103, this chapter explains and uses the classical definition of stability which is very similar

2 e.g. US Government FAA, "Federal Aviation Regulations; Sec. 25.233—Directional Stability and Control," in *Part 25*, ed. FAA (Washington, DC: Federal Aviation Administration, 1992).

3 Michael Peter Kennedy, "Bifurcation and Chaos," in *The Circuits and Filters Handbook, Second Edition*, ed. Wai K. Chen (Boca Raton: Taylor & Francis, 2002): 1105–7.

4 Hans True, "Nonlinear Vehicle Dynamics," in *Road and Off-Road Vehicle System Dynamics Handbook*, ed. G. Mastinu and M. Ploechl (Boca Raton: CRC Press, 2014), 129.

5 Anthony N. Kounadis, "Nonlinear Dynamic Buckling and Stability of Autonomous Dissipative Discrete Systems—Potential Systems," in *Nonlinear Stability of Structures: Theory and Computational Techniques*, ed. Anthony N. Kounadis and Wilfried B. Krätzig (Vienna: Springer 2014), 142.

6 E.g. Soodeh Dadras, Ryan M. Gerdes, and Rajnikant Sharma, "Vehicular Platooning in an Adversarial Environment" (paper presented at the Proceedings of the 10th ACM Symposium on Information, Computer and Communications Security, 2015).

7 Peter Turchin, *Complex Population Dynamics: A Theoretical/Empirical Synthesis (Mpb-35)* (Princeton: Princeton University Press, 2013), 142, 43.

8 Leah Edelstein-Keshet, *Mathematical Models in Biology* (New York: Random House, 1988), 55, 56.

9 US Government NTSB, "Aircraft Accident Report Ntsb/Aar-92/06" (Washington, DC: NTSB-National Transportation Safety Board, 1992), 102.

10 "Aircraft Accident Report Ntsb/Aar-99/01" (Washington, DC: NTSB-National Transportation Safety Board, 1999).

11 Carl Sagan, *Dragons of Eden: Speculations on the Evolution of Human Intelligence* (New York: Ballantine Books, 2012).

12 Carl Sagan and Ann Druyan, *The Varieties of Scientific Experience: A Personal View of the Search for God*, Kindle edition (London: Penguin, 2006), 2701.

13 Eric Schwitzgebel, "Human Nature and Moral Education in Mencius, Xunzi, Hobbes, and Rousseau," *History of Philosophy Quarterly* 24, no. 2 (2007).

14 Carlo Rovelli, "Aristotle's Physics: A Physicist's Look," *Journal of the American Philosophical Association* 1, no. 1 (2015): 23–40.

15 Brett K. Hayes, Evan Heit, and Haruka Swendsen, "Inductive Reasoning," *Wiley Interdisciplinary Reviews: Cognitive Science* 1, no. 2 (2010): 278–92; Evan Heit,

"Properties of Inductive Reasoning," *Psychonomic Bulletin & Review* 7(2000): 569–92 ; Evan Heit and Caren M. Rotello, "Relations between Inductive Reasoning and Deductive Reasoning," *Journal of Experimental Psychology: Learning, Memory, and Cognition* 36, no. 3: 805 (2010); W. Brian Arthur, "Inductive Reasoning and Bounded Rationality," *The American Economic Review* 84, no. 2 (1994): 406–11.

16 Carlo Arduini, *La Primogenita Di Galileo Galilei Rivelata Dalle Sue Lettere Edite Ed Inedite* (Florence: Felice Le Monnier, 1864), 57.

17 Steven Gimbel, *Exploring the Scientific Method: Cases and Questions* (Chicago: University of Chicago Press, 2011), 1.

18 Jerome R. Ravetz, *Scientific Knowledge and Its Social Problems* (Milton Park: Taylor & Francis, 2020), Ch. "What is Science."

19 Ibid.

20 Andrew J. Parker, "Revealing Rembrandt," *Frontiers in Neuroscience* 8 (2014): 76.

21 Ball, Philip. "The physical modelling of society: a historical perspective." *Physica A: Statistical Mechanics and its Applications* 314, no. 1–4 (2002): 1–14.

22 H. Eugene Stanley, Professor Emeritus at Boston University; former editor of Physica A, one of the pioneers of interdisciplinary science.

23 Immanuel Kant and J. M. D. Meiklejohn, *Critique of Pure Reason* (New York: Colonial Press, 1899).

24 Colby Teeman, "Does Chicken Soup Really Help When You're Sick?," *The Conversation*, https://theconversation.com/does-chicken-soup-really-help-when-youre-sick-a-nutrition-specialist-explains-whats-behind-the-beloved-comfort-food-213847.

25 Ibid.

26 Marcella Martos and Meredith Turnbough. "Protein Parts," Arizona State University School of Life Sciences Ask a Biologist, https://askabiologist.asu.edu/venom/building-blocks-protein.

27 Philip C. Calder, "Omega-3 Fatty Acids and Inflammatory Processes: From Molecules to Man," *Biochemical Society Transactions* 45, no. 5 (2017): 1105–15.

28 Ronald Eccles, "Mechanisms of Symptoms of Common Cold and Flu," *Common Cold* (2009): 23–45.

29 Barbara O. Rennard et al., "Chicken Soup Inhibits Neutrophil Chemotaxis in Vitro," *Chest* 118, no. 4 (2000): 1150–57.

30 The editors of Encyclopedia Britannica, "S.V. Inflammation," in *Encyclopedia Britannica on Line* (Chicago: Encyclopaedia Britannica, Inc., 2024).

31 Fred Rosner, *The Medical Legacy of Moses Maimonides* (Hoboken: KTAV Publishing House, 1998), 242.

32 Sagan and Druyan, *The Varieties of Scientific Experience: A Personal View of the Search for God*, 472. Obviously, Sagan meant human life; the theory can easily be proven wrong concerning chickens' life;

33 Teeman, "Does Chicken Soup Really Help When You're Sick?"

34 Ancient Rome: John D. Durand, "Mortality Estimates from Roman Tombstone Inscriptions," *American Journal of Sociology* 65, no. 4 (1960): 365–73; Peter W. Van der Horst, *Ancient Jewish Epitaphs* (Louvain: Peeters Publishers, 1991); Walter Scheidel, *Debating Roman Demography* (Leiden: Brill, 2001); Europe: Ohlin P. Göran, "The Positive and the Preventive Check: A Study of the Rate of Growth of Pre-Industrial Populations" (PhD Thesis, Cambridge, MA, Harvard, 1955); Georges

Duby, *The Early Growth of the European Economy* (Ithaca: Cornell University Press, 1978).

35 E.g. OECD, *Pensions at a Glance 2019 OECD and G20 Indicators* (Paris: OECD Publishing, 2019).

36 Miguel S. Porta, *A Dictionary of Epidemiology* (Oxford: Oxford University Press, 2016).

37 Dave S. Steinberg, *Vibration Analysis for Electronic Equipment* (Hoboken: Wiley-Interscence, 2000); *Cooling Techniques for Electronic Equipment* (Hoboken: Wiley, 1991).

38 Piero Olliaro, Els Torreele, and Michel Vaillant, "Covid-19 Vaccine Efficacy and Effectiveness—the Elephant (Not) in the Room," *The Lancet Microbe* 2, no. 7: (2021): e279–e80.

39 Randolph C. Byrd, "Positive Therapeutic Effects of Intercessory Prayer in a Coronary Care Unit Population," *Southern Medical Journal* 81, no. 7 (1988): 826–29.

40 Ibid.

41 Ibid.

42 Francis P. F. Reay-Jones, "Pest Status and Management of Corn Earworm (Lepidoptera: Noctuidae) in Field Corn in the United States," *Journal of Integrated Pest Management* 10, no. 1 (2019): 19.

43 Eric H. Cline, *1177 B.C.: The Year Civilization Collapsed*, Kindle edition (Princeton: Princeton University Press, 2015).

2

Physics of Equilibrium and Stability

Summary

Reasonably, scholars with analytical interest in *resilience of democracies* are teaching and researching sociopolitical patterns. The intended audience of this book consists of readers interested in that domain. This book bridges between exact sciences and the field of my intended audience which can be political science, law, sociology, or any other related discipline.

The impetus behind this book consists of equivalence between societal resilience and stability of natural systems; if one agrees to the interpretation of *societal resilience* given in the *Introduction,* this equivalence is valid. Chapters 3–10 develop the message of this book (see *Introduction*) with as little mathematical jargon and equations as possible. Nevertheless, for the sake of readers who are curious about the mathematical backing of the message, and in order to make the case for its validity, this chapter abounds in algebraic expressions. In other words, this chapter deals with the mathematical demonstration of the inverse relationship between social complexity and *societal resilience.* Readers are invited to read it; however, the message of the book will not be lost if readers skip this algebraically loaded chapter.

Equilibrium

The barrel of Figure 2.1 is at rest. It does not move forward, x, sideways, y, upward, z, and it does not roll or heave.

The position coordinates x, y, z, φ determine the status of the barrel. When at rest these coordinates are constant; however, in general they could vary in time. At any point in time their value defines the *state* of the barrel. Therefore, they are called *state variables.* Currently the barrel is at rest and the *state variables* are constant. It is customary to represent the rate of change of a variable x with $\dot{x}$ (pronounced x dot). Then the expression for a resting barrel is $\dot{x} = \dot{y} = \dot{z} = \dot{\varphi} = 0$. In society there are also *state variables* that determine the state of a town, an institution or a nation. For example the House of Commons in the Parliament of UK has 650 MPs, the House of Lords about 800 members, the cabinet consists of about 25 senior ministers, about half a million civil servants and one monarch. These are *state variables.* At a point in time

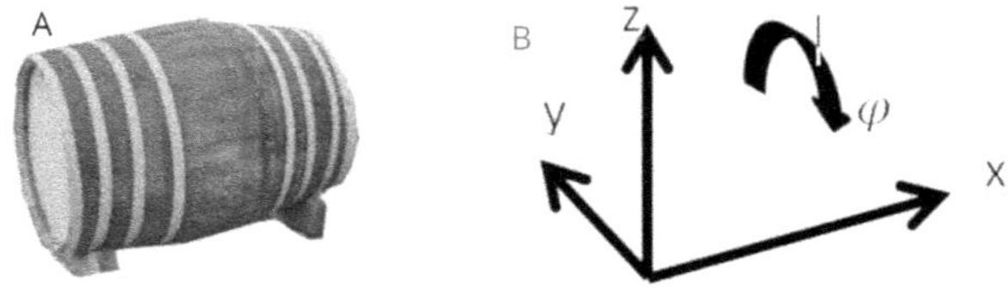

Figure 2.1 A. Body at rest. Picture taken by author. B. Location coordinates of barrel. Author's work.

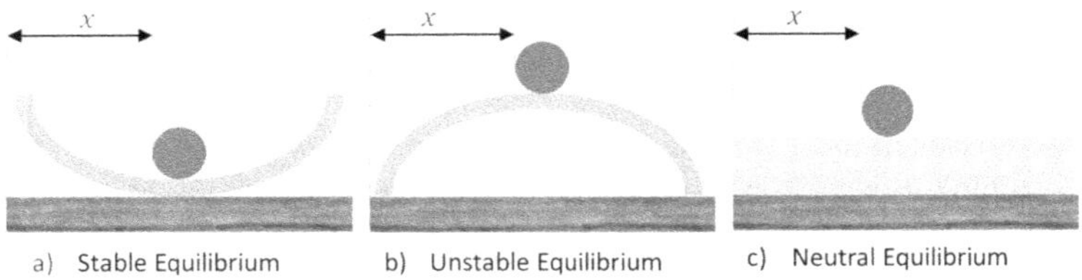

Figure 2.2 Equilibrium. Public Domain. Attribution: By Ordinary Artery, Own work.

$x = 650, y = 798, z = 25, u = 526{,}092, R = 1$. For practical purposes the state variables change very little in a yearly interval; the system is practically at equilibrium and one arrives at the same equation $\dot{x} = \dot{y} = \dot{z} = \dot{u} = \dot{R} = 0$.

Stability

Not everything is in equilibrium, nor is equilibrium permanent.

> The Cretaceous-Paleogene boundary ~65.5 million years ago marks one of the three largest mass extinctions in the past 500 million years. The extinction event coincided with a large asteroid impact at Chicxulub, Mexico.[1]

The Chicxulub event was quite a breathtaking example of disequilibrium. Nevertheless, Google Scholar reports only 619 researches dated after 2020 about the event. The event is fascinating and raises many questions. However, I guess it is not practical to agonize about keeping the planet in equilibrium in the event of a future collision with a similarly large asteroid. Without researching the event I feel brave enough to affirm that from the dinosaurs' evolution point of view the term *instability* is appropriate. Yet, if we interrogate Google Scholars about *equilibrium and stability of complex systems* the answers offers 28,000 results for the same period of 2020–4.

At this point the chapter is ready to explain what *stability* means in practical considerations. Figure 2.2 portrays three situations of a ball in equilibrium. In case a) if one impacts the ball with a slight touch, the ball returns to its position. This is called *stable equilibrium.* In case b) the ball rolls away—*unstable equilibrium*; in case c) the ball rolls a little bit and comes at rest at another point of the surface—*neutral equilibrium.*

Following a small *nudge* not all the state variables are constant. At least the horizontal coordinate, x, of the ball is subject to change or $\dot{x} \neq 0$.

Therefore *stability* is the property of a system in equilibrium to return to the previous values of its state variables following a small *disturbance.*

Nature: Prey and Predator Equation Derivation

Predators have hunted prey since one species specialized in consuming another. Two mathematicians determined that this is a typical equilibrium and stability subject. They both worked independently and arrived at the same mathematical model: the Lotka-Volterra model.

As any mathematical model, the prey and predator model is an idealization. In this case the justification of the Lotka-Volterra model[2] starts with two questions:

1. What would happen to the bison population if there were no wolves or other predators hunting them?

Every female bison gives birth to a certain number of offspring per unit of time. Let us denote the size of the population at time *t* as $x(t)$; $\dot{x}(t)$ denotes the growth rate of the population. The growth rate is the increment of population in a unit of time. A unit of time could be a generation, a year, a week, and so on. (If the growth rate is *r* bison/generation, then it is *r/3* bison/year because a cow is mature enough at age 3 to give birth.[3]) If in her lifetime a cow gives birth to two offspring, then the growth rate of the population is $\dot{x} = 0$. If in a lifetime the number of offspring of a cow exceeds two calves, then we can talk about a positive growth rate. If a cow gives birth to a calves in a life time, then the population will grow by $a - 2$ bison/generation because the new generation size is a bison and the old generation that dies consists of two bison: a bull and a cow.[4] The population at time *t* consists of $x(t)$ bizon or $\frac{x(t)}{2}$ couples then the next generation it will count $x(t+1) = \frac{x}{2}(a-2) = x\left(\frac{a}{2} - 1\right)$ $\dot{x} = \frac{x}{2}(a-2) = x\left(\frac{a}{2} - 1\right)$ bison. If in a generation the population grows $\left(\frac{a}{2} - 1\right)$ times, then in a year it grows $\frac{1}{3}\left(\frac{a}{2} - 1\right)$ times and in a week $\frac{1}{3 \times 52}\left(\frac{a}{2} - 1\right)$. Let us denote $\alpha = \frac{1}{3 \times 52}\left(\frac{a}{2} - 1\right)$; we obtain one term of the *Lotka-Volterra* model $\dot{x}(t) = \alpha x(t)$. It expresses that if there were no predators the population of bison will multiply α times every week.

2. What would happen to the wolf population if the bison or other prey disappeared? If the wolf population is $w(t)$ strong at time *t*, then one

week later a proportion β will die of starvation and at time *t+1* it will count $w(t+1)=w(t)-\gamma w(t)$ wolves. The increment per unit time is $\dot{w}(t)=w(t+1)-w(t)=-\gamma w(t)$. Another term of the *Lotka-Volterra* model is $\dot{w}(t)=-\gamma w(t)$. It expresses that the population of wolves decreases γ times every week.

3. It is time to become more realistic and to relax the assumption that the bison live without predators and the wolves live without prey.
   a. The bison population increases α times per week; however, every wolf consumes weekly a proportion β of the bison population. Since there are w wolves the bison population decreases weekly by βxw bison. Therefore, the rate of change of the bison population is the weekly rate of increase due to natural growth (αx) minus βxw or the number of bison consumed weekly by the wolves or:

$$\dot{x}(t)=\alpha x-\beta xw$$

   b. The presence of prey stops the devastation of the wolf population. The natural growth of the wolf population will increase the population δ_0 times. We saw earlier that in the absence of prey this will not happen. Realistically, the more bison are around, the more wolves survive to multiply. The mathematical expression $\delta_0 \times \delta_1 x$ represents that the surviving wolf population grows proportionally to the prey population by a factor of $\delta_1 x$ and its natural growth further multiplies the population δ_0 times its size. Or in algebraic terms: $\dot{w}(t)=\delta_0 \times \delta_1 xw-\gamma w$. Replacing $\delta_0 \times \delta_1$ by δ one obtains the second equation of the Lotka-Volterra model:

$$\dot{w}(t)=\delta xw-\gamma w$$

4. The Equations are:

$$\begin{cases}\dot{x}(t)=\alpha x-\beta w\\ \dot{w}(t)=\delta xw-\gamma w\end{cases} \qquad \text{Equation 2.1}$$

5. Equilibrium of prey and predator model

At equilibrium, the state variables x and w are constant or $\dot{x}(t)=\dot{w}(t)=0$. Or:

$$\begin{cases}0=\alpha x-\beta xw=x(\alpha-\beta w)\\ 0=\delta xw-\gamma w=w(\delta x-\gamma)\end{cases} \qquad \text{Equation 2.2}$$

Let us denote $x^*, y^*, \dot{x}, \dot{y}, x^*, w^*$ as the values of the two state variables at equilibrium. Two sets of solutions satisfy the set of Equation 2.2:

The trivial solution $x^* = w^* = 0$ Equation 2.3

The natural solution is : $x^* = \gamma/\delta ; w^* = \alpha/\beta$ Equation 2.4

The trivial solution only confirms that if both populations become extinct the system will not change anymore. The natural solution confirms the intuition that the bison population size at equilibrium grows when the wolves starve faster and when the wolves reproduce at a slower pace. Similarly the wolf population size at equilibrium is bigger when the bison population size grows faster and when the wolves are weaker hunters.

Society: Police and Criminals Equilibrium

The analogy of police hunting criminals is simplistic; the main dissimilarity consists of the fact that populations of living beings grow according to laws of nature' while police size is dictated by government decisions. Nevertheless, the analogy is reasonable; a government refusing to imitate nature will end up either with a growing police force with no criminals to chase or with a society with a weakening police and growing criminality. The conditions of equilibrium are identical, and consequently for a defined time interval the society will live at equilibrium. The size of criminal population is determined by the size of police and its capability to detect and incarcerate criminals. A numerical example is discussed in Chapter 3.

Society: Police and Criminals Stability

The system is stable when after a small change of an equilibrium both state variables return to their value at equilibrium which are $x = \gamma/\delta ; w = \alpha/\beta$ (Figure 2.1, a). In this case Equation 2.1 consists of two nonlinear equations with two state variables. Stability is tested for a small deviation from equilibrium. Consequently one can use the Taylor expansion of a function of several variables to linearize the nonlinear equations.[5]

The linear approximation of a function of two variables is:[6]

$$F\left(x^* + \Delta x, w^* + \Delta w\right) = F\left(x^*, w^*\right) + \frac{\partial F\left(x^*, w^8\right)}{\partial x}\Delta x + \frac{\partial F\left(x^*, w^*\right)}{\partial w}\Delta w$$

In our case $F\left(x^*, w^*\right)$=0 and consequently the linearized Equation 2.1 is:

$$\begin{cases} \dot{x}(t) = \left(\alpha - \beta w^*\right)\Delta x - \beta x^* \Delta w \\ \dot{w}(t) = \delta w^* \Delta x + \left(\delta x^* - \gamma\right)\Delta w \end{cases}$$ Equation 2.5

Inserting the values of the *natural solution* found earlier one obtains:

Equation 2.5 becomes:

$$\begin{cases} \dot{x}(t) = \alpha(\Delta x) - \beta\left(\Delta x \frac{\alpha}{\beta}\beta\right) - \beta\frac{\gamma}{\delta}\Delta w \\ \dot{w}(t) = \delta\frac{\alpha}{\beta}\Delta x + \left(\delta\frac{\gamma}{\delta} - \gamma\right)\Delta w \end{cases} \qquad \text{Equation 2.6}$$

Or

$$\begin{cases} \dot{x}(t) = -\beta\frac{\gamma}{\delta}\Delta w \\ \dot{w}(t) = \delta\frac{\alpha}{\beta}\Delta x \end{cases} \qquad \text{Equation 2.7}$$

In matrix form

$$\begin{bmatrix} 0 & \beta\frac{\gamma}{\delta} \\ \delta\frac{\alpha}{\beta} & 0 \end{bmatrix} \begin{Bmatrix} \Delta x \\ \Delta w \end{Bmatrix} = \begin{Bmatrix} \dot{x} \\ \dot{w} \end{Bmatrix} \qquad \text{Equation 2.8}$$

The matrix $\left[\mathfrak{J}\right] = \begin{bmatrix} \frac{\partial F_1}{\partial x} & \frac{\partial F_2}{\partial w} \\ \frac{\partial F_2}{\partial x} & \frac{\partial F_2}{\partial w} \end{bmatrix} = \begin{bmatrix} 0 & \beta\frac{\gamma}{\delta} \\ \delta\frac{\alpha}{\beta} & 0 \end{bmatrix}$ is the matrix form of the left-hand side of the linearized equation calculating the rate of change of the two state variables; this matrix is called Jacobian.

The system is stable if the real parts of all the *eigenvalues* of the Jacobian $\left[\mathfrak{J}\right]$ are negative.[7] This theorem is not intuitive even for exact scientists; consequently it is worth justifying it. λ_k is an eigenvalue of a square matrix $[A]$ if $[A]\{\breve{x}\} = \lambda_k\{\breve{x}\}$. For example $[A]\{\breve{x}\}$ can be the left-hand side of a system of equations like $[A]\{x\} = \{b\}$; $\{x\}$ represents the unknowns of the equation and $\{b\}$ is the vector obtained by the matrix operation $[A]\{x\}$. It is not very likely that the solution $\{b\}$of the equation is proportional to $\{x\}$. For a certain eigenvalue λ_i there is only one vector $\{\breve{x}\}$ of knowns that would generate a solution $\{\dot{x}\}$that is proportional to $\{\breve{x}\}$;

For example in our case Equation 2.8 an eigenvalue λ means that:

$$\begin{bmatrix} 0 & \beta\frac{\gamma}{\delta} \\ \delta\frac{\alpha}{\beta} & 0 \end{bmatrix} \begin{Bmatrix} \Delta x \\ \Delta w \end{Bmatrix} = \lambda \begin{Bmatrix} \Delta x \\ \Delta w \end{Bmatrix} \qquad \text{Equation 2.9}$$

Or:

$$\begin{bmatrix} -\lambda & \beta\frac{\gamma}{\delta} \\ \delta\frac{\alpha}{\beta} & -\lambda \end{bmatrix} \begin{Bmatrix} \Delta x \\ \Delta w \end{Bmatrix} = \begin{Bmatrix} 0 \\ 0 \end{Bmatrix} \qquad \text{Equation 2.10}$$

It is time to refresh a few characteristics of square matrices.

Math a) Equation 2.10 is a system of two homogeneous equations with two unknowns; it can only have nonzero solutions if its determinant is zero, or $\begin{vmatrix} -\lambda & \beta\frac{\gamma}{\delta} \\ \delta\frac{\alpha}{\beta} & -\lambda \end{vmatrix} = 0$.[8] This condition leads to a quadratic equation.[9] It has two solutions λ_1 and λ_2. These are called eigenvalues of the Jacobian matrix $[\mathfrak{I}] = \begin{bmatrix} 0 & \beta\frac{\gamma}{\delta} \\ \delta\frac{\alpha}{\beta} & 0 \end{bmatrix}$.

Math b) The nontrivial solution $\{\varphi\}_1 = \begin{Bmatrix} \varphi_{11} \\ \varphi_{12} \end{Bmatrix}$ to the equation $\begin{bmatrix} -\lambda_1 & \beta\frac{\gamma}{\delta} \\ \delta\frac{\alpha}{\beta} & -\lambda_1 \end{bmatrix} \begin{Bmatrix} \varphi_{11} \\ \varphi_{12} \end{Bmatrix} = \begin{Bmatrix} 0 \\ 0 \end{Bmatrix}$ is called an eigenvector of the Jacobian matrix $[\mathfrak{I}]$. Obviously the Jacobian in this case of two state variables will have another *eigenvector* $\{\varphi\}_2$ obtained by solving $\begin{bmatrix} -\lambda_2 & \beta\frac{\gamma}{\delta} \\ \delta\frac{\alpha}{\beta} & -\lambda_2 \end{bmatrix} \begin{Bmatrix} \varphi_{21} \\ \varphi_{22} \end{Bmatrix} = \begin{Bmatrix} 0 \\ 0 \end{Bmatrix}$.

Math c) A system of *n* state variables will have *n eigenvalues* and *n eigenvectors.*

Math d) If one inserts λ_1 in the first row of Equation 2.9 one obtains

$$\beta\frac{\gamma}{\delta}\Delta w = \lambda_1 \Delta x + \lambda_1 \Delta w$$

Math e) T$\sum_{k=1}^{n}$he sum of the eigenvalues of a square matrix [A] is the sum of its diagonal terms. In algebraic notation $\sum_{k=1}^{n}\lambda_k = \sum_{k=1}^{n} A_{kk}$.[10] This sum is called the *trace* of matrix [A].

Math f) The product of the *eigenvalues* of a *square matrix* [A] is equal to the value of the determinant $|A|$.[11]

Math g) If a *square matrix* $[\Im]$ has j distinct *eigenvalues,* then any vector $\begin{Bmatrix} \Delta x_1 \\ \Delta x_2 \\ \dots \\ \Delta x_j \end{Bmatrix}$ can be expressed as a linear combination if its j eigenvectors or $\begin{Bmatrix} \Delta x_1 \\ \Delta x_2 \\ \dots \\ \Delta x_j \end{Bmatrix} = \sum_{i=1}^{j} c_i \{\varphi\}_i$.[12] In the particular case of the two state variable prey and predator problem $\begin{Bmatrix} \Delta x \\ \Delta w \end{Bmatrix} = c_1 \{\varphi\}_1 + c_2 \{\varphi\}_2$

Now we can return to our example and explain why the eigenvalues of the Jacobian determine whether a system is stable. The sum of the *eigenvalues* of the Jacobian (see Equation 2.8) is the trace of the Jacobian and or $\lambda_1 + \lambda_2 = 0$ 0. The product is$\lambda_1 \lambda_2 = \dfrac{-\delta\alpha\beta\gamma}{\beta\delta} = -\alpha\gamma$. One can easily verify that $\lambda_1 = i\sqrt{\alpha\gamma}$ and $\lambda_2 = -i\sqrt{\alpha\gamma}$, where $i^2 = -1$ verifies both the sum and the product of the *eigenvalues*. Thus, our *eigenvalues* are:

$$\lambda_1 = i\sqrt{\alpha\gamma} \text{ and } \lambda_2 = -i\sqrt{\alpha\gamma} \qquad \text{Equation 2.11}$$

The system is at the natural equilibrium (Equation 2.4). To test the response to a small unbalance one needs to calculate $\dot{x}$ the rate of change of the criminal population size and $\dot{w}$, the rate of change of the police size for adding an unbalance consisting of Δx criminals and Δw policemen. Since Δx and Δw are small one can use the linearized approximation of Equation 2.8:

$$\begin{bmatrix} 0 & \beta\dfrac{\gamma}{\delta} \\ \delta\dfrac{\alpha}{\beta} & 0 \end{bmatrix} \begin{Bmatrix} \Delta x \\ \Delta w \end{Bmatrix} = \begin{Bmatrix} \dot{x} \\ \dot{w} \end{Bmatrix} \qquad \text{Equation 2.12}$$

However, the vector $\begin{Bmatrix} \Delta x \\ \Delta w \end{Bmatrix}$ may be replaced by a linear combination of two *eigenvectors* (see Math-g). Or:

$$\begin{Bmatrix} \Delta x \\ \Delta w \end{Bmatrix} = C_1 \begin{Bmatrix} \varphi_{11} \\ \varphi_{12} \end{Bmatrix} + C_2 \begin{Bmatrix} \varphi_{21} \\ \varphi_{22} \end{Bmatrix} \qquad \text{Equation 2.13}$$

If the unbalance were $\begin{Bmatrix} \Delta x \\ \Delta w \end{Bmatrix} = \begin{Bmatrix} \varphi_{11} \\ \varphi_{12} \end{Bmatrix} = \{\varphi\}_1$ then the response would be:

$$[\Im]\{\varphi\}_1 = \lambda_1\{\varphi\}_1 = \{\varphi\}_1 \qquad \text{Equation 2.14}$$

This implies that $\{\varphi(t)\}_1 = \{\varphi(0)\}_1 e^{\lambda_1 t}$ because then Equation 2.14 is verified

Similarly if the unbalance were $\{\varphi\}_1$ then the response would be:

$$[\Im]\{\varphi\}_2 = \lambda_1\{\varphi\}_2 = \{\varphi\}_2 \text{ which implies that } \{\varphi(t)\}_2 = \{\varphi(0)\}_2 e^{\lambda_2 t}$$

Since the unbalance is $C_1\{\varphi\}_1 + C_2\{\varphi\}_2$ the response is $C_1\{\varphi\}_1 e^{\lambda_1 t} + C_2\{\varphi\}_2 e^{\lambda_2 t}$
Inserting the *eigenvalues* of Equation 2.11 the response to the unbalance is:

$$\Delta\begin{Bmatrix} x(t) \\ w(t) \end{Bmatrix} = C_1\{\varphi\}_1 e^{i\sqrt{\alpha\gamma}t} + C_2\{\varphi\}_2 e^{-i\sqrt{\alpha\gamma}t} \qquad \text{Equation 2.15}$$

The time history of the criminal population and law enforcement sizes is
$\begin{Bmatrix} x(t) \\ w(t) \end{Bmatrix} = \begin{Bmatrix} x(0) \\ w(0) \end{Bmatrix} + C_1\{\varphi\}_1 e^{i\sqrt{\alpha\gamma}t} + C_2\{\varphi\}_2 e^{-i\sqrt{\alpha\gamma}t}$ or replacing $\begin{Bmatrix} x(0) \\ w(0) \end{Bmatrix}$ with the values at equilibrium (Equation 2.4) one obtains:

$$\begin{Bmatrix} x(t) \\ w(t) \end{Bmatrix} = \begin{Bmatrix} \gamma/\delta \\ \alpha/\beta \end{Bmatrix} + C_1\{\varphi\}_1 e^{i\sqrt{\alpha\gamma}t} + C_2\{\varphi\}_2 e^{-i\sqrt{\alpha\gamma}t} \qquad \text{Equation 2.16}$$

Equation 2.16 represents a cyclical fluctuation of police size and criminal population size (see for example Figure 3.7). This means that rather than reaching precise equilibrium one ends up in *steady* state., At steady state the state variables are not constant; however, their mean value is constant.

The real part of both *eigenvalues* is zero. As a consequence, for every state variable the average of the *steady state* is the average of the previous *steady state* or *equilibrium*. That means that we are dealing with a neutral equilibrium.

Society: The General Case

In the general case we deal with n state variables. The rate of change of each state variable is a function of the other state variables. For example:

$$\dot{x}_1 = F_1\left(x_1 x_2,,, x_j,,, x_n\right)$$
$$\dot{x}_2 = F_2\left(x_1 x_2,,, x_j,,, x_n\right)$$
$$\dot{x}_j = F_j\left(x_1 x_2,,, x_j,,, x_n\right)$$
$$\dot{x}_n = F_n\left(x_1 x_2,,, x_j,,, x_n\right)$$

Equation 2.17

At equilibrium $\dot{x}_1 = \dot{x}_2 = \ldots \dot{x}_j = \ldots \dot{x}_n = 0$; Therefore, the *state variables* settle at equilibrium at values that satisfy the set of equations:

$$0 = F_1\left(x_1 x_2,,, x_j,,, x_n\right)$$
$$0 = F_2\left(x_1 x_2,,, x_j,,, x_n\right)$$
$$0 = F_j\left(x_1 x_2,,, x_j,,, x_n\right)$$
$$0 = F_n\left(x_1 x_2,,, x_j,,, x_n\right)$$

Equation 2.18

In order to determine the stability of the equilibrium one linearizes the system using the Taylor expansion as we did in the system of two *state variables*. The Jacobian is:

$$\left[\Im\right] = \begin{bmatrix} \frac{\partial F_1}{\partial x_1} & \frac{\partial F_1}{\partial x_2} & \cdots & \cdots & \frac{\partial F_1}{\partial x_n} \\ \frac{\partial F_2}{\partial x_1} & \frac{\partial F_2}{\partial x_2} & \cdots & \cdots & \frac{\partial F_2}{\partial x_n} \\ \cdots & \cdots & \cdots & \cdots & \cdots \\ \cdots & \cdots & \cdots & \cdots & \cdots \\ \frac{\partial F_n}{\partial x_1} & \frac{\partial F_n}{\partial x_2} & \cdots & \cdots & \frac{\partial F_n}{\partial x_n} \end{bmatrix}$$

Equation 2.19

The n *eigenvalues* of $\left[\Im\right]$ are $\lambda_1, \lambda_2, \ldots, \lambda_n$. The n *eigenvectors* of $\left[\Im\right]$are $\{\varphi\}_1, \{\varphi\}_2, \ldots \{\varphi\}_n$. If the change for equilibrium were $\{\varphi\}_1$ then the response would be $\{\dot{x}\} = \left[\Im\right]\{\varphi\}_1 = \lambda_1 \{\varphi\}_1$ implying that$\{\dot{x}\} = \{x^*\} e^{\lambda_1 t}$. If the change from equilibrium were $\{\varphi\}_j$ then the response would be $\{\dot{x}\} = \left[\Im\right]\{\varphi\}_j = \lambda_j \{\varphi\}_j$ implying that$\{\dot{x}\} = \{x^*\} e^{\lambda_j t}$. In reality the change from equilibrium is an ordinary vector $\{\Delta x\}$. Since $\{\Delta x\} = \sum_{j=1}^{n} C_j \{\varphi\}_j$ the response will be $\{x\} = \{x^*\} + \sum_{j=1}^{n} C_j \{\varphi\}_j e^{\lambda_j t}$.

$$\{x\} = \{x^*\} + \sum_{j=1}^{n} C_j \{\varphi\}_j e^{\lambda_j t} \qquad \text{Equation 2.20}$$

Equation 2.20 reveals that:

a. If the real part of at least one *eigenvalue* of the Jacobian is positive, then the system is not stable (Figure 2.2b). For example if $\lambda_k = s + id; s > 0$ then the component k will be $C_j \{\varphi\}_j e^{st} e^{idt}$. The term grows away from equilibrium.
b. If the real part of all the *eigenvalues* is 0, then the equilibrium is neutral (Figure 2.2c). The system will oscillate above and below the average of the steady state.
c. Otherwise, if the real part of all the *eigenvalues* are negative, then the equilibrium is stable (Figure 2.2a).

Society: The Ideal Case

Typical government responsibilities are legislation, justice, defense, law enforcement, finance, infrastructure, safety regulations (e.g., ground, air, sea, food, drugs, communication, and trade), education, and spread of knowledge. Each department of government is assigned to keep a desired equilibrium in its field. Typically the department administration detects deviation in a certain state variable and acts to correct it by adding, deleting, or replacing regulations. (This social function works similarly to temperature adjustment in humans: one sweats when it is too hot and one shivers when it is too cold.)

If x is a control variable and it deviates from its desired value x^*, then the administration will issue a correction:

$$\dot{x} = -\gamma x \qquad \text{Equation 2.21}$$

The time history of the response is:

$$x(t) = x^* + (x^* + \Delta x)e^{-\gamma t} \qquad \text{Equation 2.22}$$

In this ideal system every state variable is controlled by the appointed administration. The Jacobian of such a system is:

$$[\Im] = \begin{bmatrix} -\gamma_{11} & 0 & \dots & \dots & 0 \\ 0 & -\gamma_{22} & \dots & \dots & 0 \\ \dots & \dots & \dots & \dots & \dots \\ \dots & \dots & \dots & \dots & \dots \\ 0 & 0 & \dots & \dots & -\gamma_{nn} \end{bmatrix} \qquad \text{Equation 2.23}$$

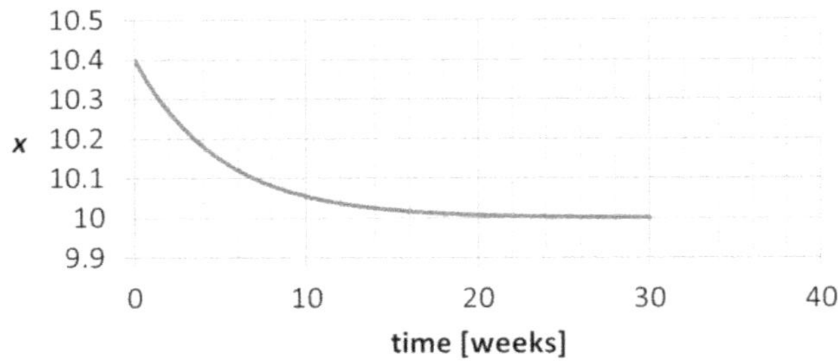

Figure 2.3 Illustration of Equation 2.22. x*=10; Δx=0.4; γ=0.2. Author's work.

The eigenvalues of the system are the diagonal terms of $\left[\mathfrak{J}\right]$. All the eigenvalues are negative; the system is stable. The sum of the eigenvalues is $\mathbf{tr}\left(\mathfrak{J}\right)$or the trace of the Jacobian. Then the term $-\mathbf{tr}\left(\mathfrak{J}\right)$ represents the cost of fixing all the deviations. If one added one state variables, then $-\mathbf{tr}\left(\mathfrak{J}\right)\sum_{k=1}^{n+1}\gamma_{kk}$ will increase by $\gamma_{k+1,k+1}$. However, at a certain value of $n=\bar{n}$ the cost of fixing all the deviation cannot increase because of budgetary constraints. Or:

$$\lim_{n\to\infty}\sum_{k=1}^{n}\gamma_{kk}=\sum_{k=1}^{\bar{n}}\gamma_{kk} \qquad \text{Equation 2.24}$$

If the negative of the trace is constant and the number of its terms increases, then many of the γ_{kk} terms will decrease. As the number of state variables increases, some eigenvalues approach zero. At limit one of them will be zero and the determinant of the Jacobian will also be$\left|\mathfrak{J}\right|=0$. At this point the equilibrium will be *neutral* (Figure 2.1c). The number of state variables of an ideal system can grow indefinitely, and practically it will remain stable.

Society: The Practical Case

The previous analysis suggests that in a functioning society the equilibrium can become unstable if the number of state variables exceeds a certain threshold. In societies the state variables are interdependent and the Jacobian is not a diagonal of correction factors. The diagonal terms of the Jacobian represent the *good* intensions of administrators, hence the symbol γ for the diagonal terms. Good intensions have side effects, and usually they are harmful. For example, in the expression $\dot{x}_k=-\gamma_{kk}x_k+\beta_{kj}x_j$ the term γ_{kk} quantifies the good intention of the administration to reduce the deviation of state variablex_k. However, good intentions may have bad side effects. One side effect

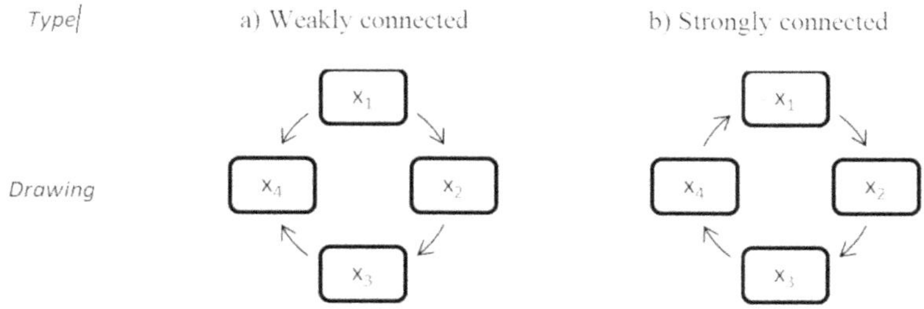

Figure 2.4 Weakly connected and strongly connected state variables; in b) one can reach any state variable from any state variable; in a) one cannot reach x_1 from any of the other variables. Author's work.

of state variable x_k is proportional to state variable x_j. The proportionality coefficient of this potentially bad outcome should be symbolized by the letter β. This coefficient acts on x_k and multiplies x_j; therefore, its full designation is β_{kj}. With this understanding the Jacobian of a practical government system is:

$$[\mathfrak{J}] = \begin{bmatrix} -\gamma_{11} & \beta_{12} & \cdots & \cdots & \beta_{1n} \\ \beta_{21} & -\gamma_{22} & \cdots & \cdots & \beta_{2n} \\ \cdots & \cdots & \cdots & \cdots & \cdots \\ \cdots & \cdots & \cdots & \cdots & \cdots \\ \beta_{n1} & \beta_{n2} & \cdots & \cdots & -\gamma_{nn} \end{bmatrix} \qquad \text{Equation 2.25}$$

A published research investigated the effect of off-diagonal terms on the determinant of the Jacobian $\mathfrak{J}$.[13] In some cases adding an off-diagonal term has no effect. In other cases it drives the value of $\mathfrak{J}$ toward 0. The condition is that the *directed graph* of the involved state variables is *strongly connected*.[14] Figure 2.4 displays the *directed graph* of four state variables $x_1, x_2, x_3, x_4,$.

In column a) of Figure 2.4 x_1 has a damaging effect on x_2 and x_4; x_2 damages x_3 and x_3 damages x_4.

In column b) of Figure x_1 has a damaging effect on x_2; x_2 damages x_3; x_3 damages x_4 and x_4 damages x_1. In this directed graph every variable marker is reachable from every other variable marker. This directed graph is strongly connected. Column a) shows a weekly connected directed graph.

The investigation[15] shows that:

1. In the ideal government system if one increases the number of state variables some eigenvalues approach zero because $-\mathbf{tr}(\mathfrak{J})$ is constant and the number of its terms increases. As one eigenvalue is almost zero, the determinant of the ideal government model is also close to 0.

2. In the practical government system, if one increases the number of state variables, the Jacobian receives more off-diagonal terms (Equation 2.25). Off-diagonal terms may
   a. Either leave the eigenvalues unchanged
   b. Or bring some of them closer to zero or even beyond zero i.e one ore more eigenvalues change signs from negative to positive.

Equation 2.20 shows that if the real part of at least one eigenvalue is positive, then the government system is at an unstable equilibrium (Figure 2.2b).

Recapitulating the Principal Logic of the Model

The model of n interrelated *state variables* consists of a system of n nonlinear equations with n unknowns; this is true regardless if the *state variables* represent magnitudes in nature, physics, technology, society, or a mixture of any of the above. The right-hand side of these equations consist of terms $\dot{x}_i$ representing the rate of change in time of state variable number i as function of the value of all the state variables. The system of equation has solutions satisfying the condition that$\dot{x}_j = 0; j = 1,2,\ldots,n$; these solutions represent sets of values of the state variable at *equilibrium*. One can "linearize" the system of equations at every point of equilibrium. The "linearized" system represents the behavior of the system for a small disturbance. Any linear system of n equations with n unknowns can be expressed in a matrix form $\left[\mathfrak{I}\right]\{x\} = \{\dot{x}\}$. The matrix $\left[\mathfrak{I}\right]$ is called the Jacobian. The eigenvalues of $\left[\mathfrak{I}\right]$ can be calculated, and they will be of the form $\lambda_j = a_j + b_j i$. The system is stable if $a_j < 0, j = 1,2,\ldots n$; in other words if the real part of all n eigenvalues is negative. The sum of the eigenvalues (trace) is $\sum_{j=1}^{n} \lambda_j = \sum_{j=1}^{n} a_j$ because for every solution $a_j + b_j i$ there will be a solution$a_j - b_j i$. Consequently, in a stable system the trace is negative.

At this point, the problem of a governmental system possesses a particular limitation. The sum of the diagonal terms of the Jacobian $\sum_{j-1}^{n}(-\gamma_{jj})$represents the totality of corrective actions taken for cancelling deviations from equilibrium. This sum is limited because it is related to the taxing capability of the government. If the economic growth is zero or negligible, then the sum $\sum_{j-1}^{n}(-\gamma_{jj})$cannot grow beyond a ceiling. Since $\sum_{j=1}^{n}(-a_j) \leq \sum_{j-1}^{n}(-\gamma_{jj})$ the sum $\sum_{j=1}^{n}(-a_j)$is also limited by a ceiling. Thus if $\sum_{j=1}^{n}(-a_j)$ is constant and n grows then at least one of the $(-a_j)$ terms must approach 0. When one of the $(-a_j)$ terms becomes 0, then the system is at neutral equilibrium. The next increment in n takes the system to unavoidable instability or sudden collapse.

From Model to Reality

The model shows that a government system with a growing number of state variables approaches the point of instability. This is true whether the diagonal and off-diagonal terms of the Jacobian are known or rough estimates. As the number *n* of state variables grows the Jacobian is populated with off-diagonal terms which represent a potential of instability. In terms of *here and now*, the more functions the government manages, the less stable its societal equilibrium is. The off-diagonal terms represent unintended side effects of well-intended governmental interventions. These side effects tend to close positive feedback loops; as the model shows, the real parts of its eigenvalues approach zero. In complex societies this signifies neutral equilibrium; in everyday terms it is equivalent to the brink of the cliff.

At this point one additional government function will transfer the society to a state of ungovernable disorder.

Notes

1 Peter Schulte et al., "The Chicxulub Asteroid Impact and Mass Extinction at the Cretaceous-Paleogene Boundary," *Science* 327, no. 5970 (2010): 278–92.

2 Vito Volterra, "Variations and Fluctuations of the Number of Individuals in Animal Species Living Together," *ICES Journal of Marine Science* 3, no. 1 (1928): 92, 93; Alfred J. Lotka, *Elements of Physical Biology* (Baltimore: Williams & Wilkins, 1925).

3 E.g. Carolina Acevedo and Jennifer P. Barfield, "Review: Reproductive Physiology of Bison and Application of Assisted Reproductive Technologies to their Conservation," *Animal* 17 (2023), doi.org/10.1016/j.animal.2023.100842.

4 "Under natural conditions male to female ratios will be close to 1:1" ibid.

5 E.g. Johannes J. Duistermaat and Johan A. C. Kolk, *Distributions: Theory and Applications* (New York, Dordrecht, Heidelberg, and London: Birkhäuser, 2010), Ch. 6.

6 E.g. Ibid.

7 E.g. Thierry van Cutsem and Costas Vournas, *Voltage Stability of Electric Power Systems* (New York: Springer, 2007), 142.

8 E.g. Clarence R. Wylie J.R., *Advanced Engineering Mathematics* (New York: Mc-Graw-Hill, 1966), 454. Corollary 1.

9 E.g. Ibid., 477. Subsection (1).

10 E.g. Ibid., 479. Theorem 2.

11 E.g. Ibid., 478. Subsection (4).

12 E.g. Ibid., 481–2.

13 Joseph Livni, "Investigation of Collapse of Complex Socio-Political Systems Using Classical Stability Theory," *Physica A: Statistical Mechanics and Its Applications* (2019): 553–62.

14 Ibid.

15 Ibid.

3

Stability of Simple Systems

Objective

This chapter intends to familiarize the reader with concepts of stability and control in technology, nature, and society.

The chapter will introduce and explain the related terms used by specialists in the domain and will dwell on the logical analogy of all systems in which stability is maintained by a controller. Consequently, the same mathematical expressions are proper for all the study of equilibrium and stability of all systems (e.g., autopilot, cruise-control of ground vehicles, prey and predator population, financial stability, crime control, and, most importantly for this book, sociopolitical stability).

The discussion opens with a simple technological example. A hot water tank is not considered as a technological novelty. Even the solar water tank concept is more than 100 years old (Figure 3.1). All water tanks need to keep water temperature within a range typically 110–120°F. Section *Physics: Hot Water* Temperature control discusses how this temperature range is maintained, recapitulating the applicability of the terms, equilibrium, stability and collapse for this particular technological application. Section *Nature: Prey and Predator* will transpose the reader into the realm of biology. Here again the section discusses and repeats the concepts of stability, control, and collapse in order to underline the cross-disciplinary analogy. This section makes one step forward by treating a case where two magnitudes are controlled: the prey population and the population of predators. Section *Crime Control Simple Model* brings us closer to the main theme of the book: stability of social systems. The section discusses a model developed in a health science discipline studying the spread of infectious diseases. The crime control section will help substantiating the analogy between natural and social systems and their stability. Crime control is discussed as controlling three magnitudes; however, the chapter will bring an example of an analysis where additional social metrics have been taken into account. This opens the door to real-life stability and control issues where numerous social parameters play in an intricate process of mutual interference. Chapter 5 discusses equilibrium, control, and stability of such complex sociopolitical schemes.

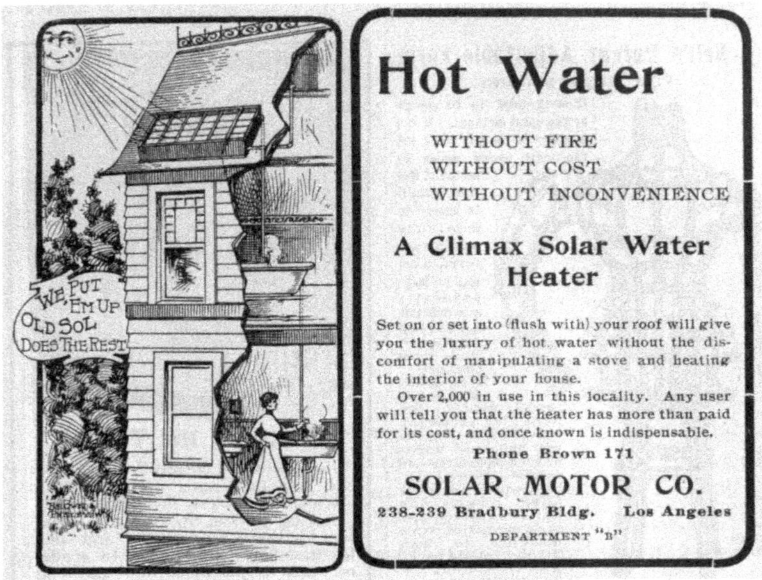

Figure 3.1 Solar water heater in 1902. By Solar Motor Co. Public Domain.

Physics: Hot Water Temperature Control

Figure 3.2 is a schematic illustration of a typical hot water tank. The water in hot water tanks is heated with oil, natural gas, wood, coal or other fuel. The tank of Figure 3.2 happens to be heated with natural gas. If the gas continuously burned, the temperature of the water would increase until all the water becomes vapor. If the tank had no relief valve, the tank would explode; the tank we talk about has a pressure/temperature relief valve; consequently this tank is safe as far as building up of vapor pressure is concerned. However, this is not our concern. The water tank of Figure 3.2 has another device called *thermostat and gas valve*. This is the controller device that keeps the water temperature within the desired range, for example, 110–120°F. If the water is too cold, then not only it is not comfortable for a shower, but also it allows harmful bacteria such as *legionella* to grow in the water tank.[1] If the water is too hot, it can cause burns. Consequently the thermostat is an essential component of the water tank. Its operation is easy to understand. The thermostat has a temperature transducer which is an element that changes with temperature: it may bend, expand, shrink, increase or decrease its electric resistivity, and so on. These changes activate or deactivate either mechanically or electrically the valve of the thermostat. When the water is below the required temperature, the valve is activated to open the gas entry turning on the gas burner; as a consequence the water heats up. When the water temperature is above the required range, the thermostat closes the valve, turning off the burner and the water cools down. This system keeps the mean temperature constant; in other words

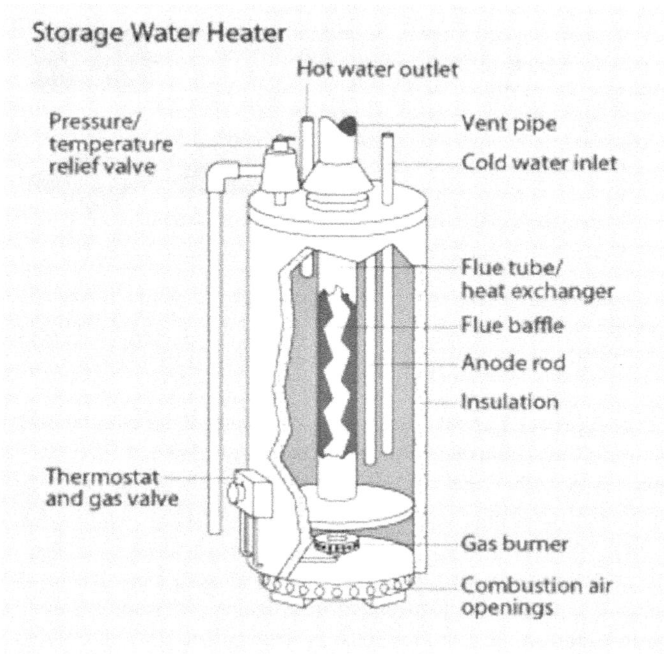

Figure 3.2 Hot water tank. US Department of Energy. Public Domain.

the water temperature is in equilibrium. The monitored magnitude here is the water temperature. Stability and control specialists call the monitored magnitude *state variable.* The state variable in this case is kept within limits; in the specialists' lexicon the temperature is in equilibrium. If one disturbs the equilibrium, for example, by overusing the hot water, the water will cool down perhaps below the prescribed range. However, the system will return to the prescribed range. Stability and control specialist describe such equilibrium as *stable.* If the thermostat fails to open or to close the valve, then the equilibrium will arrive either at the boiling temperature of the water or at room temperature. This equilibrium is *unstable* because the state variable reaches undesired magnitudes. Without adequate control the stability of the system is compromised.

Society: Simple Business Control Model

The purpose of business is to make a profit. Business administration checks the balance between income and expenditure (Figure 3.3). Expenses are salaries, dividends, travel expenses, maintenance, equipment purchase, interest payments, insurance payments, contractor payments, and so on. If the income is higher than the expenses, the difference is reinvested increasing the capital of the business; else the administration

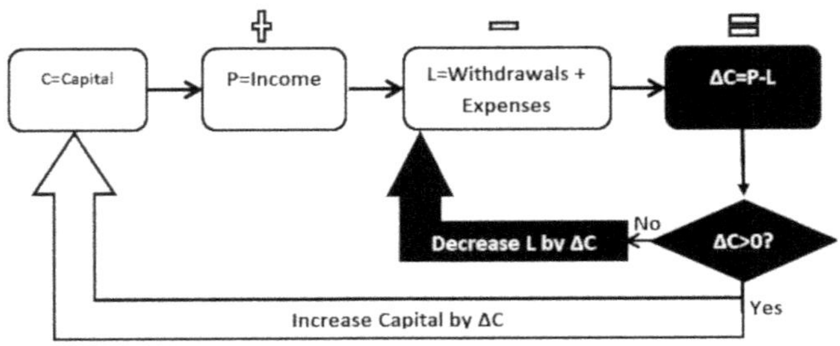

Figure 3.3 Business financial control model; black on white boxes are operation functions; white on black boxes are control functions; if control malfunctions the capital constantly decreases until the business collapses. Author's work.

needs to reduce expenses accordingly. If the administration repeatedly declines to take corrective actions, the capital decreases, the debt increases and, ultimately, the business fails. Without a responsible finance control the system is in an unstable equilibrium.

The purpose of discussing the temperature control of a hot water tank temperature and the business control model is to show how similar they are. True, hot water tanks are products of technology. Probably their ancestry goes back to the discovery of fire. Maintaining capital in a business is more recent. Babylonian tables concerned with compound interest calculations indicate that calculation procedures involving capital have been around for close to 4,000 years.[2] Our interest is in the fact that both processes are concerned with equilibrium. One example maintains the temperature; the other preserves the capital. Both monitor deviations and activate corrective actions when deviations are detected. Figure 3.4 illustrates the analogy between the two equilibrium related tasks. The examples illustrate that closely related problems have similar solutions even when one belongs to technology and the other to society. All these systems consist of a closed loop (see Figure 3.4) where deviations are detected and corrective actions are initiated and transmitted back to the current value to cut down the deviation. Therefore, in specialists' jargon these loops are called *negative feedback loops.*

The thermostat controls temperature; the financial administrator controls the invested capital. Both control *state variables.* The examples of Figure 3.4 deal with very simple models with one single *state variable.* The next sections will extend the discussion to examples where more than one *state variable* are necessary to investigate the equilibrium and stability of the system.

Nature: Prey and Predator

The biosphere of our planet houses a diversity of living creatures. They live in a large system of interdependent species. Some bacteria live within more evolved organisms which feed them, and the bacteria either harm or help the host creatures. Some species

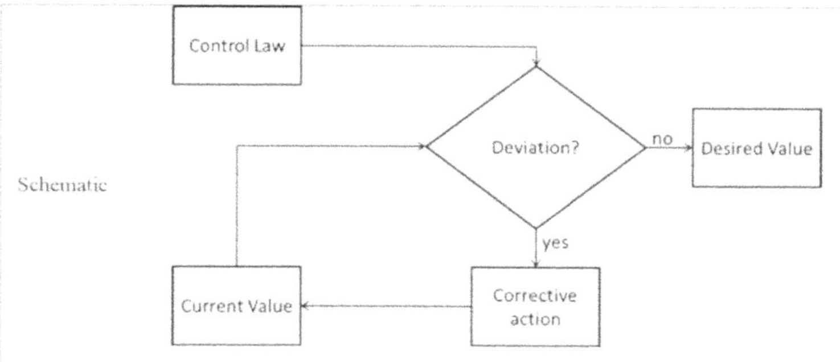

	a) *Thermostat*		b) *Simple Business Control*	
Control Law	Keep Temperature at 145°F		Prevent Capital Decrease	
State Variable	Temperature		Capital	
Deviation	Is temperature too high or too low?		Is income higher or lower than expense?	
Answer	Yes		No	
Corrective Action	Too high	Switch power off	Higher by $x	Invest $x
	Too low	Switch power on	Lower By $x	Cut expenses by $x

Figure 3.4 Comparison between two simple control models: (a) Physics—thermostat and (b) Society—simple business control. The resemblance allows using the same stability and control judgments, calculations, analysis, etc. Author's work.

help each other in a symbiotic relationship. Some natural species are endangered species. Some will go extinct. No doubt for the species in question extinction is collapse. However for the biosphere it is perhaps a normal event: "Extinction is the rule. Survival is the exception."[3] This does not imply that the biosphere is on the brink of collapse. Evolution is responsible for the extinction of species; evolution also guarantees the survival of other species and the appearance of new species. The diversity of species is on an exponential growth curve.[4]

"Accidents that eradicate successful species have always accompanied life."[5] Some disruptions were calamities generating mass extinctions. After each violent upset a new *steady state* was achieved. In terms of stability of systems, life on Earth is not in equilibrium; however, this complex system of living beings has experienced a series of equilibria disrupted by grand-scale perturbations.[6] Equilibria collapsing because of a major blow are not considered as either stable or unstable. The study of equilibrium and stability is not interested in excessive upheavals of nature. The study of stability and control is intended to keep systems stable when exposed to small perturbations. Science and technology is far from fantasizing winning over extraordinary natural catastrophes. After all during the last 540 million years, which are believed to be the biosphere, Earth has experienced only five mass extinctions. Therefore, stability and control specialists worry about airplane crash, buckling of buildings, and, in our case, collapse of democracy.

It is time for the chapter to come *back to earth* and examine useful examples of system equilibrium of Earth's living beings. Chapter 2 explains with mathematical tools how to determine conditions of equilibrium and stability of a prey and predator system. The section will recap in plain English the equilibrium and stability examination of the coexistence of two species: one is predator and the other is prey (Figure 3.5).

Figure 3.6 illustrates how nature controls prey and predator populations.

1. Abundance in prey increases the predator population.
2. More predators bring about more hunting and prey shortage.
3. Predators starve and their population dwindles; less predation allows for more prey.
4. Predator population recovers and we are back to a new loop.

Lotka[7] and Volterra[8] developed and proved a mathematical model of this loop (see details in Chapter 2). Figure 3.7 graphically illustrates how the model predicts the cyclical growth and decline of rabbits and foxes. In terms of equilibrium and stability, the two population sizes are *state variables.*

None of these *state variables* is constant; however, the outcome of Figure 3.7 is similar to equilibrium because the average of both curves over time is constant. Scholars call this type of equilibrium *dynamic equilibrium* or *steady state*. The Lotka-Volterra

Figure 3.5 Prey and predator or cat and mouse. By Jengod. Public Domain. Creative Commons Attribution-Share Alike 4.0 International.

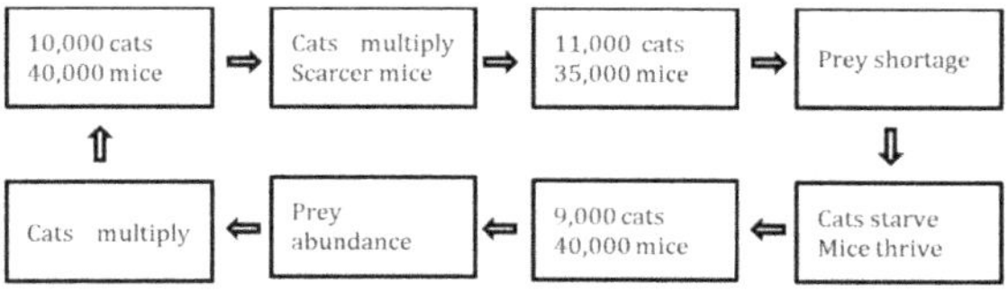

Figure 3.6 Prey and predator natural control loop. Author's work.

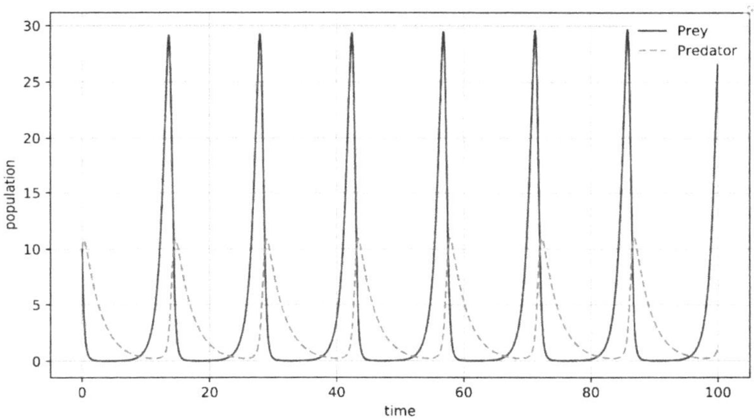

Figure 3.7 Prey: rabbit. Predator: fox. Public Domain. Credit: Ian Alexander and Krishnavedala CC BY-SA 4.0 DEED Attribution-ShareAlike 4.0 International.

model explains how nature maintains *steady state* of animal populations. However, it is not difficult to extend the prey-predator concept to society. For example, *criminals* have a predator called *police*. It is easy to see the analogy. Therefore, one can use the model to make simplistic predictions regarding the *steady state* of criminal population for a given average police force. Obviously, society has more complex situations than police chasing criminals. For example in society criminals are predators of property owners and prey of police. This is a slight complication of the original Lotka-Volterra model. The model was modified accordingly by adding a third state variable, studied and published.[9]

The Lotka-Volterra model illustrates that a simplified model of two-state variables is a basic model explaining the principles of maintaining *steady state*. In society as in nature, the *two-state-variable* model is not always sufficient; after all wolf population size depends on more factors than their most abundant prey; other factors like competition with other predators, human hunters, and even bacteria may be taken into account in some studies.

The use of Lotka-Volterra model in a social context opens the window to discuss the value of analogy of police as predators and criminals as prey. As any model, the two-state variable Lotka-Volterra model solves the idealized problem of prey and predator population sizes in a world in which they depend on each other and only on each other. Ignoring other factors simplifies the problem, and in most cases, it provides adequate understanding of how and why steady state is achieved. Borrowing the cat-and-mouse model to study the police and criminal relationship is valid as long as one understands that the results reflect a situation in which the criminal population size depends only on the police size and vice versa. The analogy of all applications of the model is valid as long as the idealization of a two-state variables study is representative.[10] When necessary, adding more state variables is feasible.[11] Nevertheless, this discussion bridges the domain of social sciences with exact and natural sciences as far as application of models of equilibrium and stability is concerned. For readers familiar with algebra, Chapter 2 illustrates how identical equations apply for all these prey and predator family of stability studies. Now, this chapter is ready to discuss the crime control function of government.

Crime Control: Simple Model

Crime and its punishment are among the oldest problems faced by the human kind.[12] To be more precise a justice system combatting criminals is as old as civilization; it started more than 5,500 years ago.[13] It is not a coincidence that civilization and development of fortified cities began at the same time.[14] Moving to cities protected citizens from invaders; living outside kinship networks opened the need for established conventions protecting property, or laws. Where there is *law*, there is *lawlessness*.[15]

A more representative idealization of crime control is also borrowed from another science: health sciences. Health science studies the spread of infection using a mathematical model which is a three-state-variable version of the Lotka-Volterra model. It is known as the Kermack and McKendrick epidemics model.[16]

Figure 3.8 illustrates the interrelations between the three *state variables* of the model. In the health science variant the public consists of three populations: *Susceptible*, *Infected*, and *Recovered*. Infected people are contagious and transmit their

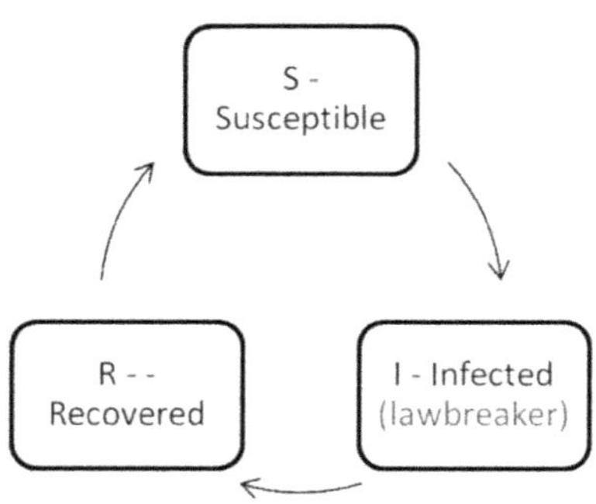

Figure 3.8 Schematic of the Kermack-McKendrick epidemics model. Author's work.

disease to susceptible individuals. Infected individuals recover, become immune (not susceptible) joining the population of recovered. Recovered people may lose their immunity and become susceptible.

The easiest way to substantiate the analogy of infection with social deviation is by using an example that bridges infectious disease with social deviation: drug addiction. The title of Rossi's paper (*The Role of Dynamic Modelling in Drug Abuse Epidemiology*[17]) indicates that the association of drug abuse and epidemics is widely accepted. The article indeed uses the Susceptible-Infected-Recovered (SIR) initial *state variables* (Figure 3.8); later Rossi extends it into seven state variables distinguishing between light drug users, hard drug users, recidivist drug users, dead users, and so on. The more state variables, the more realistic the idealization becomes. However, the value of this reference for our purposes consists in spanning between contagion of diseases and contagion of social deviation.

The next step in the analogy is spotting in the drug addiction idealization a significant *state variable*: the drug dealer. With this state variable, the model crosses the bridge into the domain of crime. Economists argue that crime pays if one ignores the risk of capture and punishment.[18] Economists do weigh the benefit against the risk of crime:

> Subject to data problems, almost all analyses conclude that crime pays a higher hourly rate than legitimate work but that the work from crime is sufficiently intermittent and risky that annual crime incomes may be lower than the annual income the criminal could get from legal work.[19]

Since we are still in the realm of addiction the reader will notice that gambling is also an addiction. Does gambling pay? Needless to say the gambler is convinced that it does; he/she is *infected* by this persuasion. A *susceptible* has a chance to conclude that crime pays because he/she underestimates the risks. The income of a criminal is attractive, and major lawbreakers take advantage of this incentive to recruit minor delinquents. On the other hand, a punished criminal may recalculate the odds and arrive at the conclusion that crime does not pay. Such a change of attitude transposes the infractor into the population of resistant individuals; the resistant is immune to the "crime pays" recruitment ad. Under certain circumstances the resistant individual will lose immunity; he/she may consider lapsing into breaking the law in spite of knowing the odds of being captured and punished. Figure 3.8 illustrates the cycle of susceptible-infractor-resistant in the sociopolitical realm of crime control. The mathematical equation of this $S \rightarrow I \rightarrow R \rightarrow S$ cycling (Figure 3.8) is known as the SIRS model; it is found in the mathematical epidemiology literature.[20]

The crime control analogy of the model is consistent with the earlier mentioned precept that crime pays if the expectation of its *benefits* exceed its expected *cost*. Thus, the probability of converting a susceptible (category S in Figure 3.8) is proportional to crime's *benefit* and inversely proportional to its *cost*. Thus, one can define a *Crime Deterrence* ratio:

$$Crime\ Deterrence = \frac{Crime\ Cost}{Crime\ Benefits}$$

The next conversion is from infractor category (I in Figure 3.8) to resistant (R in Figure 3.8). This happens due to detection, capture, and punishment applied by justice administration.

As described earlier, some infractors realize that after all crime does not pay; the analogy to acquiring immunity after getting infected is apparent. The next conversion is from resistant category to susceptible, or $R \to S$ in Figure 3.8. There are many reasons for this conversion; Chapter 5 discusses sociological theories explaining the occurrence. For the time being, suffice to mention that scholars research *recidivism*;[21] consequently it exists.

Reasonably, the efficiency of law enforcement or cost of crime is directly proportional to immunity retention. The combined failures of recidivism are grouped into a magnitude that behaves as *loss of immunity* in epidemiologic studies. The combined *Immunity Retention* is:

$$Immunity\ Retention = \frac{Crime\ Cost}{Immunity\ Loss}$$

The equations of the SIRS model (Figure 3.9) may be used to arrive at the value of each state variable at equilibrium. We are interested in the proportion of criminals at equilibrium, I^*. The system's equations predict that this ratio is:

$$I^* = \frac{1 - Crime\ Deterrence}{1 + Immunity\ Retention} \qquad \text{Equation 3.1}$$

Figure 3.9 graphically displays the results of equilibrium and stability examination using Equation 3.1.

In understandable words, as long as the expectation of cost of crime exceeds its benefits, the model predicts a stable crimeless equilibrium. However, when crime deterrence is less than 1, the crimeless equilibrium becomes unstable. This outcome is not surprising; if crime pays, that is, the cost of crime is less than its benefit, then the appearance of the first successful criminal spawns an epidemic of crime. After a period of volatility the system arrives at a new equilibrium. The new equilibrium is a society in which crime is endemic. Most civilized societies are in this category. The lower the *Crime Deterrence* ratio, the higher the percentage of endemic criminality will be at steady state. For example on the line of *Immunity Retention* of 1.0, at the *Crime Deterrence* ratio of 0.8 the endemic criminality at steady state is 10%. If the *Crime Deterrence* ratio is only 0.5, the criminality settles down at 25% (Figure 3.9). As the Immunity retention declines, the endemic criminality grows. At a *Crime Deterrence* ratio of 0.8 the criminality is 10% if the *Immunity Retention* is 1.0; if the *Immunity Retention* is 0.1, then the criminality settles at 18%.

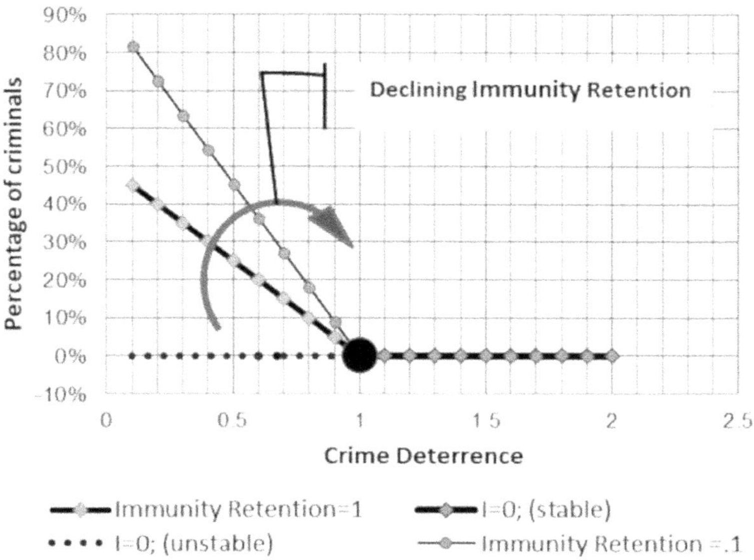

Figure 3.9 Parametric SIRS investigation of equilibrium and stability of criminality; Three equilibria are obtained: (a) stable zero criminality; (b) unstable zero criminality; (c) stable positive criminality. Author's work.

Equilibrium and Stability of Societies with Many State Variables

The previous example of three state variables criminality analysis is helpful to examine the problem of combatting crime where the foremost priority of the administration is law and order. Complex societies simultaneously tackle more and more public concerns; as a consequence, their *equilibrium and stability* system consists of a growing number of *state variables*. For example Table 3.1 lists seventeen conceivable governmental departments of the deceased Roman Empire and the corresponding seventeen *state variables*.[22] Sociologists and political scientist may analyze a government dissecting its public departments. Socio-physics examines the measurable state variables to arrive at conclusions; in this case the purpose of the examination is related to equilibrium and stability of a government system.

Figure 3.10 illustrates that public concerns are not decoupled; reducing deviations of one state variable from desired level may cause nonconformities of other *state variables*. For example increased taxation caused land abandoning that reduced agricultural supply.

An examination of the Roman Empire's government shows that some variables are strongly connected (Figure 3.10). Intuitively, one observes positive feedback loops predicting disaster. For example increasing the loading and unloading of ships at ports

Table 3.1 Functions and State Variables of the Roman Empire

#	Department	State Variable
1	Defense	Number of incursions
2	Defense	Size of the army
3	Public works	Worker availability
3	Welfare[a]	Number of poor
5	Transportation[b]	Road transport duration
6	Transportation[c]	Expected time a boat is tied up at dock
7	Justice[d]	Time and cost for resolving a commercial dispute
8	Health/epidemics	Number of death cases
9	Agriculture[e]	Square meters of unused arable land
10	Trade and Industry[f]	Probability of acceptable exchange of goods
11	Housing	Housing density
12	Revenue	Tax cheaters
13	Agriculture	Agriculture product supply
14	Trade and industry	Import from Egypt
15	Trade and industry	Product supply
16	Trade and industry	Consumer price index (CPI)
17	Revenue[g]	Number of smugglers

Source: Compiled by the author using information from:
[a] Alan Bowman, "Quantifying Egyptian Agriculture," in *Quantifying the Roman Economy. Methods and Problems, Oxford*, edited by Alan Bowman and Andrew Wilson (Oxford: Oxford University Press, 2009).
[b] Edward Gibbon, *The History of the Decline and Fall of the Roman Empire* (Boston: Little, Brown, 1854), 242.
[c] Maria T. Boatwright, *Hadrian and the Cities of the Roman Empire* (Princeton: Princeton University Press, 2000), 119.
[d] Cameron Hawkins, "Contract, Coercion, and the Boundaries of the Roman Artisanal Firm," in *Work, Labour, and Professions in the Roman World* (Leiden: Brill, 2017), 36–61.
[e] Joseph A. Tainter, *The Collapse of Complex Societies* (Cambridge: Cambridge University Press, 1990), 145.
[f] Ruth Kassinger, *Gold: From Greek Myth to Computer Chips* (Brookfield, CT: Twenty-First Century Books, 2003), 19.
[g] Gibbon, *The History of the Decline and Fall of the Roman Empire*, Kindle Location 4929; Stanley Bonner, *Education in Ancient Rome: From the Elder Cato to the Younger Pliny* (New York: Routledge, 2012), 317; William Smith, *Dictionary of Greek and Roman Antiquities* (London: C.C. Little and J. Brown, 1853), 945.

is feeding several boxes. Two of them, namely, worker availability and duration of load transport, back-feed the *boats' time at dock* box; the result is an additional decline of product supply, which ultimately closes two vicious circles (Figure 3.10).

This positive feedback loop continuously degrades all the variables in the loop. For the purpose of clarity Figure 3.10 does not mention interactions among all the function of the imperial administration. Nevertheless, these boxes feed functions that are not in the chart. For example, increasing poverty increases criminality, which decreases the ruler's legitimacy. This indicates that as the number of state variables grows the additional variables potentially generate more vicious circles within the system. This is consistent with the theory of *growing complexity* potentially bringing government system to instability.

Chapter 4 discusses various interpretation of the term *social complexity.* One of them hits the nail on the head clarifying that the problem is related to "the interwoven economic, social, religious and political organizations that structure societies."[23] I do not raise objections to other definitions of complexity like the number of strata in the social hierarchy. However, when the context is stability or resilience, then science

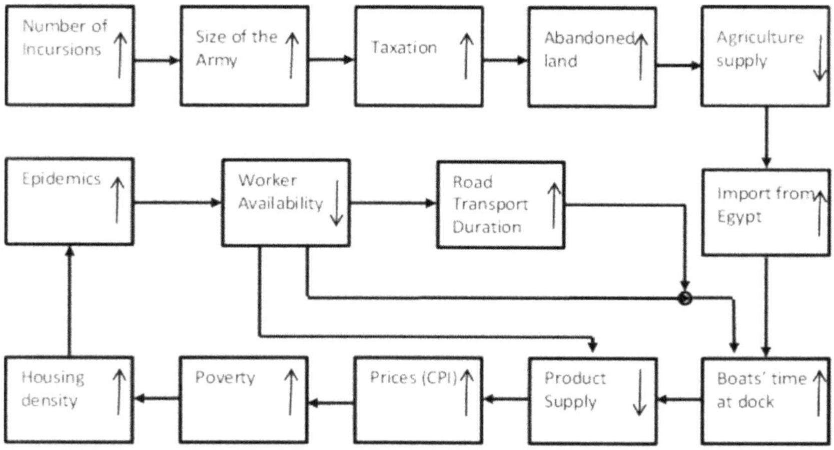

Figure 3.10 Interaction among selected functions of the administration of the Roman Empire. Author's work.

raises its eyebrows. It would be appealing if all disciplines would agree to use identical terms for the same magnitude. Naturally, the difficulty of inconsistent jargon in interdisciplinary dialogue is out of scope.

My mathematical derivation[24] uses classic equilibrium and stability theory confirming that as the number of state variables grows their intertwined functions proliferate; if the economic growth is not fast enough, then one reaches the point when many state variables exponentially spiral into total failure of the whole system.

Conclusion

This chapter offered a commonsense explanation to the theory that growing social complexity is destabilizing. It starts with practical simple explanation of how simple control systems work (thermostat) and how such a simple system can fail if the control unit violates control laws (financial business example). The chapter then illustrated how systems where two or more controlled variables interact with each other reach equilibrium. The system is more complex because both state variables need to reach such a constant value that mutually neutralize the undesired effect of one state variable on the other. The chapter discussed that there is a steady state of prey and predator populations so that they mutually assure each other's survival; at steady state there are not too many predators to depopulate the prey and not too few prey to exterminate the predators. The chapter justified the analogy of this coexistence with a social analogue: criminals and law enforcement. Finally, the chapter focused on growing complexity of social systems.

If a government deals with a growing number of state variables and if the interaction of these state variables is more and more intricate, then the equilibrium tends to reach instability.

This chapter substantiates the validity of the analogy of epidemics control by health administration with crime control by law enforcement.

The chapter explained the control of the water temperature of hot water tanks; this a technological application of control theory. Subsequently the chapter wandered into natural sciences discussing how nature controls prey and predator populations. Then it crossed into the field of government wisdom stating that justice administration is one of the oldest and therefore primary functions of the early states. Therefore, the prophetic instructions related to administering justice on the occasion of the return of Jews from the Babylonian exile serve as a proper closing:

> These are the things you are to do: Speak the truth to each other, and render true and sound judgment in your courts.[25]

Notes

1 Goverment of Canada, "Water Temperature and Burns/Scalds" (Ottawa: Health Canada, 2011).
2 Otto Neugebauer, *The Exact Sciences in Antiquity*, Second edition (New York: Dover Publications, 1969), 44.
3 Carl Sagan and Ann Druyan, *The Varieties of Scientific Experience: A Personal View of the Search for God*, Kindle edition (London: Penguin, 2006), Kindle Location 702.
4 Michael J. Benton and Brent C. Emerson, "How Did Life Become So Diverse? The Dynamics of Diversification According to the Fossil Record and Molecular Phylogenetics," *Palaeontology* 50, no. 1 (2007).
5 Michael L. Rosenzweig, "Loss of Speciation Rate Will Impoverish Future Diversity," *Proceedings of the National Academy of Sciences* 98, no. 10. (2001): 5404–10.
6 Ibid.
7 Alfred J. Lotka, "Contribution to the Theory of Periodic Reactions," *The Journal of Physical Chemistry* 14, no. 3: 271–74. (1910); Alfred J. Lotka, *Elements of Physical Biology* (Baltimore: Williams & Wilkins, 1925); *Analytical Theory of Biological Populations* (New York: Plenum Press, 1998).
8 Vito Volterra, "Variations and Fluctuations of the Number of Individuals in Animal Species Living Together," *ICES Journal of Marine Science* 3, no. 1 (1928): 3–51.
9 Juan C. Nuño, Miguel A. Herrero, and Mario Primicerio, "A Triangle Model of Criminality," *Physica A: Statistical Mechanics and Its Applications* 387, no. 12 (2008): 2926–36.
10 See for example using this simple model in an extremely complex of question regarding arms race competition, Joshua M. Epstein, *Nonlinear Dynamics, Mathematical Biology, and Social Science: Wise Use of Alternative Therapies* (Boca Raton: CRC Press, 2018), Lecture 1, Equation (1.1).
11 three state variables used in Gustav Feichtinger, Christian V. Forst, and Carlo Piccardi, "A Nonlinear Dynamical Model for the Dynastic Cycle," *Chaos, Solitons & Fractals* 7, no. 2: 365–85 (1996); five state variables used in Haiyun Zhao, Zhilan Feng, and Carlos Castillo-Chavez, "The Dynamics of Poverty and Crime," MTBI-02-08M (2002): 365–85.

12 Mark Jones and Peter Johnstone, *History of Criminal Justice* (Waltham: Elsevier, 2012), 1.
13 Mayson Kirby, *History of Civilizations* (Waltham Abbey: EDTECH, 2018), 91.
14 Ibid., 7.
15 Law does not produce lawlessness; however, how can one be lawless if there is no law? Before law and lawlessness existed, there were offenses of people against other people; an offense is a subjective injustice and its existence is determined by the offended party; in those pre-civilized societies, offenses were dealt by *restorative* justice; justice was restored by acts that "fit between hot blooded revenge and cold blooded deterrence." Alan M. Dershowitz, *The Genesis of Justice* (New York: Warner Books, 2000).
16 William O. Kermack and Anderson G. McKendrick, "A Contribution to the Mathematical Theory of Epidemics" (paper presented at the Proceedings of the Royal Society of London A: Mathematical, Physical and Engineering Sciences, 1927).
17 See also Carla Rossi, "The Role of Dynamic Modelling in Drug Abuse Epidemiology," *Bulletin on Narcotics* LIV, no. 1 and 2): 33–44 (2002); Michael A. Irvine et al., "Distribution of Take-home Opioid Antagonist Kits during a Synthetic Opioid Epidemic in British Columbia, Canada: A Modelling Study," *The Lancet Public Health* 3, no. 5 (2018): e218–e25.
18 Richard B. Freeman, "The Economics of Crime," *Handbook of Labor Economics* 3 (1999): 3529–71.
19 Ibid.
20 E.g. Matt J. Keeling and Pejman Rohani, *Modeling Infectious Diseases in Humans and Animals* (Princeton and Oxford: Princeton University Press, 2011), 40.
21 E.g. Roderic G. Broadhurst and Ross A. Mailer, "The Recidivism of Prisoners Released for the First Time: Reconsidering the Effectiveness Question," *Australian & New Zealand Journal of Criminology* 23, no. 2: 88–104 (1990): 88–104; Matthew R. Durose and Leonardo Antenangeli, "Recidivism of Prisoners Released in 34 States in 2012: A 5-year Follow-up Period (2012–2017)" (Washington, DC: Bureau of Justice Statistics, 2021).
22 I compiled a similar list of twenty-nine state variables; see Joseph Livni, "Nomadism and the Sociological Seed of Pre-Monarchic Israel," in *A Civil Society with No Hierarchy*, ed. Ilie Bădescu and Joseph Livni (Lanham: Lexington Books 2023), 13. Table 1.1.
23 Jennifer C. Ross and Sharon R. Steadman, *Ancient Complex Societies* (New York and London: Taylor & Francis, 2017), 2.
24 Joseph Livni, "Investigation of Collapse of Complex Socio-Political Systems Using Classical Stability Theory," *Physica A: Statistical Mechanics and Its Applications* (2019): 553–62.
25 Zechariah 8:16.

4

Socio-Physical Analysis of Complex Government Systems

Initial Remarks

The title of this chapter promises confusion. Every word of the title except for the word *government* is at least ambiguous if not pretentious to be ignorance covered up by *scientific mumbo-jumbo.* This strategy of promoting nonsense has been quite widespread for quite a while. After all, the phrase "they muddy the water to make it seem deep" is attributed to Nietzsche who lived in the nineteenth century; a historical chart of using the term *muddy the waters* goes back to 1650.[1] Consequently I owe the reader an explanation proving that this chapter is not selling muddied water; the easiest way is to translate the title to plain English.

Government

I will start therefore with the term *government.* I admitted earlier that the term *government* is less equivocal than the others. In spite of that, it is worthwhile to delimit the meaning of the term for the purpose of this book in general and this chapter in particular. We all learned that government decrees laws, enforces the law, and makes sure that laws and law enforcement are kept within a framework of fairness.

Historians help us understand how this came about. The agricultural revolution allowed human kind to expand in demographic terms and gave birth to large villages, towns, and cities. Life with kinfolks gave way to living with hundreds and thousands of people; the town and the city transposed the term *kinship* from its real meaning into an imaginary perception. The urban life came into being because cultivation of food allowed it; nevertheless, it could subsist only if the residents came to a general agreement about how to determine and protect property, how to solve internal disputes, and how to protect themselves against enemies and natural disasters[2] This general understanding divided human kind not only into *us* and *them* but also into *just* and *unfair*. In other words governments had power; however, their legitimacy[3] depended on indefinable spiritual concepts of faith, fear of god, and ideology. The art of governing is determined by an invisible societal feedback loop setting limits to how far autocracy can go:

> Even the most powerful and the most despotic government cannot hold a society together by sheer force; to that extent there was a limited truth to the old belief that governments are produced by consent.[4]

History is also useful to illustrate this postulation. Roman emperor Valentinian decreed a law authorizing police to detain senators. The repeal of that law by Emperor Gratian balanced concessions to aristocrats in favor of increased legitimacy. Unenforceable decrees, enforcement of unlawful orders, and excursions of power beyond the limits of legitimacy are unwise, unpractical, and dangerous.

Legitimacy of rulers reflects equilibrium between the power of government and consent of the governed. Not all societies arrive at the same equilibrium. In tyrannies the freedom of government outweighs the freedom of the governed. Tyrannies have existed for millennia; this empirical evidence indicates that autocracies have an inclination toward stability. A state of equilibrium in a tyranny implies that the consent of the governed guarantees the government a wide mandate. In other words the *cognitive map* of the governed regards collective obligations well above individual freedoms. A society of this state of equilibrium may experience an upheaval intended to redistributing power. History posits that the new equilibrium will consist of a similar tyranny.[5] Transfer from tyranny to liberal government is evolutionary, slow, and conditioned by incremental changes of the consent of the governed; in other words "societies do not hop models."[6]

Socio-physical Analysis

It is time to stop dwelling on the "easy" term *government* and examine the term *socio-physical analysis.* The term directs us to the notion of *science*. Etymology guides us to the Latin *scientia* meaning knowledge. A proposed taxonomy of knowledge into four compartments is helpful: Humanities, Social Sciences, Natural Sciences and Life Sciences.[7] No doubt physics belongs to Natural Sciences and the prefix *socio* points at Social Sciences. Socio-physics therefore bridges between the two categories upholding that difficult is not impossible. One of the difficulties consists of the fact that, "apart from the Humanities, all other scholars use the term *science* to describe their work."[8] Bridging two sciences should not be difficult. However, natural scientists consider science to be knowledge acquired through the three phases of the *scientific method*: observation, theory, and proof. Social science is characterized by scientific work, scientific theories, and scientific ethics.

In other words natural sciences presume that every question has only one correct answer and many wrong answers. In social science many scientific theories coexist even if they contradict each other. "Furthermore, many social scientists have distaste for quantitative approaches."[9] Bridging the two is therefore difficult, but not impossible. The socio-physicist observes an analogy between social and physical phenomena. For example the equilibrium between prey and predator populations is analogous to the balance between crime and law enforcement. The Lotka-Volterra model can examine both. The stability of these equilibria follows the same quantitative rules. The socio-physicist assumes that there is only one correct answer to any given equilibrium examination: it is neutral, stable, or unstable. Once one quantitatively determines the correct answer, the wrong answer is ruled out. That does not mean that any controversy in social science can be or must be quantified. It only means that if an analogy can be defended then there is "a need for a new interdisciplinary field, 'socio-physics,' which combines sociology with the methodology of physics."[10]

Complex Government Systems

This brings us to the question of the analogy between *complex government systems* with complex systems in physics. For that purpose, it is useful to define the term *complex government systems*. The term *complexity* has been introduced in Social Sciences independently of its use as *complex systems* in physics. One of the definitions of social complexity is:

> The extent of functional differentiation among social units, [which] may be vertical or horizontal; vertical complexity is hierarchical governance with a degree of concentration in decision making and power, [whereas] horizontal complexity is the differentiation of a population into various roles or subgroups.[11]

This definition is useful to clarify that Mesopotamia, Pharaonic Egypt, Communist China, and Cameroun are complex societies. Archaeologists can accordingly convey the following:

> While the archaeological data for the development of Maya civilization in the southern lowlands are difficult to synthesize, investigations over the last century have revealed a civilization with great complexity.[12]

Readers can relate to Maya civilization having strongly hierarchical governance, a significant degree of concentration in decision-making and power, and a differentiated population. No doubt archaeologists can talk to each other and perhaps even understand each other. Archaeologists interested in social complexity did indeed hypothesize that growing complexity drives society toward collapse. Both archaeologists[13] and economists[14] subscribed to the relation between growing complexity and social collapse. Applying Feinman's definition to examine stability of complex societies is awkward. Growth implies a measurable magnitude. Hierarchy is vertical and numerically measurable by the number of layers from top to bottom. But how can one compare one hierarchy with another. If growing complexity drives toward collapse how do we determine the complexity of a society with a given horizontal and vertical complexity? Is it height times width? Even archaeologists who intuitively subscribe to the relationship between social complexity and social stability express doubt in the practicality of such a definition:

> in suggesting that complexity theory should be brought to bear on the analysis of the causes of the Late Bronze Age collapse, we may just be applying a scientific (or possibly pseudoscientific) term to a situation in which there is insufficient knowledge to draw firm conclusions. It sounds nice, but does it really advance our understanding?[15]

In physical systems complexity is related to the number of *state variables* determining the system. For example the study of aero-elastic stability of aircraft started with a two-state-variable analysis of the wing, tail, or control surface. The two variables were bending and torsion. For straight wing aircraft (Figure 4.1), these two state variables were sufficient.[16]

However, modern aircraft have swept wings (Figure 4.2); their aerodynamic surfaces cannot be modeled as cantilevered beam. Assuming decoupling between torsion and bending is unrealistic. Fortunately, with the introduction of computers more complex models were derived and the whole aircraft is analyzed by models having several state variables known in that field as normal vibration modes.

The number of state variables of problems in physics varies from one application to another. Naturally, the more state variables are needed in an application, the more complex the analyzed system is. Therefore, in physics of equilibrium and stability

Figure 4.1 P-40 Warhawk. Source: National Museum of the U.S. Air Force, photo 050215-F-1234P-065. Public Domain.

Figure 4.2 Tupolev-144 at Technikmuseum Sinsheim, Germany. Public Domain. Credit: Froideval67.

the term *complex system* relates to the number of state variables its model requires. Sociologists similarly observe that societies "slowly augment in mass; they progress in complexity of structure; at the same time their parts become more mutually dependent."[17] This process is similar in nature, physics, and technology, and it is what this work calls growing complexity.

Fortunately, there are archaeologists that see complexity in the same way:

> One school of theory examines complexity in terms of the interacting and integrated "systems" of a society; these systems are the interwoven economic, social, religious and political organizations that structure societies.[18]

This definition of social complexity indicates that complex physical systems like the aircraft of Figure 4.2, and complex societies of the Maya civilization, for example, follow the same rules of equilibrium and stability. My experience taught me that postulating such an analogy requires a vigorous defense.

I still hear the reaction of a brilliant archaeologist who rebuked me, "your aircraft are dead things made of metal and plastic, put together with bolts and nuts, according to plans following laws of nature; my ancient societies consisted of human beings, gathered together in an unpredictable combination of agreements and disagreements; mathematical models are not helpful, are they?" No doubt, the affirmation that all societal questions are quantifiable is false. For example consider the following axiom:

> Equality of the general rules of law and conduct, however, is the only kind of equality conducive to liberty and the only equality which we can secure without destroying liberty.[19]

The algebra indeed cannot help examining Hayek's affirmation. As a matter of fact I admit that in social studies the unfeasibility of algebraic substantiation is the rule; questions that can be answered using algebraic manipulations are the exception. In any case the analyst bears the burden of evaluating the validity of the mathematical idealization.

Precisely for this discussion I placed Chapter 3 before this chapter. The bio-mathematical model of prey and predator grew from natural observations of a natural cycle (Figure 4.3). Police hunt criminals; it is not news. Nevertheless, sometimes police reporters keep the public up-to-date about the progress of the hunt against criminals:

> After a two-month undercover operation dubbed "Operation Summer Heat," the New Orleans Police Department announced the arrest of seventy-one street-level drug dealers as of Monday, along with arrest warrants for fifty-four additional suspects.[20]

Replace the term *predator* with *police* and *prey* with *criminals* in Figure 4.3, and the analogy of leopard hunting impalas with police hunting down criminals is straightforward. Similarly, the analogy of spread of infection with spread of drug addiction is quite reasonable; the next step is extending drug addiction to an improved model of crime control; this model has three state variables. It takes into account that law enforcement not only catches criminals, but the mission of its correction department is

> to reduce criminal behavior by providing individualized treatment and education to offenders, resulting in successful community reintegration through accountability and positive change.[21]

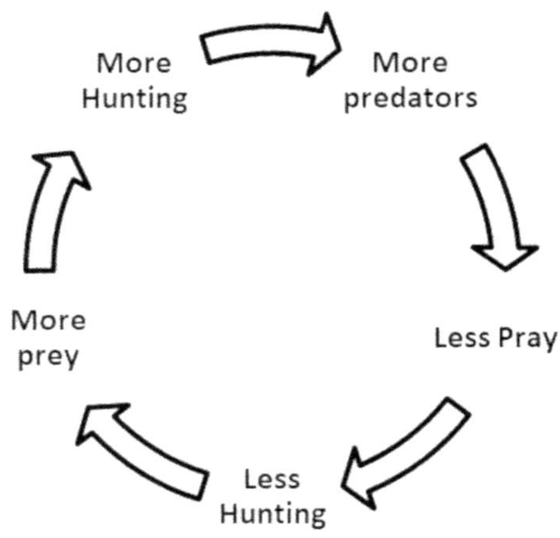

Figure 4.3 Prey and predator cycle. Prepared by author.

This excursion explains that human beings may seem more complex than bridges and aircraft; however, society consists of institutions acting to keep it within predetermined limits, detecting deviations, and applying corrective action. Safe flight requires commanding several systems like flight controls, landing gears, hydraulic system, electric system, communication system, fuel system, and environmental control system. Figure 4.4 illustrates pilots' instruments, devices, levers, switches, and handgrips needed to command an aircraft in flight. Similarly, the complexity of governing a society consists of many institutions and the interaction between constituent functions. This analogy confirms that growing complexity in the sense of adding more and more government responsibilities (*state variables*) is the quantifiable way to explain collapse.[22]

In plain English the mathematical investigation conveys that every corrective action consists of a well-intended measure reducing the harmful deviation of a state variable beyond desired limits. I will reuse the decree of Emperor Valentinian permitting arrest of senators to illustrate this statement. The intention was fighting senatorial misbehavior. However, the side effect was a decrease of imperial legitimacy. Apparently, the side effect was evident and Emperor Gratian repealed it. However, the side effects are mostly hidden, and they negatively act on many other state variables. This creates new corrective actions and more negative responses. The more state variables there are, the higher the chance of creating a chain reaction of a vicious circle in which intended corrections not only do not reduce the state variable, but also the correction capability diminishes approaching zero. Figure 4.5 illustrates one of the many possible ways a corrective action of Emperor Valentinian of the Roman Empire may have produced a vicious circle that has the potential to bring the empire to collapse. Naturally, this does not suggest that this decree was the reason for the empire's downfall. We know that Emperor Gratian repealed the decree, and this particular vicious circle was terminated before it could create too much harm.

Figure 4.4 Cockpit. Pilot is responsible for safe flight, from takeoff to landing at destination. Attribution: OV Squadron. Public domain.

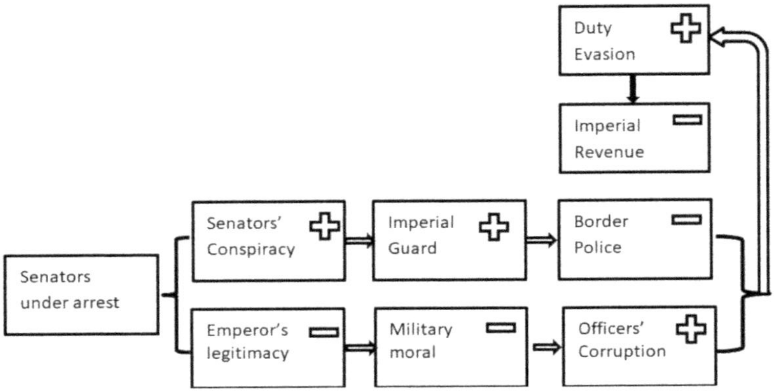

Figure 4.5 Roman Empire: Valentinan's Decree allowing police to arrest senators generating vicious circle. Author's work.

The discussion of the following sections deals with factors promoting the chances for such vicious circles.

Branches of Government, Power Distribution, and Power Flow

Any civil society legislates and executes the law. Less obviously, civil societies limited legislation by ethical boundaries set by an abstract concept called justice. This formulation requires a justification. For some societies like constitutional democracies there is no need to explain the legal constraints of a Constitution. No doubt, in other societies governments act with no constitutional constraints. Nevertheless, the perception of justice of the governed has played a role in governmental decision-making. Living in towns and cities outside kinship borders owning property like land and crops gave birth to an awareness of justice (see also Chapter 3, *Crime Control Simple Model* and Chapter 5, *Résumé*).

Rulers and governments either acted in fairness or at least they projected an image that they do so. Therefore the three branches of government: legislative, executive, and judicial have been part and parcel of civilization, even though they were not distinct. In terms of equilibrium and stability, every society established a unique balance between the way the citizens are governed and "the way they would wish to be governed."[23] Even despots could not make arbitrary excursions from equilibrium. Empires and kingdoms were indeed stratified. Hierarchies and oligarchies characterized various degrees between monarchs and aristocracy. For example, we are told that in the Roman Empire

> Political and military power resided in one man, but was of necessity modulated, communicated, and interpreted through an existing structure of aristocratic

> power-brokers. This system was the result of an uneasy and, at best, invisible compromise between the positions of the emperor and the aristocracy.[24]

Similarly in England the Magna Carta (1215) was the first of a series of unsuccessful "attempts in 1215, 1244, 1258, 1265 and 1311 (to name only the best-known instances), of subjecting the King to the dictation of a Committee of his adversaries."[25]

That said, these are not expressions of constitutional rule of law. They are primitive practices of balancing government activities. These compromises relate to constitutional checks and balances as the practice of adding wood to the fire when the room is cold relates to modern thermostat controlled room temperature. Civilization came to existence as a response to the need of defense against attempts to misappropriate land or crops. The conflict between individual and collective good required a compromise between individual and collective constraints. Naturally, this compromise may vary from one individual to another. Individuals may have different claims of mutual collaboration within the collective; "they nevertheless acknowledge a common point of view from which their claims may be adjudicated."[26] The very existence of that particular society proves the presence of such a shared point of view. Justice is a reflection of the shared collection of punishable offenses, their adjudication, and correction. Justice therefore was different in Sparta than in Athens, and justice in South Korea is different from justice in North Korea because the balance between individual rights and collective responsibilities diverges. In surviving societies the equilibrium is between the two extremes: liberty and servitude; its position is determined by the sense of justice.

In constitutional democracies the balance is strictly controlled by a tangible set of rules that clearly limit government. The Constitution of the United States is the first written set of such rules in effect today. The separation of the three branches of government—*legislative, executive,* and *judicial*—is an effective mechanism limiting the government.

Not every regime possessing a Constitution is a constitutional democracy. For example articles 83 and 102 of the Russian Constitution 2020 "empower the Federation Council, on the advice of the president, to dismiss from office the chairs and judges of the Constitutional and Supreme Courts."[27] A difference between constitutional democracies and domineering oligarchies is that in the later the Constitution empowers, while in constitutional democracies the Constitution limits government. Vladimir Putin, the top of the executive pyramid, proposed articles 83 and 102 to parliament; the legislative branch promptly approved the subordination of the judiciary to the executive. The blurring between the three branches clarifies the distinction between this type of government and constitutional democracies.

Currently, the Russian government system is in equilibrium. In 1991 the Soviet Union collapsed and disintegrated into several republics. As far as the Russian republic is concerned, the new steady state was achieved only after a transient of up-and-down fluctuation of individual freedoms; the steady state was achieved at a degree of individual freedoms in the vicinity of the liberty in the Soviet dictatorship.

The current Russian system started with Ivan the Terrible. Many changes have occurred since then. However, very little of those changes were in the direction of limiting government; on the contrary, most "reforms" empowered the government, even further including the reforms introduced by the Soviet revolution.

Centralization of Power

This section examines power centralization with tools of equilibrium and stability. The section will show that counterintuitively power centralization decreases stability. No doubt, an infinitely competent autocrat governs a state with justice, peace, and prosperity. Opposed to that a decentralized federation arrives at decisions reconciling conflicting aspirations of the constituting confederates. Autocracies promise a long steady state where wise rulers govern and happy governed willfully consent.

However, the practical situation involves rulers with random wisdom and limited understanding of questions brought to the decision-making table. The most common way of overcoming this constraint is the ancient solution of imperial bureaucracy.[28] If the ruler's wisdom is not infinite, then the pyramid of loyal and competent forecasters comes to the rescue. Scholars noted that this formula raises a question in need of examination: loyal or competent? Disloyal bureaucrats endanger stability by obvious reasons; incompetent counsel creates damaging decisions provoking unrest "local riots, in which violence was confined within a province, and mass rebellions, in which violence spread across several provinces."[29] The give and take between loyal and competent government machine is not the decisive factor of stability. The stability of autocratic systems is explained by "a combination of meritocracy and patronage in bureaucratic selections."[30] A strategy of an administrative pyramid populated by experts and local officials at regional levels and loyal overseers at top level explains the longevity of empires. The Roman Empire also used the strategy of mixing patronage on one hand and promotion of experts on the other.[31] Chapter 2 addresses the question why, after all, empires collapse. Control and stability theory demonstrates that system collapse due to vicious circles generated by chains of corrective actions that trigger unintended side effects linked to other side effects. As societies grow more and more complex, the probability of such vicious circles, increases (see for example Figure 4.5). Once many such positive feedback loops is close, neither loyalty nor competence prevents system disintegration. Competent advisors will come up with a well-intended fix of a new problem. However, if the fix triggers an unintended response that activates a chain of other unintended outcomes ending up with deteriorating the initial problem, then the advisor will upturn the initial correction. A critical number of such loops cause sudden collapse.

That is why neither loyalty nor competence of the administrators explains the stability of a centrally controlled government system. The danger of destabilization consists of centralization of power because centralized administration handles more *state variables*.

Decentralized systems handle local problems at local levels, county and state problems at county and state levels, respectively, and federal issues at federal level. In a decentralized constitutional government system the constitution limits the power of federal legislators to encroach on lower level authority. For example, "The powers not delegated to the United States by the Constitution, nor prohibited by it to the States, are reserved to the States respectively, or to the people."[32]

It is very unlikely that considerations of equilibrium and stability drove the framing fathers of the Constitution and of the Tenth Amendment to protect state powers from federal encroachment. Nevertheless the amendment significantly increases the resilience of the American Constitutional Democracy.

The social organization of pre-revolutionary American colonies shaped the concept of federative union of sovereign states keeping most of their powers while delegating some essential ones to the federal level. The combination of decentralized structure and bottom to top power flow were unusual in the Old World. Nevertheless, this concept was imported from there into the New World on the board of vessels bringing Puritans to America.[33] This power structure set up "the destiny of America embodied in the first Puritan who landed on those shores, just as the human race was represented by the first man."[34] The Puritans did not design their political power structure from scratch. "Puritanism was not merely a religious doctrine, but it corresponded in many points with the most absolute democratic and republican theories."[35] Not surprisingly the concept of decentralized structure and bottom-up power flow is the same in both: the Puritan Church organization and political arrangement (Figure 4.6).

The pattern is common to every Calvinist church. The local community and church oversaw the compliance of individuals with church rules and discipline.[36] This consisted of detecting deviations and applying corrective actions. The presbytery served as a regional council debating and deriving guidelines for reconciling unprecedented conflicts. The synod was a top-level council harmonizing standards of behavior all over the national domain.

The advantage of this arrangement in terms of stability is that each level controls less state variables. Moreover most state variables are controlled in the fundamental unit of the town: full participation of the constituents in detecting, judging, and punishing deviations aligns government with the communal perception of justice.

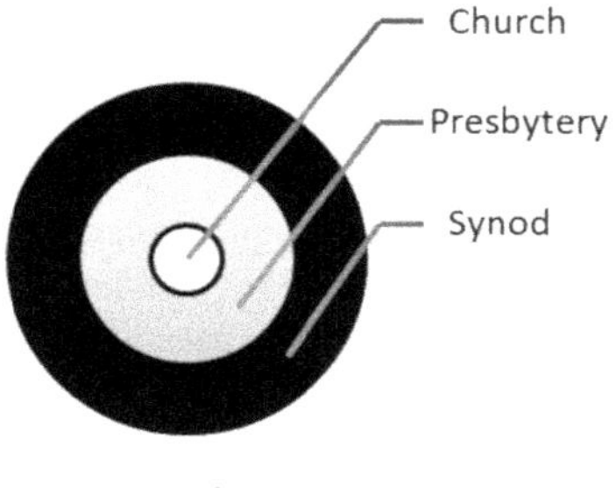

Figure 4.6 Puritan organization. Author's work.

The Constitution of the United States[37] has continued the colonial political formula of older Puritan practices. Constitutional limits set on the federal powers therefore constitute a significant factor of resilience of federal constitutional democracies; political initiatives ignoring these constitutional safeguards entail destabilizing factors.

Stratification

The introduction to this chapter mentioned scholars who agree that growing *social complexity* destabilizes sociopolitical arrangements. However, the notion of *social complexity* is not necessarily clear and scholars may disagree on what it covers. Reasonably, the Roman Empire was socially more complex than its predecessor the Roman Republic. The introduction mentioned Feinman's scale of complexity, namely, as the combination of vertical complexity (hierarchic stratification) and horizontal complexity (differentiation of roles and subgroups). This section discusses the practicality of quantifying complexity on a scale of stratification and/or functional differentiation.

Stratification is a tangible term. Archaeologists use criteria of detecting stratification like house size, grave contents, tomb sizes, wasteful construction and monuments, burial practices, and human osteology.[38] Archaeologists challenged the assumption that unranked societies are the default.[39] In other words, from the Neolithic onward ranking was the rule, unranked societies were the exception.

Nevertheless sociologists of modern societies refer to stratification equivocally. For example Chmielewski cites Baker[40] stating that cognitive skills "replace direct inheritance as the only legitimate source of social stratification."[41] Another source affirms that "the structure of social stratification can be defined as the distribution of resources in society, such as income, wealth, occupation, education, and power."[42] Chmielewski determines that cognitive skill places people in the proper layer; Beeghley adds four additional criteria: class, race, ethnicity, and gender. No one has the courage to claim that *race*, *ethnicity*, and *gender* are ambiguous terms. However, as far as *class* is concerned things change when one is told that

> As a system of domination, class is rather new in history. It arose along with economic development and democracy (the two are related) over the last few centuries.[43]

The term *class* is ancient. An ancient Latin text[44] uses the term *class* in the phrase "Ipse interea milites scribere, non more maiorum neque ex *classibus*, sed ut lubido quoiusque erat, capite censos plerosque."[45] New or ancient, which is it? To reconcile the apparent confusion one can reasonably admit that capitalism and democracy added a new flavor to the ancient class distinction.

Since the terms are ambiguous this book introduces its own flavor of the terms *stratification* and *class*. I shall start out from Beeghley's words. Mentioning the nineteenth-century Beeghley specifies: "Before that time, people's place in society was pretty much fixed at birth."[46]

I would propose to define *class* accordingly; *class* is one's place in society determined at birth. The term *stratification* henceforth is ranking individuals in *classes*; each *class* possesses different roles, rights, privileges, and duties. This understanding of *stratification* is in conflict with associating *class* with cognitive skills, income, and wealth. No one acquires cognitive skills at birth. One does inherit wealth; however, income and wealth change during a lifetime, and as a consequence, income or wealth does not reflect one's situation at birth. British series like *Upstairs Downstairs* or *Downtown Abbey* better illustrate what *class* is about. Therefore, I dare claim that if cognitive skills replace inheritance as a source of ranking then we talk about replacing *aristocracy* with *meritocracy*. Aristocracy is a symptom of *stratification*; meritocracy opposes it.

This definition of *stratification* allows me to question another truth: "In all societies, parents pass on whatever advantages and disadvantages they have to their children."[47] No doubt, there is some truth to this observation. The mechanism is mostly through providing education to one's offspring. Chmielewski researches precisely this postulation. She plots the time history of the difference between measured results in math and reading of children of highly educated and poorly educated parents.[48] No doubt the approach is promising. The information comes from test results; as a consequence, for every cohort one can obtain the mean achievement of children of high education and of children of parents with poor education. The difference between achievements of the two categories of parents is plotted on a curve. In order to obtain a trend, the investigation calculates a cubic curve-fit.

To illustrate, explain, and validate the procedure, I propose to apply the approach of measured data of two almost unrelated variables. Figure 4.7 illustrates a time history of a patient's blood pressure (systolic and diastolic).

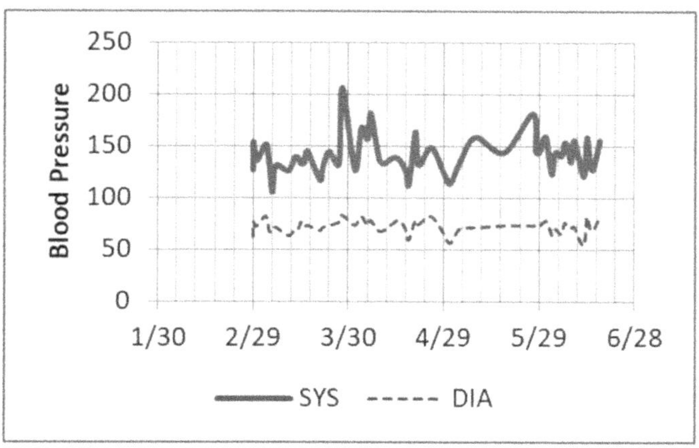

Figure 4.7 Blood pressure time history. Author's work.

Reasonably, the two are weakly related because otherwise one would need only one to diagnose patients. Nevertheless we calculated the mean difference between systolic and diastolic on each day of the week (Table 4.1).

Figure 4.8 plots the data of Table 4.1 and a cubic curve-fit indicating a trend. The trend is a weekly oscillation of the difference between the two unrelated blood pressure measurement with highs on Saturdays and Mondays and lows on Thursdays. Obviously the trend is misleading. That does not necessarily disqualify the methodology. The calculation of the trend comes with a statistics calculating the confidence in the curve-fit. In this case the statistics called R-squared is $R^2 = .67$. This R-squared figure is considered to be a bad curve-fit.

Unfortunately, Chmielewski did not provide the R-squared of her curve-fits. Since her trends are reasonable, I will comment on her findings. She applied the methodology in various countries where the time history of the income gap is known.

Table 4.1 Mean Difference Systolic-Diastolic on Days of the Week

Day of the Week	Mean Difference Sys-Dia
Sunday	68.625
Monday	69.6
Tuesday	69
Wednesday	70.375
Thursday	66.5
Friday	64.81818
Saturday	73.69231

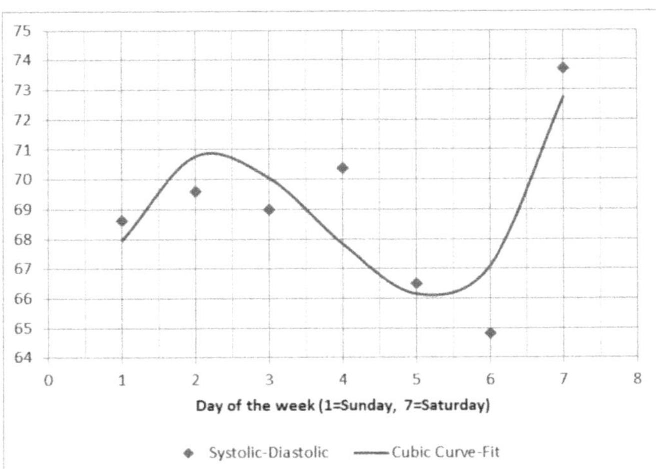

Figure 4.8 The difference between systolic and diastolic on days of the week. Author's work.

An interesting finding says:

> In low-income countries, increasing income inequality is positively associated with increasing SES achievement gaps, as expected, an association that is in part driven by declining income inequality in several Latin American countries and increasing income inequality in several post-Soviet countries. In contrast, in high-income countries, increasing income inequality is unexpectedly associated with decreasing gaps, driven by countries with increasing income inequality, very high levels of educational and occupational attainment, and stable or declining gaps, including the United States, England, Finland, Israel, and Japan.[49]

The R-squared statistics of the curve-fits are unknown; rather than claiming that the curve-fit is not appropriate, one can rationalize that parents' income is not a dominant component in children's' test results. For example:

> Although often significant in explaining differences in test scores for some groups, social class variables do not adequately explain the high test scores of Vietnamese who often have low levels of parental education and income.[50]

The driving force in children's achievements is not necessarily the income or education level of the parents. There is a cultural component of family tradition related to expectations of escaping poverty through education; this culture is characteristic to immigrant populations. A research of Caribbean-American women entrepreneurs in Massachusetts concluded:

> Individuals who start from a place of confidence in themselves, their products, and the system in which they ply products for money can be satisfied with building up capital of various kinds, not simply financial. This piece has suggested that diversifying business discourse and assumptions away from neoliberal capitalist notions about entrepreneurship, innovation, and worthy personhood can expand the funding imagination for how personal economic growth and productive community relations can be supported in their work as *reciprocal* development processes in U.S. cities.[51]

The immigrants migrate precisely because they believe that the Promised Land (e.g., the United States, England, Canada, Australia, or Denmark) enables mobility from poverty to material comfort. In the past masses of Irish, Italian, and Jewish migrants underwent similar trends. Currently Asian students follow their footsteps:

> Compared with other racial groups, including whites, Asian Americans achieve higher standardized test scores, obtain better grades, and complete more advanced courses. Asian Americans are less likely to repeat grades. They are more likely to finish high school and to receive bachelor's and postgraduate degrees. As suggested earlier, Asian Americans are also overrepresented at first-tier universities). In

> short, the higher educational achievement of Asian Americans in the U.S. school system is not a myth but a generally observed empirical regularity, at least on average for this group as a whole.[52]
>
> This finding questions another sociological truth:
>
> Class is maintained by means of a simple mechanism: discrimination, the unequal treatment of individuals and groups based on their personal characteristics.[53]

The extraordinary achievements of first-generation Asian Americans are factual. Asian Americans have been treated with discrimination and prejudice; that is also a fact. They succeeded. This indicates that identifying ethnic minorities as class is not quite adequate; after all class determines one's future social position at birth. Undeniably, discrimination holds back; however, in a constitutional democracy, success in competition for academic achievements is possible because the constitution prescribes equality before law; constitutionalism enforces it.

This section started from the topic of stratification. It concludes that in a constitutional democracy, stratification plays a minor role if any because of mobility thanks to learned and innate skills. Stratification is not a clear measure of social complexity and of sociopolitical stability.

Administration and Civil Service

Not surprisingly, the birth of government administration coincides with the beginning of civilization.[54] Section *Branches of government, power distribution and power flow* of this chapter mentioned the association between emergences of land ownership and of justice. Essential tools of administration appeared with the beginning of urbanization and trade.[55]

As urban areas grew in size,[56] social relations required unprecedented skills. Cities and towns grew where the necessary administrative capabilities became available. Managing urban agglomerations required administrative proficiencies, the main ones being reading, writing,[57] counting[58] and other arithmetic operations.[59] Trade allowed further population growth; needless to say, trade development was also facilitated by the concept of currency;[60] once money became an accepted means of exchange financial operations followed with interest and compound interest calculation.[61] Social management saw the transition from households to tribal councils to towns. Administered population size could grow because bureaucrats with various skills appeared and administered city-states and kingdoms. Bureaucracy "as a technical arrangement for the implementation of certain goals and provision of services"[62] is essential in any civilized existence.

Nevertheless the term *bureaucracy* sounds similar to notions like autocracy, democracy, and aristocracy.[63] A Marxist research states: "The real massive ascendancy of bureaucracy as a distinct and separate social group came only with the development of capitalism."[64] Criticism of Marxist philosophy being out of scope, this section will try to accept some of the reasoning behind this affirmation. The source rationalizes that the roots of bureaucracy are in "market economy, money economy and the continuous and deepening division of labor." However, all these factors appeared four to five millennia before even the term *capitalism* was coined. The question is when bureaucracy became an agent of state power. Reasonably, knowledge of reading, writing, and solving quadratic equations gave some status to the ancient Mesopotamian, Chinese, and Egyptian bureaucrat. No cuneiform tablet or papyrus text can give us a credible account how much power a king or a pharaoh conceded to his wise administrators. However, later antiquity left clearer insight: the Roman Empire witnessed "an increased professionalization of the military and state bureaucracy at the expense of senatorial traditions."[65] Consequently, some degree of sharing power between ruling class and bureaucrats took place at least as early as the third century.

This brings us to the question whether bureaucracy plays a role in the equilibrium and stability of a constitutional democracy.

One distinguishes between *static equilibrium*, *steady state*, and *transient*. *Static equilibrium* defines a constant ratio of the power of elected officials to the power of bureaucratic institutions. The higher the ratio, the more democratic the equilibrium is.

When the ratio oscillates above and below a constant average, it is rigorous to talk about a *steady state*. The average of the ratio of the power of elected officials to the power of bureaucratic determines how democratic the equilibrium is.

A *transient* state is not equilibrium; it describes a change from one state of equilibrium to another. Nature- and government-induced calamities create transients. The values of state variables change in order to rebalance the system. Examples of natural causes for *disequilibrium* are draught, flood, earthquake, epidemic, ice storm, heat wave, parasite causing production loss in livestock, and plant pathogens. One of the consequences of nature-induced unbalance is that bureaucrats gain power; often they practically take over the steering wheel. Often unelected officials piloting across storms further the disequilibrium with government-induced unbalance. For example, during the Potato Famine in Ireland (1845–52), Lord Russel, the elected prime minister of the UK, was unable or reluctant to override Trevelyan, an unelected civil servant,[66] who after a trip to Ireland became the expert on how to handle the crisis.[67] Consequently "the governmental strategy for Ireland was based on what was, in effect, a blueprint for depopulation drawn up by Trevelyan."[68]

Government-induced *transients* (e.g., economic volatility) are, for example, inflation, deflation, currency devaluation, and economic depression; societal imbalance may be the consequence of other manmade actions like military coup, rebellion, and civil war.

Not every change in equilibrium is collapse. *Ordinary transients* happen when *values* of state variables change. *Collapse* occurs when the *number* of state variables is suddenly and significantly reduced.

One should not conclude that bureaucracy is the opposite of democracy. Although bureaucracy has existed long before democracy, democracy cannot exist without bureaucracy.

"Max Weber considers the bureaucracy to be the epitome of rationality and efficiency, the most rational means of implementing a given goal."[69] No doubt, Weber the thinker talks about the *Ideal-Type* of bureaucracy; the *Ideal-Type* is an abstract, idealized image of an entity "it aims at directing at formation of hypotheses."[70] My personal education and experience makes me appreciate this approach. During the years of engineering studies, students solve idealized concepts such as mass and spring systems, rigid bodies, pendulums, frictionless hinges, insulators. Students get more and more frustrated realizing that these things do not exist in reality and hopelessly grasping that the real things as bridges, wings, and printed circuit boards are not part of the curriculum. There is a point in time when the engineer finds out that solution of masses and springs systems are applicable to predicting the response of an elastic wing to landing impacts. True, the wing is not made of springs joining point masses. Nevertheless, tests proved that adequate models of masses and springs produce sufficiently accurate predictions. The *Ideal Type* of Weber helps understanding how an organization of apolitical experts can better rationalize the ways to achieve goals.

The reality is, however, different. The *Ideal Type* of the elected official or of the civil servant has a common goal: serving the public. However, in practice, the primary goal of both is getting a promotion; the ways of climbing the ladder diverge. The career of elected official depends, among others, on their standing with his constituents; on the other hand, the practical way of a civil servant consists of promotions by extending the range of responsibilities and increasing the number of subordinates. This adds state variables to the system which is proven to be destabilizing.[71] As opposed to the *Ideal-Type,* unchecked bureaucracy does not stop growing. In a tyranny the growth of bureaucracy is checked by the ruler. In a democracy, the elected officials and their constituents keep the growth of civil service in check.

Political Participation

The correct answer to the test of Figure 4.9 is *C.* I am aware that there are scholars and students of law at Harvard who disagree with me. After all, one of their professors authored a book dedicated to the thesis implying that A is the correct answer.[72] Klarman's book discusses how "throughout American history political actors have invoked the wisdom and virtue of the Framers as arguments against constitutional change."[73]

The Constitution of the United States is "the oldest written constitution still in effect today."[74] The Framers accomplished an admirable task to put it together; however, they did not conceive the need for a constitution. Constitutions of American colonies guided government starting with the Mayflower Compact (1620). The framers followed a blue print of government framework engraved in the practice towns and colonies:

> I have already observed that the origin of the American settlements may be looked upon as the first and most efficacious cause to which the present prosperity of the United States may be attributed.[75]

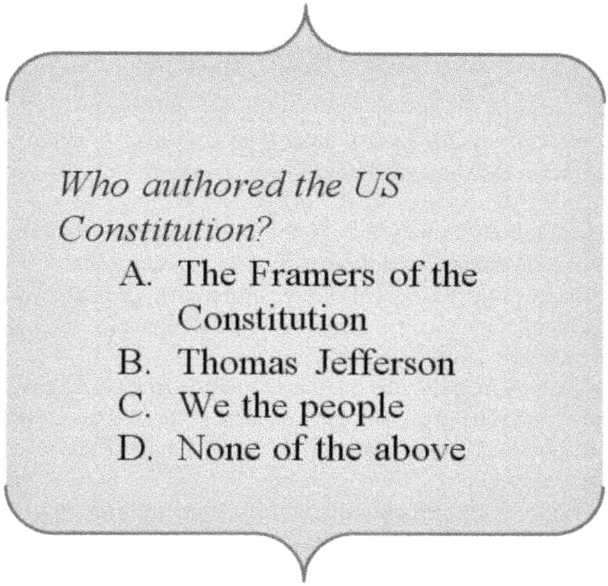

Figure 4.9 Multiple choice test. Author's work.

Principles of government in Colonial America were inscribed in the daily practice of the seventeenth century. They reflected public accords founded on free consent, a common mutual interest in the laws governing their town, and a shared responsibility of the members to uphold the welfare of the community.[76]

In the Old World, Enlightenment anticipated a transition to a new social contract addressing the "dignity of man."[77] Individual freedoms are essential to political participation. In the Old World there were no such freedoms in the seventeenth century. The Enlightenment formulated the need of revision of "contractual theories of the relation between ruler and ruled"[78] from tracks of spiritual obedience to paths of rational guidelines based on "humanity, justice and free exercise of reason."[79] Inspired by scientific discoveries and the introduction of mathematical methods in philosophy often attributed to Newton, Descartes, and Spinoza,[80] the promoters of the Enlightenment reasoned that the new era introduces the notion of individual rights growing from the human nature. In the pre-Enlightenment Old World individual rights were neither theory nor practice;[81] the Enlightenment argued that individual rights were inalienable because they are *natural* rights.[82] As long as individual rights are not practiced political participation is confined and feeble.

In the New World individual freedoms like freedom of religion, of speech, of press, of peaceable assembly, and of petition to the government have been stamped in the public life before their appearance in the First Amendment. Here they were unalienable because *constitutionalism* made certain that no one could or would alienate them.

As a consequence, in the New World the political participation of the public was a natural outcome of the way the settlements functioned:

> The New Englander is attached to his township, not only because he was born in it, but because it constitutes a social body of which he is a member, and whose government claims and deserves the exercise of his sagacity.[83]

The town of Plymouth pioneered, among others, the principle of community control over office holders. For example, ministers[84] or military commanders[85] with tendencies of domination had to bow to the will of the community. The Old World elaborated these prophetic ideas of political participation in philosophical dissertations; the New World printed them in day-to-day social practices.

Other towns of New England like Boston, Quincy, Salem, Lexington, and Concord in Massachusetts or Hartford, Wethersfield, and Windsor in Connecticut were established and practically administered by the residents. Each town maintained its law. However, natural population exchange dictated the need of harmonization. County and colony councils of representatives took care of smoothing inconsistencies between legal and illegal, between acceptable and punishable. The power flow was from town to county to colony. It is not a coincidence that this practice mirrors the Puritan Church administration (Figure 4.6). The source of authority is the Congregation; presbytery councils standardize practices of nearby congregations and the cluster of several presbyteries is harmonized by eventual synods. The Framers did not invent the American decentralized political reality; we do owe credit to the Framers for conserving it and elevating it to the status of constitutional decree. The Framers were not aware that this decentralized administration reduces the number of state variables of governments and consequently it increases the resilience of the future union. My thesis is that the Framers understood that the blueprint of sociopolitical framework is the will of the people and therefore it needs to be conserved. Therefore, the answer to the multiple answer question of Figure 4.9 is *C*: "We the people."

Other Constitutions followed the US model. Individual liberties have been decreed; in Western democracies individual liberties grew into being an integral part of the social contract; political participation played a dual role in this shift: it was cause and effect (see more in Chapter 7).

Elections are planned instances of political participation. Reasonably, as long as people freely participate in elections they expect that their vote has an impact. Beyond this trivial observation the subject is out of scope. The significance of elections in democracies is amply discussed in the literature.[86]

In the New World the participation at school board meetings, at town meetings, holding membership of boards and committees[87] has been inherited from early colonial town government practice.

Other forms of political participation entail "such activities as signing petitions, blocking traffic, donating money, or fighting with the police,"[88] "or taking part in demonstrations and strikes."[89] Another opportunity of the public to make an impact consists of membership in associations like "women's rights groups, animal protection organizations, or the global justice movement."[90]

In democracies where freedom of speech and of association are granted, the consent of the governed is unequivocal. Multitudes of free citizens express their consent by not protesting. Silence is not always a symptom of consent. In societies where bureaucrats are more powerful than elected officials, nonparticipation is a symptom of "disillusioned citizens."[91]

Sometimes consent is not expressed passively. I was most impressed by a brave active statement of consent with government in Catania, Italy. Shops posted signs of the grassroots movement *Addiopizzo* affirming that the owner refuses to pay extortion fees to organized crime.

Political participation is sometimes for or against nongovernmental institutions. For example in the nineteenth century, in France anti-Dreyfusards marched against Jews and in support of Church and Army.

The press is active in the process of political participation. Journalists are supposed to factually inform the public and comment on political debates and events. Recently, the press in the free world is more inclined to influence the political participation rather than report it. Political campaigning also known as *propaganda* is not new. Coincidentally the term was coined in the Old World about the time when New England settlements started to appear. The term was derived by the Roman Curia of the Catholic Church from the Latin *propagare* in the context of *propagating the faith* (*Propaganda Fide*). Under Pope Pius IX (1846 to 1878) the journal *Civiltá Cattolica* battled the cause of Church[92] with the same commitment to one particular political creed as do most of the media in recent years. Unquestioned devotion of a periodical to a cause damages the credibility of the press. Consequently, press propaganda is self-damaging; however, it is not necessarily destabilizing.

Institutions of higher education constitute a more powerful influencer of public participation; it is difficult to challenge the credibility of higher education. As a consequence, section *Education* of Chapter 8 further details the damaging potential of academic education and research in the United States.

DEI is not the only destabilizing persuasion fed to our students. Surprisingly, even law schools lecture destabilizing conceptions of constitutionalism. I will pick one example to illustrate how bad unproven innovative brainstorming can be. Among others the research of a Harvard Law professor teaches:

> freedom conceived as an *individual* right operates as a "trump" against legislative majorities. Yet freedom conceived as a *political* right entails the capacity of democratic majorities to control their destinies through legislation.[93]

Before civilization wrestled with the idea of constitutionalism despots freely controlled the destiny of the ruled through legislation. Freedom conceived as an *individual right* did not exist. *Democracy* appeared in Athens; it was not our kind of democracy, it displayed "polarities between citizen and metic, free and slave, Greek and barbarian, or men and women."[94] Nevertheless, scholars agree that Athens was the first democracy;

reasonably it was the first manifestation of "the capacity of democratic majorities to control their destinies through legislation." Many centuries later constitutionalism was noticed. Scholars[95] who paid attention to constitutionalism summarized that a constitution is not a government; it is antecedent to government; it defines limits of legislation, and "any exercise of authority beyond these limits is an exercise of 'power without right.'"[96]

No doubt a Harvard law student learning from both Klarman and McIlwain can conclude only one of the possible conclusions:

1. Klarman is right and the freedom of individual needs to be balanced by the freedom of government.
2. McIlwain is right.
3. Both are right.

My background teaches that when in doubt a test helps. The capitalist world is inundated by migrants escaping countries with capacity of "democratic majorities to control their destinies through legislation." They are seeking residence and hoping for a better life in countries where the government is limited by constitution. Klarman's version of freedom is destabilizing. McIlwain wins!

The political participation of academic institutions is powerful; however, the confidence in the claim that the academy increases the stability of constitutional democracies is not justified.

Groups obsessed with destabilizing the democratic system and the rule of law are various and embrace different and sometimes contradictory persuasions. Nevertheless there is some commonality. They share the same reliance of intellectual justification[97] of the need to a struggle against the current mistreatment of their kind (race, class, and ethnicity) wrapped in a promise of a future righting the wrong; this struggle includes "forcible overthrow of all existing social conditions,"[98] legal and illegal acts. Only a minority of these action groups rule out violence and bloodshed.

Checks and Balances

Chapter 2 discussed the principles of equilibrium in simple and complex systems. The common strategy of maintaining equilibrium consists of checking deviations in state variables and balancing them with corrective actions.

Autocratic systems maintain equilibrium the same way. The dominant state variable in an autocracy is obedience. Autocracies maintain special police forces spying on dissenters and deciding when and how to punish them. Socialist autocrats interfere in the economy,[99] education,[100] sport activities,[101] arts,[102] and so on to maintain many state variables at desired levels.

Democracies take freedoms seriously. We saw earlier that scholars note that individual freedom may clash with the principle of governing majority. Checks and balances of constitutional democracies have functioned as controls impeding deviations toward "tyranny of majority."[103] The Framers knew a colonial America with a rudimentary separation of powers. By the mid-seventeenth century the executive power of American colonial system was in the hands of a governor appointed by the king. Governors could impose legislation of a faraway English Parliament. They did not! Seeking as much approval as possible from the local population they consulted with a House of Representatives. The representatives were elected by free man.[104]

Naturally, some legislation by a council of elected representatives created conflicts with the will of the Governor. The legislative power was therefore shared between the House of Representatives (Lower House) and a Governor's Council (Upper House); it was either nominated by the Crown or elected by the House and confirmed by the Governor (for example in Virginia). This pattern of separation of powers reminds of current governments in North America. By its nature it offered operational checks and balances and the Framers of the Constitution were wise to adopt it.

The invention of the separation of the three branches of government is attributed to Montesquieu.[105] Among others Montesquieu was a judge. The American colonies practiced the separation of the executive and legislative branches. The judicial branch was mainly controlled by the executive branch.[106] The Framers were wise to implement Montesquieu's scheme separating the judicial power also; it gave way to ordered and efficient reconciliation of disputes between the other two branches of government and of legislative conflicts between federal and state levels.

Conclusion

Chapter 2 formulated methods of equilibrium and stability extensively using mathematical equations. This chapter tells the story of the resilience of constitutional democracies without equations. It submits that stability requires separation of powers, decentralization of the government system, a rigorous education of science, technology, engineering and math, a balanced education of conflicting persuasions, control of unelected administrators by elected officials, individual rights and liberties, political participation, and political checks and balances.

Notes

1 Candace Osmond, "Muddy the Waters – Idiom, Meaning, and Origin," The Grammarist, https://grammarist.com/idiom/muddy-the-waters/.
2 Yuval N. Harari, *Sapiens: A Brief History of Humankind* (New York: HarperCollins, 2015), Ch. 6 Building Pyramids.
3 See for example The Social Organism in Herbert Spencer, *Essays, Scientific, Political, and Speculative* (New York: D. Appleton, 1892), 267.
4 George H. Sabine and Thomas L. Thorson, *A History of Political Theory* (Oxford: Oxford and IBH Publishing, 2018), 731. Cited by Bas Dianda, *A History of the*

Seventies: The Political, Cultural, Social and Economic Developments That Shaped the Modern World (Wilmington: Vernon Press, 2019), 347.

5 See for example the 1917 October Revolution in Tsarist Russia, the 1979 overthrow of the Pahlavi dynasty; and the 2011 Arab Spring in Egypt.

6 Joseph Livni and Ilie Bădescu, "The Battle of the Covenantal Society against Elitism—an Overlooked Chapter in the History of Social Inequality," *Romanian Journal of Sociological Studies, New Series*, no. 1 (2020): 3–36.

7 Henk Wesseling, "History: Science or Art?," *European Review* 6, no. 3 (1998) 265–67.

8 Ibid.

9 Alex E. S. Green, "Socio-Physics: Should We Take It Seriously?," *Quarterly Journal of the Florida Academy of Sciences* 34, no. 3/4 (1971): 161–71.

10 Summary of ibid.

11 Gary M. Feinman, "The Emergence of Social Complexity," in *Cooperation and Collective Action: Archaeological Perspectives*, ed. David M. Carballo (Boulder: University Press of Colorado, 2012).

12 Arlen F. Chase and Diane Z. Chase, "Complex Societies in the Southern Maya Lowlands," in *The Oxford Handbook of Mesoamerican Archaeology*, ed. Deborah L. Nichols and Christopher A. Pool (Oxford: Oxford University Press, 2012), 265.

13 E.g. Eric H. Cline, *1177 B.C.: The Year Civilization Collapsed*, Kindle edition (Princeton: Princeton University Press, 2015); Joseph A. Tainter, *The Collapse of Complex Societies* (Cambridge: Cambridge University Press, 1990).

14 E.g. Crawford S. Holling, "Understanding the Complexity of Economic, Ecological, and Social Systems," *Ecosystems* 4, no. 5 (2001): 390–405; Gregory G. Brunk, "Why Do Societies Collapse? A Theory Based on Self-Organized Criticality," *Journal of Theoretical Politics* 14, no. 2 (2002): 195–230.

15 Cline, *1177 B.C.: The Year Civilization Collapsed*, Kindle Locations 3405–8.

16 E.g. Marty A. Ferman, *A Wing Design Method for Aerospace Students and Home Builders: Strength, Weight, Flutter, Divergence, Buckling, Deflection, and Twist* (Bloomington: Trafford Pub., 2011), 16.

17 Spencer, *Essays, Scientific, Political, and Speculative.*

18 Jennifer C. Ross and Sharon R. Steadman, *Ancient Complex Societies* (New York and London: Taylor & Francis, 2017), 2.

19 Fridrich A. Hayek, *The Constitution of Liberty* (Chicago: University of Chicago Press, 1978), 85.

20 Michael Perlstein, "NOPD Says 71 Arrested in Recent Weeks; Murders, Shootings Down through June," *4WWL* (2018). https://www.wwltv.com/article/news/crime/nopd-says-71-arrested-in-recent-weeks-murders-shootings-down-through-june/289-583661618

21 Australian Bureau of Statistics, "National and State Information About Adult Prisoners and Community Based Corrections, Including Legal Status, Custody Type, Indigenous Status, Sex" (Canberra: Corrective Services, Australia, 2023).

22 see also Joseph Livni, "Investigation of Collapse of Complex Socio-Political Systems Using Classical Stability Theory," *Physica A: Statistical Mechanics and Its Applications* 524 (2019).

23 J. K. Feibleman, *Justice, Law and Culture* (Springer Netherlands, Dordrecht, 2012), 27.

24 Paul Jarvis, "Commodus' Court: Conspiracy and Consequences," *Ancient History Bulletin* 37, no.1–2 (2023): 53–79.

25 William S. McKechnie, *Magna Carta: A Commentary on the Great Charter of King John* (New York: Burt Franklin, 1914), 127.
26 John Rawls, *A Theory of Justice: Original Edition* (Cambridge, MA: Harvard University Press, 2005).
27 Elizabeth Teague, "Russia's Constitutional Reforms of 2020," *Russian Politics* 5, no. 3 (2020): 301–28.
28 "As early as 3200 B. C.2, the 'gift of the Nile' was being administered by a completely organized governmental machine centered in the person of a God-King, and requiring the cooperative effort of a vast number of officials directly or indirectly responsible, down to the least of the innumerable village scribes, to that God-King," Casper J. Kraemer, "Bureaucracy and Petty Graft in Ancient Egypt," *The Classical Weekly* 20 (1927).
29 Claudia Moreau et al., "Polygenic Risk Scores of Several Subtypes of Epilepsies in a Founder Population," *bioRxiv* (2019): 728816.
30 Ibid.
31 E.g. « un certain nombre de procurateurs était choisi pour des types de postes bien précis, en raison de compétences particulières » S. Demougin, "Considérations Sur L'avancement Dans Les Carrières Procuratoriennes Équestres," in *Administration, Prosopography and Appointment Policies in the Roman Empire* ed. Lukas De Blois (Leiden: Brill, 2001), 24–34.
32 Tenth Amendment of the US Constitution.
33 See more in Peter Mazzacano, "From Covenant to Compact to Contract: The Legal Transplantation of Puritan Jurisprudence to America," in *A Civil Society with no Hierarchy*, ed. Ilie Bădescu and Joseph Livni (Lanham: Lexington Books, 2023), 208–27.
34 Alexis de Tocqueville, *Democracy in America*, trans. Henry Reeve, Kindle edition, vol. 1 (Project Gutenberg, 2006), 233.
35 Ibid., 12.
36 See more Chapter 8 of Joseph Livni, *The Biblical Roots of American Constitutionalism—from "I Am the Lord" to "We the People"* (Lanham: Lexington Books, 2021), 93–6.
37 The Constitutions of Canada and Australia followed later a similar pattern; e.g., Dara Lithwick, *A Pas De Deux: The Division of Federal and Provincial Legislative Powers in Sections 91 and 92 of the Constitution Act, 1867* (Ottawa: Library of Parliament, 2015); Leeka Kheifets et al., "The Sensitivity of Children to Electromagnetic Fields," *Pediatrics* 116, no. 2 (2005): e303–e13.
38 Kenneth Ames, "The Archaeology of Rank," in *Handbook of Archaeological Theories*, ed. R. Alexander Bentley, Herbert D. G. Maschner, and Christopher Chippindale (Lanham: AltaMira Press, 2007), 487–513.
39 Michael W. Diehl, "Some Thoughts on the Study of Hierarchies," *Hierarchies in Action: Cui Bono* (2000); cited by Ames, "The Archaeology of Rank."
40 David P. Baker, *The Schooled Society: The Educational Transformation of Global Culture* (Stanford: Stanford University Press, 2014).
41 Anna K. Chmielewski, "The Global Increase in the Socioeconomic Achievement Gap, 1964 to 2015," *American Sociological Review* 84, no. 3 (2019): 517–44.
42 Leonard Beeghley, *The Structure of Social Stratification in the United States, the, Coursesmart Etextbook* (London and New York: Routledge, 2015), 1.
43 Ibid., 2.
44 Crispus C. Sallustius and Charles Anthon, "Jugurthine War." (New York: Harper, 1840).

45 Lukas De Blois, "Army and General in the Late Roman Republic," in *A Companion to the Roman Army*, ed. Paul Erdkamp (Malden, Oxford, and Victoria: Blackwell, 2007), 167.
46 Beeghley, *The Structure of Social Stratification in the United States, the, Coursesmart Etextbook*, 22.
47 Ibid., 1.
48 Chmielewski, "The Global Increase in the Socioeconomic Achievement Gap, 1964 to 2015."
49 Ibid.
50 Arthur Sakamoto, Kimberly A. Goyette, and ChangHwan Kim, "Socioeconomic Attainments of Asian Americans," *Annual Review of Sociology* 35 (2009).
51 Ping-Ann Addo, "'Is It Entrepreneurship, or Is It Survival?': Gender, Community, and Innovation in Boston's Black Immigrant Micro-Enterprise Spaces," *Societies* 7, no. 3 (2017): 20.
52 Sakamoto, Goyette, and Kim, "Socioeconomic Attainments of Asian Americans."
53 Beeghley, *The Structure of Social Stratification in the United States, the, Coursesmart Etextbook*, 11.
54 Richard L. Schott, "The Origins of Bureaucracy: An Anthropological Perspective," *International Journal of Public Administration* 23, no. 1 (2000): 53–78; Richard Swedberg, *Max Weber and the Idea of Economic Sociology* (Princeton: Princeton University Press, 2018), 63.
55 Guillermo Algaze, *Ancient Mesopotamia at the Dawn of Civilization: The Evolution of an Urban Landscape* (Chicago and London: University of Chicago Press, 2009), 20.
56 Seth Abrutyn, "Pollution-Purification Rituals, Cultural Memory and the Evolution of Religion: How Collective Trauma Shaped Ancient Israel," *AJCS* 3, no. 1 (2015): 123–55.
57 Schott, "The Origins of Bureaucracy: An Anthropological Perspective," 67.
58 Ibid.
59 A. Leo Oppenheim, "On an Operational Device in Mesopotamian Bureaucracy," *Journal of Near Eastern Studies* 18, no. 2 (1959); Ancient Mesopatmians used multiplication tables, reciprocal tables, fractions with a common denominator (i.e. 60); solutions to some quadratic equations; Pythagoras triangle calculations Otto Neugebauer, *The Exact Sciences in Antiquity*, Second ed. (New York: Dover Publications, 1969), 29–52.
60 Algaze, *Ancient Mesopotamia at the Dawn of Civilization,* 20.
61 Neugebauer, *The Exact Sciences in Antiquity*, 44.
62 Shmuel Noah Eisenstadt, "Bureaucracy and Bureaucratization," *Current Sociology* 7, no. 2 (1958): 99–124.
63 Aristotle, Benjamin Jowett, and Henry William Carless Davis, *Politics*, Kindle edition (Mineola: Dover Publications, 2000).
64 Isaac Deutscher, "Roots of Bureaucracy," *Canadian-American Slavic Studies* 3, no. 3 (1969): 453–72.
65 Michele Renee Salzman, *The Making of a Christian Aristocracy: Social and Religious Change in the Western Roman Empire*, Kindle edition (Cambridge, MA: Harvard University Press, 2002).
66 Tim P. Coogan, *The Famine Plot: England's Role in Ireland's Greatest Tragedy* (New York: St. Martin's Publishing Group, 2012), 175.

67 Ibid., 60.
68 Ibid., 175.
69 Eisenstadt, "Bureaucracy and Bureaucratization."
70 Glynn Cochrane, *Max Weber's Vision for Bureaucracy: A Casualty of World War I* (Cham: Springer International Publishing, 2017), 68.
71 Livni, "Investigation of Collapse of Complex Socio-Political Systems Using Classical Stability Theory."
72 Professor Michael J. Klarman is the Charles Warren Professor of Legal History at Harvard Law School.
73 Michael J. Klarman, *The Framers' Coup: The Making of the United States Constitution* (Oxford and New York: Oxford University Press, 2016), 4.
74 The Editors of Encyclopaedia Britannica, "Text of the Constitution of the United State," in *Encyclopedia Britannica*, https://www.britannica.com/topic/Constitution-of-the-United-States-2231775.2023.
75 Tocqueville, *Democracy in America*, 1:233.
76 Mazzacano, "From Covenant to Compact to Contract: The Legal Transplantation of Puritan Jurisprudence to America." see also; Winthrop, John. *Winthrop Papers*, ed. Robert Charles Winthrop Jr., Vol. 3 (Boston: Massachusetts Historical Society, 1947).
77 Hannah Arendt, *The Origins of Totalitarianism* (San Diego, New York, and London: Harcourt Brace Jovanovich, 1973), 298.
78 Dorinda Outram, *Panorama of the Enlightenment* (Los Angeles: J. Paul Getty Museum, 2006), 52.
79 Ibid.
80 Ibid., 14.
81 Pre-Enlightenment mainstream thought and practice consisted of privileges (arisrtocracy, clergy and monarchs) and of duties (commoners).
82 Arendt, *The Origins of Totalitarianism*, 298.
83 Tocqueville, *Democracy in America*, 1:42.
84 Nathanel Philbrick, *Mayflower: A Story of Courage, Community, and War*, Kindle edition (New York: Penguin Publishing Group, 2006), Kindle Locations 317.
85 Ibid.
86 For example a search in Google Scholars "elections and democracy in the EU" for year 2024 produced 10,400 resuts.
87 Zoning Appeals, Health, Library, Finance are only a few example of about 50 boards and committees of Winchester, MA see Town of Winchester, "Boards and Committees" (Winchester, 2024), https://www.winchester.us/251/Boards-and-Committees.
88 Jan W. Van Deth, "Studying Political Participation: Towards a Theory of Everything" (paper presented at the Joint Sessions of Workshops of the European Consortium for Political Research, Grenoble, 2001).
89 Joakim Ekman and Erik Amnå, "Political Participation and Civic Engagement: Towards a New Typology," *Human Affairs* 22 (2012): 283–300.
90 Ibid.
91 Ibid.
92 David I. Kertzer, *The Kidnapping of Edgardo Mortara* (New York: Vintage, 2008), 56, 57, 71, 113–15, 35, 38, 57, 244, 57.

93 Michael J. Klarman, "Rethinking the History of American Freedom (Review Essay of Eric Foner, the Story of American Freedom (1998))," *William & Mary Law Review* 42 (2000): 265–88.
94 Kostas Vlassopoulos, "Free Spaces: Identity, Experience and Democracy in Classical Athens," *The Classical Quarterly* 57, no. 1 (2007).
95 E.g. Charles Howard McIlwain, *Constitutionalism: Ancient and Modern* (Clark: Lawbook Exchange, 2005).
96 Ibid., 9.
97 Giovanni Gentile, *Origins and Doctrine of Fascism: With Selections from Other Works* (New York: Taylor & Francis, 2017).
98 Karl Marx and Fridrich Engels, *The Communist Manifesto* (Redwood City: SoftBook Press, 2020).
99 Frederic L. Pryor, "The Red and the Green: The Rise and Fall of Collectivized Agriculture in Marxist Regimes" (2014) https://works.swarthmore.edu/fac-economics/91.
100 Even science is bent in a Marxist education system in order to align though with the projects of the Great Leaders Douglas R. Weiner, "The Roots of 'Michurinism': Transformist Biology and Acclimatization as Currents in the Russian Life Sciences," *Annals of Science* 42, no. 3 (1985).
101 John M. Hoberman, "The Transformation of East German Sport," *Journal of Sport History* 17, no. 1 (1990): 62–68.
102 Veneta Todorova Ivanova, "Occult Communism: Culture, Science and Spirituality in Late Socialist Bulgaria" (Urbana: University of Illinois at Urbana-Champaign, 2017).
103 Tamás Nyirkos, *The Tyranny of the Majority: History, Concepts, and Challenges* (New York: Routledge, 2018); Bradley Dart, "Tyranny of the Majority" (2021) https://www.researchgate.net/publication/360147380_Tyranny_of_the_Majority.
104 Peverill Squire, *The Rise of the Representative: Lawmakers and Constituents in Colonial America* (Ann Arbor: University of Michigan Press, 2017), 14.
105 Charles de Secondat baron de Montesquieu, *The Spirit of Laws* (London and New York: Colonial Press, 1900).
106 John F. Burns, *Controversies between Royal Governors and Their Assemblies in the Northern American Colonies* (Boston: Wright and Potter Printing Company, 1923), 167.

5

Crime Control

Résumé

"If you do not enforce appropriate punishments against those who utterly refuse to mend their ways evil will increase, and the kingdom will be destroyed."[1] Reasonably, the perception of *justice* emerged with the appearance of private property; about 8,000 years ago in the Near East, land held in common became the property of private owners.[2] Common land and crops need less protection than private land and its yields.

Borders between owned lands had to appear; reasonably they consisted of *straight* lines. These straight lines delimited rights to the land; 5,000 years ago Sumerians were aware of such rights and "resented any encroachment on them."[3] Words for straight and right have intertwined for millennia. In Indo-European languages the root for the geometric term *straight* and the legal term *just* (*Recht in* German, *droit* in French *right* in English) share a common etymological ancestor, namely, the Proto-Indo-European root *reĝ*.[4] The hypothesis that both geometry and justice started bundled together with land ownership is reasonable; its negation consists of coincidence. However, in Semitic cultures the geometric and legal notions also converge.[5] This brings the negative hypothesis to the level of double coincidence. If a coincidence had a probability of one in a hundred, its probability to occur twice would be one in ten thousand.

The pantheon of Pharaonic Egypt included Maat, Goddess of Order, Truth and Justice.[6]

> A man of Ma-a-t is one who practices justice in every respect. All government officials, and above all the pharaoh, are called to put Ma-a-t in practice.[7]

Themis, Yama and Justitia were goddesses of law, order, and justice in ancient Greece, ancient India, and ancient Rome respectively. These gods do not prove that Pharaoh or Emperor Augustus ruled fairly. However, the rituals consecrated to worship these deities indicate that rulers tried to project the image of being guided by ethical values of fairness. I will borrow a convincing argument for a similar, however not identical, prevalent value:

> Even if the textual evidence is no more than propaganda, its very existence proves that there was an audience for it.[8]

Justice was the main reason why town folks agreed to bow to rulers. As early as Sumerians populated cities, they decreed laws[9] and instituted means of law enforcement.[10] Crime and crime control therefore have been primary duties of rulers of all kinds from despots to democratic governments.

This chapter first discusses the causes of crime. It distinguishes between causes related to normal and abnormal individuals. The chapter discusses crime perpetrated by normal people; the abnormal cases are out of scope. As mentioned earlier, civilization required law; this opened an opportunity for lawlessness. The chapter examines theories of justice, incarceration, and deterrence. It also looks at the argument that rational people disobey the law if in their judgment crime pays. One observes that societies in which a portion of inhabitants disobey the law are the rule; crimeless societies are the exception. Therefore, the case for the argument that *if crime pays then crime exists* is compelling.

The chapter discusses the factors determining the equilibrium of crime, that is, the situation in which the average portion of criminals is constant. It brings up two mathematical approaches: one borrowed from models of epidemiology and the other one from game theory. Not surprisingly, the examination arrives at the conclusion that the dominant factor is the difference between the benefit and the cost of crime. Nevertheless, the epidemiology model reveals that recidivism is another factor determining the ratio of criminals at equilibrium. Therefore the chapter turns to examine effects, causes, and treatment of recidivism.

The Causes of Crime

Hartung lists several theories explaining crime.[11] One group of theories blames the society; it assumes that the criminal is normal. Another group finds the criminal not normal (Table 5.1).

Theories attributing causes of crime to abnormality rule out the presence of normal people in the criminal population. Conversely, the high number of psychologically

Table 5.1 Hartung's List of Theories Explaining the Causes of Crime

Criminal	Crime	Rebuttal
Normal	Current disorganized society	Crime has existed in every civilization
	Rational, Inherent to society	No rebuttal
Not normal	Neurologically abnormal	Al Capone, Charles Ponzi, and O.J Simpson were normal
	Psychopath	Only 16% of US convicts are psychopaths[a]
	Mentally deficient	Mentally deficient cannot rob a bank
	Psychoanalytic Disorders	Had everyone in the Gambino family such disorders?

Source:
[a] Kent A Kiehl and Morris B Hoffman, "The Criminal Psychopath: History, Neuroscience, Treatment, and Economics," *Jurimetrics* 51 (2011).

normal convicts rules out the validity of these theories. Of the two remaining categories we are left with the theory claiming that most criminals are rational and crime is inherent in civilized society. I emphasized *civilized* society because before civilization there were no laws; consequently there was no lawlessness. Therefore, any examination assuming that crime is caused by abnormal societies or irrational people will explain only criminal behavior of those particular societies and people. These particular cases are out of scope. Therefore, we shall deal with normal societies and rational criminals.

Crime Does Not Pay

Some say that this proverb originates from Victorian England; it encourages moral behavior. It is easy to prove that under the assumption of normal society and rational people this proverb states a fiction. A rational person will not engage in anything with higher cost than benefit. Therefore, if crime does not pay no rational person would become criminal. However, practically every society deals with criminals. Therefore, at least in criminals' opinion crime does pay; their opinion matters.

Before the Enlightenment, pre-industrial societies prevented crime applying harsh sentences. The Sumerians, one of the earliest known civilizations, knew that crime prevention requires tough punishments.[12] Not surprisingly, tyrannies punished. The theorists of the Enlightenment had new concepts in mind like rationalism, liberty, and equality. Rationalism of liberty postulates that one's liberty cannot encroach on someone else's liberty. Among others crime is the negation of liberty and liberty requires crime prevention. Promoters of the Enlightenment realized that in order to stop rational citizens turning to crime its cost must exceed its benefit. The new age shall not abolish punishment; it should keep it in proportion:

> In order for a punishment not to entail violence of one or many against a private citizen it essentially needs to be public, prompt, necessary, as lenient as possible in the given circumstances, proportional to the infraction, and prescribed by the laws.[13]

Not surprisingly, rationalism rejected irrational assumptions about lawbreakers (born evil, Satan worshipper, sorcerer, heretic, etc.) on one hand, and irrational theories regarding rulers on the other hand. In early times rulers were pronounced God, divinity, or possessing divine rights to rule.[14] Punishment was an act of faith, or *auto da fé* in Portuguese:

> Repentant victims were mercifully strangled or beheaded before being burned at stake, while unrepentant defendants were spared no indignity and were burned alive.[15]

The new era sought truth through intuitive knowledge backed by empirical evidence. For example the previous quote from Beccaria upholds punishment and dismisses cruelty. By intuition punishment deters crime; extremely cruel punishment like flogging, beating, branding, mutilation, blinding, the use of the stock and pillory,[16] and the earlier mentioned *auto da fé*[17] had no place in the New Era.

The link between Enlightenment and Democracy is probably in consensus.[18] The wisdom of Beccaria has matured and scholars have taught it and reiterated it. For example:

> it is important to recognize that deterrence depends on the difference between the expected punishment costs that a citizen faces when he is guilty and the costs he faces when he is innocent.[19]

However, in our times some thinkers crossed limits beyond old rationalism. The school of classical rationalism of the *Enlightenment* gives way to *inductive reasoning*. This exploratory approach questions even intuitive knowledge backed by empirical evidence. This chapter is about crime; consequently I shall illustrate my claim by examples of crime deterrence theories. For example Lewis[20] agrees with Beccaria in principle; however he finds his thought impractical. He agrees that punishment should be known in public, and the perceived cost should exceed the expected benefit. However he argues that:

a. Individuals "often use their own moral intuitions to guess at legal rules without any actual knowledge of the legal code."
b. "Those who commit crime tend to be impulsive and risk-seeking in general, and often intoxicated when they do."

The Rational Lawbreaker

This post-Enlightenment insight challenges the practicality of empirically proven wisdom; it argues for a more cautious approach postulating that people have little idea that crime may be punished. I am aware that science proved that intuitive observation may be erroneous. We all understand that the world is not flat. However, this erroneous perception is disproven by facts. Not only nothing backs the stipulation of naïve criminals, but also actual data disprove it beyond reasonable doubt (see Table 5.2). Viscusi's investigation[21] interrogated a sample of criminals asking whether they consider the chance of being arrested, convicted, and sentenced to prison to be high, medium, or low. He proposed that the high, medium, and low chances correspond to 0.75, 0.50, and 0.25 respectively. The answers of the criminals were recorded as the proportion of respondents assessing each chance to be high, medium, or low. There are twenty-seven combinations from [High arrest, High conviction, High prison sentence =HHH] to [Low arrest, Low conviction, Low prison sentence =HHH] (see Table 5.2)

Table 5.2 Investigation of Viscusi—Anticipations of Criminals to Be Arrested, Convicted, and Incarcerated

		Chance Of			**Ratio of Criminals**			**Chance of Prison**
#	**Combination**	**Arrest**	**Conviction**	**Prison**	**Arrest**	**Conviction**	**Prison**	
1	HHH	0.75	0.75	0.75	0.06	0.44	0.13	0.001448
2	HHM	0.75	0.75	0.5	0.06	0.44	0.13	0.000965
3	HHL	0.75	0.75	0.25	0.06	0.44	0.75	0.002784
4	HMH	0.75	0.5	0.75	0.06	0.33	0.033	0.000184
5	HMM	0.75	0.5	0.5	0.06	0.33	0.5	0.001856
6	HML	0.75	0.5	0.25	0.06	0.33	0.17	0.000316
7	HLH	0.75	0.25	0.75	0.06	0.22	0	0
8	HLM	0.75	0.5	0.25	0.06	0.22	0.25	0.000309
9	HLL	0.75	0.25	0.25	0.06	0.22	0.75	0.000464
10	MHH	0.5	0.75	0.75	0.21	0.16	0.55	0.005198
11	MHM	0.75	0.5	0.75	0.21	0.16	0.09	0.000851
12	MHL	0.75	0.5	0.25	0.21	0.16	0.36	0.001134
13	MMH	0.75	0.5	0.5	0.21	0.25	0.33	0.003248
14	MMM	0.5	0.5	0.5	0.21	0.25	0.47	0.003084
15	MML	0.5	0.5	0.25	0.21	0.25	0.2	0.000656
16	MLH	0.75	0.5	0.25	0.21	0.39	0.12	0.000921
17	MLM	0.5	0.5	0.25	0.21	0.39	0.19	0.000973
18	MLL	0.5	0.25	0.25	0.21	0.39	0.69	0.001766
19	LHH	0.25	0.75	0.75	0.73	0.02	0.6	0.001232
20	LHM	0.75	0.5	0.25	0.73	0.02	0.2	0.000274
21	LHL	0.25	0.75	0.25	0.73	0.02	0.2	0.000137
22	LMH	0.75	0.5	0.25	0.73	0.03	0.17	0.000349
23	LMM	0.5	0.5	0.25	0.73	0.03	0.5	0.000684
24	LML	0.5	0.25	0.25	0.73	0.03	0.33	0.000226
25	LLH	0.25	0.25	0.75	0.73	0.95	0.06	0.00195
26	LLM	0.5	0.25	0.25	0.73	0.95	0.09	0.00195
27	LLL	0.25	0.25	0.25	0.73	0.95	0.86	0.009319
Average chance to be sentenced to prison								0.0016

Source: W Kip Viscusi, "The risks and rewards of criminal activity: a comprehensive test of criminal deterrence," Journal of Labor Economics 4, no. 3, Part 1 (1986).

For example category HML

a. a proportion of 0.06 of criminals consider a 0.75 chance to be arrested;
b. of these 0.06 criminals a proportion of 0.33 consider a 0.50 chance to be convicted;
c. and of these 0.06*0.33=.02 a proportion of 0.17 criminals consider a 0.25 chance to end up in prison.

The total chance of being arrested for the HML category is:

$$0.06 \times 0.33 \times 0.17 \times .75 \times .50 \times .25 = 0.000316 \text{ or less than one in 3,164.}$$

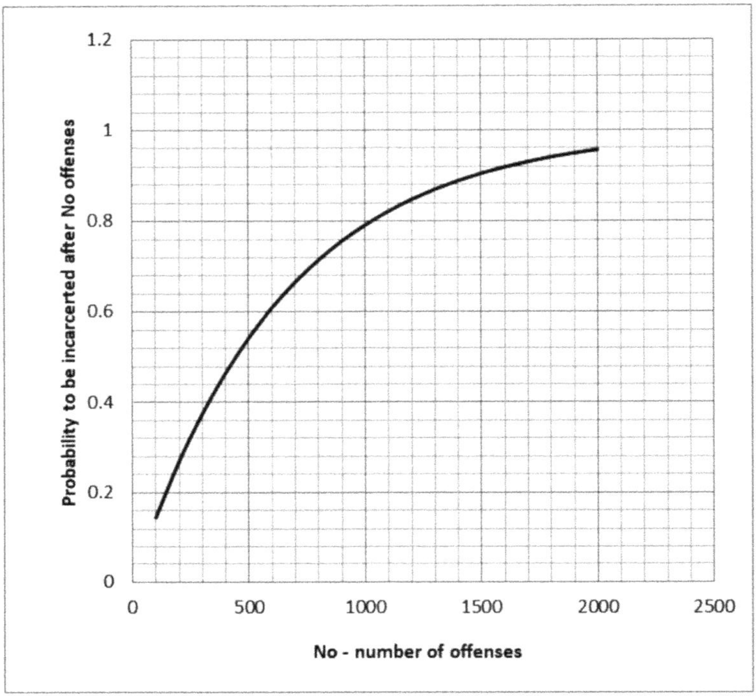

Figure 5.1 Probability of incarceration after no offenses. Author's work.

The average chance a criminal expects to be incarcerated is . 0.0016 or one in 639 (Table 5.2).

Figure 5.1 illustrates that at this risk a criminal "working" three times a week will likely get imprisoned by the end of one year. Perhaps, a criminal guided by the chart of Figure 5.1 would not commit crimes. However, before any new opportunity, the typical rational criminal considers that his chance to be incarcerated is one in 639 and, consequently, will chance it.

The Impulsive Lawbreaker

The second argument relating crime with "impulsive and risk-seeking in general, and often intoxicated"[22] individuals is, on the other hand, defended by an actual fact-finding research carried out by Junger, West, and Timman.[23] This time the argument loses its effect when we find out that it is concluded by a research about traffic violations; no doubt traffic accidents are a result of impulsive and risk-seeking moods and of DUI. I doubt that bank robbers are impulsive, risk-seeking, or intoxicated while actively pursuing their vocation.

Justice

The justice system of decreeing criminal law, detecting lawbreakers, bringing them to justice, judging the evidence, and punishing the violators is called *retributive justice.* Punishments may vary between lenient and harsh. As mentioned earlier, Enlightenment thinkers like Beccaria promoted proportional punishment. The earlier mentioned speculation denying the proportional relationship between deterrence and harshness of punishment has been an extrapolation of a recent trend of *inductive reasoning.* Another expression of this schooling consists of questioning the empirically validated institution of *retributive justice.* For example *Transform Justice,* a nonprofit organization based in the UK opposing classical proportional punishment, urged the *Sentencing Council of England and Wales* to carry out an academic examination of the deterring effect of incarceration. *Transform Justice* published the finding:

> The academics have done no original research, but they have reviewed relevant, reliable studies which throw a light on the effectiveness of current sentences. They find literally no evidence to say deterrence works.[24]

The publication argues against the rational criminal assumption because "the evidence points in the opposite direction, most crime being spontaneous, often driven by temper, mental health issues, drink or drugs."[25] This *inductive reasoning* contradicts not only measured data (Table 5.2) and empirical knowledge[26] but also actual quantitative research. For example quantitative researches conclude that:

1. Dedicated deterrence strategies effectively control street gang violence.[27]
2. The evidence reveals that the marginal decrease in crime due to incarcerating juveniles is "at least as large as the corresponding crime reduction for adults."[28]

Transform Justice dismisses the value of deterrence; the implication is to dismiss incarceration altogether. Let me illustrate how destabilizing the consequences of such inductive reasoning are.

For the sake of argument I shall admit the hypothesis that in most cases of crime "driven by temper, mental health issues, drink or drugs"[29] the deterrence does not help.

The simple cat-and-mouse model of crime reveals that the police—criminal confrontation arrives at steady state (Equation 2.4). The factors determining the equilibrium are:

1. Benefit of crime—the growth rate of the criminal population in absence of police.
2. Cost of crime—the rate of removal of criminals by police i.e. deterrence.
   Figure 3.7 shows a time history at steady state for such an example.

The more complex model with three state variables also points at a predictable steady state. This time three factors determine the values of the state variables at steady state (Figure 3.9):

1. benefit of crime
2. cost of crime
3. correction efficiency expressed by recidivism

Now we are ready to examine the outcome of accepting the advice to abolish incarceration because "for most crimes deterrence does not work." By hypothesis spontaneous crime levels will not be affected by a *no-punishment policy*. However, canceling incarceration does affect planned crimes like robbery, burglary, intentional homicide, drug or sex trafficking, fraud, corruption, terrorism, espionage, and treason. Figure 3.9 shows that at an *Immunity Retention* ratio of 0.1 and at no crime deterrence, the planned crime ratio settles at 80%. This result is an underestimate because under a policy of no incarceration repetition of crime is almost guaranteed; as a consequence the *Immunity Retention* ratio is less than 0.1. In conclusion, under a no-punishment policy, spontaneous crimes remain stable; however, planned crimes spiral up to 80–100%.

The inductive reasoning of *Transform Justice* is understandable. No one wants a society with crime and punishment. As a consequence, the suggestion that one can achieve a crimeless society by first canceling punishment is destabilizing. This particular publication came from one academic researcher;[30] however, the notion is widespread in Western academic circles.[31]

One can also argue that the *Transform Justice* advocacy amounts to no justice. Aiming at a no-crime-no-punishment equilibrium is commendable. However, as long as crime persists, a no-punishment policy inevitably punishes the victim; that is no justice.

A more radical *inductive reasoning* proposes to return to *restorative justice*. This approach not only cancels the punishment but also eliminates even the notion of crime:

> Rather than viewing crime simply as the violation of the criminal law, restorative justice advocates reframe crime as a harm done to another person or a community.[32]

Rossner and Taylor describe *restorative justice* as a novel movement of the twentieth to twenty-first centuries.[33] In reality this type of justice is very old, and most likely it preceded *retributive justice*. The long-standing Mohawk Longhouse Justice System has solved offenses by mediation between perpetrator and victim, through an arbitration that "is not a process grounded upon fact-finding toward a determination of guilt and allocation of punishment."[34] A similar system of offense, followed by a cycle of retaliations ending with a negotiated "*sulkha*," or forgiving ceremony, has been practiced in Arab towns and villages for centuries.[35] Reasonably, this system of restoring peace after offense and repeated reprisals started much earlier. Current law experts familiar with the biblical source dissect the case of Jacob's sons who "where understandably outraged by the crime against their maiden sister."[36] The brothers searched for justice; they arrived at excessive violence: "The mass murder of the clan of Hamor by Dina's brothers fits somewhere between hot-blooded revenge and cold-blooded deterrence."[37]

The historicity of this story is of minor importance. The story is ancient; its origins are even earlier customs.

> What we can derive from the stories of Genesis is the *need* for an agreed-upon and enforceable code of conduct with procedural safeguards against arbitrary enforcement and unfair application.[38]

Naturally, before light there was darkness; before law, there was unruliness. There were offenders, retaliations of victims, negotiations and finally peace was restored. That is what restorative justice is about. Its current proponents affirm that *restorative justice* is not about violating the law, but it is about reconciling the victim's demands with the offender's needs for rehabilitation. I admit the proponents of return to *restorative justice* do not envisage the need of violence to bring the sides to mediation. Nevertheless, it is reasonable that some convincing has to be taken into account. Even if offenders were eager to settle right after the offense this suggestion brings us back to early lawlessness. There are two reasons for such an outcome:

1. Let us assume that Peter steals Paul's dinnerware. Arbitration establishes that Peter should return the stolen property. Peter complies and later tries another victim. Nine times he is obliged to return the stolen item. The tenth attempt ends up with arbitration in Peter's favor. Peter has appropriated a dinnerware at no cost. Peter can now try to obtain more appliances. If the chance of getting a favorable verdict is 1 in 10, then one tries 9–15 times and one arrives at a well-equipped kitchen. *Restorative justice* encourages the offender; it is not justice.
2. By definition *restorative justice* ignores criminal law, or any law. What about Dershowitz's wisdom regarding the "need for an agreed-upon and enforceable code of conduct with procedural safeguards?" What about the rule of law?

Equilibrium

Chapter 3 discussed a simple model of crime control. It is an analogy to infectious disease control; the chapter justifies the analogy. Figure 3.8 illustrates the schematic of the model. This chapter repeats it to make it easier for the reader. The model describes how some susceptible individuals become infractors; this $S \rightarrow I$ conversion occurs because crime pays (see section *The causes of crime).* Some infractors are arrested, convicted and punished; consequently there will be an $I \rightarrow R$ conversion; some infractors decide that crime does not pay after all. These infractors become resistant to temptation of crime; they acquire immunity. Finally some resistant individuals lose immunity and return to the susceptible population. The next section (*Recidivism or* $R \rightarrow S$ *conversion*) discusses this transfer.

The transition from one *state variable* to another is a dynamic process. Each of the categories accepts and loses members; therefore, the size of each *state variable* can grow, decline, or remain unchanged. *Equilibrium and stability* scholars define *equilibrium* a situation in which every *state variable* maintains a constant magnitude. That does not mean that at equilibrium there are no $S \to I, I \to R$, and $R \to S$ conversions. For example, if the number of $S \to I$ conversions equals the number of $I \to R$ conversions, then the number of infractors remains constant.

The mathematical model expresses relations between the state variables at a point in time and their rate of change; in our case the rate of change is the growth rate of each state variable *S, I,* or *R*. Obviously if one or two state variables grow, then at least one of them must decline. Mathematicians easily overcome this argument; they use the term *negative growth* for *decrease. Equilibrium* is, however, neither growth nor decline; equilibrium is, therefore, neither positive nor negative; it is zero growth. In the particular case of three state variables, the condition of zero growth in the relationship leads to a system of three equations with tree unknowns. Show me a mathematician who does not love systems of n equations with n unknowns! Algebra taught us how to find the values of *S, I,* and *R* at equilibrium. Chapter 3 explains that two ratios determine these values *Crime Deterrence* and *Immunity Retention*. Crime deterrence expresses whether crime pays or not. If it is greater than unity, then crime does not pay. *Immunity Retention* measures the rate of $I \to R$conversions. The more such conversions take place the less *Immunity Retention* is. Figure 3.9 shows that *Crime Deterrence* is a major factor determining the equilibrium; if it is greater than unity, then no matter what *Immunity Retention* is, the equilibrium is a crime-free society. In other words, if crime does not pay, there is no crime. No wonder Victorian moralizers formulated the *crime does not pay* cliché. However, the fact that many scholars, politicians, and civil servants still struggle with crime proves that the proverb is not effective. Figure 3.9 illustrates that when crime pays then the combination of both ratios determines at what value of the *state variables* equilibrium is achieved. Figure 3.9 also shows that three equilibria are possible:

a. a stable crime-free equilibrium
b. an unstable crime-free equilibrium
c. an endemic crime equilibrium

Apparently an investigation of Schrag and Scotchmer[39] contradicts these predictions of the *SIR* model. I will ask you to bear with me to reconcile the conflict. Not surprisingly, I will start with their Equation 1. The investigation affirms that "the citizen will take all crime opportunities that satisfy":

$$\pi(m,e,\rho,q) = m - M - K(e,\rho,q) \geq 0.$$ [40] Eq Schrag and Scotchmer 1

I shall work around the detailed meaning of symbols and summarize that $m - M$ stands for benefit of crime and $K(e,\rho,q)$ symbolizes its cost. The symbols e,ρ,q

represent probabilistic parameters regarding one's chance of ending up incarcerated. As a consequence if the benefit exceeds the cost crime prevails; this is consistent with what this chapter postulates: crime exists if crime pays.

Then the investigation turns to *game theory* in order to show that "the level of enforcement does not uniquely determine the crime rate." The symbol *m* is a variable representing the benefit of crime; the investigation introduces a critical magnitude of crime benefit, or cut-off crime benefit; below the cut-off value crime is prevented and above it crime is warranted. The study then assumes that "each citizen has the same cutoff"; it is a reasonable assumption if one is interested in the overall strategy of the citizenry. This general threshold is represented by the symbol m*. The purpose of this is to establish that

> A symmetric Nash equilibrium is a strategy m* such that for each citizen i $\pi(m,e,0,q)_i \leq 0$ for $m \leq m^*$ and $\pi(m,e,p,q)_i \geq 0$ for $m \geq m^*$.[41]

Let me first translate the mathematical mumbo jumbo to human language and only then discuss what Nash equilibrium is. The expression $\pi(m,e,0,q)_i \leq 0$ for $m \leq m^*$ comes from Eq Schrag and Scotchmer 1 and its translation is that a citizen will not commit a crime if he/she considers its benefit not above the cut-off benefit m^*. Similarly $\pi(m,e,p,q)_i \geq 0$ for $m \geq m^*$ should be read as affirming that a citizen will commit a crime if he/she considers its benefit to be above the cut-off benefit, m^*. An examination of the two expressions is that in the second statement the left-hand side is $\pi(m,e,p,q)_i$ while in the first statement it is $\pi(m,e,0,q)_i$. The third parameter in one is a positive probability and 0 in the other. This third parameter is a probability parameter; it represents the likelihood to be punished for a crime one did not commit. Thus $\pi(m,e,p,q)_i$ means the cost and benefit analysis assuming that there is some chance to be punished even if one did not commit the crime. Similarly $\pi(m,e,0,q)_i$ translates to the cost and benefit analysis of committing a crime under the rule 'no crime no punishment.'

Now we are ready to return to our theme: equilibrium. The two expressions are inequalities one for $m \leq m^*$ and one for $m \geq m^*$ What happens if $m = m^*$? The two inequalities can be true only if $\pi(m^*,e,0,q)_i = 0$ and $\pi(m^*,e,p,q)_i = 0$. The two inequalities became equalities at the cut-off crime benefit,m^*. In human language this says that at the threshold m^* the citizen is at a balanced point between committing a crime or staying out of trouble, hence the term *equilibrium* or *Nash equilibrium*.

Before, we stated that equilibrium corresponds to a status where *state variables* are constant. The balance is between increasing and decreasing the magnitude of each state variable.

The Nash equilibrium balances the incentive with the disincentive to choose a strategy. At this point, I need to affirm that the two are not the same. The *constant state variable* interpretation comes from *equilibrium and stability* lingo while the *Nash equilibrium* is in *game theory* lingo. This is consistent with my experience concluding that interdisciplinary study is stressful but not impossible.

The term *equilibrium* used by game theorist has an equivalent in *equilibrium and stability* jargon: *bifurcation point* (see for example the point corresponding to Crime Deterrence = 1 and Percentage of Criminals = 0 on Figure 3.9).

The objective of this excursion was to examine how the investigation of Schrag and Scotchmer[42] concluded that "the level of enforcement does not uniquely determine the crime rate." They arrive at the following proposition:

> PROPOSITION 1: Let m_1 and m_2 satisfy' $\pi(m_2,e,0,q)=0$ and $\pi(m_1,e,p,q)=0$ then any m* such that $m_1 < m^* < m_2$ is a symmetric Nash equilibrium. If $(m_1) < C(m_2)$, there are symmetric Nash equilibria with different crime rates.

Let us talk English again. Some individuals consider that the justice system does not punish the innocent and they derive accordingly their strategy to commit a crime. Their strategy will be that if the crime benefit is measured by m_1 then the benefit balances the cost. Other individuals take into account that innocent people may be convicted of a crime and they arrive at a different threshold, m_2 across which crime pays. Can the crime rates arrive at different equilibria? I will ask your permission to use the *equilibrium and stability* meaning of equilibrium. I will use the term *tipping point* for levels of crime benefits were the benefit is in balance with the cost.

As explained by Schrag and Scotchmer,[43] the tipping point of the "no crime no punishment" persuasion is at a higher crime benefit m_2 because his incentive to keep away from trouble is stronger; the cynical individual hesitates less and commits the crime at the lower benefit m_1 (see Figure 5.2)

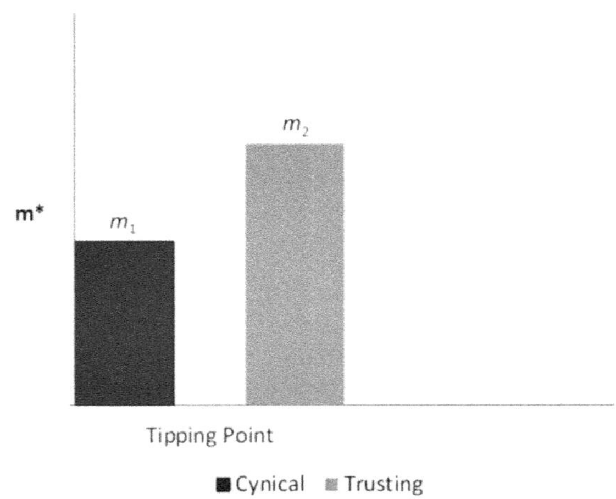

Figure 5.2 The cynical has a lower tipping point; his cost analysis considers that even if he does not commit the crime, he has a chance to pay for it; he hesitates less and the balance tips for action at the lower cost m1. Author's work.

As long as the benefit of crime is less thanm_1, both individuals will not commit the crime. The criminality will be the stable crime-free equilibrium of Figure 3.9 because the cost of crime is higher than its benefit, that is, the *Crime Deterrence* ratio is higher than 1. If the benefit of crime is between m_1 and m_2 then cynical individuals will commit crimes while trusting individuals will keep away from trouble. The Deterrence Ratio of the public will be the average of all individuals. The more cynical individuals are in town the lower the average Deterrence Ratio will be. As the crime benefit increases getting closer to m_2 the Deterrence Ratio declines. At a certain level the Deterrence Ratio and the equilibrium will settle at the stable endemic crime equilibrium (Figure 3.9). If the crime benefit exceeds m_2 the Percentage of Criminals will be positive (endemic crime) because all susceptible individuals will consider that crime pays.

In Eq Schrag and Scotchmer 1 the magnitude of cynicism is represented by p the probability one assigns to be incarcerated even if one is innocent. If all the cynical individuals had the same *p*, and if one could distinguish between cynics and trusting individuals by gender, persuasion, race, and so on, then one could plot on Figure 3.9 two separate crime rates at equilibrium: one for cynics and one for trusting individuals

More realistically, the probability distribution of cynicism is more continuously distributed than in two blocks: cynical and trusting. For example Figure 5.3 is a probability density function that decreases from about 0% of the population extremely cynical $\left(p=80\%\right)$ and about 22% completely trusting individuals. In such a realistic case, for every magnitude of crime benefit there is only one equilibrium. Schrag and

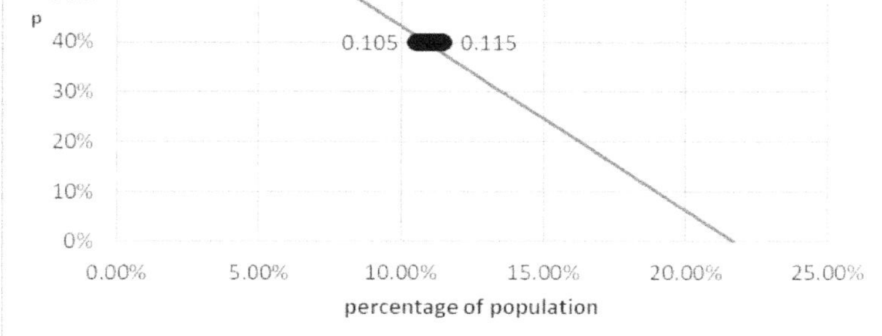

Figure 5.3 Probability density distribution of p; it should be read, for example, that between 10.5% and 11.5% of the population expects a 40% chance to be punished for a crime he/she did not commit; around 22% of the population are trusting individuals. Author's work.

Scotchmer[44] affirm that there are multiple equilibria because they call tipping point equilibrium.

Then why does the investigation[45] focus on the difference between trusting and cynical individuals? The answer is given by a hypothetical situation:

> Now suppose that the enforcement budget is fixed, and therefore the probabilities of apprehension are endogenous to the crime rate.[46]
>
> the probability of arresting the perpetrator goes down, whereas the probability of arresting an innocent citizen could go up.[47]

Without getting into quantitative details, the investigation[48] observes that under budgetary constraints the proportion of imprisoned innocents grows; consequently the proportion of cynical individuals grows. The tipping point of the cynical individuals is lower; as a consequence the crime rate increases. Schrag and Scotchmer conclude that law enforcement increases crime rather than reinforcing it. In the words of the authors:

> These effects increase the incentive for crime, and therefore high crime and randomness in indictments are mutually reinforcing.[49]

Let me debug this conclusion. The investigation[50] correctly determines that the equilibrium of such a scenario is at higher crime rates than the crime rates in effect before the budgetary constraints had to be considered. Questioning the stability of this equilibrium would shed light on the fact that this scenario is not possible. If the increasing crime rate is not met by increased deterrence then this equilibrium is in a positive feedback loop; as a consequence it is unstable. The prey and predator model (Chapter 2) inherently increases the number of predators when the prey increases; conversely when the predators' number grows there will be less prey. In nature there are no unstable loops because they go extinct. In society one can hypothesize that a society will defund the police or keep its budget constant even when crime rates grow. Nevertheless such a society will cease to exist because crime will keep growing as long as law enforcement will stay underfunded. At a point crime rates will reach intolerable levels guaranteeing the extinction of the society. Chapter 2 argued that societies collapse due to the growing number of state variables and their interdependence. There are two state variables that can bring down societies even when they act alone: crime and defense. Defunding police or defense forces are evidently destabilizing.

Recidivism or $R \to S$ conversion

Chapter 3 explained that two ratios determine the proportion of criminals at equilibrium:

a) Crime Deterrence—represents the cost/benefit analysis of the criminal
b) Immunity Retention—this magnitude is inversely proportional to the rate of freed prisoners who turn to be susceptible (Figure 3.9) to repeated offense (recidivism).

Figure 3.9 illustrates that decreasing the immunity retention increases the criminality reached at equilibrium. This section will show a practical example illustrating the critical effect of this conversion on the equilibrium of endemic crime in Australia.

Then the section will scan theories regarding the causes of recidivism, and examine proposed corrective actions.

Effect of Recidivism—Australian Example

Table 5.3 shows that the prisoner population of Australia amounts to 0.203% of the adult population; the prisoner proportion among aboriginals is 2.524%. One can approximate that the proportion of prisoners also represents proportion of criminals (see Figure 5.1). I calculated combinations of *Crime Deterrence* and *Immunity Retention* corresponding to the endemic criminal proportion for each population (Table). Figure 5.4 plots the data of Table 5.3 on the chart of Figure 3.9.

The chart shows that the *Crime Deterrence* of both the general population and the aboriginal population is remarkably high. However, the *Immunity Retention* of the aboriginal population is significantly lower than the one of the general population; this explains why the criminal proportion of the aboriginal population is significantly higher. This low *Immunity Retention* is consistent with the observation that "four out of every five male Aborigines returned [to crime and jail],"[51] while the recidivism among the general population is "two out of every five non-Aborigines."[52]

Causes of Recidivism

Some researchers link the causes of recidivism to prisoners as follows:

> Black, Latino, and poor defendants in criminal cases are more likely to have prior convictions than their white and wealthy peers.[53]

Table 5.3 Proportion of Incarceration in Australia

	General Population	Aboriginals
Incarcerated proportion of adult population 2023*	0.203%	2.524%
Corresponds to *Crime Deterrence* (Figure 3.9)	.996	.972
Corresponds to *Immunity Retention*	1.0	.12

Source

* Australian Bureau of Statistics, "National and state information about adult prisoners and community based corrections, including legal status, custody type, Indigenous status, sex" (Canberra: Corrective Services, Australia, 2023).

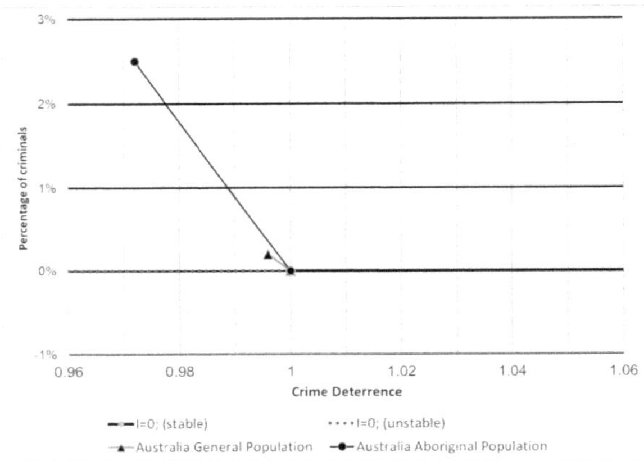

Figure 5.4 Australia: Equilibrium of proportion of criminals; Immunity Retention of general population = 9; Immunity Retention of aboriginal population = 0.05. Author's work.

This observation offers an opportunity to examine some possible causes of recidivism. Our assumption is that Black, Latino, poor, white, and wealthy criminals are rational individuals; they commit offenses if crime pays. In the case of wealthy criminals, a research that interviewed 133 inmates guilty of embezzlement concluded that the "problems were all related" to the "status-seeking or status-maintaining behavior of the violators."[54] Status improvement is not a trait of white or rich. Every reasonable person strives to climb a status ladder. If crime pays then crime is a means to achieve results for rich and poor.

White or Black embezzlers commit their offenses alone. After being caught, punished, and released, the embezzler loses his status and his appetite to improve it. Reasonably this applies to other white-collar crimes like fraud and forgery. Most Black, Latino, and poor commit gang-related crimes[55] rather than single operator delinquencies. Reasonably, after discharge from penitentiary, a return to one's gang opens new opportunities to relapse.

Several scholars blame society for recidivism. The causes attributed to society can be divided into two categories:

a. Prison conditions "which tend to alienate and dehumanize the inmate."[56]
b. Circumstances after release consisting of "a range of common problems that contribute to returning to criminal behaviors."[57]
c. Replacement effects—This suggestion claims that "incarcerating one person for a market-driven offense—for example, trafficking an addictive drug like heroin—can open up new, lucrative criminal opportunities for someone else."[58] The suggestion relates this effect to recidivism:

> Replacement effects are likely to be stronger for offenders with prior convictions than those without. [59]

No evidence or rational is offered to clarify why replacement effects get stronger with recidivism. Nevertheless this suggestion foresees that the corrective action of incarceration increases the number of criminals. This renders the *replacement effect* theory both wrong and destabilizing.

Figure 3.9 shows why the theory is wrong. If one incarcerates a criminal, then the infractor population size decreases by one. On the other hand the replacement effect increases the infractor population size by one; the combined effect is that the population size is constant.

The *replacement effect* is neutral; however the replacement effect theory is destabilizing. Incarceration increases the cost of crime; consequently it elevates the threshold of benefit that would trigger a crime. In other words incarceration is a negative feedback element of crime control as is the thermostat in temperature control. As shown in Chapter 3, the effect of incarceration is bringing the SIR system to equilibrium. The function of the incarceration therefore is to keep the number of infractors constant which is achieved at equilibrium (see Figure 3.9). Suggesting that incarceration increases the crime rate is destabilizing because someone might adopt the theory and reduce or eliminate incarceration. Reducing incarceration decreases the *Crime Deterrence* ratio; Figure 3.9 illustrates that at a lower *Crime Deterrence* ratio one arrives at a higher *Percentage of Criminals* at equilibrium. Eliminating incarceration destroys the controller element of the SIR system and the Percentage of Criminals quickly spirals to 100%. Thus, implementing the Replacement Effects theory is destabilizing.

The research of Lewis[60] concludes that applying harsher sentences to recidivists is not a deterrent. No doubt, research is beneficial for all of us. However, in this case the arguments of Lewis based the *irrational delinquent* assumption. Lewis invokes the research of Junger, West, and Timman[61] investigating traffic accidents to infer that infractors including recidivists are irrational:

> Those who commit crime tend to be impulsive and risk-seeking in general, and often intoxicated when they do.
>
> There is no prima facie reason to think the recidivist sentencing premium is an exception to any of these general trends. Therefore, justifying that principle [of harsher punishments for recidivists] on the basis of its deterrent effect is a tall task from the start.[62]

I mentioned earlier that traffic accident statistics is rich of irrational infractors. Earlier I also agreed that not all delinquents are rational. (see section *The impulsive lawbreaker*). Irrational lawbreakers exist, and I agree that for them the Figure 3.9, the SIR model, the *Crime Deterrence ratio*, and the *Immunity Retention* ratio do not apply. Treating irrational people is out of scope. Deterrences apply for rational criminals and they exist (see for example Table 5.2).

Treatment

Regardless whether society is liable or not, for recidivism society benefits from cost-effective measures reducing reoffending.

Table 5.4 lists treatments proposed to increase *Immunity Retention* among convicts. The table has two columns for treatments: one during detention and the other following the release to freedom. The purpose of this examination is determining the stabilizing effects of the proposed measures on the equilibrium. The examination of cost effectiveness of the treatments is out of scope, and it can be found in the literature.[63]

Table 5.4 Corrective Actions for Reducing Recidivism

	Treatment	
1	**In Prison**	**After Release**
21	Education[a]	Find employment[b]
32	Psychotherapy[c]	Get housing[d]
43	Behavioural therapy[e]	Get Welfare[f]
54	Therapeutic Community[g]	Reuniting with family members[h]
65	Diversion[i]	Rebuilding convict's life[j]
66	Substance abuse treatment[k]	Accessto services[l]
77	Accountability of prison staff for recidivism[m]	Accountability of Parole officer for recidivism[n]
88		Revoking stigma attached to convicts[o]

Sources

[a] Cesare Beccaria, Dei delitti e delle pene (Livorno, Italy: Marco Coltellini, 1764), 102; Christopher Lewis, "The paradox of recidivism," Emory LJ 70 (2020); Santiago Redondo Illescas, Julio Sánchez-Meca, and Vicente Garrido Genovés, "Treatment of offenders and recidivism: Assessment of the effectiveness of programmes applied in Europe," Psychology in Spain 5, no. 1 (2001); Lise McKean and Charles Ransford, Current strategies for reducing recidivism (Center for Impact Research Chicago, IL, 2004).

[b] Lewis, "The paradox of recidivism"; McKean and Ransford, Current strategies for reducing recidivism.

[c] Illescas, Sánchez-Meca, and Genovés, "Treatment of offenders and recidivism: Assessment of the effectiveness of programmes applied in Europe"; McKean and Ransford, Current strategies for reducing recidivism.

[d] Lewis, "The paradox of recidivism"; McKean and Ransford, Current strategies for reducing recidivism.

[e] Illescas, Sánchez-Meca, and Genovés, "Treatment of offenders and recidivism: Assessment of the effectiveness of programmes applied in Europe."

[f] Lewis, "The paradox of recidivism."

[g] Illescas, Sánchez-Meca, and Genovés, "Treatment of offenders and recidivism: Assessment of the effectiveness of programmes applied in Europe."

[h] McKean and Ransford, Current strategies for reducing recidivism.

[i] Illescas, Sánchez-Meca, and Genovés, "Treatment of offenders and recidivism: Assessment of the effectiveness of programmes applied in Europe."

[j] McKean and Ransford, Current strategies for reducing recidivism.

[k] Ibid.

[l] Ibid.

[m] Ibid.

[n] Ibid.

[o] Joel Schrag and Suzanne Scotchmer, "The self-reinforcing nature of crime," International review of Law and Economics 17, no. 3 (1997).

The measures of column "In Prison" consist of corrective actions consistent with the theory that the responsibility for proper behavior lies with the individual; society is interested in treating the prisoner because it helps retaining his immunity after discharge. The measures are stabilizing with one striking exception: accountability of prison staff for recidivism. This measure transfers accountability from the individual to society. I will explain later that this proposal is destabilizing.

The corrective actions in the "After Release" column consist of remedial measures consistent with the concept that responsibility for keeping individuals out of trouble rests with the society. Measures 1–6 and 8 affect the equilibrium; treatment number 7 is destabilizing. Measures 1–6 and 8 of the right-hand-side column decrease the cost of crime. These measures reward the criminal with guaranteed employment, housing, welfare, family, straightforward access to services, and with canceling stigma. Applying any of these measures changes the cost and benefit calculation of a susceptible. The increased benefits will result in a higher incentive to commit a crime. Reducing *Crime Deterrence* increases the crime rate at equilibrium (Figure 3.9). As far as measure 7 on both columns of Table 5.4 is concerned, assigning accountability to either prison staff or parole officers regarding recidivism is an empty measure, counterproductive, irresponsible, and, ultimately, destabilizing. It is an empty measure because if remedial measures include education, therapies, substance abuse treatment, housing, employment, and family life, then prison wards would be made accountable for acts they cannot control. It is counterproductive because it assigns accountability to the wrong actors; consequently it enlightens the burden of accountability of functions that should be responsible. Assigning accountability on officers of law enforcement for results they cannot control is more questionable when this idea comes from academics; the staff of higher education is protected by academic tenure. This is not to say that one should cancel tenure for academic staff. The only thing that is worse than keeping tenure is terminating it. Accountability is necessary for healthy administration. It should be assigned mostly by people who themselves are accountable for their actions. Tenure is also necessary for progress of science. People protected by academic tenure should be hesitant stipulating accountability of others especially when such stipulations stand on feeble validation. Most importantly, the provision of accountability of law enforcement officers for reducing recidivism is destabilizing because it may negatively impact the career of valuable officers.

Stigma

Measure no. 8 of Table 5.4 needs special attention. Complex societies inherited the institute of stigma from simpler societies. We have institutes that grade honest behavior not only for convicts but also for law obeying citizens. Credit rating is used in financial transactions, security clearance helps receiving employment offers, and good behavior certificates are issued by police for the purpose of immigration or employment.

Is inflicting stigma an acceptable means of punishing offenders? Not surprisingly there is a split among scholars regarding the answer. State inflicted stigma "invites the public to punish the offenders."[64] That is true. However, the same scholar further condemns official stigma "for it invites the *mob* to tyrannize over whoever they happen not to like."[65] That is questionable. A bank regulation may or may not allow employing bank robbers, embezzlers, or other violators of the law. Is a regulation not to employ such an offender a tyrannical persecution of disliked individuals? Or, perhaps, it is reducing the risk of account holders to be victimized.

Credit rating, security clearance, and good behavior certificates may harm some citizens and may benefit others. Punishing people who do not pay back their loans impoverishes the poor. However, eliminating credit rating impoverishes customers in need for a loan that do pay back their loans in a timely manner. I brought these examples precisely because so does stigma inflicted by law enforcement. Earlier I admitted that inflicting stigma invites the public to punish the offender. It is worthwhile examining the consequences of protecting the offender from public punishment. I will first use the examination of a specialist of Social and Political Theory, and then I will reevaluate the example using Equilibrium and Stability Theory.

The example was raised by Nussbaum,[66] the opponent of inflicting stigma on lawbreakers. She considers the impact of using stigma on drunk drivers by a regulation "requiring the convicted offender to display for some period of time a 'DUI' message on his car license plate indicating that he has been convicted of driving under the influence of alcohol."[67] Arneson agrees that a license plate with such a message is "antithetical to human dignity."[68] At this point Arneson answers the question of what is the effect of not allowing the "DUI" message on the license plate. He argues that if such a message is considered a deterrent from drunk driving, then "foregoing the shaming penalty brings it about that some innocent people are killed or maimed."

Equilibrium and Stability Theory can be useful to examine the conflicting views. This chapter explained that the percentage of drunk drivers in society is determined by two ratios: *Crime Deterrence*" and "*Immunity Retention*." The *Crime Deterrence* is directly proportional to crime cost in the view of the potential drink driver. A potential drunk driver would decide not to drive under the influence precisely because among other factors he worries about "human dignity." This increased cost of DUI increases the *Crime Deterrence*. Figure 3.9 illustrates that the effect reduces the percentage of drunk drivers; this is consistent with Arneson's argument affirming that the final outcome is less "innocent people are killed or maimed."

It is more remarkable that in simple societies stigma is an effective punitive measure while incarceration is not even practiced. In an eye-opening exposition, Adela Şerban describes social deviation control in traditional Romanian villages.[69] The portrayal of this simple society not only reveals simple and effective means of social control but also suggests at likely methods employed by simple societies at the beginning of civilization. Stigma has been an efficient instrument of keeping individuals out of trouble.

Conclusion

1. The primary conclusion of this chapter reinforces an old wisdom: *crime exists if crime pays*. Conversely only a society where crime never pays will be crimeless.

2. The percentage of criminals in a society is determined by two ratios: Crime Deterrence and Immunity Retention. The first ratio is related to the cost and the benefit of crime; the second ratio is related to recidivism.
3. Proportional punishment increases the cost of crime. Increasing the cost of crime reduces the percentage of criminals. Conversely policies of not punishing crime increase the percentage of criminals. Theories claiming that "less punishment decreases crime" are destabilizing.
4. Recidivism is an important factor determining the percentage of criminals. Our knowledge about causes of recidivism is immature.
5. Education seems to be a generally accepted means of recidivism prevention. It is true that educated people are less inclined to repeat their offenses; however, educated people commit crimes which are tricky to repeat.
6. If education advocates theories opposing incarceration or stigma, then it is more harmful than beneficial.

Notes

1 Jamgon Mipham and José I. Cabezon, *The Just King: The Tibetan Buddhist Classic on Leading an Ethical Life* (Boulder: Shambhala, 2017), 35.

2 Richard L. Schott, "The Origins of Bureaucracy: An Anthropological Perspective," *International Journal of Public Administration* 23, no. 1 (2000).

3 Samuel N. Kramer, *The Sumerians: Their History, Culture, and Character* (Chicago: University of Chicago Press, 2010), 4.

4 Julius Pokorny, *Indogermanisches Etymologisches Wörterbuch* (Bern: Francke, 1959), 854–+; see also David W. Anthony, *The Horse, the Wheel, and Language: How Bronze-Age Riders from the Eurasian Steppes Shaped the Modern World* (Princeton: Princeton University Press, 2010), Kindle Location 3185.

5 Yashar in the Hebrew Bible means a road being straight (1 Samuel 6:12), a just life (Proverbs 11:5), right in the eyes of someone (Judges 14:3, 17:6).

6 Anna Mancini, *Maat Revealed, Philosophy of Justice in Ancient Egypt* (Buenos Aires: Buenos Books America, 2004), 10.

7 Claas J. Bleeker, "The Religion of Ancient Egypt," in *Historia Religionum, Volume 1 Religions of the Past*, ed. Claas J. Bleeker and G. Widengren (Leiden, New York, Copenhagen, and Köln: E.J. Brill, 1988), 57.

8 Avraham Faust, *Israel's Ethnogenesis: Settlement, Interaction, Expansion and Resistance* (London: Equinox Pub., 2006), 105.

9 Kramer, *The Sumerians: Their History, Culture, and Character*, 4.

10 Ibid., 83, 84.

11 Frank E. Hartung, "Methodological Assumption in a Social-Psychological Theory of Criminality," *The Journal of Criminal Law, Criminology, and Police Science* 45 (1954): 65.

12 e.g. Kramer, *The Sumerians: Their History, Culture, and Character*, 83, 84.

13 perchè ogni pena non fia una violenza di uno , o di molti contro un privato cittadino, dev ' essere essenzialmente pubblica , pronta , necessaria , la minima delle possibili nelle date circostanze , proporzionata ai delitti , dettata dalle Leggi Cesare Beccaria, *Dei Delitti E Delle Pene* (Livorno: Marco Coltellini, 1764), 104, author's translation.

14 Irene Winter, "Touched by the Gods: Visual Evidence for the Divine Status of Rulers in the Ancient near East" (paper presented at the Oriental Institute Seminars 4, Chicago, 2008); Henry F. Lutz, "Kingship in Babylonia, Assyria, and Egypt," *American Anthropologist* 26, no. 4 (1924); Angelos Chaniotis, "The Divinity of Hellenistic Rulers," *A Companion to the Hellenistic World* (2003); Stephen Houston and David Stuart, "Of Gods, Glyphs and Kings: Divinity and Rulership among the Classic Maya," *Antiquity* 70, no. 268 (1996); Melvyn Bragg et al., "The Divine Right of Kings," in *In Our Time*, ed. Melvyn Bragg (London: BBC Radio 4, 2007).
15 Gretchen Starr-LeBeau and Kimberly Lynn, "Inquisitions," in *Judging Faith, Punishing Sin*, ed. C. H. Parker and G. Starr-LeBeau (Cambridge: Cambridge University Press, 2017), 63.
16 In 1901 the pillory was still in use in Delaware.
17 Starr-LeBeau and Lynn, "Inquisitions," 63.
18 e.g. Stephen E. Bronner, *Reclaiming the Enlightenment: Toward a Politics of Radical Engagement* (New York: Columbia University Press, 2004), 41; Jonathan Israel, *A Revolution of the Mind: Radical Enlightenment and the Intellectual Origins of Modern Democracy* (Princeton: Princeton University Press, 2010).
19 Joel Schrag and Suzanne Scotchmer, "The Self-Reinforcing Nature of Crime," *International Review of Law and Economics* 17, no. 3 (1997): 325–35.
20 Christopher Lewis, "The Paradox of Recidivism," *Emory Law Journal* 70 (2020).
21 W. Kip Viscusi, "The Risks and Rewards of Criminal Activity: A Comprehensive Test of Criminal Deterrence," *Journal of Labor Economics* 4, no. 3, Part 1 (1986): 317–30.
22 Lewis, "The Paradox of Recidivism."
23 Marianne Junger, Robert West, and Reinier Timman, "Crime and Risky Behavior in Traffic: An Example of Cross-Situational Consistency," *Journal of Research in Crime and Delinquency* 38, no. 4 (2001).
24 Penelope Gibbs, "The Myth That Tough Sanctions Deter Crime – Revealed by the Sentencing Council," Transform Justice, https://www.transformjustice.org.uk/news-insight/the-myth-that-tough-sanctions-deter-crime-revealed-by-the-sentencing-council/.
25 Ibid.
26 Anthony A. Braga and David L. Weisburd, "The Effects of Focused Deterrence Strategies on Crime: A Systematic Review and Meta-Analysis of the Empirical Evidence," *Journal of Research in Crime and Delinquency* 49, no. 3 (2012).
27 Anthony A. Braga, David M. Hureau, and Andrew V. Papachristos, "Deterring Gang-Involved Gun Violence: Measuring the Impact of Boston's Operation Ceasefire on Street Gang Behavior," *Journal of Quantitative Criminology* 30 (2014).
28 Steven D. Levitt, "Juvenile Crime and Punishment," *Journal of Political Economy* 106, no. 6 (1998).
29 Gibbs, "The Myth That Tough Sanctions Deter Crime – Revealed by the Sentencing Council."
30 Research Associate, Department of Criminology, Kellogg College, University of Oxford.
31 e.g. Sherry F. Colb, "Freedom from Incarceration: Why Is This Right Different from All Other Rights," *New York University Law Review* 69 (1994); Hannah T. S. Long, "The Inequability of Incarceration," *The Columbia Journal of Law and Social Problems* 31 (1997); David Cole, "Turning the Corner on Mass Incarceration," *Ohio*

State Journal of Criminal Law 9 (2011); Todd R. Clear and James Austin, "Mass Incarceration," *Reforming Criminal Justice: A Report of the Academy for Justice on Bridging the Gap between Scholarship and Reform* 4 (2017); Andrew D. Leipold, "Is Mass Incarceration Inevitable," *American Criminal Law Review* 56 (2019); Heba Shahaed, Sai Surabi Thirugnanasampanthar, and Dale Guenter, "Make or Break: Succeeding in Transition from Incarceration," *PLoS One* 19, no. 1 (2024); Thomas Guiney and Henry Yeomans, "Explaining Penal Momentum: Path Dependence, Prison Population Forecasting and the Persistence of High Incarceration Rates in England and Wales," *The Howard Journal of Crime and Justice* 62, no. 1 (2023).

32 Meredith Rossner and Helen Taylor, "The Transformative Potential of Restorative Justice: What the Mainstream Can Learn from the Margins," *Annual Review of Criminology* 7 (2024).

33 Ibid.

34 Jane Dickson-Gilmore, "Resurrecting the Peace: Traditionalist Approaches to Separate Justice in Kahnawake Mohawk Nation," in *Law & Anthropology*, ed. René Kuppe and Richard Potz (The Hague: Martinus Nijhoff Publishers, 1996). See also Teresa L. Amott and Julie A. Matthaei, *Race, Gender, and Work* (Cambridge, MA: South End Press, 1996); Sharon O'Brien, *American Indian Tribal Governments* (Norman: University of Oklahoma Press, 1993).

35 Jacob Bercovitch, *Resolving International Conflicts: The Theory and Practice of Mediation*, ed. Jacob Bercovitch (Boulder: Lynne Rienner Publishers, 1996).

36 Alan M. Dershowitz, *The Genesis of Justice* (New York: Warner Books, 2000), 157.

37 Ibid., 156, 57.

38 Ibid., 205.

39 Schrag and Scotchmer, "The Self-Reinforcing Nature of Crime."

40 Equation 1 of ibid.

41 Ibid.

42 Ibid.

43 Ibid.

44 Ibid.

45 Ibid.

46 Ibid.

47 Ibid.

48 Ibid.

49 Ibid.

50 Ibid.

51 Roderic G. Broadhurst and Ross A. Mailer, "The Recidivism of Prisoners Released for the First Time: Reconsidering the Effectiveness Question," *Australian & New Zealand Journal of Criminology* 23, no. 2 (1990).

52 Ibid.

53 Lewis, "The Paradox of Recidivism."

54 Jay S. Albanese, "White Collar Crimes and Casino Gambling: Looking for Empirical Links to Forgery, Embezzlement, and Fraud," *Crime, Law and Social Change* 49 (2008).

55 Lewis, "The Paradox of Recidivism."

56 Kristen Bailey, "The Causes of Recidivism in the Criminal Justice System and Why It Is Worth the Cost to Address Them," *Nashville Bar Journal* 6, no. 11 (2007): 6–9.

57 Lise McKean and Charles Ransford, *Current Strategies for Reducing Recidivism* (Center for Impact Research Chicago, 2004).
58 Lewis, "The Paradox of Recidivism."
59 Ibid.
60 Ibid.
61 Junger, West, and Timman, "Crime and Risky Behavior in Traffic: An Example of Cross-Situational Consistency."
62 Lewis, "The Paradox of Recidivism."
63 E.g. Santiago Redondo Illescas, Julio Sánchez-Meca, and Vicente Garrido Genovés, "Treatment of Offenders and Recidivism: Assessment of the Effectiveness of Programmes Applied in Europe," *Psychology in Spain* 5, no. 1 (2001).
64 Martha C. Nussbaum, *Hiding from Humanity: Disgust, Shame, and the Law* (Princeton: Princeton University Press, 2009), 234.
65 Ibid.
66 Ibid.
67 Richard J. Arneson, "Shame, Stigma, and Disgust in the Decent Society," *The Journal of Ethics* 11 (2007).
68 Ibid.
69 Adela Şerban, "Brief Theoretical Perspective on Traditional Society," in *A Civil Society with No Hierarchy: The Covenantal Societal Model*, ed. Ilie Bădescu and Joseph Livni (Lanham: Lexington Books, 2023).

6

Weimar and Nazi Germany

Law and Science

Constitutionalism: Foundation of Constitution

Encyclopedia Britannica defines Constitution as "the body of doctrines and practices that form the fundamental organizing principle of a political state."[1] The same encyclopedia sheds light on the term *constitutionalism;* it is a doctrine that a government's authority is determined by a body of laws or constitution. I prefer an alternative definition of *constitutionalism*:

> *Constitutionalism* is the name given to the trust which men repose in the power of words engrossed on parchment to keep a government in order."[2]

I prefer Hamilton's designation because the term *trust* is more suitable than *doctrine.* An anecdotal memory can better explain the difference between the two terms. I had a small talk discussion in Canada with a Chinese-Canadian expert of aerodynamic stability and control. He asked me why the Canadian Chief of the Defense Staff[3] does not take over the government. I answered, "because he trusts that the current system is an optimal arrangement"; I explained why replacing it with a junta government would be bad for him, for his family and for every Canadian. I asked him in return, why the Chief Commander of the Chinese Army does not take over? The stability and control colleague explained that in China there are four chiefs of four Armies: East, West, North, and South; each commander needs to conspire with at least two others to have a chance; therefore he has no hope of success. As a consequence, the Chinese system is in stable equilibrium. Both the Canadian and the Chinese systems subscribe to principles of equilibrium. The Canadian version, however, stems from the "the trust in the power of words" of the Canadian Constitution. The North American creed is constitutionalism, and that is why Hamilton's definition appeals to me.

We shall ignore those Constitutions that have nothing to do with the actual functioning of government because we focus on democracies. There is a chicken and egg question that comes to mind: What came first—the Constitution or constitutionalism? From Hamilton's definition of *constitutionalism* one deducts that *constitutionalism* preceded the Constitution, because *constitutionalism* establishes the need of a *Constitution.*

The American reality confirms this deduction.

> In America, on the other hand, it may be said that the township was organized before the county, the county before the State, the State before the Union. In New England townships were completely and definitively constituted as early as 1650.[4]

The early towns developed political standards and conducts that for generations to come were "of primary importance in the shaping and perpetuation of a coherent set of political ideas and practices."[5] Mazzacano terms these "doctrines and practices" as "contractual constitutionalism." They determine limits on government; these limits stem from the liberties engraved in the everyday life of the seventeenth-century New Englander and New England's laws derived from it:

> In the laws of Connecticut, as well as in all those of New England, we find the germ and gradual development of that township independence which is the life and mainspring of American liberty at the present day.[6]

In America *constitutionalism* preceded the *Constitution.*

A Constitution without Constitutionalism

As opposed to the American Revolution, the Weimar Republic came about as the results of the fall of the German Empire and its monarchic order. Germany was odd even compared to other European parliamentary systems of that time:

> In other Western democracies the established Western parliamentary democracies had benefited from a period in which parliamentary practices had been established on a far from democratic basis.[7]

The new Republic preserved a significant portion of the previous imperial order (see Figure 6.1). As a consequence, the new concept of government was marked by "only a fairly weak and highly unorganized constitutional insertion into the surviving authoritarian system [Obrigkeitssystem]."[8] The transition from the previous Imperial system of assigned authorities to the Weimar Republic is another example of the observation that "societies do not hop models."[9] Doblin's words summarize the outcome as "a republic with no instruction manual."[10]

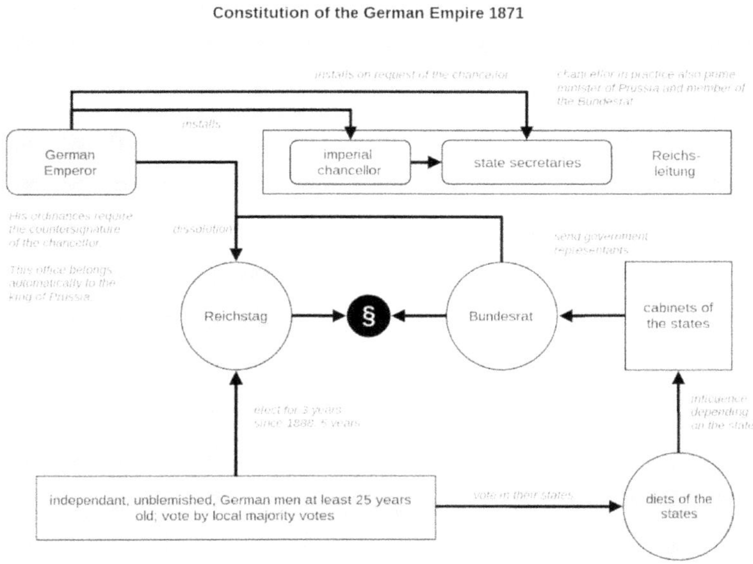

Figure 6.1 The Constitution of the German Empire 1871. Public Domain. Credit: Ziko van Dijk.

The old imperial system did have an instruction manual. It was inscribed in procedures and regulations of a well-established imperial bureaucracy entrusted and trained to be active managers and passive as far as political bias is concerned:

> True, it has been shown that some branches of the German *Beamtentum* attempted to sabotage many of the Weimar reforms and never did become fully loyal to the Weimar Republic. But at the same time their political passivity and non-participation made them an easy tool in the hands of the Nazis and their very neutrality and (official or unofficial) willingness to accept political masters of any kind (even if they did not serve them with good heart) facilitated the rise of the Nazi régime.[11]

The Weimar Constitution was framed "to combine the political and economic principles of both liberalism and socialism."[12] The Constitution heralded a new beginning.

> No man in the world would be more free than the German. No government would be more democratic than his. At least on paper.[13]

The Germans, however, showed "a lack of active commitment to the new order."[14] Many professors opposed democratic values such as freedom of speech and freedom of press.[15]

In America constitutionalism legitimized the constitution; In Weimar Germany absence of constitutionalism produced distrust.

Legal scholars examined the text to exhaustion. The thesis of this work is that a system fails in the absence of negative feedback loops which in terms of constitutional scholars are known as checks and balances. Let me show you how my thesis sheds light on the case of Republic of Weimar.

Judicial Review

The weakness of judicial review prescribed by the Weimar Constitution foretold a high likelihood of instability. The next paragraphs detail the main faults.

The Imperial Constitution of 1871 assigned the courts authority to review the constitutionality of rules and regulations (*Verordnungen*).[16] Not surprisingly, the Weimar Constitution also authorized the Supreme Court to review the constitutionality of rules or regulations.[17] However, the Constitution did not authorize the court to revoke unconstitutional rules and regulations; the court empowered lower courts to disregard unconstitutional regulation.[18]

The Constitution authorized the Supreme Court to pronounce constitutional judgments regarding disputes between the federal government and a state government or between two states.[19] This authority of the Supreme Court should not be grasped as a relaxation of the centralized top-to-bottom power flow of the imperial order. The Weimar Constitution clearly stated that federal law overrides state law.[20] The authority of the Supreme Court was, therefore, restricted to judge whether a particular state law does or does not contradict federal law.[21] This understanding was also inherited from the Constitution of 1871.[22]

As opposed to rules and regulations federal laws could not be reviewed directly. It is important to compare the American evolution of the notion of constitutionality with the German history. The American Framers grew up in Colonial America which, among others, had Puritan roots. Puritans landed in America with a persuasion of supremacy of covenants, compacts, or constitutions over royal authority. This persuasion spawned the perception that laws contradicting covenanted rules may and should be revoked. Colonial America had a dual government: one in London represented by a governor and one in the colony. Governors balanced royal authority with customs and aspirations of the governed. For example governor "Belcher's achievement rested on his ability to strike a balance between the indigenous moral order and royal authority."[23] Belcher governed Massachusetts and New Hampshire (1730–41) caring "to promote the Interest and honour of the Crown and at the same time to preserve the Liberties and Privileges of the People."[24] These liberties and privileges had been around for a century and remained deeply rooted in the hearts and minds of the townsfolk:

> He was protector of a legacy that was rooted in that moment when a covenanted people had swarmed out of England to plant a "wilderness Canaan."[25]

Protecting a covenanted legacy is not yet judicial review. However, balancing a covenantal order practiced by the New Englander against dictates of the Crown germinated the concept that laws may be subject to review.

Contrastingly, the German states of the eighteenth century responded to "the rapid growth of democratic ideas all over the world"[26] by princes embracing *enlightened despotism*. The princes retained their power; however they strived to exercise it "for the good of the people."[27] The rulers learned and appreciated ideas of the enlightenment;[28] nevertheless, they held the sole authority to determine what the *good of the people* consists of. A motto attributed to Joseph II, emperor of Austria, "everything for the people, nothing by the people,"[29] illustrates the sociopolitical distance between German princes and Colonial America's reality

Not surprisingly, the framers of the Weimar Constitution did not hurry to fully implement judicial review of legislation. However, they decreed that the justices in their capacity of judging conflicts between federal and state law may find that the federal law is unconstitutional and consequently rule in favor of the state law.[30] This tortured opening toward judicial review illustrates that social order does not leap from one blueprint to another; instead, models of society crawl ahead.

Everything for the People, Nothing by the People

The Weimar Republic inherited a sociopolitical reality that crystallized with the creation of the German Empire. As before unification, in Germany, "the norms of civic conduct were still being determined by the canons of enlightened despotism."[31]

Therefore Joseph II's catchphrase describing *enlightened despotism* deserves to be explored. The first part of the motto sounds hollow propaganda; the second appears honest.

Historians credit the German unification to Wilhelm I and to Otto von Bismarck.[32] Bismarck's rule was autocratic; nevertheless, we are told that it was socially engaged in people's concerns like administration of law, education, town management, healthcare, anti-poverty provisions, and unemployment.[33] This section explores the transition from aristocracy to meritocracy[34] in pre-Weimar Germany through the prism of industrialization. Pre-Weimar Germany began with the rule of Wilhelm I and ended with the rule of his grandson, Willhelm II.

Figure 6.2 illustrates a comparison of economic growth in the relevant time interval (1870–1910).The source of the data is the investigation of Alvarez-Palau, Díez-Minguela, and Martí-Henneberg,[35] The economic growth of unified Germany was surpassed only by Denmark and Switzerland. As opposed to the United Kingdom and the United States, the German autocratic government played an active role by financial stimuli.[36] The involvement of the government also consisted of imperial or state[37] ownership of industries, subsidies, and tariffs.[38] Other factors contributing to the economic growth are railroad infrastructure,[39] subsidized shipping,[40] new technologies and skilled workers, "notably chemical engineering, electrical engineering, and mechanical engineering."[41]

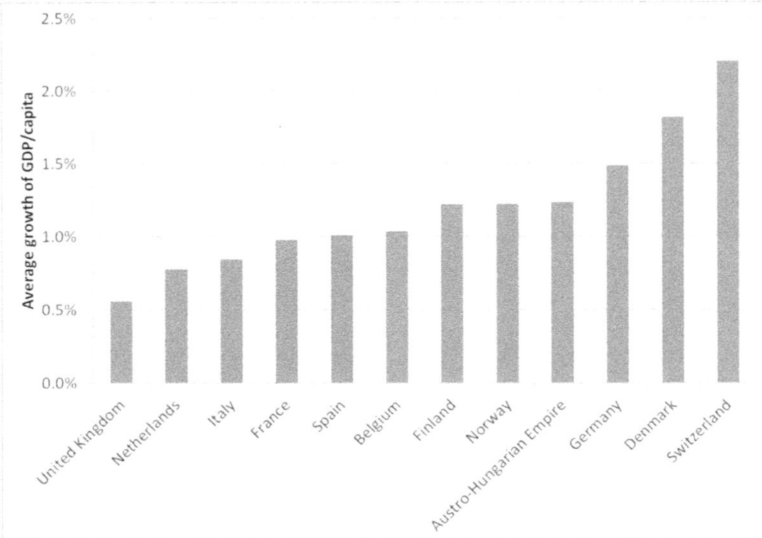

Figure 6.2 West European average GDP/capita growth 1870–1910. Author's work.

Surprisingly, Figure 6.2 indicates that the UK, the *engine of the Industrial Revolution*, had the lowest economic growth rate. In absolute values the UK GDP/capita exceeded the German one[42] (see Figure 6.3). However in the UK growth rate was slower precisely because the Industrial Revolution of the UK started earlier; consequently, the time interval (1870–2010) is not relevant for the UK.

The constituent states continued the benign autocracy of pre-unification times. At the municipal level authorities were busy setting up sanitary and hygienic infrastructure, central water supply and sewage; they installed disinfection facilities and regulated food products,[43] Municipalities supplied pasteurized milk to the population, and distributed milk for babies.[44]

At the state level bureaucratic institutes managed healthcare; the staff was trained in law and consulted experts in medical sciences.[45]

The previous discussion illustrates that the pre-Weimar government incentivized economic growth and social security; however, I suggest that the "everything for the people, nothing by the people" approach inhibited constitutionalism. Enlightened despotism of the empire and its constituent states improved the standard of living of the people and their social security while denying their participation in public life. Rights, liberties, and equality are incompatible with "nothing by the people." Government-owned enterprises, subsidies, and tariffs deny equal opportunity because they monopolize sections of the economy, unfairly favor certain endeavors, and protect well-connected entrepreneurs. As long as the results were positive, constitutionalism had no chance to appear. Successful entrepreneurs feared calls for *equality*. After all, they enjoyed governmental stimuli, subsidies, and trade protection while out-of-favor competitors did not.

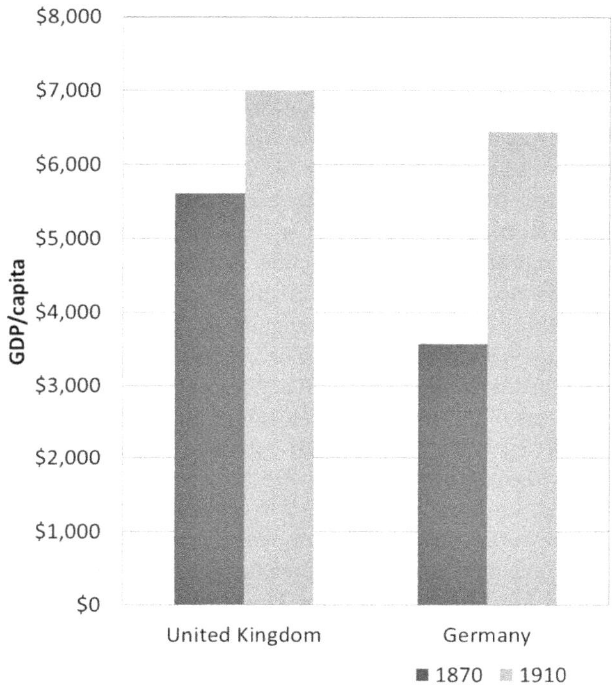

Figure 6.3 GDP/capita 1870–1910—Germany and UK. Author's work.

In America the Industrial Revolution built prosperity because of equal opportunities, constitutional liberties, and respect for rights. Pre-Weimar citizens accepted what the enlightened despotic state offered and internalized freedom as an ideal "achieved by the individual in and through the organized state."[46] Not surprisingly, the Weimar Republic did not inherit from the defunct empire even one centiMorgan[47] of constitutionalism in its DNA.

Perhaps it is not a coincidence that the two most hazardous ideologies of the modern era stemmed from this imperial "nothing by the people" experience: Marxism and Nazism. They both preserved the model of German autocratic rule with its privileged ruling clique. Marx and Engels pledged diverting privileges from the "financial and industrial bourgeoisie"[48] to the "exploited working class."[49] Only this radical mutation guarantees that the "everything for the people" dream comes true. In following Marxist experimentations, the dream developed into a nightmare. The Nazi ideology also departed from tracks laid by the German Empire. They preached that "for the people" refers to people of the Aryan Race; consequently, only the German Nazi party under its Führer can assure the triumph of Germany. This ideology also ended up in disaster.

In spite of inequality, aristocratic privilege, autocratic rule of the empire, there was some flexibility of movement from one social stratum to another. That was not because of constitutionally imposed equality but because the economic project of the autocrat required it. Here are some famous examples:

Ernst Werner Siemens grew up in the Kingdom of Hanover; he came from the "higher educated upper middle class."[50] In spite of his parents being poor,[51] he founded the well-known Siemens Electrical and Telecommunication Corporation; he was involved in inventions like electric streetcar, locomotive, and elevator.

Alfred Krupp came from Essen, the Ruhr district. His father Friedrich was himself an entrepreneur, who tried and failed.[52] In spite of his impoverished parents, Alfred Krupp initiated a large army supply corporation. Among others he pioneered a health insurance scheme for his employees.[53] This can be viewed as a top-to-bottom radiation effect of the "everything for the people, nothing by the people" philosophy.

Karl Benz grew up in Karlsruhe, Baden-Württemberg.[54] His father was a locomotive driver; his mother had no hopes for Karl; in her eyes he "was a liability rather than an asset."[55] Benz was one of the pioneers of the automobile. He held the patent for the Benz-Patent-Motorwagen (Figure 6.4). Karl Benz was one of the three founders of Benz & Companie Rheinische Gasmotoren-Fabrik.

Gottlieb Daimler was born in Schorndorf, Württemberg. His father was a baker.[56] His inventions were in the domain of the gasoline internal combustion engine. As an entrepreneur he founded the Daimler Motoren Gesellschaft.

One can deduct from these reports that Pre-Weimar Germany was a mixture of aristocracy and meritocracy. It was an *enlightened despotism* conserving aristocratic privileges; however, the social stratification did not consist of classes the membership of which was strictly determined by birth. The "everything for the people" was not a guarantee for "life, liberty and pursuit of happiness";[57] however, it created an "offer of occupational services on the labor market or successful applications for free positions."[58] As mentioned earlier, the Marxist perspective of *class struggle* implying

Figure 6.4 Benz Patent-Motorwagen. Public domain.

rigid stratification also originated in pre-Weimar Germany. Opposed to Marx, Max Weber observed that "transitions from one class to another vary greatly in fluidity."[59] The earlier examples illustrate that *enlightened despotism* tolerated transition from one layer to another based on meritocratic evaluation. Liberty and equality were not constitutionally granted; however, in practice, people were free to try. Friedrich Krupp tried and failed; his son Alfred tried and succeeded.

Governing by Decree

The most frequent controversy regarding the Weimar Constitution is about article 48. This article authorized the President to suspend constitutional practices and to govern by decree.[60] Scholars note that the provision was not outright antidemocratic because the Parliament was authorized to annul such Presidential decree.[61] More problematically, Carl Schmitt argued that article 48 served the "security and defense of the constitution as a whole."[62]

The effectivity of checks and balances is examined by their use in practice. The state of emergency was invoked twenty-four times until the end of 1920 enabling extraordinary courts and summary trials both denying defendants' right of appeal.

Article 48 is often criticized; however, it was not necessarily the main weakness of the Weimar Republic. After all, the article's intention was to save democracy.[63] Scholars rightly observe that "it was not the constitutional power of the president that was the biggest problem. It was the persistence of conceptions of the power of the state that long pre-dated the Weimar Republic."[64]

The antidemocratic outcome of the application of article 48 is not because of the *constitution* but because of lack of *constitutionalism*. In America constitutional practices rested on a quarter-century-long history of covenantal practices established by the passengers of the Mayflower.[65] The German tradition came from a historical line dominated by "the union of personal and territorial power in the princely right of domination."[66]

Framing the Weimar Constitution

The academic elite of Weimar played a primary role in putting democracy in practice. The fall of the empire required a replacement. Hugo Preuss, a former professor,[67] was in charge of the political design of Weimar.[68] His previous studies inferred that the wrong choice consists of "an impotent, disorganized populace."[69] Preuss indeed specified the guidelines:

> The differentiation of the legally normativized and organized expression of the common will through a plurality of organs is, in contrast to the absolute state, the conceptual essence of the constitutional Rechtsstaat.[70]

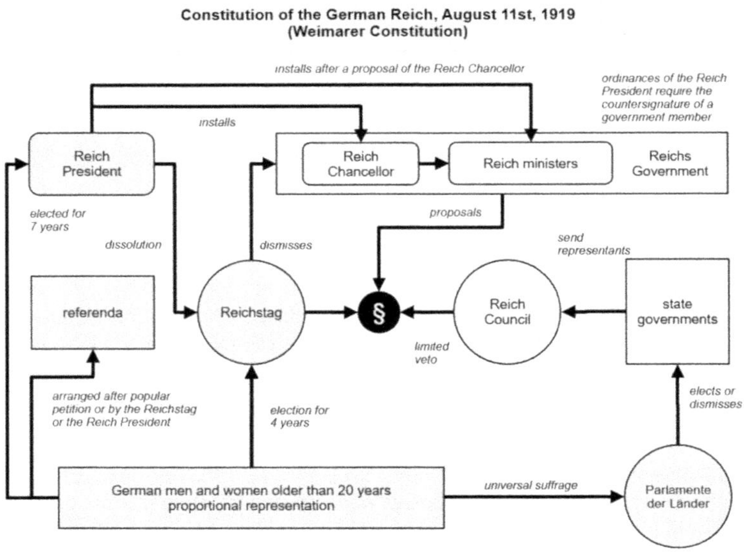

Figure 6.5 The institutions of the Weimar Republic. Public Domain. Credit: Ziko van Dijk.

The question to what extent this specification helps is beyond my expertise and experience. Nevertheless, the term "plurality of organs" may hide the idea of checks and balances. Let us examine not the intent but the outcome (Figure 6.5).

At first sight the Weimar organization chart is very similar to the organization chart of the empire (Figure 6.1). One should note the following differences:

1. In the Weimar Republic the Reichstag can dismiss the executive government including the Chancellor; the Imperial Reichstag could not. However, the representatives of the states—the Reich Council—had no such authority entailing an unbalance in favor of centralization. The Reich Council of Weimar had a limited veto authority over legislation. This should not mislead the reader; the Weimar Constitution introduced no additional mechanism of checks and balances in favor of the states. The opposite is true. In the Imperial Constitution the legislation power was shared by the Reichstag and the Bundesrat (Reich Council). That potentially balancing power has been replaced by a *limited veto.* The new veto power consisted of the authority to reject a law; however if the Reichstag resubmitted the law to a vote and obtained a majority of two-thirds the veto was overridden.[71] Even in the case of obtaining a majority of two-thirds the president had a choice to submit the law to a referendum or to abolish the law. So far the new Constitution scored two-zero for unbalanced centralization.

2. In Figure 6.1 the emperor has the authority to dissolve the Reichstag. That is understandable under the concept of "nothing by the people"; in Figure 6.5 the president has the same power; moreover the President has the right to bring any legislation of the Reichstag to a referendum. At first glance, this also hints at checks and balances. It is absolutely the opposite. A judicial review can reject a law if it is unconstitutional. The American Constitution assigns unalienable rights to individuals and limited authority to state governments. The Weimar Constitution (Figure 6.5) entitles the president to arbitrarily submit to referendum laws protecting such rights. The result would be potential removal of minority rights by majority vote. Actually, there were referenda that recommended approving expropriating private assets:
    a. The 1921 Berlin referendum known as "Expropriate Deutsche Wohnen & Co." proposed transferring the property of private real-estate companies owning 3,000 or more units to public ownership. The city referendum passed; however it was not binding.
    b. The 1926 referendum—the German public voted on a proposal to confiscate the assets of the abdicated monarch and his family. It is known as the Princes' Referendum. The referendum failed.[72]

Both referenda failed. In the Weimar Republic, both referenda complied with the Constitution; however both contradicted *constitutionalism;* moreover, they were uncivilized. *Constitutionalism* is the trust of the public that words of the Constitution can stop governmental injustice. The American Constitution forbids expropriation without "due process of law."[73] One cannot speak about *constitutionalism* in the German Empire; however it is inconceivable that the governed consented to arbitrary expropriating one's property. Chapter 5 mentioned that protecting one's assets was the fundamental reason of people's concessions to rulers. This principle is consistent with *justice*; it is 5,000 years old. Chapter 5 argues that the linguistic ancestors of the Germans, the proto-Indo-Europeans had a word *reĝ* from which the German word *Recht* (law, right, justice) has descended. In modern German a judge is called *Richter.*[74] The referenda failed because *justice* had existed for five millennia. People who resented the proposals did not necessarily empathize with the targets; they understood that voting for injustice, one votes against oneself. The two referenda were not only an attempted assault on individual or minority rights, they were an assault on *justice*.

3. The authority of the president to bring any law to referendum empties the legislative authority of the Reichstag.[75] Checks and balances consist of separation of powers not of encroachment of authority.
4. One-tenth of the population could require a referendum.[76] As argued in point 1 above, this entitlement is *unjust* and *uncivilized.*

The Constitution replaced the "plurality of organs" by a president with imperial power to govern by decree if circumstances require such a move.

Some attribute this outcome to the influence of Redslob on Preuss, some point the finger at Max Weber.[77] Interestingly, Redslob understood that the American Democracy possesses an inherent resilience because of its *national tradition and mentality*.[78] Let me convince you that the American tradition and mentality in question is *constitutionalism*. Consider the following:

a. Redslob also notices that such mentality was missing in France of 1848.[79]
b. Redslob compares the mentality regarding government between France and England:
    i. In France the national mindset leads to one institution that governs. In 1848 the Constitution assigned power to an elected President;[80] the Constitution of 1799 designated the First Consul that led to the rule of Napoleon I;[81] the Constitution of 1875 decrees Parliament's absolute rule.[82] This national conviction is incompatible with a balance of power because it calls for the supremacy of one single will.
    ii. In England the national mentality evolved from practice, history and tradition; consequently, this practical approach is consistent with a government equilibrating opposite forces.[83] This mentality of proven traditional expression of a practiced mutual agreement between government and governed is *constitutionalism*. A practiced rule of behavior does not need a *constitution*. The simplest example consists of marriage. The wedding vow promises *to have and to hold from this day forward, for better, for worse, for richer, for poorer, in sickness and in health, to love and to cherish, until parted by death*. The real constitution of a married couple crystallizes during years of better days and worse days, successes and failures, dinners with parents and dinners with in-laws. Not all marriages are resilient *until parted by death*. Resilient partnerships develop a *constitution* with mutual understandings how to survive disputes, failures, sickness, and other unforeseen difficulties.

In Germany, as in France, the Constitution was not preceded by constitutionalism. In France, the striving for "liberty, equality, fraternity" came from demands of the third estate to remove aristocratic and royal obstacles to free trade, manufacture, cultural and political expression. In this respect, there was a *general will* and the Constitutions of France respected it. Weimar Germany did not need to deal with freedom for trade and industry initiatives. The empire took care of them.

The Framers of Weimar maintained the previous system of Imperial autocracy replacing the "nothing by the people" with "something by the people." Some call this variant Führer-Democracy.[84] A strong president with a counseling Parliament is *enlightened despotism* 2.0. The old motto "everything for the people nothing by the people" became "something for the people, something by the people."

The authoritarian empire started with German unification; it terminated trade barriers between states; it remarkably accelerated a State and Crown directed German Industrial Revolution. It maintained a healthy level of decentralization "with a high degree of variation in administrative structures and legislative enactments."[85] The Weimar changes weakened the constituent states and empowered the president.

The empire collapsed not because it hindered industrial development but because it gambled on total victory in the First World War, and it ended up in total defeat. The old *enlightened despotism* with aristocratic privileges and meritocratic advantages perished; its resurrection was unlikely. The people lost faith in the old regime and had no faith in the new one. The framers of the Weimar Constitution ignored this public atmosphere; they sanctioned an abstract *general will*, even though the framers could only guess what that means in Weimar's uninspired reality; they invented theoretical adjustments boosting an intangible *general will* ending up with unintended unfairness.

If the American Constitution were a result of a "Framers' Coup,"[86] it would look like the Weimar Constitution.

Enlightenment

The Enlightenment in continental Europe "involved the revaluation of all values, established a new order of thought, and transformed the standards of humanity."[87] The resurrection of the ancient Aristotelian notion of *democracy* generated the need to coin the term *general will*. Rousseau claimed that there is a *general will* and everyone is constrained to obey it.[88] In America there was no need to abstract terms to talk about public engagement in government. Pre-Revolutionary America willfully obeyed covenants, compacts, and Constitutions.

Revolutions in France came from a tyranny imposing aristocratic privileges. The General Estates consisted of a council of three Estates: aristocracy, clergy and the rest. The Third Estate rebelled because of the privileges of the two other Estates, and in the spring of 1789, it voted in the General Estate that the Third Estate alone is the National Assembly.[89] Naturally, Louis XVI disagreed; the only source of legitimacy of a vote of majority was in theoretical publications of proponents of the Enlightenment. In my view, the clearest interpretation of the term *general will* has been formulated by Weirich: the general will is the abstract imperative that *should* govern society; however, in the *concrete* reality Rousseau proposes the majority rule as its best practical approximation.[90] Eighteen years earlier, in 1771, Louis XV the grandfather of Louis XVI dismissed rebellious members of parliament, revoking their membership.[91] What changed? I suggest that not the Enlightenment pamphlets changed royal attitudes but the American Revolution. The Treaty of Paris of 1783 and the concessions of George III of Great Britain altered the chances of resisting the National Assembly; in 1789 the majority vote of the National Assembly prevailed, and in Europe democracy scored 1–0 against tyranny.

A second victory followed; the National assembly decreed the "Declaration of the Rights of Man and of the Citizen," 1789. It is a constitutional act because it establishes constitutional principles; however, it did not stem from *constitutionalism*. Constitutionalism would be the *trust* of people in the words inscribed in the *declaration*. The *Declaration* announced a "break with a thousand years of history." Consequently, in Europe of 1789 one cannot speak of a trust in the brand new principles of the declaration.

In America "the final authority to interpret the American Constitution—and thus the obligation to prevent infringement of the rights which it purported to confer—rested in the hands of an independent judiciary."[92]. In continental Europe the enforcement of the Declaration was premature. Four years after its proclamation, the Declaration was systematically violated during the period known as *Reign of terror.*[93] Subsequently, the declaration was ignored in the Dreyfus affair,[94] and crushed by the unconstitutional acts of the Pétain government 1940–3. The principles of the Declaration resurrected with the liberation in1944.

Enlightenment in Germany

In Germany, the Declaration of the Rights of Man and of the Citizen had an indirect impact. The *Enlightened Despotism* echoes the demands of the 1848 Revolution.[95]

Scientific knowledge in Germany took off as early as the Enlightenment. Leibniz is considered one of the earliest promoters of the Enlightenment.[96] Figure 6.7 offers the genealogical schematic of the scientific lineage of Richard Kroner. During the Weimar Republic Kroner was a neo-Hegelian philosopher, professor at Kiel University. Unfortunately for him, one of his biological ancestors happened to be Jewish. The Nazis dismissed Kroner from Kiel University because of his Jewish ancestry; he continued to teach at the Union Theological Seminary, New York.[97]

However, before dealing with Leibniz's heritage of metaphysical reasoning, I suggest going from easy to difficult; let me turn to Leibniz the mathematician. After all, Leibniz's legacy in exact sciences equally shaped the post-Enlightenment era of the world in general and Germany in particular.

Leibniz was a great thinker, hard worker, connected counselor, and many other things; however, there is no evidence that he was a formal teacher. Nevertheless, every scholar of exact sciences or technology is a pupil of Leibniz because Newton and Leibniz co-founded calculus.

Adolf Hurwitz taught at Albertus Universität in Königsberg, Germany, during the Empire. During the Weimar Republic he held a chair at Eidgenössische Polytechnikum, Zürich. He is known for his publication establishing the Routh–Hurwitz stability criterion.[98] This criterion is crucial in determining the stability of any control system. In particular, a mathematical application of Hurwitz's theory extended the solution to sociopolitical systems[99] (see also Chapter 2 of this book); this application made this book possible.

Figure 6.6 illustrates a teacher to pupil succession with Leibniz and ending with Adolf Hurwitz. The great industrial expansion described earlier (section *Everything for the people, nothing by the people*) should be principally credited to the substantial network of institutes of interacting research and education.[100] Admission to these institutes was selective based on meritocratic criteria.[101]

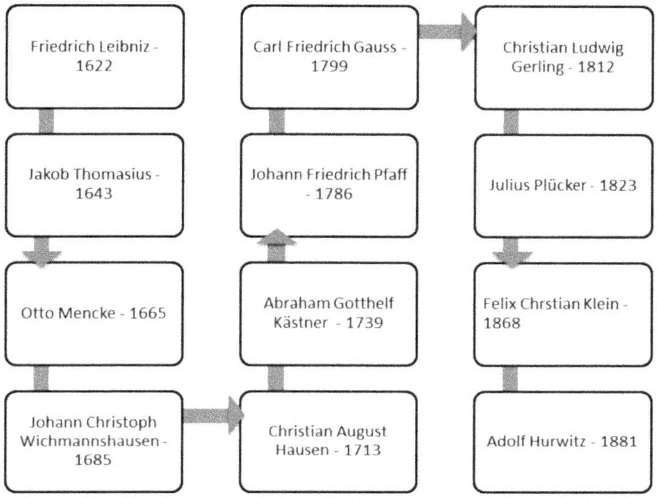

Figure 6.6 A genealogical exact science lineage of Adolf Hurwitz from the beginning of Enlightenment; years represent date of doctoral degree. Author's work.

The University of Göttingen stands out as a central node of this network. It was established in 1734 to spread the ideals of the Enlightenment. Figure 6.6 mentions five scholars serving on its staff: Abraham Gotthelf Kästner, Carl Friedrich Gauss, Christian Ludwig Gerling, Felix Chrstian Klein, and Adolf Hurwitz.

Table 6.1 lists German scholars who were awarded a Nobel Prize in Physics, Chemistry, or Medicine during the German Empire.

Democracy in the Weimar Republic

Table 6.2 lists Nobel Prize winners in the Weimar Republic.

Returning to Richard Kroner, his scientific lineage also starts with Leibniz (Figure 6.7). He was inspired by Hegel. Hegel met Fichte at Jena University and studied his thinking.[102] Hegel and Fichte are relevant to this chapter in view of their teachings regarding freedom and equality.

Fichte's affirmation that "original rights" (*Urrechte*) are "conditions of personality"[103] is inconsistent with the practical constitutionalist term of *unalienable rights*. Fichte's point inspires social interactions to respect each other's *original rights*. Hegel's criticism of Fichte sheds more light on how Fichte's self-defined right may be interpreted. Hegel illustrates it by an example: "the relationship of lordship and bondage is an economic relationship of domination and subordination."[104] Hegel argues that in a "master-slave" relationship Fichte's concept of rights is "compatible with, and which to a certain extent facilitates, gross economic inequality."[105]

Table 6.1 German Nobel Price Winners—Physics, Chemistry, or Medicine—German Empire

	Physics	*Chemistry*	*Medicine*
Name	Wilhelm Conrad Röntgen	Hermann Emil Fischer	Emil Adolf von Behring
Prize Year	1901	1902	1901
University	Munich University	Berlin University	Marburg University
Name	Philipp Eduard Anton von Lenard	Johann Friedrich Wilhelm Adolf von Baeyer	Robert Koch
Prize Year	1905	1905	1905
University	Kiel University	Munich University,	Institute for Infectious Diseases, Berlin
Name	Wilhelm Wien	Eduard Buchner	Albrecht Kossel
Prize Year	1911	1907	1910
University	Würzburg University	Landwirtschaftliche Hochschule Berlin	University of Heidelberg
Name	Max von Laue	Wilhelm Ostwald	
Prize Year	1914	1909	
University	Frankfurt-on-the-Main University	Leipzig University	
Name	Max Karl Ernst Ludwig Planck	Otto Wallach	
Prize Year	1918	1910	
University	Berlin University	Goettingen University	
Name		Richard Martin Willstätter	
Prize Year		1915	
University		Friedrich-Wilhelms-Universität, Berlin,	
Name		Fritz Haber	
Prize Year		1918	
University		Kaiser-Wilhelm-Institute for Physical Chemistry Berlin	

Table 6.2 German Nobel Prize Winners—Physics, Chemistry, or Medicine—Weimar Republic

	Physics	Chemistry	Medicine
Name	Johannes Stark	Walther Hermann Nernst	Otto Heinrich Warburg
Prize Year	1919	1920	1931
University	Greifswald University	Berlin University	Kaiser-Wilhelm-Institute for Biology
Name	Albert Einstein	Richard Adolf Zsigmondy	
Prize Year	1921	1925	
University	Physics Kaiser-Wilhelm-Institut, Berlin	Goettingen University	
Name	James Franck	Heinrich Otto Wieland	
Prize Year	1925	1927	
University	Goettingen University	Munich University	
Name	Gustav Ludwig Hertz	Adolf Otto Reinhold Windaus	
Prize Year	1925	1928	
University	Halle University	Goettingen University	
Name	Werner Karl Heisenberg	Hans Fischer	
Prize Year	1932	1930	
University	Leipzig University	Technische Hochschule Munich	
Name	Erwin Schrödinger	Carl Bosch	
Prize Year	1933	1931	
University	Berlin University	Heidelberg University	

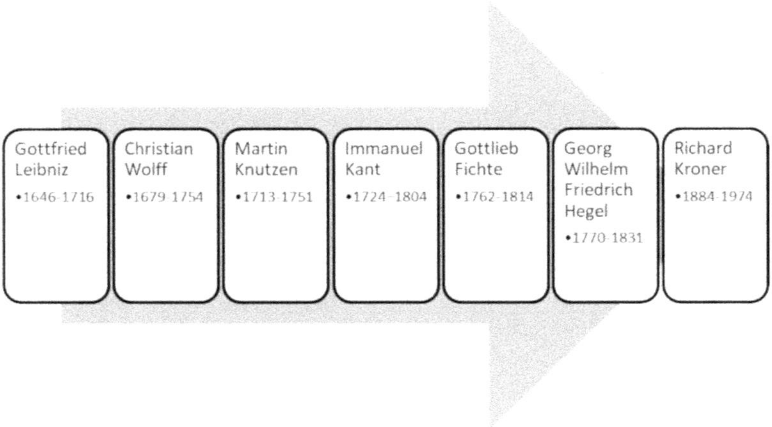

Figure 6.7 A genealogical succession of thought from the Enlightenment to Weimar Republic. Author's work.

Fichte's concept of *rights* is also incompatible with *constitutionalism* because it is not enforceable. *Constitutionalism* grew from practical reality hence it is enforceable. Hegel's concept of rights may be enforceable. However, it is not compatible with constitutionalism because leveling economic inequality entails violating the right to own property; as argued earlier (see *Framing the Weimar Constitution*, point 2) that is unjust and uncivilized. Constitutionalism entails equality before the law.

As discussed, constitutional concepts such as liberty and rights were located high in the troposphere of the considerations of the intelligentsia of Weimar. Consequently, even democracy was subject to confusing abstract deliberation. For example Carl Schmitt, a constitutional lawyer[106] affirms the following:

> Every actual democracy rests on the principle that not only are equals equal but unequals will not be treated equally. Democracy requires, therefore, first homogeneity and second—if the need arises—elimination or eradication of heterogeneity.[107]

The mathematical blunder about unequal equals may be an irritant for some readers familiar with equations. However, does "eradication of heterogeneity" allude to a future "Final Solution?" The answer is given by Carl Schmitt himself:

> To preserve the unity of their national life, a people can admit emigrants from alien races only if within a reasonable time they show willingness and a capacity to amalgamate ideally as well as racially with them.[108]

Needless to say, Schmitt was never an admirer of functioning democracies either in France, the United States, or the United Kingdom.

The *Enlightened Despotism* complied with some constitutional demands; however, it was not a result of German *constitutionalism.* As mentioned earlier, *constitutionalism* is a mentality. Mentality is hard to copy, impossible to invent and not likely to be transmitted through academic lectures or seminars.

Therefore, the understandings of the Weimar framers were purely theoretical. History proved that the Weimar design had little chance of survival. The constitutionalism of the Weimar Republic population was absent because it was absent in its predecessor, the *Enlightened Despotism*.

Education in the Weimar Republic

The Weimar experience followed the tradition of the Empire; this was also true as far as mass education is concerned. This education scored remarkable achievements in exact, natural, health, and social-sciences (see for example Table 6.2). Nevertheless, as far as promoting democracy is concerned, the Weimar Republic failed miserably. In my view, this failure disproves the widely accepted axiom claiming that education promotes democratic values.[109]

In the Weimar era, Carl Schmitt condemned parliamentary democracy for many reasons. One of them was that it cannot guarantee "the education of a political elite."[110] He anticipated a positive feedback loop (Figure 6.8) of so-called *education to democracy* in which the people's will is shaped by the "people's education"; the loop is

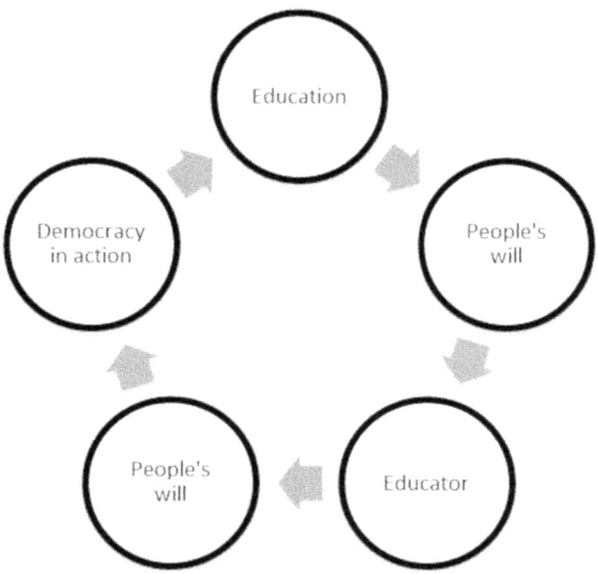

Figure 6.8 Carl Schmitt's positive feedback loop of education to "democracy"; this schematic faithfully represents Nazi, Fascist, and Communist education to "loyal citizenship." Author's work.

closed because people's education means "nothing else but that the educator identifies his will at least provisionally with that of the people."[111]

Schmitt himself concluded that "this educational theory is a dictatorship that suspends democracy in the name of a true democracy that is still to be created."[112] Schmitt explained this affirmation "clarifying" that "dictatorship is not antithetical to democracy."[113] This example illustrates that indeed in the democratic Weimar Republic advocates of antidemocratic education systems were easy to find. However, what about current Western democracies? How many would agree that current trends also envision an "education for democracy" similarly following the logic of Figure 6.8. For example:

> Education should be for a democracy that offers possibilities for radical collective transformation, the re-imagining of societies and the reconstruction of institutions, including education, in the interests of those who are currently least advantaged.[114]

Doesn't this plan evoke the destabilizing loop of Figure 6.8? Educating for democracy to reconstruct institutions, including education so that one educates for democracy to reconstruct institution and so on. One asks oneself how the "currently least advantaged" are supposed to benefit from this Schmitt scheme. Past experience hints that the answer is: not much.

The Weimar Republic featured antidemocratic education and anti-democratic educated elite that "opposed individual basic rights and parliamentary democracy."[115] Levinson and Ericksen edited a remarkable collection of works disproving the myth that the reason for Germany turning for the worse consisted of an uneducated mob seizing power.[116] The collection proves that high education of the democratic Weimar Republic created and spread evil. Allow me to reiterate some of these neglected facts in this chapter. Academic elites embraced Nazi ideology and mindsets before Hitler came to power.[117]

> Many legal scholars had been hard at work preparing Hitler's path to power by setting the stage for the dismantling of the Weimar Republic and its constitution.[118]

In 1921, during the Weimar Republic, Gerhard Kittel gave a lecture in Sweden deploring that Germany "had sold out to the Enlightenment."[119] The academic elite needed no reskilling in order to educate a generation of graduates enthusiastically engaged in Nazi projects. Seven of the fifteen men who met at the Wannsee conference in January 1942 to plan the murder of European Jews had earned doctorates.[120] Michael Wildt researched 221 SS officers who served in the Main Office of the Reich Security; two-thirds of them held a university degree and one-third held doctorates.[121]

Physicians,[122] lawyers,[123] pastors, and professors of theology, historians, and other scholars of humanities "found a comfortable place within Hitler's Germany, often with considerable enthusiasm."[124]

It is difficult to determine who participated because of sincere belief and who in spite of it.[125] Obviously, those who spread Nazi ideology during the Weimar period became genuine devotees to the Nazi "up-to-date culture." Thus, young campaigners of the Nationalist Socialist German Students Association propagating the evil message from 1926[126] were truly wicked.

The evil impregnated students of science and engineering reaching even the most despicable Nazi enterprise: the death camps.

> [T]he death camps in Nazi Germany would not have been possible without the many engineers that designed, constructed, and maintained them.[127]

And

> the death camp operations were highly efficient, so these technological professionals knew what they were doing: they were, so to speak, good engineers. Beyond that many of these engineers were convinced Nazi-adherents, the fact remains that many simply acted according to the altered extrinsic incentive structure of the Third Reich.[128]

Many professors during the Third Reich were students in 1926. Reasonably those who were genuine Nazis in 1926 became even more enthusiastic Nazis spreading malicious messages through both: education and research.

Nevertheless, many joined the trend because it paid. Once a Nazi Government was established it instituted a process of coordination (*Gleichschaltung*) of all activities, including academic education and research with the leadership of the Nazi Party.[129] "1700 faculty members, comprising 15 percent teaching staff lost their jobs."[130] Furthermore, "a new policy to be implemented was overturning the historical practice of selecting rectors and deans by faculty election and instead making these positions political appointments."[131] The rector appointed professors[132] and shaped the curriculum.[133] This is an example of a destabilizing vicious circle in which the more politically aligned a scholar is the more he is valued; the result is "inevitable decline in standards whether in mathematics, the sciences or humanities."[134]

Education to Democratic Values

It is widely accepted that in democratic societies education promotes democratic values. Notwithstanding, there are questions regarding this postulation.

Weil concluded that in various times and countries education had no positive effect on attitudes regarding democratic values.[135] Table 6.3 summarizes Weil's survey.

Many educators in Germany and Italy of the late 1950s received their "Ein Volk, Ein Reich, Ein Führer"[136] education in the Third Reich or in the Ballilla youth movement (Figure 6.9). No wonder, the democratic values they imparted were fragile. In the mid-1970s educated individuals showed less respect for freedom of assembly or freedom of speech than uneducated countrymen in Germany and Austria; that is bad news for the theory claiming that education promotes democratic values. The good news

Table 6.3 The Effect of Education on Nurturing Liberal Values according to Weil

Attitude	Where		When
	Education had no effect	Education had effect	
Valuing democratic institutions	W Germany, Italy	US, UK, Mexico	Late 1950s
Respecting freedom of assembly	W Germany, Austria	US, UK, Netherlands	Mid 1970s
Anti-semitism	Eastern Europe		Early 1970s
Tolerating free speech	W Germany	US	1970s

Figure 6.9 Children in the Ballilla Italian Fascist children's organization (1936). In the late 1950s some of these children educated the next generation. Public Domain by Italian Photographer.

is that the United States, Mexico, the United Kingdom, and the Netherlands showed promising results. Then there is the question of the . . . *question*. Higher education involves lectures, seminars, research projects, dissertations, tests, and final exams. In summary a PhD degree requires answering thousands of questions. A remarkable study on anti-Semitism in democracies raised an original concern:

> The finding that anti-Semitism is associated with lower levels of education may just be a function of who is caught by the measure, not a true relationship between education and antipathy toward Jews.[137]

Let us examine how a Weil finding[138] was extracted. The question was:

> Would you be in favor of a law saying that groups who disagree with our form of government could not hold public meetings or make speeches, or would you be opposed to it?[139]

I have no doubt that a graduate of Erasmus University Rotterdam knows how to answer the question. On the other hand, one cannot rule out that a clever taxi driver in Amersfoort, the Netherlands, Lockerbie, Scotland or El Paso, Texas reckons that disagreeing with democracy contradicts democracy. Answering that allowing antidemocratic speech is democratic does require years of hitting the books. In other words, knowing the correct answer to a sneaky question requires getting a degree; fixing a vacuum cleaner does not. On the other hand tolerating intolerable speech is without doubt a democratic value. The US results of Table 6.3 do not necessarily reflect deeper democratic values on US campuses than everywhere else in the democratic world.

Yad Vashem—The World Holocaust Remembrance Center has not yet made a study about the social status of the Righteous Among the Nations, that is, non-Jews who rescued Jews during the Holocaust.[140] However, Bejski, a member of the Yad Vashem Commission for the Designation of the Righteous, observes:

> my distinct impression from years of work on the Commission has been that the majority were from the lower classes—poverty-stricken common folk, poor people who had difficulty providing for their own families yet found it possible to share their meager fare with those whom they took under their protection.[141]

Table 6.4 reproduces finding of a survey[142] illustrating that education had little impact on positive attitudes toward Jews in Nazi-occupied Europe.

Table 8.4 lists twenty US universities; they happen to be the top twenty as far benefiting from the public purse is concerned. All the twenty display a considerable DEI staff. As a consequence, their capacity to impart democratic values is less in doubt than the capacity of Harvard of Cotton Mather (Figure 6.10).

DEI embodies the intellectual opposition to meritocracy. Diversity, equity, and inclusion stop short of including Asian or Jewish students. Asian students are perceived

Table 6.4 Education Was Not a Determining Factor of Rescuing Jews during the Holocaust

Source	Judgment
Bejski[a]	Majority of rescuers were "lower classes"
Tec[b]	Middle Class and Working Class rescuers were proportional to their share in the overall population
	Intelectuals were somewhat more represented
	Peasants were somewhat less represented
Oliner and Oliner[c]	Even distribution in terms of occupational status

Information Source

[a] Moshe Bejski, "The Righteous Among the Nations and their Part in the Rescue of Jews," in *The Nazi Holocaust*, ed. Michael R. Marrus (1989).

[b] Nechama Tec, *When Light Pierced the Darkness: Christian Rescue of Jews in Nazi-occupied Poland* (Oxford: Oxford University Press, 1987).

[c] Samuel P. Oliner and Pearl Oliner, *Altruistic Personality: Rescuers Of Jews In Nazi Europe* (New York: Touchstone, 1992).

as tough competitors. Meritocracy implies inclusion of gifted Asian students. Opposed to it, DEI is about easing the competition, not about toughening it up. Reasonably, anti-Semitic attitudes on US and European campuses have been nurtured through similar prejudice.

Universities are essential to progress. Educating for democratic values would help if it were promising. The evidence is not encouraging. We are not in Nazi Germany; however, as far as democratic values are concerned, some facts indicate that current Western higher education replicates failures of Weimar.

Conclusion

This work considers that it is not the Constitution that makes or breaks the system but constitutionalism. The weakness of the Weimar Constitution and the absence of an appropriate judicial review were due to little or no spirit of constitutionalism. Lack of constitutionalism caused Weimar's "endless debate and discussion" and the esteem for an "image of the man of action and decision."[143]

Constitutionalism by definition advocates limiting the power of government by separating branches of government and by encouraging debate and judicial review. The Framers of the American Constitution understood the trust of "we the people" in words engraved in the Constitution.

The Weimar Constitution did not copy the checks and balances of the American Constitution. That is not the only reason for its demise. When "economic activity and social conditions reached a point of crisis, there were few reserves of legitimacy on which the Republic could draw, and the search for stabilizing political solution proved fruitless."[144]

Figure 6.10 Cotton Mather (about 1700). Mather's book *Wonders of the Invisible World* inspired the Salem Witch Trials. By Peter Pelham, artist. Public Domain.

Notes

1 H. John Spiro, "Constitution," in *Encyclopaedia Britannica* (Chicago: Encyclopædia Britannica, Inc., 2024), https://www.britannica.com/topic/constitution-politics-and-law.

2 Walter H. Hamilton, "Constitutionalism," in *Encyclopedia of the Social Sciences*, ed. Edwin R. A. Seligman and Alvin Johnson (New York: Macmillan, 1931).

3 In Canada the Commander in Chief is the King; the highest ranking -member of the Canadian Armed Forces is the Chief of Defense Staff.
4 Alexis de Tocqueville, *Democracy in America*, trans. Henry Reeve, Kindle edition, vol. 1 (Project Gutenberg, 2006), 20.
5 Peter Mazzacano, "From Covenant to Compact to Contract: The Legal Transplantation of Puritan Jurisprudence to America," in *A Civil Society with no Hierarchy*, ed. Ilie Bădescu and Joseph Livni (Lanham: Lexington Books, 2023), 242.
6 Tocqueville, *Democracy in America*, 1, 20.
7 Peter Stirk, "Hugo Preuss, German Political Thought and the Weimar Constitution," *History of Political Thought* 23, no. 3 (2002), 497–516.
8 Ibid.
9 Joseph Livni and Ilie Bădescu, "The Battle of the Covenantal Society against Elitism—An Overlooked Chapter in The History of Social Inequality," *Romanian Journal of Sociological Studies*, New Series, no. 1 (2020).
10 H. Lethen and D. Reneau, *Cool Conduct: The Culture of Distance in Weimar Germany* (Berkley, Los Angeles, and London: University of California Press, 2002), 42.
11 Shmuel Noah Eisenstadt, "Bureaucracy and Bureaucratization," *Current Sociology* 7, no. 2 (1958), 99–124.
12 The Editors of Encyclopaedia Britannica. "Hugo Preuss." *Encyclopedia Britannica*, October 24, 2024. https://www.britannica.com/biography/Hugo-Preuss. (2022).
13 William L. Shirer, *Rise and Fall of the Third Reich: A History of Nazi Germany* (New York: Simon & Schuster, 1990), 57.
14 Lethen and Reneau, *Cool Conduct: The Culture of Distance in Weimar Germany*, 42.
15 Introduction Bernard M. Levinson and Robert P. Ericksen, eds., *The Betrayal of the Humanities: The University during the Third Reich* (Bloomington: Indiana University Press, 2022), 9.
16 Bernd J. Hartmann, "The Arrival of Judicial Review in Germany Under the Weimar Constitution of 1919," *Brigham Young University Journal of Public Law* 18 (2003): 111.
17 Ibid., 114.
18 Ibid.
19 Ibid., 113.
20 Ibid., 114.
21 Ibid., 115.
22 Ibid., 113.
23 Michael C. Batinski, *Jonathan Belcher, Colonial Governor* (Lexington: University Press of Kentucky, 1996), 137.
24 Ibid., 62.
25 Ibid., 68.
26 Bayard Taylor, *A School History of Germany: From the Earliest Period to the Establishment of the German Empire in 1871* (New York: D. Appleton & Company, 1874), 486.
27 Ibid.
28 Frederick the Great, ruled contemporarily with Governor Belcher; he was an admirer of Voltaire. Roger Pearson, *Voltaire Almighty: A Life in Pursuit of Freedom* (London: Bloomsbury Publishing, 2010), Ch. 9.

29 Robert Bideleux and Ian Jeffries, *A History of Eastern Europe: Crisis and Change* (New York and London: Taylor & Francis, 2006), Ch. 9.
30 Hartmann, "The Arrival of Judicial Review in Germany Under the Weimar Constitution of 1919," 116.
31 Theodore S. Hamerow, *Social Foundations of German Unification, 1858–1871, Volume II: Struggles and Accomplishments* (Princeton: Princeton University Press, 2015), 3.
32 e.g. David G. Williamson, *Bismarck and Germany: 1862–1890* (London and New York: Taylor & Francis, 2013).
33 Charles H. Herford, "The Intellectual and Literary History," in *Germany in the Nineteenth Century: Five Lectures*, ed. John H. Rose et al. (Manchester: Manchester University Press, 1912), 76.
34 See Heywood's definition in the *Introduction.*
35 Eduard J. Alvarez-Palau, Alfonso Díez-Minguela, and Jordi Martí-Henneberg, "Railroad Integration and Uneven Development on the European Periphery, 1870–1910," *Social Science History* 45, no. 2 (2021): 261–89.
36 Germany cashed substantial payments as war indemnity paid by France (1871); consequently a certain powerful industrial stimulus was brought into play by the provision of a new fund of capital. Edward C. K. Gonner, "The Economic History," in *Germany in the Nineteenth Century: Five Lectures*, ed. Rose et al., 91.
37 The empire was a confederation of constituent states (*Länder*).
38 Gonner, "The Economic History," 94–5.
39 Alvarez-Palau, Díez-Minguela, and Martí-Henneberg, "Railroad Integration and Uneven Development on the European Periphery, 1870–1910"; Gonner, "The Economic History," 95.
40 Gonner, "The Economic History," 95.
41 Ulrich Pfister, Jan-Otmar Hesse, Mark Spoerer, and Nikolaus Wol, *An Economic History of the First German Unification* (London and New York: Routledge, 2023).
42 Alvarez-Palau, Díez-Minguela, and Martí-Henneberg, "Railroad Integration and Uneven Development on the European Periphery, 1870–1910."
43 Jörg Vögele and Wolfgang Woelk, "Public Health and the Development of Infant Mortality in Germany, 1875–1930," *The History of the Family* 7, no. 4 (2002), 585–99; W. Robert Lee and Jörg P. Vögele, "The Benefits of Federalism? The Development of Public Health Policy and Health Care Systems in Nineteenth-century Germany and their Impact on Mortality Reduction" (paper presented at the Annales de démographie historique, 2001).
44 Vögele and Woelk, "Public Health and the Development of Infant Mortality in Germany, 1875–1930."
45 Lee and Vögele, "The Benefits of Federalism? The Development of Public Health Policy and Health Care Systems in Nineteenth-Century Germany and their Impact on Mortality Reduction."
46 Herford, "The Intellectual and Literary History."
47 Unit of genetic distance see for example Paul Berg and Maxine Singer, *Dealing with Genes: The Language of Heredity* (Mill Valley: University Science Books, 1992).
48 Karl Marx and Fridrich Engels, *The Communist Manifesto* (Redwood City: SoftBook Press, 2020).
49 Ibid.
50 Wilfried Feldenkirchen, *Werner Von Siemens: Inventor and International Entrepreneur* (Columbus: Ohio State University Press, 1994), 29.

51 Ibid.
52 Harold James, *Krupp: A History of the Legendary German Firm* (Princeton: Princeton University Press, 2012), 21–2.
53 Ibid., 72.
54 St John C. Nixon, *The Invention of the Automobile—(Karl Benz and Gottlieb Daimler)* (Ancarano: Edizioni Savine, 2016), Ch. II, Karl Benz the Student.
55 Ibid.
56 Ibid., Chapter VI Gottlieb Daimler.
57 United States Declaration of Independence.
58 Max Weber and Talcott Parsons, *The Theory of Social and Economic Organization* (New York: Simon & Schuster, 2009), Ch. 21.
59 Ibid., Ch. IV.
60 Stephen J. Lee, *The Weimar Republic* (London: Taylor & Francis, 2013), 38.
61 Detlev Peukert, *The Weimar Republic* (New York: Farrar, Straus and Giroux, 1993), 214.
62 Carl Schmitt and Ellen Kennedy, *The Crisis of Parliamentary Democracy*, ed. Carl Schmitt (Cambridge, MA and London: MIT Press, 1988), Introduction by Ellen Kennedy.
63 Lee, *The Weimar Republic*, 38.
64 Stirk, "Hugo Preuss, German Political Thought and the Weimar Constitution."
65 e.g. Joseph Livni, *The Biblical Roots of American Constitutionalism—From "I am the Lord" to "We the People"* (Lanham: Lexington Books, 2021); Mazzacano, "From Covenant to Compact to Contract: The Legal Transplantation of Puritan Jurisprudence to America"; Daniel J. Elazar, *Covenant & Constitutionalism: The Great Frontier and the Matrix of Federal Democracy* (New Brunswick: Transaction Publishers, 1997); Donald S. Lutz, *The Origins of American Constitutionalism* (Baton Rouge: Louisiana State University Press, 1988).
66 Stirk, "Hugo Preuss, German Political Thought and the Weimar Constitution," 510.
67 *Berliner Handelshochschule.*
68 Stirk, "Hugo Preuss, German Political Thought and the Weimar Constitution," 510.
69 Ibid.
70 Hugo Preuß, "Über Organpersönlichkeit: eine begriffskritische Studie," *Jahrbuch für Gesetzgebung, Verwaltung und Volkswirtschaft im Deutschen Reich* (1902); cited by Stirk, "Hugo Preuss, German Political Thought and the Weimar Constitution."
71 Robert Redslob, *Le régime parlementaire: étude sur les institutions d'Angleterre, de Belgique, de Hongrie, de Suède, de France, de Tchécoslovaquie, de l'Empire allemand, de Prusse, de Bavière et d'Autriche* (Paris: M. Giard, 1924), 290.
72 Franklin C. West, *A Crisis of the Weimar Republic: A Study of the German Referendum of 20 June 1926* (Philadelphia: American Philosophical Society, 1985).
73 Fifth Ammendment of the US Constitution.
74 *jemand, der in die richtige Richtung lenkt.*
75 Redslob, *Le régime parlementaire: étude sur les institutions d'Angleterre, de Belgique, de Hongrie, de Suède, de France, de Tchécoslovaquie, de l'Empire allemand, de Prusse, de Bavière et d'Autriche*, 291.
76 Ibid., 294.
77 Preuß, "Über Organpersönlichkeit: eine begriffskritische Studie"; cited by Stirk, "Hugo Preuss, German Political thought and the Weimar Constitution."

78 Redslob, *Le régime parlementaire: étude sur les institutions d'Angleterre, de Belgique, de Hongrie, de Suède, de France, de Tchécoslovaquie, de l'Empire allemand, de Prusse, de Bavière et d'Autriche*, 168.
79 Ibid.
80 Ibid.
81 Ibid., 259.
82 Ibid.
83 Ibid., 260.
84 Bryan S. Turner, *Max Weber: From History to Modernity* (London and New York: Taylor & Francis, 2002), 199.
85 Lee and Vögele, "The Benefits of Federalism? The Development of Public Health Policy and Health Care Systems in Nineteenth-Century Germany and their Impact on Mortality Reduction."
86 Allusion to Michael J. Klarman, *The Framers' Coup: The Making of the United States Constitution* (Oxford and New York: Oxford University Press, 2016).
87 Frederick B. Artz, *The Enlightenment in France* (Kent: Kent State University Press, 1968), 30.
88 Jean-Jacques Rousseau, Quintin Hoare, and Christofer Bertram, *Of the Social Contract and Other Political Writings* (London: Penguin Books Limited, 2012), Book I–Ch. 7.
89 Susan Dunn, *Sister Revolutions: French Lightning, American Light* (New York: Farrar, Straus and Giroux, 2000), Ch. The French Nation One and Indivisible.
90 Paul Weirich, "Rousseau on Proportional Majority Rule," *Philosophy and Phenomenological Research* 47, no. 1 (1986), 111–26.
91 Thomas Wright, *The History of France: From the Earliest Period to the Present Time* (London and New York: London Print and Publishing Company, 1858), 373.
92 see Marbury v. Madison, 5 U.S. (I Cranch) 137 (1803) in Vincent Robert Johnson, "The Declaration of the Rights of Man and of Citizens of 1789, the Reign of Terror, and the Revolutionary Tribunal of Paris," *Boston College International and Comparative Law Review* 13 (1990):1–45.
93 Ibid.
94 Leslie Derfler, *The Dreyfus Affair* (Westport and London: Greenwood Press, 2002); Winthrop E. Dwight, "An Episode in the Affaire Dreyfus," *The Yale Law Journal* 8, no. 6 (1899): 272–9.
95 Dieter Langewiesche, "Revolution in Germany," in *Europe in 1848*, ed. Dieter Dowe, et al. (New York and Oxford: Berghahn Books, 2008), 128.
96 Arthur Strum, "What Enlightenment Is," *New German Critique*, no. 79 (2000): 106–36.
97 See for example Richard Kroner, "The Year 1800 in the Development of German Idealism," *The Review of Metaphysics* 1 (1948): 1–31.
98 Adolf Hurwitz, "Ueber die Bedingungen, unter welchen eine Gleichung nur Wurzeln mit negativen reellen Theilen besitzt," *Mathematische Annalen* 46, no. 2 (1895): 273–84.
99 Joseph Livni, "Investigation of Collapse of Complex Socio-Political Systems Using Classical Stability Theory," *Physica A: Statistical Mechanics and Its Applications* (2019): 553–62.

100 Michael Sadler, "The History of Education," in *Germany in the Nineteenth Century: Five Lectures*, ed. Rose et al., 120.
101 Ibid., 121.
102 Georg W. F. Hegel, *The Difference between Fichte's and Schelling's Systems*, ed. H. S. Harris and W. Cerf (Albany: SUNY Press, 1984). First published in 1801 by Jena University.
103 James Alexander Clarke, "Fichte and Hegel on Recognition," *British Journal for the History of Philosophy* 17, no. 2 (2009): 365–85.
104 Ibid.
105 Ibid.
106 Ellen Kennedy, *Constitutional Failure: Carl Schmitt in Weimar* (Durham and London: Duke University Press, 2004).
107 Schmitt and Kennedy, *The Crisis of Parliamentary Democracy*, 9.
108 endnote 26 ibid., 90.
109 e.g. Allan T. Wood, "What is Renewal, Why Now?," in *Education and the Making of a Democratic People*, ed. J. I. Goodlad, R. Soder, and B. McDaniel (Milton Park: Taylor & Francis, 2015), 32; Edda Sant, "Democratic Education: A Theoretical Review (2006–2017)," *Review of Educational Research* 89, no. 5 (2019); Magnus Dahlstedt and Maria Olson, *Education, Democracy, Citizenship—Utbildning, demokrati, medborgarskap* (Malmö: Gleerups Utbildning AB, 2013).
110 Schmitt and Kennedy, *The Crisis of Parliamentary Democracy*, 7.
111 Ibid.
112 Ibid.
113 Ibid.
114 Stewart Riddle and Michael W. Apple, "Education and Democracy in Dangerous Times," in *Re-imagining Education for Democracy*, ed. Stewart Riddle and Michael W. Apple (London: Routledge, 2019), Ch. 1.
115 Oren Gross, "Hitler's Willing Law Professors," in *The Betrayal of the Humanities: The University during the Third Reich*, ed. Levinson and Ericksen, 367.
116 Levinson and Ericksen, *The Betrayal of the Humanities: The University during the Third Reich.*
117 Ronald M. Smelser, "Hitler and the DNSAP. Between Democracy and Gleichschaltung," *Bohemia* 20, no. 1 (1979): 137–55.
118 Gross, "Hitler's Willing Law Professors," 367.
119 Introduction Levinson and Ericksen, *The Betrayal of the Humanities: The University during the Third Reich*, 9.
120 Michael Wildt, *An Uncompromising Generation: The Nazi Leadership of the Reich Security Main Office* (Madison: University of Wisconsin Press, 2009), 18; cited by Levinson and Ericksen, *The Betrayal of the Humanities: The University during the Third Reich*, 2.
121 Levinson and Ericksen, *The Betrayal of the Humanities: The University during the Third Reich.*
122 Christian Pross, "Breaking through the Postwar Coverup of Nazi Doctors in Germany," *Journal of Medical Ethics* 17, no. Suppl (1991).
123 In October 1933 in Leipzig, '[t]en thousand lawyers gathered in front of the Supreme Court building and swore, with their right arms raised in the Nazi salute, "'by the soul of the German people'" that they would "'strive as German jurists to

follow the course of our Fuehrer to the end of our days' Matthew Lippman, "They Shoot Lawyers Don't They: Law in the Third Reich and the Global Threat to the Independence of the Judiciary," *California Western International Law Journal* 23 (1992): 257–318.

124 Levinson and Ericksen, *The Betrayal of the Humanities: The University during the Third Reich*, 3.

125 Suzanne L. Marchand, "The 'Orient' and 'Us,'" in *The Betrayal of the Humanities: The University during the Third Reich*, ed. Levinson and Ericksen.

126 Stephen J. Lee, *Hitler and Nazi Germany* (London: Taylor & Francis, 2013), 56.

127 Beth-Anne Schuelke-Leech, "The Place of Wicked Problems in Engineering Problem Solving: A Proposed Taxonomy" (paper presented at the 2020 IEEE International Symposium on Technology and Society (ISTAS), 2020); citing Eric Katz, "The Nazi Engineers: Reflections on Technological Ethics in Hell," *Science and Engineering Ethics* 17 (2011): 571–82.

128 Jardar Lohne et al., "Homines Oeconomici or Moral Saints? On the Purpose of Educating Civil Engineers" (paper presented at the Proceedings of the 9th Nordic Conference on Construction Economics and Organization, 2017); citing Katz, "The Nazi Engineers: Reflections on Technological Ethics in Hell."

129 Bernard M. Levinson, "Gerhard von Rad's Struggle against the Nazification of the Old Testament," in *The Betrayal of the Humanities: The University during the Third Reich*, ed. Levinson and Erickse, 154; Aristotle Kallis, "Nazi Propaganda and 'Coordination': The Haphazard Path to Totalitarianism," *European Review of History: Revue européenne d'histoire* 13, no. 1 (2006): 115–39.

130 Gross, "Hitler's Willing Law Professors," 364.

131 Levinson, "Gerhard von Rad's Struggle against the Nazification of the Old Testament," 155–66.

132 See for example the appointment of Heinz Eisenhuth by the rector of Jena University ibid., 173.

133 Ibid., 175; Lee, *Hitler and Nazi Germany*, 56.

134 Lee, *Hitler and Nazi Germany*, 56.

135 Frederick D. Weil, "The Variable Effects of Education on Liberal Attitudes: A Comparative-Historical Analysis of Anti-Semitism Using Public Opinion Survey Data," *American Sociological Review* 50, no. 4 (1985): 458–74.

136 One People, One Empire, One Leader.

137 Jay Greene, Albert Cheng, and Ian Kingsbury, "Education and Anti-semitism" Education Reform Faculty and Graduate Students Publications, University of Arkansas, Fayetteville, (2021).

138 Weil, "The Variable Effects of Education on Liberal Attitudes: A Comparative-Historical Analysis of Anti-Semitism Using Public Opinion Survey Data."

139 Ibid., 471.

140 Moshe Bejski, "The 'Righteous Among the Nations' and their Part in the Rescue of Jews," in *The Nazi Holocaust* 5, ed. Michael R. Marrus (Westport, Conn. 1989).

141 Ibid.

142 Norman Geras, "Richard Rorty and the Righteous among the Nations," *Journal of Applied Philosophy* 12, no. 2 (1995).

143 Gross, "Hitler's Willing Law Professors," 385.

144 Peukert, *The Weimar Republic*, 6.

7

Democracies Outside North America

Democracy

"Democracy is a system in which parties lose elections."[1] It is a challenge to disagree with such a brilliant and simple definition of a complex concept. Nevertheless, allow me to propose a tiny, but significant, correction: democracy is a system in which parties lose election and *that matters*.

True, a system where parties do not lose elections is not a democracy. Consider a system in which parties lose elections, yet the new broom sweeps as the old one. Is such a system a democracy?

In the United States democratic and constitutionalist practices had been established during the colonial era. The transition to a constitutional democracy was smooth; the revolutionary struggle removed the power of the Crown replacing it with a federal government; however, it did not have to reform existing local and state governments and their constitutional authorities.

Elsewhere democracies germinated from the ashes of fallen tyrannies;[2] they evolved as democratic mutations of previous concepts of government. The new democratic variants replaced the authoritarian ruler with democratically elected institutions. Nevertheless, the new order conserved previous top-to-bottom transmission of rule and administration. Parties lost elections. It is worthwhile examining examples how much it mattered.

Constitutionalism

Chapter 6 quoted Hamilton's definition of the term Constitutionalism. The rest of the book will refer to constitutionalism accordingly except where it is otherwise specified.

Civilization imposed on residents of cities and countryside to agree on what is right, to proclaim and to oppose what is wrong, and to seek for civilized ways to solve disputes. These measures are covered by the term *justice*. Most civilized societies entrusted the function of justice to rulers. A small minority of social arrangements trusted a covenant commanding what is right, what is wrong, how to judge, and how to punish evil. These societies are called covenantal societies. Their tradition of trusting a "parchment" rather than a ruler gave rise to constitutionalism.[3] Chapter 6 is dedicated to the most fragile democracy, the Weimar Republic. Chapter 8 deals with the most resilient democracy, the United States. This chapter covers democratic or quasi-democratic societies in America, Europe, Australia, and the Middle-East. Asian democratic or quasi-democratic societies like India, Japan, South Korea, Taiwan, Indonesia, and the Philippines are out of scope.[4]

Latin America

Mexico has a liberal constitution and elections. That could mislead us to define Mexico as a constitutional democracy. It is not. Mexico is characterized by its "highly centralized control of a single institution that dominates access to all public office."[5] Not surprisingly, scholars define Mexican government system as authoritarian constitutionalism. The term *authoritarian* indicates lack of democracy. The term *constitutionalism* in the Mexican context is also misrepresentative. In Mexico the constitution is a written document perpetuating the will of the elites.[6] The decree of judicial review reform of 2021[7] justifies the reform because earlier in Mexico "inbreeding and cronyism have produced deep-rooted clientelist networks, in which positions are trafficked, favours are exchanged, or worse, a price is put on justice."[8]

Scholars of the Mexican government system distinguish between a political and legal environment empowering the ruling elite and a common determination to limit government. They call the latter *constitutional culture.* In current Mexico *constitutional culture* is still an intellectual idea waiting to reach the hearts and minds of Mexicans[9].

Argentina offers a valuable lesson regarding questions of constitutional democracy. Argentina has held elections since 1852. In spite of elections, Argentina was not a democracy until 1916 because electoral fraud prevented a certain party from losing elections.[10] The period 1916–30 is remembered as a transition to constitutional democracy. Argentina has possessed a written Constitution since 1853. The Constitution does limit government; it "places a duty on public authorities—both federal and provincial—to comply with constitutional provisions, federal laws and international treaties."[11] Nevertheless the image of the judicial review is tarnished being "slow and corrupt";[12] it is carried out by a court which "automatically adheres to government views or prevailing public opinion."[13]

Since 1865 the Supreme Court stated that "the duty of each individual judge to verify the conformity of the law to be applied to the specific case with the Constitution."[14] Nevertheless, Argentina was plagued with military coups seven times: in 1930, 1943, 1955, 1962, 1966, and 1983. There are two possible explanations:

a. Argentina was never a true democracy.
b. Argentina had a perfect Constitution, judicial review, and other checks and balances; however, these were not inspired by popular constitutionalism that evolved during the colonial experience but by copying foreign systems properly functioning elsewhere.

The second explanation is more convincing. In North America no army general contemplates fixing the system by a military putsch. Above all, his/her constitutionalism would prevent him/her to lead a military insurrection. Moreover, the constitutionalism of his/her family, of his/her community ties,[15] and, most importantly, of other commanders of the Armed Services would render hardly possible to plan a putsch.

Brazil also started its experience with constitutional control from an imperial beginning. During the imperial past neither the judiciary nor other institution could limit government by declaring acts and laws unconstitutional.[16] The text of the first republican *Constitution* of 1891 was strongly inspired by the American Constitution. The constitutional practice preceding the Constitution authorized the Supreme Court to overrule lower courts in case state laws conflicted with federal laws, treaties, or the Constitution. Overruling decisions of lower courts on constitutional ground does not control government; it controls lower components of the judiciary; only declaring laws or acts of government unconstitutional limits the government.

This power of the courts to judge in favor of federal laws and treaties indicates a top-to-bottom government philosophy. It reminds more of the Weimar Republic than of the decentralized government model of the United States. The competence of judicial review evolved; however, the constitutional practice limited the judiciary and not the executive. For example, in the 1970s only the Attorney General of the Republic, an executive position, authorized the Supreme Court to judge cases of conflicts with the Constitution.[17] This limitation was partially removed only in 1988[18] when the list of authorities allowed requesting judicial review became longer. Limits on the judiciary were slowly lifted; in 2004 a procedure called *súmula vinculante* extended the authority of controlling constitutionality over all federal executive and judiciary branch. The legislative branch is excluded from judicial review; state governments are controlled by lower courts.

The constitutional experience of Brazil has a history that started from imperial unconstitutionality; it did not evolve from the constitutionalism of people who have faith in the power of words printed on the Constitution; instead it evolved from practices of top-to-bottom rules with constitutional mutations that relaxed the limits on the judicial control of government. The judicial review in Brazil is currently experimenting with an excursion into adjudicating extraconstitutional issues such as "socioeconomic rights as a distributive justice."[19] Since such rights are not guaranteed by the constitution, the judicial is engaged in a dialogue with other government branches. This futile negotiation process not only blurs the separation of powers but it also weakens the capability of the Supreme Court. The court is flooded with "an unmanageable number of lawsuits"[20] preventing it to effectively function as an independent judicial adjudicator of true constitutional rights,

Venezuela is an extreme example of "democracies" holding elections that do not matter.

> Chávez was able to use his total control over the constitution-making process in 1999 to construct a competitive authoritarian regime, where elections continue to be held, but where Chávez's political movement has systematic advantages over the opposition (although he does not always win).[21]

No doubt, the Chávez system does not comply with Przeworski's concise definition of democracy.

Table 7.1 Constitutionalism and Democracy in Latin America

Country	Elections	Elections Matter	Constitution	Bottom-Up Constitutionalism	Judicial Review
Mexico	Yes	No	Yes	No	Weak
Argentina	Yes	Since 1916	Yes	No	Weak
Brazil	Yes	Yes	Yes	No	Inefficient
Venzuela	Yes	No	Yes	No	None

In terms of stability analysis, the top-to-bottom constitutionalism and the weak balance of the feedback-loop of judicial review diminish the stability of the democratic equilibrium of the three democratic Latin American nations of Table 7.1 As far as Venezuela is concerned, the current equilibrium is not democratic.

Europe

Medieval Europe consisted of empires, kingdoms, principalities, and city-states. The evolution toward democracy was slow. The oldest known constitutional document appeared in 1117 in Pistoia, Italy.[22] The *Constitutum consulum Communis Pistoriae* contained directives regarding:

a. Relations between secular and religious authorities
b. Protection of municipal signs
c. Electoral mechanisms and competences of consuls
d. Institutions and procedures of civil and criminal justice
e. Freedom and protection of citizens and their property
f. Custody of places
g. Rules and penalties on work compensation

An English Parliament existed in 1207. Nevertheless, it is wise considering that modern European democracy was born after the French Revolution of 1789.

Modern France is a democracy with constitution. It is worthwhile examining whether that makes France a constitutional democracy.

The president of the Republic decides to submit a question to referendum; his powers are:

a. Nominate the prime minister
b. Dissolve Parliament
c. Appeal to popular referendum

No doubt, a binding referendum is democratic; however, it is not necessarily constitutional.[23] The Constitutional Council gives its opinion on this text, but it is a simple opinion, not published. The Council has judgment whether the submitted question is sufficiently clear in order to ensure that the answer is binding.[24] Amendments to the Constitution may be subject to a referendum. As a consequence, in theory a judicial review may not reject a referendum proposal on grounds that it violates the current Constitution.

The system of Figure 7.1 illustrates a mutation from a monarchy with constitution in transition to a democratic republic. It exhibits unbalance of power in favor of the executive branch, mostly of the office of the President. This unbalance is not in spite of the Constitution; the Constitution stipulates it. Left and Right, the usual political labels, enthusiastically supported it or opposed it. This sentiment is not according to the partisan label itself but to the political circumstance of each wing. The Left opposed the constitutional arrangement when in opposition;[25] when in power the Left embraced the excessive power of the executive branch because its agenda needed it even more than the Right.[26]

This illustrates two misconceptions regarding the European debate about constitutionalism:

a. The terms Left and Right are not necessarily adequate in the context of a constitutional debate. This misconception is also valid in North America.
b. Every executive requires more power than it has. European Constitutions removed the inherited authority of rulers. In America the Constitution is the brake stopping power accumulation by the executive. The Framers echoed the colonial experience; the act of replacing a King with a President did not reflect the anticipations of "We, the People." Even a president elected by the majority of the people is hungry for power. The long coexistence of covenantal community practice with the Crown taught the New World that excessive power of the head of state is the problem; whether he/she ascended to the position by elections or by inheritance is a minor factor.

A remarkable feature of constitutional amendments of the Fifth Republic consists of the constant increase of executive power. European idealism optimized efficiency over safety. In engineering jargon this is called a *design taking success for granted*.[27] It follows a political theory postulating that "the strength of the French executive was also in tune with the necessity for a modern state to handle a very complex machinery of government."[28] Opposed to this, American constitutionalism prevails by maneuvering through constitutional checks and balances mirroring a reverse concept of government. To be precise, I shall paraphrase Rousselier: the sustainability of the US executive is in tune with a series of checks and balances raised by the legislative and judicial branches; these are necessary to circumvent the executive of a modern state to mishandle a very complex machinery of government. The French Democracy stands on a constitution empowering the executive branch of government. The French government system is more efficient. The American Democracy developed from a constitutionalist experience; it advocates restraining government. The American Constitutional Democracy is more stable.

The ratification of the Treaty establishing a Constitution for Europe (2005) offers an example illustrating how unsafe a constitutional referendum is. In France the Constitutional Council approved the question to the referendum:

> Do you approve the bill authorising the ratification of the treaty establishing a Constitution for Europe?[29]

This question is not a clear question. The Treaty comprises 448 articles divided into 4 parts. Many people hire a lawyer when purchasing real estate. How many lawyers are needed to disagree with one of 448 articles? The text is clear; the question is not!

The Constitutional Council has the authority to ask for a clearer text; it did not. I do not blame the Council. The text could not be clearer. The Constitutional consequences of answering yes/no, however, are unforeseeable. In France the people answered NO. I do not blame them.

In Belgium there was no referendum. Fortunately for Belgians, binding plebiscites are not allowed in their country. Belgium ratified the European Constitution by a majority vote of the House, of the Senate, and of five regional/language community Parliaments.

The question was equivocal. The participants had to decide whether the EU Constitution would change their status for better,[30] for worse, or not at all?[31]

EU referenda are subject to judicial review.

> Observance of the above rules will be subject to judicial review. This is exercised, in the final instance, by the Constitutional Court—if it exists—or by the Supreme Court. In particular, judicial review will focus on:
>
> - the franchise;
> - the completion of popular initiatives;
> - the procedural and substantive validity of the texts submitted to referendum, which should be subjected to preliminary review;
> - domestic law determines whether this control is obligatory or optional;
> - respect for free suffrage;
> - the results of the ballot.[32]

However, the guidelines do not allow for the court to reject the particular referendum on constitutionality grounds. Theoretically, an executive can submit to referendum proposals that are overtly or covertly undermining long-established norms of justice, law enforcement, penalties, health care guarantees, education practices, and so on. The typical risk ignoring EU outlook closes doors; however, it leaves windows open to abuse. A cautious, risk-mitigating constitutionalism would allow canceling referenda in general or certain plebiscites in particular.

The European Commission consists of unelected individuals. They are mostly experienced in government administration; they possess management skills and hold university degrees.[33]

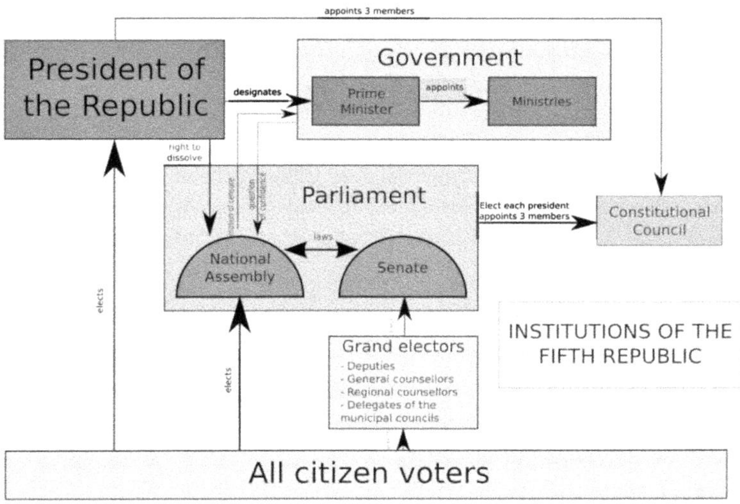

Figure 7.1 Schematic of the constitutional system of the Fifth Republic of France. Public Domain. Credit: Nicoz.

> However, the European Commission was never intended to fit models of democratic accountability as we might now understand them. Dominant amongst those now seen as its "founding fathers" was expertise in top-down planning, largely in France, and the Commission officials of the 1950s and 1960s were heralded as a "technocratic elite" answerable only to the "European ideal."[34]

Residents of Liège, Belgium—Utrecht, Netherlands—Pitigliano, Italy—Nyíregyháza, Hungary—or Turnu-Severin, Romania work, earn, pay taxes, and educate children like my neighbors in Woburn, MA. They also vote in elections. In these election parties win and lose. According to Przeworski's definition they live in democracies. They probably enjoy freedom of speech, of association and of press. They live under the rule of law. However, when they vote they have very little impact on the "canonosphere" of directives[35] and regulations[36] that envelope a cloud of constraints on their choices (see examples in Table 7.2). They vote for a Member of Parliament. But laws are legislated by the European Commission consisting of unelected technocrats. At the EU level, the Commission has *monopoly* over legislation. At the National state level their Parliament has legislative authority. However, in case of conflict between a National Law and EU Regulation the Supranational Regulation wins.

The Constitutional Council of France has to ensure that national laws obey EU Treaties. The Romans used to utter: *Dura Lex sed Lex*. Today their descendants feel what it means. Yes, they vote, parties win and lose; however it matters less and less. The participation of other actors than elected government in regulating public affairs reduces public participation in citizen's deliberations, transparency, and the expectations to reasonable response to public aspirations.[37] One can still use the term *democracy* for the system of the folks of Liège and of Turnu-Severin. However, Constitutional democracy is a stretch. My understanding of constitutionalism requires that a Constitution limits government and not citizens.

The essential question in a stability investigation is the capability of controlling deviation from equilibrium of state variables concerning democracy and constitutional rights and freedoms. For that purpose it is useful to compare the current EU democracies with the Weimar Republic. A comparison of the North-American constitutional democracies with EU democracies is treated in Chapter 8, "The United States of America."

There are striking resemblances between the EU constitutional arrangements and the Weimar Republic:

a. Both came to existence after disastrous failures of a world war
b. Both perpetuated earlier understanding of civil order in which kings, emperors, and princes ruled and citizens obeyed. That said, both discontinued inherited legitimacy to rule and replaced them by legitimizing democratically elected rulers.

Both maintained the principle of top-to-bottom sovereignty. The Weimar Republic Constitution accorded supremacy of federal law over states' (*Länder*) law. Similarly, the EU supranational regulations supersede national laws

We find an essential difference between the Weimar democracy and the current EU democracies. The difference is related to the perception of the primacy of human rights. We shall discuss this difference first in terms of philosophy then of stability

a. Philosophy and Law

> Before the Enlightenment the European individual respected other human beings according to religious and moral rules of the Christian faith. The Scientific Revolution challenged Church Doctrines. This gave rise to ideas free of previous ecclesiastic constraints because sometimes they contradict science.The new philosophy known as Enlightenment extended the Christian understanding that all humans are equal before the eyes of God to equality before law. Christianity preaches to "love thy neighbor as thyself."[38] The Human Rights of the Enlightenment *impose* on laws to respect the rights of liberty, property, safety, and resistance against oppression. With this respect there is a difference between Weimar and EU constitutions. In Weimar:
>
> The constitution contained an innovative catalogue of fundamental rights, but this was not very relevant in practice because it was generally interpreted to be merely programmatic, not enforceable in court.[39]

The example of the Fifth Republic shows that the Declaration of the Rights of Man and of the Citizen is part of the Constitution

Table 7.2 A Few Examples of Regulations, Directives, and Domains of Competence of EU Commissioners

Regulation	Domain
The Radio Spectrum Decision	
The BEREC Regulation	
The Roaming Regulation	Telecommunication
The Telecoms Single Market Regulation	
The Union Programme for education and training, youth and sport	
The production and development of statistics on education and lifelong learning (Text with EEA relevance)	Education And Sport
The Framework Programme for Research and Innovation, laying down its rules for participation and dissemination	Research and Innovation
The comparability of fees related to payment accounts, payment account switching and access to payment accounts with basic features Text with EEA relevance	
The European system of national and regional accounts in the European Union Text with EEA relevance	Finance
Medical devices	
In vitro diagnostic medical devices	
The application of patients' rights in cross-border healthcare	Health Care
Programme for the Union's action in the field of health ("EU4Health Programme") for the period 2021–7	
Cross-border transportation of euro cash by road	
Rules for the compilation of statistics regarding goods carried by road	
Roadside inspections of the safety of commercial vehicles	
Road safety: EU database on road traffic accidents	
Road infrastructure safety management	
Transportable pressure equipment	
Testing to ensure the safety of vehicles and trailers	
Tachographs in road transport	Road Transport
The deployment of intelligent transport systems in Europe	
Driving time and rest periods in the road transport sector	
Joint rules on access to the EU road haulage market	
Hiring of vehicles for the carriage of goods	
Loading and unloading of bulk carriers	
Freight transport logistics action plan	
Bus and coach passengers' rights	

(Continued)

Table 7.2 (Continued)

Regulation	Domain
Commercial air transport operations	
Safeguarding competition in air transport	
Safety regulation of aerodromes	
Rights of people with reduced mobility—air travel	
Unmanned aircraft systems—design and manufacture requirements	
Unmanned aircraft—operating rules and procedures	
Single European Sky—EU rules on air navigation services	
Statistics in respect of the carriage of passengers, freight and mail by air	
The EU's aviation strategy	Air Transport
Air traffic flow management	
Allocation of time slots at European Union airports	
Airworthiness and environmental certification	
Aircrew regulation	
Air service agreements between EU and non-EU countries	
Air carrier passenger and baggage liability	
Agreements on air services	

b. Stability

The schematic of Figure 7.1 shows that the constitutional system of the Fifth Republic contains a check point called Constitutional Council. One function of this institution consists of verifying that laws do not conflict with the Declaration. This is a key function for the stability not only of the democracy but of its constitutionality. Another component responsible for this stability is the people. As explained in the previous paragraph, the actors of Enlightenment inscribed in the hearts and minds of the people the principles of the Declaration. Some Europeans added these principles to their previous Christian beliefs regarding respect for their neighbor; other Europeans replaced their Christian attitude to other humans with the humanistic values of the Enlightenment. Regardless, the Declaration morally constrained governments to act accordingly. It is not easy to tell how deep and how vital any faith is. In this case, however, the faith was put once to test. The Declaration was also part of the Constitution of the Third Republic. During the Nazi occupation the local government brutally disregarded the Declaration.

> The functionaries of the French state overwhelmingly assisted in the execution of the regime's program. Indeed, Robert Paxton and Eberhard Jäckel have demonstrated that members of the Vichy government sought more extensive collaboration than Germany envisioned.[40]

This is consistent with the relatively low proportion of Resistance members actively opposing the occupation and its evils: 523 in 100,000 residents.[41] Did the faith in the

Rights of Man fade away or was it always only a superficial behavioral standard required by norms of decency prevailing before the occupation? This work offers no answer; it only points at the questionable strength of the faith factor in stabilizing constitutional support in that particular place, time, and circumstances.

This brings us to the question of the resilience of EU democracies. Have these democracies sufficient stability controls? If they were stable then the answer would be yes. However, looking at it as a complex system of many state variables, the EU appears to be a system in constant transient. It started as a clearly defined Economic Union. Today it is a giant supranational political endeavor controlling everything but itself. Is Brexit a unique accident or the dawn of disintegration? The system is fluid with little steering, and a weak braking capability. The safest bet is that it is too soon to tell.

The UK, Canada, Australia, Israel, and New Zealand

These countries share a democratic model of government known as parliamentary system inherited from the UK. They are all monarchies except for Israel, which is a Republic. Nevertheless, they share a function called Head of State which mostly detain ceremonial honors and duties. In the three non-British monarchies these functions are delegated to a governor general; in Israel the head of state is the president. All five countries were under British rule and continued the British parliamentary system in which sovereign power is contained by the Parliament; the executive is elected by Parliament, which can terminate the term of a government by a motion of no-confidence.

All five countries have a judicial review. All five countries share the spirit of constitutionalism. Canada, Australia, and New Zealand have a written constitution; the constitutional practice of Israel and of the UK consist of fundamental laws, proclamations of rights and liberties of citizens and conventional schemes of bringing together the three branches of government.

As Table 7.3 illustrates, in the UK and New Zealand the sovereignty of Parliament does not permit canceling laws on grounds of unconstitutionality. The five countries share a type of constitutionalism that grew up from customary practice rather than theoretical ideals of liberalism. The most ancient component of the English constitutionalism is related to liberty. Liberty here is in the sense of opposition to captivity or imprisonment without a fair trial. Scholars postulate that the English

Table 7.3 Judicial Review in Westminster Parliamentary Systems of Democracies

	Acts of Parliament (Laws)	Acts of Executive
UK	No	Yes
Canada	Yes	Yes
Australia	Yes	Yes
Israel	Yes	Yes
New Zealand	No	Yes

custom of trial by peers goes back to Anglo-Saxon history; ancient records of those times reveal "sound and vital spirit, the love of freedom and of justice."[42] The ancient spirit of freedom enabled acts like the writ of Habeas Corpus (1166), Magna Carta (1215), and the Petition of Rights (1628).[43]

The notion of equality in the eyes of the law is even more ancient. The Hebrew Bible proclaimed equality in the eyes of the Lord. Early Christians copied the covenantal organization, institutions, and practices of covenantal Jewish communities.[44] These practices entailed a justice system of equality in the eyes of the Law. The post-Constantine Roman Empire actively engaged in mass-conversion to Christianity. In order to convert the senatorial aristocracy the Church adopted the old Roman hierarchic philosophy.[45] Ambrose of Milan was the first aristocrat ordained bishop in 374.[46] The Church doctrine steered away from classlessness and adopted elitist birthright distinctions such as *nobilitas*.[47] Most of Christianity abandoned egalitarian models and returned to hierarchical governments.

A few islands of covenantal Christians conserved the covenantal arrangements mostly in mountainous regions: the traditional Romanian villages in the Carpathians,[48] the Waldensian network in the Alps,[49] and the vicinal network in the Pyrenees.[50] The decentralized organization, institutions, and egalitarian spirit of the Waldensian covenantal communities served as practical model to Calvinist community doctrine.[51] The Puritans were Calvinists.[52] They were the first champions of equality before the law on English soil. Isaac Dorislaus was the first to claim that the king is subject to the law at Cambridge University in 1627.[53] In 1644 a seminal work, *Lex Rex,* substantiated Dorislaus' concept.[54] In 1649 the Puritan uprising excessively applied the theory that the King is subject to the Law. The insurgents submitted the king to a trial, found him guilty, condemned him to death, and beheaded him. In 1689 the Bill of Rights was enacted. It limited the powers of the monarch, it recognized the rights of Parliament, including the right to approve taxes, and it established free elections. The Bill of Rights also pronounced individual rights, including the prohibition of cruel and unusual punishment. A model of Parliamentary Constitutional Monarchy took off. The model prescribed elections with winners and losers. The results of the elections mattered. The Parliamentary model of England was a constitutional democracy.

In modern UK an unexpected mutation appeared in the "unwritten Constitution." In 2015 the government called for a referendum. For the first time, the government transferred the political debate from Parliament to the people. The debate was not about a trivial issue. It was about Brexit. For better or for worse the UK ceased to be a member of the EU.

Canada, Australia, New Zealand, and Israel inherited the constitutional blueprint of England. In Canada the federal government proposed a constitutional amendment significantly challenging the constitutional equilibrium. The proposal known as "The Meech Lake Accord of 1987" proposed to declare that Quebec is a *distinct society* defying the principle of equality of provinces. The Constitution required, among others, the consent of all ten provinces to such an amendment. Newfoundland and Manitoba voted against the proposal, underlining that in Canada the source of constitutional authority also consists of "we the people."

In Australia the High Court forced the resignation of some Members of Parliament because their dual citizenship violated article 44 of the Constitution.

One can determine that the UK, Canada, Australia, New Zealand, and Israel share a distinct variant of constitutional democracy characterized by a bottom-up constitutionalism and a an efficient and stabilizing judicial review. It is known as the constitutional parliamentary model.

Conclusion

1. The Republic of Weimar was a democracy with a Constitution inherently unstable because of lack of constitutionalism and absence of checks and balances.
2. The largest Latin American nations are democracies, with a constitution, elections, a feeble constitutionalism, and weak checks and balances. The stability of their democratic equilibrium is not convincing.
3. The EU is a confederation of democracies with elections; however, the legislative function of the confederation is shared by an unelected bureaucracy that initiates bills and an elected Parliament sanctions them into regulations and directives. The stability of the confederation was challenged by Brexit. It is too soon to evaluate the impact of this first crack.
4. France, a typical member of the Union, is a democracy with a constitution. France possesses a top-down constitutional philosophy; it spread from liberal principles of the Enlightenment. The judicial review in France adequately controls deviations from the Declaration of Human Rights, from other constitutional provisions and from international treaties. The constitutional democracy of France possesses strong elements of stability.
5. The UK, Canada, Australia, New Zealand, and Israel are constitutional democracies. Their bottom-up constitutionalism grew from ancient traditions and customs. The judicial review of these parliamentary democracies is robust. These systems of government are stable.

Notes

1 A. Przeworski, *Democracy and the Market: Political and Economic Reforms in Eastern Europe and Latin America* (Cambridge: Cambridge University Press, 1991), 10.

2 Peter Stirk, "Hugo Preuss, German Political Thought and the Weimar Constitution," *History of Political Thought* 23, no. 3 (2002).

3 Joseph Livni, *The Biblical Roots of American Constitutionalism—From 'I am the Lord' to 'We the People'* (Lanham: Lexington Books, 2021); Daniel J. Elazar, *Covenant and Polity in Biblical Israel: Volume 1, Biblical Foundations and Jewish Expressions: Covenant Tradition in Politics* (London and New York: Routledge, 2018); Mazzacano, "From Covenant to Compact to Contract: The Legal Transplantation of Puritan Jurisprudence to America" in *A Civil Society with no Hierarchy*, ed. Ilie Bădescu and

Joseph Livni (Lanham: Lexington Books, 2023, 227–52; Adela Șerban, "Romanian Traditional Society—Social Control and Social Order," in *A Civil Society with no Hierarchy*, ed. Ilie Bădescu and Joseph Livni (Lanham: Lexington Books, 2023, 207–26); Mădălina Măndiță, "The Covenant as Ideal Type, A Sociological Study of A Covenanted Community Model,' in *A Civil Society with no Hierarchy*, ed. Ilie Bădescu and Joseph Livni (Lanham: Lexington Books, 2023, 171–26; Everett H Emerson "Calvin and Covenant Theology," *Church History* 25, no. 2 (1956): 136–44; Joseph Livni and Ilie Bădescu, "The Battle of the Covenantal Society Against Elitism. An Overlooked Chapter in ihe History of Social Inequality," *Romanian Journal of Sociological Studies*, New Series, no. 1 (2020): 3–36; David Novak, *Covenantal Rights, A Study in Jewish Political Theory* (Princeton: Princeton University Press, 2000); Irving Louis Horowitz, "Daniel J. Elazar and the Covenant Tradition in Politics," *Publius: The Journal of Federalism* 31, no. 1 (Winter 2001): 1–7; D. J. Elazar et al., *The Covenant Connection: From Federal Theology to Modern Federalism* (Lexington Books, 2000); Daniel J. Elazar, *Covenant & Constitutionalism: The Great Frontier and the Matrix of Federal Democracy* (New Brunswick: Transaction Publishers, 1997); Steven Alan Samson, "Covenant Origins of the American Polity," *Faculty Publications and Presentations. 5* (Liberty University, 1994); Lynn D. Wardle, "The Constitution as Covenant," *Brigham Young University Studies* 27, no. 3 (1987); Shaun A. De Freitas, "Samuel Rutherford on Law and Covenant: The Impact of Theologico-Political Federalism on Constitutional Theory" (University of the Free State, 2003); Bernard M. Levinson and Jeffrey Stackert, "Between the Covenant Code and Esarhaddon's Succession Treaty: Deuteronomy 13 and the Composition of Deuteronomy," *Journal of Ancient Judaism* 3, no. 2 (2012): 123-40; Filippo Sabetti, "Covenant Language in Canada" (paper presented at the Workshop on Covenant and Politics, Center for the Study of Federalism, Temple University, 1980); Daniel J. Elazar, *Covenant & Commonwealth: From Christian Separation through the Protestant Reformation* (New Brunswick: Transaction Publishers, 1995); Donald S. Lutz, *The Origins of American Constitutionalism* (Baton Rouge: Louisiana State University Press, 1988); Ilie Bădescu and Joseph Livni, eds., *A Civil Society with no Hierarchy* (Lanham: Lexington Books, 2023).

4 This book focuses on how constitutionalism produces constitutions; societies where the expectation is that the constitution builds constitutionalism are out of scope see for example Vijayashri Sripati, "Constitutionalism in India and South Africa: A Comparative Study from a Human Rights Perspective" (University of Alberta, 2006).

5 John A. Booth and Mitchell A. Seligson, "The Political Culture of Authoritarianism in Mexico: A Reexamination," *Latin American Research Review* 19, no. 1 (1984).

6 Ana Micaela Alterio and Roberto Niembro, "Constitutional Culture and Democracy in Mexico: A Critical View of the 100-Year-Old Mexican Constitution," in *Constitutional Democracy in Crisis,* ed. Mark A. Graber, Sanford Levinson, and Mark Tushnet (New York: Oxford University Press, 2018): 139–59, 140.

7 *la endogamia y el amiguismo han producido redes clientelares muy arraigadas, en las que se trafica con plazas, se intercambian favores, o peor aún se pone precio a la justicia* "Proyecto De Reformas Con Y Para El Poder Judicial De La Federación," ed. Poder Judicial de la Federacion (Mexico City: Government of Mexico, 2020).

8 Translation of the above by Rafael QUINTERO GODÍNEZ.

9 Alterio and Niembro, "Constitutional Culture and Democracy in Mexico: A Critical View of the 100-Year-Old Mexican Constitution," 145.
10 Lee J. Alston and Andrés A. Gallo, "Electoral Fraud, the Rise of Peron and Demise of Checks and Balances in Argentina," *Explorations in Economic History* 47, no. 2 (2010): 179–97.
11 Anna Ciammariconi, "Chapter 9—Constitutional Justice in Argentina and Brazil," in *Comparative Latin American Constitutionalism*, ed. Silvia Bagni and Serena Baldin (Triest: EUT Edizioni Universita di Trieste 2023), 169–90, 172.
12 Alejandro M. Garro, "Judicial Review of Constitutionality in Argentina: Background Notes and Constitutional Provisions," *Duquesne Law Review* 45 (2006): 409–21.
13 Ibid., 420.
14 Ciammariconi, "Chapter 9—Constitutional Justice in Argentina and Brazil," 171.
15 Church, cultural and recreational activities, high school buddies, neighborhood and kids' school and extracurricular activities.
16 Ciammariconi, "Chapter 9—Constitutional Justice in Argentina and Brazil," 177.
17 Ibid., 179.
18 Ibid., 180.
19 Vanice Regina Lírio Do Valle, "Dialogical Constitutionalism Manifestations in the Brazilian Judicial Review," *Revista de Investigações Constitucionais* 1 (2014): 59–90.
20 Ibid.
21 David Landau, "Constitution-Making Gone Wrong," *Alabama Law Review* 64 (2012): 923–80.
22 Ludovico Zoekauer, "Sui framenti i piu antichi del constituto di Pistoia," in *Rivista italiana per le scienze giuridiche,* ed. G. Fusinato and F. Schupfer (Roma: E. Loescher & Company, 1892), 72–81, 76.
23 A hypothetical binding referendum could ask to set up a special law enforcement institution reporting to the president and dedicated to detection and immediate deportation of undocumented workers Many readers would doubt the constitutionality of such a plebiscite; undocumented workers are subject to the current political debate see *Le Monde July 30th* "Immigration in France: A necessary debate"; needless to say so far in practice no such initiatives were ever taken in democratic Europe.
24 Council of Europe, "Guidelines for Constitutional Referendums at National Level," in *CDL-INF (2001) 10*, ed. Council of Europe (Strasbourg Venice Commission at its 47th Plenary Meeting 2001).
25 François Mitterrand, *Le coup d'état permanent*, vol. 296 (Paris: Plon Paris, 1964).
26 Nicolas Rousselier, "France and the Fifth Republic," in *Constitutional Democracy in Crisis?*, ed. Mark A. Graber, Sanford Levinson, and Mark Tushnet (New York: Oxford University Press, 2018), 215–225, 218.
27 A design that takes success for granted and neglects risks and mitigation is a design that may face **unexpected challenges, delays, disputes, or failures** in their projects. Design risks are the potential occurrences that may **substantially affect** the end product, such as: safety hazards, cost overruns, unforeseen events, and hidden constraints.
28 Rousselier, "France and the Fifth Republic," 218.
29 article 2 du décret no 2005-218 du 9 mars 2005 décidant de soumettre un projet de loi au référendum

30 How could Wendy Smith foresee that her pay of £50/week as opposed to a man's pay of £60/week is not in contradiction with UK Law but it contradicts EU Treaties? How could a voter foresee which law overrides the other. The EU court overrode Court of Justice of the European Communities (including Court of First Instance Decisions) 61979J0129

Judgment of the Court of 27 March 1980.

31 The contrast with the Framers of the US Constitution is striking; the Framers did not invent a new constitutional reality and asked the people to approve it. They debated the current constitutional structure by analyzing the sociopolitical sociopolitical arrangement of communities, towns, districts and colonies and agreed to maintain working arrangements for better and for worse, for richer, for poorer, in sickness and in health.

32 Council of Europe, "Guidelines for Constitutional Referendums at National Level."

33 For example Janez Lenarčič has a degree in International Law from Ljubljana University, carried out diplomatic functions in Vienna, Warsaw, and Brussels, and appointed to top-level civil service in Ljubljana carrying the rank of State Secretary; currently he is Commissioner for Crisis Management see European Commission, mission letter of Ursula von der Leyen, 2019.

34 Maryon McDonald, "Accountability, Anthropology and the European Commission," in *Audit Cultures*, ed. Marilyn Strathern (New York: Routledge, 2003), 118–44.

35 Directives require EU countries to achieve a certain result, but leave them free to choose how to do so. Unlike a regulation, a directive is not directly applicable in Member States, it must first be transposed into national law before it is applicable in each Member State.

36 Regulations are legal acts that apply automatically and uniformly to all EU countries as soon as they enter into force, without needing to be transposed into national law. They are binding in their entirety on all EU countries.

37 Ilie Bădescu, Ozana Cucu-Oancea, and Gheorghe Şişeşte, *Dicţionar de sociologie rurală* (Bucharest: Editura Mica Valahie, 2005), 665.

38 Leviticus 19:18.

39 Brun-Otto Bryde, "Fundamental Rights as Guidelines and Inspiration: German Constitutionalism in International Perspective," *Wisconsin International Law Journal* 25 (2007): 189–206.

40 Matthew Adam Kocher, Adria K. Lawrence, and Nuno P. Monteiro, "Nationalism, Collaboration, and Resistance: France under Nazi Occupation," *International Security* 43, no. 2 (2018): 117-50. They cite: Robert O. Paxton, *Vichy France: Old Guard and New Order, 1940–1944*, rev. ed. (New York: Columbia University Press, 2001); and Eberhard Jäckel, *La France dans l'Europe de Hitler* (France in Hitler's Europe) (Paris: Librairie Arthème Fayard, 1968).

41 Kocher, Lawrence, and Monteiro, "Nationalism, Collaboration, and Resistance." They cite: Paxton, *Vichy France*; and Jäckel, *La France dans l'Europe de Hitler*.

42 John Fulton, *Free Government in England and America: Containing the Great Charter, the Petition of Right, the Bill of Rights, the Federal Constitution*, S. M. Johnson is the pseudonym of John Fulton (New York: Carleton Publisher, 1864), 273.

43 Ibid., 377.

44 Livni, *The Biblical Roots of American Constitutionalism—From 'I am the Lord' to 'We the People,'* 63.

45 Michele Renee Salzman, *The Making of a Christian Aristocracy: Social and Religious Change in the Western Roman Empire* (Cambridge, MA: Harvard University Press, 2002), Kindle Location 114–15.
46 Carlo Locatelli, *Vita di S. Ambrogio* (Milano: S. Majocchi, 1874).
47 Salzman, *The Making of a Christian Aristocracy: Social and Religious Change in the Western Roman Empire*, Kindle Location 323–4.
48 Henri H. Stahl, *Traditional Romanian Village Communities* (Cambridge: Cambridge University Press, 1980); Şerban, "Romanian Traditional Society—Social Control and Social Order"; Ilie Bădescu, *Paul Anghel – the Genial Wallach. The Eight Worlds of the Romanian Literature* (Bucharest: Walachia Press, 2018); Joseph Livni, "Christianity and the Romanian Communities Named Obşte," *Romanian Journal of Sociological Studies* 1 (2016): 61–71.
49 Gabriel Audisio, *The Waldensian Dissent: Persecution and Survival c. 1170–c. 1570*, trans. Claire Davison (Cambridge: Cambridge University Press, 1999); Dennis McCallum, "The Waldensian Movement From Waldo to the Reformation" (American Waldesian Society, History: Founded in the Middle Ages, Waldenses, Global Anabaptist Mennonite Encyclopedia, 2014); Jealn Loisa Willyams, *A Short History of the Waldensian Church in the Walleys of Piedmont* (London: James Nisbet et co., 1855); William Stephen Gilly, *Waldensian Researches During a Second Visit to the Vaudois of Piemont* (London: Rivington, 1831); Philippe Pouzet, "Les origines lyonnaises de la secte des Vaudois," *Revue d'histoire de l'Église de France* 22, no. 94 (1936): 5-37; Muston Alexis, *L'Israël des Alpes: première histoire complète des Vaudois du Piémont et de leurs colonies*, vol. I (Paris: Libr. de Marc Ducloux, 1851); Reinhard Bodenmann, "Les Vaudois et la production du livre évangélique français (1525–1550)," *Revue Littératures| Université McGill* 24, no. 1 (2017): 25–30; William Stephen Gilly, *Narrative of an Excursion to the Mountains of Piemont, and Researches among the Vaudois, or Waldenses, Protestant Inhabitants of the Cottian Alps: With an Appendix Containing Copies of Ancient Manuscripts and Other Interesting Documents* (London: C. and J. Rivington, 1824); Jean Léger, *Histoire generale des eglises evangeliques des Vallees de Piemont ou Vaudoises* (Leiden: Jean le Carpentier, 1669); Gabriel Audisio, "Des Pauvres de Lyon aux vaudois réformés," *Revue de l'histoire des religions* 217 (2000): 155–66; František Šmahel, "Crypto-et semi-vaudois dans la Bohême hussite," ibid.; L. Santini, *De Pierre Valdo à l'Eglise vaudoise* (Geneva: Labor et Fides, 1974); Jean Rodolphe Peyran, *An Historical Defence of the Waldenses or Vaudois* (London: C & J Rivington, 1826); Pierrette Paravy, *De la chrétienté romaine à la Réforme en Dauphiné. Évêques, fidèles et déviants (vers 1340-vers 1350)*, vol. 1, Collection De L'école Française De Rome (Rome: École française de Rome, 1993).
50 Augustine Robert Whiteway, "The Pyrenean Neighbour; or, the Vicinal System in the Western Pyrenees," *Archaeological Journal* 58, no. 1 (1901): 182–98; Hélène Couderc-Barraud, *La violence, l'ordre et la paix: résoudre les conflits en Gascogne du XIe au début du XIIIe siècle* (Toulouse: Presses universitaires du Mirail, 2008); Gustave Bascle de Lagrèze, *Histoire du droit dans les Pyrénées—comté de Bigorre* (Paris: Imprimerie Impériale, 1867).
51 Livni, *The Biblical Roots of American Constitutionalism—From 'I am the Lord' to 'We the People,'* 61, 62; Benjamin G. Wilkinson, *Our Authorized Bible Vindicated* (Fort Oglethorpe: Teach Services, 2014), Ch. "Waldensian Bibles"; Bodenmann, "Les Vaudois et la production du livre évangélique français (1525–1550)"; Paravy, *De la*

chrétienté romaine à la Réforme en Dauphiné. Évêques, fidèles et déviants (vers 1340-vers 1350), 1:1182–3.

52 e. g. Leonard J. Trinterud, "The Origins of Puritanism," *Church History* 20, no. 1 (1951): 37–57.

53 Isaac Dorislaus, "Inaugural Lecture, DRSS6311" (University of Cambridge: Cambridge Alumni Database, 1627).

54 Samuel Rutherford, *Lex, Rex, or, the Law and the Prince* (Penn Laird: Sprinkle Publications, 1982).

8

The United States of America

Constitutionalism

The Constitution is the supreme law of the country. The law requires every individual elected or appointed to an office of honor or serving in civil service or uniformed services to take an oath to uphold the Constitution of the United States.[1]

How is the Constitution enforced? Another law specifies that the violators of this oath by advocating the overthrow of our constitutional form of government shall be fined under this title or imprisoned not more than one year and a day or both.[2]

The law is unequivocal; however, the implied use of force against a noncompliant state government is awkward.[3] In practice, these laws do not constitute an obvious impediment to overthrowing the constitutional government. One shall remember that the role of constitution is to limit the government.[4] Limiting the government is an essential stabilizing mechanism as is the proper functioning of rudder control in an airplane (Chapter 1). What if the majority of Congress wishes to govern beyond the limits of the constitution? The majority in Congress does have the authority to repeal laws, including laws criminalizing government officials who refuse upholding the Constitution. Moreover, the example of the Weimar Republic also proves that relying on legislators to protect a constitution is risky.

On the other hand the Constitution has served as supreme law of the United States for almost two and a half centuries. Often, knowing the past helps understanding the present.[5] And the past indicates that the stability of the system is assured by *checks and balances* designed by the framers using the blueprint of Colonial America's government practice; the practice started with the "first Puritan who landed on those shores."[6]

In stability engineering language, the term *checks and balances* translates to feedback loops (see Fig 3.4) controlling the equilibrium of the system. As aircraft system stability designers, the Framers also were aware that attempts of exceeding authority beyond constitutional limits are foreseeable; keeping the equilibrium against such possible disruptions required "contriving the interior structure of the government as that its several constituent parts may, by their mutual relations, be the means of keeping each other in their proper places."[7] Is this sufficient? The 225 years of stability indicate that it is.

However, there is more empirical evidence supporting the claim that the US constitutional democracy withstands shocks. The American system was not created out of nothing. The general mindset that evolved along the history of colonial America required that the government structure is conceived so "that the rights of individuals, or of the minority, will be in little danger from interested combinations of the majority."[8] In other words "The republic endures and this is the symbol of its faith."[9] That faith is constitutionalism.

Constitutionalism preceded the Constitution. Constitutionalism was the sociopolitical conviction of the American Colonial system and it shaped the Constitution. That is why the authorship of the American Constitution is rightly credited to "We the people." The blocks of Figure 8.1 are populated by Americans, and its stability loops contain signals correcting deviations from the traditional path of constitutionalism. We shall discuss five essential blocks to maintaining the stability: judicial review, government structure, academia, education, and research.

Judicial Review

Judicial review is the only block of the diagram uniquely dedicated to correcting unconstitutional deviations of other agencies. The block diagram indicates that it is mainly fed by academic knowledge and constitutional professionalism. In reality, judges have political opinions as anybody else. Ideally, their professional ability and familiarity with the constitutional text play a primary role in their decisions. The university prepares future judges; the curriculum covers many aspects discussing the difficulties of their future task. For example they learn that "the fundamental problem of constitutional fidelity" is indeterminacy.[10]

This lecture sounds scary. At first sight it even contradicts our legally uninformed intuition. Is the phrase "The number of Representatives in the House is according to the size of the population in each state" indeterminate? Or does "The President shall be elected by the Electoral College" lack determination? These constitutional edicts are of exemplary clarity compared to instruction manuals stating the following:

> When a computer is properly connected to one of the LAN ports on the rear of the Router, the LED will light. GREEN means a 10Base-T device is connected, AMBER means a 100Base-Tx device is connected.[11]

Nevertheless, the reader should realize that law school is not preparing officers of the court to understand the phrase regarding the number of representative in the house. Hopefully, they were amply qualified to interpret it long before they filled out the application to law school. As a matter of fact, the Supreme Court is busy hearing constitutional cases. This indicates that after all there are indeterminate clauses in the text.

The stability of the American Constitutional Democracy hinges on the ability of the courts to detect and correct governmental workarounds circumventing constitutional limitations. It seems that the text is not the core of the dispute. The controversy is between two schools of applying the old text of Constitution in disputes of modern days: originalism and judicial pragmatism. The first school reads the text and interprets it according to the original intent of the Framers. The *judicial pragmatist* also called *living constitutionalism* interprets the text in light of the changing circumstances and values of society.

> Living constitutionalists believe that the meaning of the constitutional text changes over time, as social attitudes change, even without the adoption of a formal constitutional amendment pursuant to Article V of the Constitution.[12]

For example for this new school the meaning of the term *liberty* varied in time.[13]

Constitutionalism has ancient roots; they stretch to biblical times.[14] In those times *liberty* meant the opposite of servitude.[15] In 1927 the US Supreme Court interpreted the term precisely with the same meaning. Ed Tumey was convicted before the mayor of unlawfully possessing intoxicating liquor. "The Mayor of the Village of North College Hill, Ohio, had a direct, personal, pecuniary interest in convicting the defendant who came before him for trial, in the twelve dollars of costs imposed in his behalf, which he would not have received if the defendant had been acquitted."[16] Not surprisingly, the Supreme Court established that the conviction is a violation of the Fourteenth Amendment

> and deprives a defendant in a criminal case of due process of law, to subject his *liberty* or property to the judgment of a court, the judge of which has a direct, personal, substantial pecuniary interest in reaching a conclusion against him in his case.[17]

The term *liberty* was the antonym of captivity when the Book of Isaiah was written and it had identical meaning in 1927. The fundamental meaning of liberty was the same in 1591, in 1791, and in 1991. Nevertheless, the term indeed evolved and covered additional specific meanings (see Table 8.1). We are ready to explore the progression of the term liberty from 1591 to 1791 to 1991.

In 1591 most of the civilization lived in empires, kingdoms, principalities, and city-states. These were ruled by sovereign rulers. Rulers respected at will[18] ancient liberties as a matter of religion, morality, leadership cleverness, and of legitimacy. There was no constitutionalism in the sense of limiting the power of government. There were, however, a few exceptional networks of communities that adhered to the concept of limited power of leadership.[19] These networks respected liberties numbered 6 to 10 of Table 8.1. These networks were regulated by a binding covenant, and some scholars call them covenantal societies.[20] It has been substantiated that the covenant persuasion of the American Puritans gave rise to the American Constitutionalism.[21] It is worth mentioning that the only civil *liberty* that was new in 1791 is freedom of assembly. Covenantal societies were governed by elders subjected to the control of a general assembly. The members were compelled to participate at the assemblies.

Table 8.1 Civil and Political Freedoms

#	Meaning	Era
1	Freedom of conscience	Seventeenth century[a]
2	Freedom of press	Seventeenth century[b]
3	Freedom of religion	Sixteenth century[b]
4	Freedom of expression	Seventeenth century[c]
5	Freedom of assembly	1791[d]
6	The right to security and liberty	Antiquity[e]
7	The right to privacy	Antiquity[f]
8	The right to equal treatment under the law and due process	Antiquity[g]
9	The right to a fair trial	Antiquity[h]
10	The right to life	Antiquity[i]

Information Source:
[a] Evan Haefeli, *New Netherland and the Dutch Origins of American Religious Liberty* (Philadelphia, PA: University of Pennsylvania Press, Incorporated, 2013), 4.
[b] Gordon Rayner, "Leveson Inquiry: British press freedom is a model for the world, editor tells inquiry," *The Telegraph* 2011.
[c] e.g Stephen M. Feldman, *Free Expression and Democracy in America: A History* (Chicago University of Chicago Press, 2009), [7].
[d] First Amendment
[e] Deuteronomy 19:21
[f] "Argue your case with your neighbor himself, and do not reveal another's secret," Proverbs 25:9
[g] Leviticus 19:15; Leviticus 19:33-34; Galatians 3:28
[h] Deuteronomy 16:18-20
[i] "Though shall not murder" Exodus 20:13 (in the Ten Commandments)

Let us examine what was new in 1991. There were three major constitutional public debate topics:

a. The Civil Rights Act (1964)
b. The freedom of abortion
c. Same-Sex marriage

The Civil Rights Act (1964)

This act is a federal law outlawing discrimination based on race, color, religion, sex, and national origin. The act empowers the federal government to enforce existing constitutional liberties by states and agencies. The act was disputed and brought to the Supreme Court in *Heart of Atlanta Motel v. United States* (1964). The Court unanimously found that Congress acted within its constitutional boundaries. This case is legally important; however, it also teaches an important lesson about the equilibrium and stability of the American System. The equilibrium authorizes Congress to legislate laws; even the Supreme Court has no authority to cancel or modify laws compliant with the Constitution. The decision in this case illustrates the stabilizing role of the Supreme Court; it consists of correcting deviation from the Constitution and not of weighing the cost and benefit of a law.

Abortion Rights

A great majority of democracies allowed abortions one way or another. Currently abortion is illegal only in twenty-one countries.[22] Reasonably, in 1973 the count was similar. In the United States some states disallowed abortions until 1973. The famous *Roe v. Wade* case has been analyzed countlessly. Nevertheless, it is a valuable example to explore it, having in mind understandings borrowed from the study of equilibrium and stability of complex systems.

The law of Texas denied the right of Jane Roe to abort. Claiming that abortion is a constitutional right, Jane Roe requested the US Supreme Court to overrule the law of Texas. The text of the Constitution, however, does not mention the right of abortion. Originalists, therefore, would arrive at the conclusion that the Framers' intent was not to include abortion as a constitutional liberty. The approach of Living Constitution reads the text in view of what liberty meant in 1973:

> This right of privacy, whether it be founded in the Fourteenth Amendment's concept of personal liberty and restrictions upon state action, as we feel it is, or, as the District Court determined, in the Ninth Amendment's reservation of rights to the people, is broad enough to encompass a woman's decision whether or not to terminate her pregnancy. The detriment that the State would impose upon the pregnant woman by denying this choice altogether is apparent.[23]

No doubt, the world changed since 1791 and prohibiting abortion restricts one's freedom. However, the United States is a constitutional democracy. Earlier we mentioned the Civil Rights Act. This example illustrates how the term *liberty* may include the freedom to abort. Moreover, "we the people" anticipated that what was wrong in 1791 may be acceptable to "We the people" of 1973. Precisely that is the reason why they designed a path to amendments. The path itself has checks and balances to assure that amendments express the will of the people.

Stability of systems (Figure 3.4) requires predefined control laws. The thermostat of Figure 3.2 is set to predetermined range of temperature (e.g., 110–120°F). In our stability analysis, the Supreme Court is also a controller; keeping equilibrium requires reading the text *as* it appears in the Constitution or its amendments. Interestingly, in the same case the same justices exemplarily followed the letter of the law in explaining that a fetus is not a person:

> The Constitution does not define "person" in so many words. Section 1 of the Fourteenth Amendment contains three references to "person." The first, in defining "citizens," speaks of "persons born or naturalized in the United States." The word also appears both in the Due Process Clause and in the Equal Protection Clause. "Person" is used in other places in the Constitution: in the listing of

> qualifications for Representatives and Senators, Art. I, Â§2, cl. 2, and Â§ 3, cl. 3; in the Apportionment Clause, Art. I, Â§ 2, cl. 3; . . . But in nearly all these instances, the use of the word is such that it has application only post-natally.[24]

The case ended upgrading the right to abortion to the status of constitutional right. The intent of this analysis is not to deplore the result itself. The Supreme Court is constitutionally authorized to decide that the Ninth Amendment is broad enough to encompass rights that are not mentioned in it; consequently, the decision did not violate the Constitution. However, this analysis finds that such shortcuts undermine constitutionalism. Constitutionalism is analogous to the hydraulic fluid in the brake system of a car. An essential component of constitutionalism consists of the respect of "We the people" for the Supreme Court.

The decision of *Roe v. Wade* did not bring to a failure of constitutional democracy. Constitutionalism, the brake fluid empowering the system, did not vanish. However, the "broad enough" novel approach is comparable to a small amount of hydraulic fluid leaking away.

The question of the freedom of abortion did not end in 1973. In 2022 it resurrected.[25] The Court was asked again to intervene in a state law regulating abortion. The law in question respected *Roe v. Wade*. This time the opinion of the Supreme Court stated that "We hold that Roe and Casey must be overruled."[26] Not surprisingly, the opinion established that the right of abortion is not "implicitly protected by any constitutional provision."[27] The opinion of the Court accepts that the Due Process Clause of the Fourteenth Amendment does "guarantee some rights that are not mentioned in the Constitution, but any such right must be 'deeply rooted in this Nation's history and tradition' and 'implicit in the concept of ordered liberty.'"

Returning to the concept of systems stability this opinion corresponds to the rule that control laws may be updated provided they have no effect on the existing equilibrium.[28] Earlier we established that *Roe v. Wade* changed the equilibrium. For a stability and control specialist this change is a change from a neutral equilibrium to another one (case c of Figure 2.2).[29] Twenty-nine years after the new equilibrium was established; the right to abortion did become settled law "deeply rooted in this Nation's history and tradition" and "implicit in the concept of ordered liberty." Consequently, its repealing signified another change in equilibrium. As *Roe v. Wade*, *Dobbs v. Jackson* did not violate the Constitution; however both damaged constitutionalism. The trust in the Constitution declines if it exhibits seesawing between constitutionally guaranteed and not guaranteed rights. *Dobbs v. Jackson* corresponds to another leak of brake fluid; it further diminished the legitimacy of regulating unconstitutional legislation.

Same-Sex Marriages

Same-sex marriage is without doubt a novel right. Many readers would admit that such a right was not in existence the day they were born. The history of the case exemplifies the process of the concept of Living Constitution. In 2020 Kim Davis, a county clerk

Table 8.2 Medieval Marriage Records of European Church Parishes

Hungary	1625[a]
England	1580[b]
France	1332[c]
Holland	1634[d]

[a] Hanna Zipernovszky, "Parish Records as a Source for Comparative Pedagogical Research," *Scriptum* (2002).
[b] Charles M Evans and Angela E Evans, "Plague–a disease of children and servants? A study of the parish records of St Peter upon Cornhill, London from 1580 to 1605," *Continuity and Change* 34, no. 2 (2019).
[c] Antoine Follain and Jean-Michel Matz, *L'argent Des Villages Du Xiiie Au Xviiie Siècle : Comptabilités Paroissiales Et Communales, Fiscalité Locale: Actes Du Colloque D'angers, 30-31 Oct. 1998* (Rennes, France: Presses universitaires de Rennes, 1999), 35.
[d] Roodenburg, *Social Control in Europe: 1500-1800*, 101.

in Kentucky, was ordered to by the US District Court to start issuing marriage licenses to same-sex couples. The right to same-sex marriage became a constitutional right in 2015 by virtue of the Supreme Court decision in *Obergefell v. Hodges*, 576 U.S. 644 (2015).

Davis refused to issue marriage licenses to same-sex couples because of her religious conviction. She appealed to the Supreme Court; both group of justices—originalists and Living Constitution—advocates denied her request. The decision of justices embracing the Living Constitution approach is not surprising. Let us review the reasoning of the originalists. First they established that the Constitution did not mention the right to same-sex marriage:

> In Obergefell v. Hodges, 576 U. S. 644 (2015), the Court read a right to same-sex marriage into the Fourteenth Amendment, even though that right is found nowhere in the text.[30]

Needless to say, such a right did not exist in 1591, or 1791 or 1991. As a matter of fact, in 1591 marriages were carried out by Church parishes:

> One of the primary functions of ecclesiastical courts was the regulation of sexual and marital behaviours.[31]

Table 8.2 lists medieval countries with medieval marriage records across Europe.

Accordingly, in 1591 one could not talk about freedom of marriage in the constitutional sense because the Constitution limits government, and not Church. In 1791 Churches were still in charge of most marriages.[32] In 1991 freedom of marriage became a constitutional right in virtue of a Supreme Court unanimous decision.[33] In 2015 same-sex marriages were also elevated to the status of constitutional rights. The majority of the Court was guided by the Living Constitution creed. Accordingly, the Supreme Court has authority and obligation to determine whether "We the People" changed our attitude regarding liberties that have not existed in the past:

> History and tradition guide and discipline this inquiry but do not set its outer boundaries, See Lawrence, supra, at 572. That method respects our history and learns from it without allowing the past alone to rule the present.[34]

Originalists caution against applying Living Constitution teachings that cross boundaries of legality:

> The majority's decision is an act of will, not legal judgment. The right it announces has no basis in the Constitution or this Court's precedent. The majority expressly disclaims judicial "caution" and omits even a pretense of humility, openly relying on its desire to remake society according to its own "new insight" into the "nature of injustice."[35]

This chapter is not intended to take sides on a legal basis. It can only offer an opinion regarding equilibrium and stability of societies. The argument that the Court must take into consideration "changed understandings of marriage" corresponds to a speeding driver claiming liberty to consider changed circumstances of traffic at 2 AM. The law does not allow such a liberty; however, this chapter brings up this analogy for the purpose of explaining that adopting such considerations endangers the stability of the traffic system.

Same-sex marriage was prohibited in the past. Later, it became tolerated. Promoting same-sex marriages to the status of constitutional liberty corresponds to a change in the control laws because it implies a modifying course of action in applying certain laws. A few items on the list of implications of legalizing same-sex marriage are:[36]

1. Preferential treatment to foreign-born spouses of US citizens
2. Attending a sick spouse granted by federal Family and Medical Leave Act
3. Evidentiary rules that protect spouses from testifying against each other
4. Workers' compensation and Social Security survivors' benefits
5. Joint tax returns
6. Health insurance coverage as a spouse
7. Hospital visitation rights
8. Health care decisions for a partner

The legal theory leading to same-sex marriages opened the question whether the future could hold recognizing polygamy as a civil marriage.[37]

Chapter 2 explains that it is not easy to determine whether the current equilibrium is stable, unstable or neutral. The Framers of the Constitution devised a guidance to test the social implication of moving from one equilibrium state to another. Working around the constitutional process of amending the Constitution may be legal or may be not; nevertheless, it weakens stability. Originalists did not agree that same-sex marriages are a constitutional right. Nevertheless, in the case of Davis in 2020 they declined to allow marriage license officers to refuse issuing same sex-marriage licenses. In terms of equilibrium and stability examination this is exactly how a controller is designed to act. Once a new equilibrium is settled the controller will oppose disturbances to the new equilibrium.

Government Configuration and Power Flow

The United States has been established as a federal government system. The US Constitution mirrored the political chart of Colonial America not only in terms of individual liberties and equality before the law[38] but also in the organizational breakdown structure; it replaced the autonomy of colonies with state sovereignty, and it replaced the powers of Parliament and Crown with Congress and President respectively. Learning from the colonial experience of power abuse by the government in London the Constitution's governmental organization chart consists of "certain enumerated powers, and of numerous state governments, which retain and exercise all powers not delegated to the Union."[39]

Reasonably, the US Constitution upheld the colonial network of autonomous governments in a Union of states not because of *equilibrium and stability* considerations. The Framers deserve credit for fixing what was broken and not fixing what was not. Nevertheless, with hindsight we can recognize that the federal system maintained the inherent resilience of the arrangement of colonial America. "Societies slowly progress in mass; they progress in complexity of structure."[40] Chapters 2 and 3 explain why growing complexity is destabilizing. In the US federal system:

a. Local governments administer local concerns (Zoning, Schools, Public Water, City Taxes, Open Spaces, Roads, Traffic Control, Sidewalks, Police, Library, etc.)
b. State Governments—Public Health, Revenue, Energy, Transportation, State Police, Corrections, Justice, Higher Education, Elections, Education, etc.
c. Federal Government—Defense, Foreign Affairs, Homeland Security, Intelligence, Federal Infrastructure, Banking, Urban Affairs, Aviation, Food and Drug Safety, Communications, National Health, Infectious Diseases, etc.)

The Constitution does not specifically authorize local government. Nevertheless, local governments regulate activities that significantly impact citizens' quality of life like the safety and value of one's property, education of children, and personal protection from criminal offenses. Nevertheless, in practice the authority of local government of colonial towns has not been reduced. For example Justice Cooley "constitutionalized" local authority declaring that "local government is a matter of absolute right; and the state cannot take it away."[41] The common wisdom is that Justice Dillon diagonally opposed the link between the will of "We the People" and the authority of local governments. Any student in law knows that the Constitution does not mention local sovereignty. However, my thesis is that the Constitution expresses the will of "We the People"; on the other hand, constitutionalism is the complete collection of the will of the people. This is not taught in Law school, and rightly so because *constitutionalism* or *the will of the people* are not terms that judges, whether federal or state, are bound to consider. Nevertheless, the will of the people does practically affect judgments when judges live in a culture of constitutionalism. Let us listen to Justice Dillon himself:

> the legislature might, by a single act, if we can suppose it capable of so great a folly and so great a wrong, sweep from existence all of the municipal corporations in the State, and the corporation could not prevent it. We know of no limitation on this right so far as the corporations themselves are concerned.[42]

Who can better argue for the functional need of local government than Justice Dillon? Perhaps the public participation in municipal boards and committees (cable advisory, climate action, naming, aging, schools, etc.) equally constitutes compelling evidence that "We the People" want to govern ourselves through local decision-making as much as common sense allows it. Nevertheless, constitutionalism is not law while the Constitution is. Dillon's "public purpose" doctrine reconciled the constitutional dilemma of the validity of municipal local government action: actions for "public purpose" are valid. From the point of view of constitutionalism Justice Cooley is not far from Justice Dillon. One of the objectives of the US Constitution is to "promote the general welfare";[43] local government's action is valid if it promotes public interest. Elected representatives promote community well-being; if they do not they are not elected. Justice Cooley authorizes acts of local government. Dillon's *public purpose doctrine* authorizes the courts to invalidate acts of government for a "private purpose."

Section *Centralization of power* of Chapter 4 argues why centralization of government functions is destabilizing. In the particular case of the United States, the police is local; it deals with local problems, local criminals, and local population; the external adversaries are the responsibility of the federal government. This arrangement is stabilizing and stems from the constitutionalism of Americans, and it is stamped in the Constitution.

Nevertheless, there are some concerns. The Weimar Republic was also a federation. It inherited a more centralized administration from Imperial Germany than the United States inherited from its colonial past. In the Weimar Republic policing was managed by the states, one level higher than in current United States.[44]

As in Weimar, the US Constitution decrees the supremacy of federal law.[45] This point deserves a second examination. The founders did not forge a union that can override established order, and powers to maintain rights and liberties of the citizens:

> An intire [*sic*] consolidation of the States into one complete national sovereignty would imply an intire [*sic*] subordination of the parts; and whatever powers might remain in them would be altogether dependent on the general will. But as the plan of the Convention aims only at a partial Union or consolidation, the State Governments would clearly retain all the rights of sovereignty which they before had and which were not by that act *exclusively* delegated to the United States.[46]

In practical terms the US Constitution distinguishes between powers delegated to the federal level,[47] powers reserved for the states,[48] and concurrent powers;[49] see examples

Table 8.3 US Power Federalism—Separation and Sharing

	Federal Powers	Reserved Powers	Concurrent Powers
1	Taxation	Local Government	Taxation
2	Borrowing Money	Education	Borrowing Money
3	Interstate and International Commerce	Intrastate Commerce	Law Enforcement
4	Naturalization and Bankruptcy	Public Safety	Public Health and Safety
5	Currency	Marruiage and Civil Law	Building Infrastructure
6	Post Offices	Health and Welfare	Charter Banks
7	Federal Courts	State Courts	Court Systems
8	Patents and Copyrights		
9	War and Defense		
10	Militia		
11	District of Columbia		

in Table 8.3; therefore only concurrent powers can potentially generate legislative conflict between state and the union where the supremacy of federal law is assured. Even in the case of courts an apparent potential conflict is removed by the so-called "abstention doctrine" stating that federal courts should defer ongoing procedures in state courts to the state court.[50]

The Weimar Republic's Constitution continued the practice of the Imperial German Constitution subordinating State Government to Central Government. The US Constitution delegates power from the states to the Union. In practice the pre-colonial powers of local governments and the overwhelming public participation in the municipal politics have been preserved in the United States. The Weimar centralized approach is destabilizing because it implies more state variables in its equilibrium model. The US government configuration of the United States is significantly more resilient than the government pattern of the Weimar Republic.

Academia

The boxes of Figure 8.1 represent complex sociopolitical functions of the American establishment. One function, however, is an exception: the Academia. This is a global function because for better or for worse science is global.[51]

Section *Judicial Review* listed the constitutional meaning of the word *freedom*. It would be appropriate if the Academia teaching of the constitutional interpretation of freedom were somewhat consistent with the Constitution. Surprisingly students receive different or sometimes contradictory lessons regarding the subject:

> Second, freedom conceived as an *individual* right operates as a "trump" against legislative majorities. Yet freedom conceived as a *political* right entails the capacity of democratic majorities to control their destinies through legislation.[52]

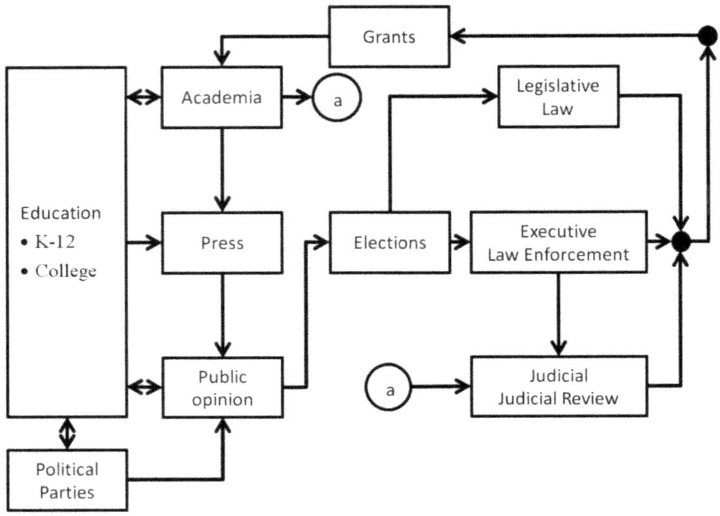

Figure 8.1 Block diagram of stability study of the US constitutional democracy. Author's work.

Law students are future officers of the court, prosecutors, judges, and defense lawyers. It would be nice if they were taught that the American Constitution was conceived in order to limit government[53] and not to establish a tyranny of the majority (see Chapter 4, section *Checks and Balances*).

Other lessons that law students may hear are not less confusing:

1. The term *freedom* may apply to claims for *freedom to own slaves*.[54] The lesson implies that at any time the Constitution legally sanctioned slavery. This affirmation is self-contradictory because the freedom to deny other people's freedom is the negation of freedom. Moreover, the lesson is misleading because the freedom to own slaves is not mentioned in the Bill of Rights. True, slavery was legal in the South. Unfortunately, prior to the Fourteenth Amendment the Constitution did not prohibit legislation in favor of this barbaric institution. However, Klarman lectures that "We the People" legalized slavery utilizing the absurd equivalence: *freedom=denial of freedom.*
2. The freedom of local communities to govern their own schools is not "persuasive" because "we no longer choose to respect the freedom of those who denigrate other human beings because of their race or to defer to the freedom of local political majorities to use their power in the service of white supremacy."[55] Local communities governed themselves from the beginning of the American experience. We argued earlier that the author of the Constitution is "We the People." Not only because the preamble declares so, but also because "[l]ocal government in colonial America was the seedbed of American

> constitutionalism."[56] This contradicts Klarman's teaching that the Constitution was a result of a "Framers' Coup." The good news about the Framer's Coup is that it instils examining legal documents from an original point of view. The bad news is that it teaches future law school graduates to walk away even from the meaning of *constitutionalism* (see Hamilton's definition in Chapter 6).

It is important to note that destabilizing theories are not exclusively spread from Law Departments. For example, a multinational multidisciplinary collection teaches a lesson against *retributive justice*. Among others it opposes punishment of offenders distinguishing between punitive and constructive means of corrections:

> We call these means constructive as, compared to punitive means, their emphasis is on healing more than hurting.[57]

I admit this observation comes from Australian psychologists and discussing it in this section dealing with US academia needs an explanation. Okimoto received his P.D in social/organizational psychology from New York University. Wenzel completed his PhD at the University of Münster (Germany) researching "justice restoration."[58] By its nature academic research is global and not national. For example, the article of Wenzel and Okimoto is a chapter of a *Handbook of Social Justice*.

This collection handling alternative approaches to "the old-time notion of justice in Western civilization"[59] consists of multinational academic studies; one-third of the contributors are from the US academia. It is multidisciplinary (psychology, sociology, economy, ethics, etc.); nevertheless, it traces without justification the Western justice approach to biblical Judeo-Christian religious customs. This Judeo-Christian origin of retributive justice is questionable due to evidence of the contrary. The Hammurabi code preexisted Judeo-Christianity for about four centuries. Punishment of offenders has been practiced, among others, in pre-Christian Rome, in African traditions[60] in Imperial China of second century BCE,[61] and in Amerindian empires.[62]

The disagreement is relevant because punishing criminals is a result of the rational theory that crime exist because crime pays. This book dedicated Chapter 5 to this argument. It is based on the rationale that most criminals are reasonable individuals. Chapters 2 and 3 teach that any government action has side effects, and side effects are potentially destabilizing. If these side effects are connected in a closed loop, then they *are* destabilizing. For example:

> Legal punishment for crimes may be deserved, but it also bears the risk of unjust social discrimination against those close to the perpetrator.[63]

This book is about equilibrium and stability, and therefore, it will not question the suitability of the expression "unjust social discrimination against those close to the perpetrator."

Even if this expression made sense, it would endorse reducing the benefit of crime and the consequential increase of criminality (Chapter 5). Allowing criminality to grow (see illustration in the chart of Figure 3.9) is socially destabilizing. Should we stop thinking, researching, and publishing opposition to a questionably defined "unjust social discrimination"? Research is a prerequisite of progress and progress is stabilizing. The message here adds on the balance the weight of social *equilibrium and stability*. The block diagram of Figure 8.1 illustrates that scholars' impact on government action is indirect. Nevertheless, it significantly matters. The ultimate factor in taking action is the executive branch of government.

The diagram of Figure 8.1 illustrates three closed loops through which considering "unjust social discrimination against those close to the perpetrator" can unhinge the social equilibrium: the loop going through the executive block, through the legislative block, and through the judicial block.

The fact that punishment of offenders has been practiced all over the civilized world is a supplementary justification of retributive justice. Not punishing offenders is therefore not only destabilizing but also uncivilized.

The theory that "the psychological problems of overstrained individuals and inferior living conditions were responsible for most crimes" has circulated in the intellectual public opinion of Weimar's Berlin.[64] It is as destabilizing as would be eliminating the thermostat of the hot water tank of Figure 3.2. This psychological stress theory of crime did not destroy the Weimar Republic; however, it contributed to its failure.

Education

Long before the Framers, colonies knew that keeping government in order requires "[t]hat Justice and Right be equally and imparshally [*sic*] administered unto all."[65] This brand of constitutionalism gave rise to the Constitution and guaranteed the resilience of the American Constitutional Democracy. Chapter 6 illustrates that the democracy of a republic with a perfect Constitution is frail in the absence of constitutionalism. Undermining constitutionalism is therefore destabilizing.

Oddly students are warned that local communities need to be prevented from deferring to local political majorities with white supremacy inclinations.[66] Consequently, Harvard students absorb the need for novel legal interpretations of *freedom* to mitigate this risk. This thinking is consistent with the concept claiming that "education remains one of the best ways to stop the proliferation of racist and discriminatory discourses and to foster intercultural exchanges."[67] "The Betrayal of the Humanities"[68] and many other references of Chapter 6 disprove that education stops racism and discrimination.

American slavery was abolished. This came about not because the staffs of Law Schools taught that slavery is wrong. More than 360,000 Union soldiers scarified their life for the freedom of American slaves. It is again "We the People" who believed, fought, and risked health and life in order to "secure the Blessings of Liberty"[69] for enslaved Americans. One may amuse law students with the concept of the framers' coup, provided one does not forget to credit "We the People" for establishing and conserving the precepts of the Constitution.

Figure 8.2 The Alamo at night, San Antonio, Texas. Credit: Danphotoman777. Public Domain.

I would like to make an exception and insert a personal account related to parents' contribution to the education of their children. One of the most attractive displays of the American good life is the "River Walk" in San Antonio. A small river divides two sides of a street, each one with rich shops, cheerful bars, and a variety of restaurants where locals and visitors wine and dine.

However, a few hundred yards from the River Walk, American parents bring their kids to the Alamo (Figure 8.2), and tell them the account of a heroic battle that once took place there. I was taken aback seeing how young Americans absorb the notion that "life, liberty and the pursuit of happiness,"[70] fully displayed on the River Walk, comes at a price, probably at the highest price one can pay.

Research

Research is the essence of progress. Researchers need grants. Some grants are provided by the private sector; however, the public sector generously funds a significant portion of research. The US taxpayer pays more than $12.7 billion/year to universities on top of the tuition fees paid by students (Table 8.4).

Research and Development (R&D) is essential for economic growth of a nation; economic growth is critical for sociopolitical stability.[71] The government directly invests about $34 billon in R&D (Table 8.5). Indirect essential investment in R&D consists of teaching sciences.[72] Therefore one cannot rule out that part of the $12.7 billion funding (Table 8.4) has a stabilizing effect on the US sociopolitical system.

Nevertheless, universities in the United States and abroad engage in propagating destabilizing philosophies. The taxpayer shells out the funds; the civil servant

Table 8.4 20 US Universities receiving the most generous federal funding[a]

Institute	Federal Funding [$ million]	DEI Chief
Johns Hopkins University	2000	Katrina Caldwell
University of Washington	961	Rickey Hall
University of Michigan	756	Tabbye Chavous
Stanford University	680	Joyce Sackey
UC San Diego	643	Becky Petitt
University of Pennsylvania	617	Mitchell J. Chang
The University of North Carolina at Chapel Hill	600	Leah Cox
Columbia University	600	Alade McKen
University of Pittsburgh	580	Clyde Wilson Pickett
Duke University	563	Kimberly Hewitt
Georgia Institute of Technology	562	Emily Monago
University of Wisconsin-Madison	551	LaVar J. Charleston
Harvard	550	Sherri Ann Charleston
UCLA	535	Anna Spain Bradley
UCSF	535	J. Renée Navarro
University of Minnesota	505	Mercedes Ramirez Fernandez
MIT	491	Kuheli Dutt
Ohio State	488	Russell Morrow
Yale	480.2	Kimberly Goff-Crews
Total Federal Funding	$12.7 billion	

Source: a) Universities Getting the Most Money from the Federal Government [https://247wallst.com/special-report/2017/03/22/universities-getting-the-most-money-from-the-federal-government/

Table 8.5 Higher Education investment in Research and Development

Economic Record US 2023	Rate	Proportion	$US
GDP			28 trillion[a]
GDP Growth	3.2%/year[b]		896 billion
National R&D investment		3.8% of GDP growth	34 billion
Higher education R&D investment[c]		12% of National R&D	4.1 billion

[a] Gross Domestic Product, Fourth Quarter and Year 2023 (Second Estimate). In. Edited by Commerce Do. Suitland, MD: Bureau of Econopmic Analysis (BEA); 2024.

[b] Ibid.

[c] Research and Development: U.S. Trends and International Comparisons. In. Edited by Foundation NS. Alexandria, VA: National Science Board; 2022.

transfers them to faculties of all kind; in the name of academic freedom the public is enriched with graduates filled with destabilizing wisdom that contributes nothing to constitutionalism, economic growth, or scientific progress.

For example federal funded universities hold DEI offices (Table 8.4). DEI is not science. It is a view that, among others, intends to replace meritocracy by an appreciation scale ensuring that "all employees feel valued."[73]

Meritocracy and DEI are not compatible. However, is *meritocracy* science? Meritocracy is a rewarding scheme favoring successful outcome. It is the fundamental compensating routine of capitalism. Rewarding success was not an invention of eighteenth- to nineteenth-century capitalists. We know that in Bronze-Age Mesopotamia mathematicians knew how to calculate compound interest.[74] Interest rewards investors in a future endeavor. Compound interest favors successive period investors over single period investors by paying for reinvested interest at the end of period. This practice of rewarding contributors to business is not an ideological invention. It is an outcome of the natural supply-and-demand rule. Rewarding a loyal and productive employee more than an average performer has been proven to be fruitful since trade, money, and market places have existed. Meritocracy has been proven to stimulate success. Ensuring that "all employees feel valued" contradicts meritocracy and promotes mediocrity; consequently its side effects are destabilizing (see mathematical substantiation in Chapter 2 and commonsense justification in Chapter 3).

I do not propose to forbid teaching DEI or any other creed; that would violate freedom of religion. However, stability concerns require mentioning in the syllabus that DEI is a persuasion and institutions of higher education should encourage students to balance their consumption of DEI with lectures opposing it.

Equilibrium and Stability

From the point of view of an overall *Equilibrium and Stability* examination, the United States is practically in equilibrium. This is true in spite of alarmist titles of excellent books.[75] If one attached *state variables* to the diagram of Figure 8.1 their yearly average values would show negligible changes.

The question is whether this equilibrium is stable. The main stabilizing factor is American *constitutionalism*; it practically surfaced in 1619, and it has matured during its four centuries of existence. Checks and balances have worked. Centralization slightly increased along the centuries; however, municipal law enforcement fights criminals; states legislate and enforce their laws; democratic elections at all levels of the federation determine who legislators and governors are.

The essential control element balancing legislative and executive actions consists of judicial review. In the United States judicial review is effective in spite of political friction producing unfortunate squeaking complaints and even attempts of de-legitimization. Politicians complain about judicial decisions; however, they realize that the only thing worse than obeying them is disobeying them. The reason for that is constitutionalism, an abstract concept that grew from the concrete sociopolitical practice and several-centuries-old traditions.

We found that there are destabilizing institutions in the system. On one hand the academic institutions have significantly contributed to the unprecedented progress in science, technology; on the other hand the same academic institutions drive destabilizing persuasions braking meritocracy.

The American Academia started off on the wrong foot.[76] It became a powerful engine of science and technology, liberal arts, and humanities. Nevertheless, the credit for American constitutionalism does not belong to the academic elites. The credit goes to "we the people." Constitutionalism constrains all the players to stay on the tracks of a mature and tested Constitution. That is the reason why of all the current democracies America is the most resilient.

Notes

1 5 U.S. Code § 3331.
2 18 U.S. Code 1918.
3 Michael J. Klarman, *The Framers' Coup: The Making of the United States Constitution* (Oxford and New York: Oxford University Press, 2016), 130.
4 Charles Howard McIlwain, *Constitutionalism: Ancient and Modern* (Clark: Lawbook Exchange, 2005), 9.
5 Paraphrasing a Quote by Carl Sagan: "You have to know the past to understand the present." (goodreads.com).
6 Alexis de Tocqueville, *Democracy in America*, trans. Henry Reeve, Kindle edition, vol. 1 (Project Gutenberg, 2006), 233.+
7 Alexander Hamilton, James Madison, and John Jay, *The Federalist Papers* (New York: Bantam Books, 1982). Federalist No 51.
8 Ibid. Federalist No 51.
9 A quote from Chief Justice Charles Evans Hughes in laying the cornerstone for the Supreme Court Building on October 13, 1932.
10 Michael J. Klarman, "Fidelity, Indeterminacy, and the Problem of Constitutional Evil," *Fordham Law Review* 65 (1997):1740–56.
11 Belkin Wireless Cable/DSL Gateway Router.
12 Steven G. Calabresi, "On Originalism in Constitutional Interpretation," National Constitution Center, https://constitutioncenter.org/the-constitution/white-papers/on-originalism-in-constitutional-interpretation.
13 For example one learns that "Roosevelt was forced to rethink the strategy of his New Deal after the Court struck down the National Recovery Act; Jack M. Balkin, "The Roots of the Living Constitution," *Bulletin Review* 92 (2012): 1129–60.
14 Joseph Livni, *The Biblical Roots of American Constitutionalism—from 'I Am the Lord' to 'We the People'* (Lanham: Lexington Books, 2021).
15 "to proclaim liberty to the captives," Isaiah 61:1-11;Liberty "is the privilege of a freeman, since, on the other hand, not to live as a man likes is the mark of a slave Aristotle, Politics 6.2.
16 Tumey v. Ohio, 273 U.S. 523 (1927).
17 Tumey v. Ohio, 273 U.S. 523 (1927).
18 Robert L. Benson et al., *Renaissance and Renewal in the Twelfth Century* (Toronto: University of Toronto Press, 1991), 6; Jean Bodin, *On Sovereignty*, ed. Julian H. Franklin, Cambridge Texts in the History of Political Thought (Cambridge: Cambridge University Press, 1992).
19 See details in Ilie Bădescu and Joseph Livni, eds., *A Civil Society with no Hierarchy* (Lanham: Lexington Books, 2023).
20 Peter Mazzacano, "From Covenant to Compact to Contract: The Legal Transplantation of Puritan Jurisprudence to America," in *A Civil Society with no Hierarchy*, ed. Bădescu and Livni; Daniel J. Elazar, *Covenant and Polity in Biblical*

Israel: Volume 1, Biblical Foundations and Jewish Expressions: Covenant Tradition in Politics (London and New York: Routledge, 2018); Mădălina Mănduță, "The Covenant as Ideal Type, a Sociological Study of a Covenanted Community Model," in *A Civil Society with no Hierarchy*, ed. Ilie Bădescu and Joseph Livni (Lanham: Lexington Books, in 2023 Everett H. Emerson, "Calvin and Covenant Theology," *Church History* 25, no. 2 (1956); David Novak, *Covenantal Rights, a Study in Jewish Political Theory* (Princeton: Princeton University Press, 2000); Irving Louis Horowitz, "Daniel J. Elazar and the Covenant Tradition in Politics," *Publius: The Journal of Federalism* 31, no. 1 (Winter 2001); Charles S. McCoy and Wayne J. Baker, *Fountainhead of Federalism: Heinrich Bullinger and the Covenantal Tradition* (Louisville: Westminster John Knox Press, 1991).

21 Livni, *The Biblical Roots of American Constitutionalism—from 'I Am the Lord' to 'We the People'*; Daniel J. Elazar, *Covenant & Constitutionalism: The Great Frontier and the Matrix of Federal Democracy* (New Brunswick: Transaction Publishers, 1997); Donald S. Lutz, *The Origins of American Constitutionalism* (Baton Rouge: Louisiana State University Press, 1988); Mazzacano, "From Covenant to Compact to Contract: The Legal Transplantation of Puritan Jurisprudence to America."

22 Andorra, Congo, Dominican Republic, Egypt, El Salvador, Haiti, Honduras, Iraq,Jamaica, Laos, Madagascar, Malta, Mauritania, Nicaragua, Palau, Philippines, San Marino, Senegal, Sierra Leone, Suriname, Tonga, West Bank and Gaza see Eloise Barry, *Time*, 2022. Originally Published: May 3, 2022.

23 Roe v. Wade, 410 U.S. 153 (1973).

24 Roe v. Wade, 410 U.S. 157 (1973).

25 Dobbs v. Jackson Women's Health Organization, 597 U.S. (2022).

26 Dobbs v. Jackson Women's Health Organization, 597 U.S. (2022).

27 Dobbs v. Jackson Women's Health Organization, 597 U.S. (2022).

28 For example an Emerson thermostat may replace a Honeywell thermostat.

29 The system did not return to the previous equilibrium; therefore, it was not a stable equilibrium; it did not collapse either; consequently, it was not in an unstable equilibrium.

30 592 U. S. ____ (2020) DAVIS v. ERMOLD—Thomas, J., dissenting.

31 Charlotte-Rose Millar, "Iii. 9 Church and Parish Records," in *Early Modern Emotions*, ed. Susan Brrohall (London and New York: Routledge, 2016); see also Audrey B. Davidson and Robert B. Ekelund Jr., "The Medieval Church and Rents from Marriage Market Regulations," *Journal of Economic Behavior & Organization* 32, no. 2 (1997): 215-45; in Switzerland 1532 Herman Roodenburg, *Social Control in Europe: 1500–1800* (Columbus: Ohio State University Press, 2004), 82–3; in Spain ibid., 268.

32 Historical Records Survey. New York, *Guide to Vital Statistics Records of Churches in New York State (Exclusive of New York City)* (WPA, 1942).

33 Loving v. Virginia, 388 U.S. 1 (1967).

34 576 U.S. 644 (2015) Obergefell v. Hodges.

35 Justice Robert's dissent 576 U.S. 644 (2015) Obergefell v. Hodges.

36 Kathleen Hull, *Same-Sex Marriage: The Cultural Politics of Love and Law* (Cambridge: Cambridge University Press, 2006).

37 Robert Leckey, "Following Same-Sex Marriage: Redefining Marriage and the Impact for Polygamy," *Les ateliers de l'éthique/The Ethics Forum* 2, no. 1 (2007): 30–5.

38 Slavery and gender inequality notwithstanding.

39 Chief Justice Marshall, in Case Gibbons v. Ogden 22 US 1 1824.

40 Herbert Spencer, *Essays, Scientific, Political, and Speculative* (New York: D. Appleton, 1892), 206.
41 The People on the relation of Henry H. Le Roy and others v. Chauncey S. Hurlbut: 24 Mich. 44 cited by Joan C. Williams, "The Constitutional Vulnerability of American Local Government: The Politics of City Status in American Law," *Wisconsin Law Review* (1986).
42 John F. Dillon, *The Law of Municipal Corporations* (New York: James Cockcroft, 1873), 475. Citied by Williams, "The Constitutional Vulnerability of American Local Government: The Politics of City Status in American Law."
43 Preamble of the US Constitution.
44 e.g. Hsi-Huey Liang, *The Berlin Police Force in the Weimar Republic* (Berkley, Los Angeles, and London: University of California Press, 2023), 10.
45 Article VI, Clause 2 of the U.S. Constitution.
46 Alexander Hamilton, "The Federalist # 32 'Founders on Line,'" https://founders.archives.gov/documents/Hamilton/01-04-02-0189; the original source: *The Papers of Alexander Hamilton*, ed. Harold C. Syrett (New York: Columbia University Press, 1962), 461–5.
47 Article I, Section 8 of the US Constitution.
48 Tenth Amendment to the US Constitution.
49 Larry E. Sullivan, *The Sage Glossary of the Social and Behavioral Sciences* (Los Angeles, London, New Delhi, Singapore, and Washington, DC: SAGE Publications, 2009), 97.
50 David A. Schultz, *Encyclopedia of the United States Constitution* (New York: Infobase Publishing, 2010), 5.
51 Except for Defense R&D.
52 Michael J. Klarman, "Rethinking the History of American Freedom (Review Essay of Eric Foner, the Story of American Freedom (1998))," *William & Mary Law Review* 42 (2000).
53 Walter H. Hamilton, "Constitutionalism," in *Encyclopedia of the Social Sciences*, ed. Edwin R. A. Seligman and Alvin Johnson (New York: Macmillan, 1931); McIlwain, *Constitutionalism: Ancient and Modern.*
54 "Southerners equally fought for freedom-the freedom to regulate their own 'domestic institutions.'" Klarman, "Rethinking the History of American Freedom (Review Essay of Eric Foner, the Story of American Freedom (1998))," 268.
55 Ibid.
56 Donald S. Lutz, *Colonial Origins of the American Constitution: A Documentary History* (Indianapolis: Liberty Fund, 1998).
57 Michael Wenzel and Tyler G. Okimoto, "Retributive Justice," in *Handbook of Social Justice Theory and Research*, ed. Clara Sabbagh and Manfred Schmitt (Heidelberg, Dordrecht, and London: Springer, 2016).
58 *Restorative justice* abandons both concepts: crime and punishment (see Chapter 5).
59 Clara Sabbagh and Manfred Schmitt, "Introduction," in *Handbook of Social Justice Theory and Research*, ed. Sabbagh and Schmitt.
60 Oladele Abiodun Balogun, "A Philosophical Defence of Punishment in Traditional African Legal Culture: The Yoruba Example," *The Journal of Pan African Studies* 3, no. 3 (2009): 43–54.

61 Xue Yang, "The Confucianization of Law and the Lenient Punishments in China," *International Journal of Criminal Justice Sciences* 10, no. 1 (2015).
62 Rafael Karsten, *A Totalitarian State of the Past: The Civilization of the Inca Empire in Ancient Peru* (Port Washington and London: Kennikat Press, 1969), 126.
63 Leo Montada and Jürgen Maes, "Introduction," in *Handbook of Social Justice Theory and Research*, ed. Sabbagh and Schmitt.
64 Daniel Siemens, "Explaining Crime: Berlin Newspapers and the Construction of the Criminal in Weimar Germany," *Journal of European Studies* 39, no. 3 (2009): 336-52.
65 The General Lawes and Liberties of the Province of New Hampshire 1679,80 cited by Lutz, *Colonial Origins of the American Constitution: A Documentary History*.
66 Klarman, "Rethinking the History of American Freedom (Review Essay of Eric Foner, the Story of American Freedom (1998))."
67 Olivier Marie, "Education Is Key to Deconstruct Racial Narratives," ed. UN (Paris: UNESCO, 2023).
68 Bernard M. Levinson and Robert P. Ericksen, eds., *The Betrayal of the Humanities: The University during the Third Reich* (Bloomington: Indiana University Press, 2022).
69 The Constitution of the United States.
70 United States Declaration of Independence.
71 Joseph Livni, "Investigation of Collapse of Complex Socio-Political Systems Using Classical Stability Theory," *Physica A: Statistical Mechanics and Its Applications* (2019): 553-62.
72 Not only common sense but even the US civil service subscribes to the primordial importance of teaching sciencehelp_outline, technology, engineering, and mathematics (STEM). For example The Committee on Science, Technology, Engineering, and Math Education (CoSTEM) was established in 2011; CoSTEM coordinates Federal programs and activities in support of STEM education.
73 Michael Boyles, "Dei: What It Is & How to Champion It in the Workplace," Harvard Business School on Line, https://online.hbs.edu/blog/post/what-is-dei.
74 Otto Neugebauer, *The Exact Sciences in Antiquity*, Second edition (New York: Dover Publications, 1969), 34, 44.
75 E. g. John DeQ. Briggs, *America in Turmoil: Essays on Politics, the Economy, Society, and the Future* (Mount Pleasant: Bublish, Incorporated, 2023).
76 Allusion to Harvard's contribution to the Salem witch hunt.

9

Grand Project

The Electric Vehicle

Objective

The previous chapters explained that the resilience of a governmental system is a function of how many *state variables* the government controls. For example, Table 3.1 listed seventeen state variables controlled by the Roman Empire. Reasonably, the empire was involved in more than the listed *state variables.* Needless to say, the current federal government of the United States and the EU council also control more than seventeen *state variables.* The control is carried out according to laws, regulations, and executive orders. Federal administration agencies detect deviations and initiate corrective actions. The previous chapters clarified that corrective actions of one agency have side effects on *state variables* controlled by other agencies. Administration agencies choose their corrective actions from several options; the choices come to the decision table with advantages and disadvantages; the decision is an informed judgment. Often, decisions come with risk mitigation actions. That said, the opportunities for side effects are significant. Consider the following proposal:

> Retraining opportunities for people who are looking to further their employment opportunities at an advanced stage of their careers should also be encouraged by government initiatives.[1]

The panel shall discuss terms like *advanced stage of their careers*, various, initiatives, forms of enrollment, retraining qualifications, employment offers, agencies, effect on other employees, budgetary constraints, travel, lodging, manpower administering the program, and so on. The opportunities for missteps are countless.

This example illustrates that most activities of the civil service involve evaluating options; commonsense discussion compares advantages, disadvantages, risks, and risk mitigation for each choice. In terms of the *theory of equilibrium and stability of complex systems*, the panel determines a corrective action of a *state variable based on* the magnitude of deviation, the range of tolerance, the risks of noncompliance, and the side effects of the corrective action.

Chapter 1 discussed that scientific knowledge requires three steps of the scientific method: observation, theory, and proof. Chapter 1 also distinguishes between various methods of proof; each method relates to a range of confidence in the scientific knowledge. The highest confidence is obtained by combined iterations of mathematical analysis followed by experimental verification until the two methods confirm each other.

There are certain mathematical procedures that cannot be experimentally verified. The most common is extrapolations. For three days in a row the wind blew from the west; stating that the fourth day the wind will also blow from the west is an extrapolation. These quantitative approaches do not result in scientific knowledge. In engineering practice such a conclusion is called *educated guess*; texts of philosophy utilize the term *inductive reasoning* for knowledge acquired by such methods.[2]

The difficulty consists of the fact that research institutions often issue reports describing extensive scientific data collection, data processing, and conclusions using inductive reasoning; these reports make their way together with reports conveying scientific knowledge to discussion tables of governmental agencies.

According to public judgment[3] decisions based on information provided by research institution deserves more confidence than determining the optimal choice in commonsense problems, like the retraining example. This assumption is risky.

Most of the time decision-makers are not aware of the certitude associated with published results; consequently the decision-making is guided by the conception that what comes from scientific institutes is *scientific knowledge*. This conception is in most cases justified; however, one cannot rule out that some reports published by scientific institutes contain conclusions and recommendations stemming from *inductive reasoning*. Making decisions based on information with some uncertainty is not always harmful. One of the cases where such decisions are risky consists of governmental decisions initiating, propping up, guiding, protecting, and funding large scale projects.[4] The greater the scale of the project, the higher the risk of harmful decisions is. This chapter intentionally chose an example of a grand-scale project in order to illustrate the shortcoming of science and technology projects directed by central governments.

The project I chose is the electric vehicle. Before discussing the details, it is important to acknowledge that the electric vehicle promises to be the future of road transportation. Technologically it is simpler than internal combustion vehicle; it has less mechanical intricacies, less moving parts, easier to control, and it promises to reduce maintenance costs. Please, revisit Figure 6.4! Who could foresee in 1885 that Karl Benz's invention will develop into a global fleet of more than a billion vehicles?[5] Who could forecast that descendants of this prototype will roam roads, fields, express ways, carrying goods and passengers, healthy and sick, rich and poor, and crisscross areas of the size of a continent? Yet the prototype evolved into cars, motorcycles, trucks, tractors, buses, and ambulances; the old horse drawn carriage gave way to its swift competitor.

The electric vehicle already possesses most of the advantages of the gasoline engine means of transportation and promises to acquire some advantages over it. However, its main disadvantage consists of cumbersome energy storage and charging. It is more than reasonable to expect that these problems will be solved. As the market forces pushed the horse-drawn carriage to corners of touristic attractions, the electric vehicle will win the economic competition against the internal combustion road transportation. This chapter is not about that competition. The chapter illustrates the risks involved in governmental interference in the pace of the contest. The destabilizing effect consists of governmental corrective actions initiated by ecological predictions coming from research institutions funded by government.

This chapter examines how government control of such a grand-scale endeavor affects the stability of modern democratic societies. The chapter explores how controlling of a typical state variable like *climate change* has side effects with undesirable consequences on other state variables. One of the measures controlling *climate change* consists of *decarbonizing ground transportation.*

Global Warming

Figure 9.1 shows findings of a geological research showing random oscillations around a stable mean temperature for the last 800 millennia.

Climatologists consider Joseph Fourier as the pioneer of the study of greenhouse gases' effects.[6] Another important scientific contribution of Fourier is known as the Fourier series.[7] It serves to analyze time histories like the one of Figure 9.1. It decomposes the history into a series of cyclical events superimposed on a noncyclical trend. One of the difficulties of such an analysis is to separate events of long periods from the noncyclical component of the time history. Fourier demonstrated that the mean of all the observations determines the noncyclical term of the series.[8] The practical difficulty of extracting this term consists of the limited length of the measurements. For example in the 800,000-year-long history the mean is not 0. Either if there is a trend of constant warming or when the measured time history has periodic components having longer than 800,000 years period, the Fourier series will show a positive mean. In other words, the chart of Figure 9.1 cannot tell whether it displays a trend of increasing temperature or a periodic variation with constant average temperature. Appendix C provides a

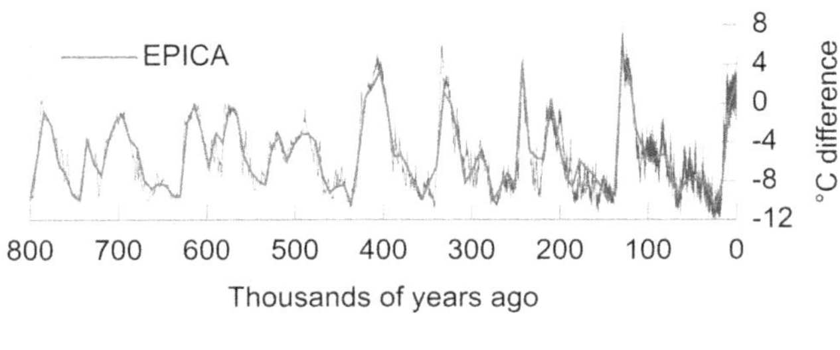

Figure 9.1 Temperature estimates relative to 1950 from over 800,000 years of the EPICA ice cores in Antarctica. The present (1950) is on the right side of the graph. Public Domain. Credit: Autopilot.

rigorous mathematical demonstration of the uncertainty of trends established from a time history like the one of Figure 9.1.

Figure 9.2 is a block diagram explaining how a planet's temperature is kept stable. The planets absorb the sun's warming heat on one hand; on the other hand the planets radiate part of the absorbed heat into the space. During the day temperature rises, and during the night, it cools down because of the outward radiation. The average temperature has been stable due to the stability mechanism of the Planck response (Figure 9.2). If the temperature of the surface rises due to an additional heat source, the radiation to the space is increased; the average temperature is restored.

There are yearly cycles and much longer cycles like the 40,000 years and 100,000 years cycle (Figure 9.1) due to the periodical variation of the Earth's tilt angle and its orbit eccentricity respectively.

Figure 9.2 illustrates natural unbalancing factors. However, there are human unbalancing factors that affect our planet's surface temperature called anthropogenic factors.[9] Human activity increases the concentration of greenhouse gases, often abbreviated as GHG. These gases obstruct earth's radiation into the space having a temperature rise effect similar to the warming effect of walls and roofs of greenhouses.

Figure 9.3 illustrates how the obstruction of the Planck response caused by greenhouse gases generates an additional heat source.

The higher the greenhouse gases concentration in the atmosphere, the higher their heating power is. The heating power, ΔF,[10] is measured in W/m^2 (Watts/meter-squared), indicating that it is a heating energy per unit time and per unit area.

The anthropogenic greenhouse gases effect is perceivable; "State of the Climate 2019"[11] cites three supporting investigations,[12] concluding that recent years show

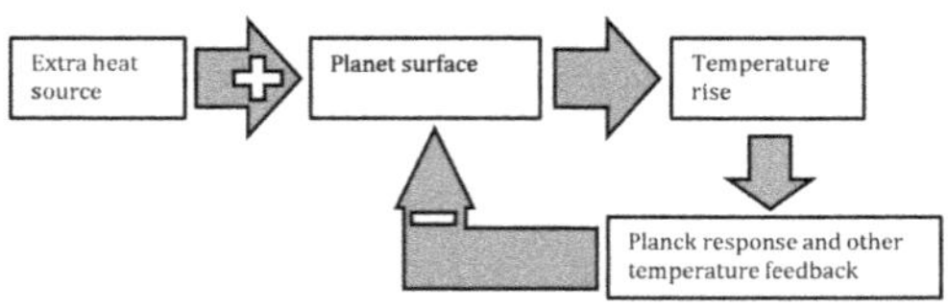

Figure 9.2 Earth Temperature Stability Mechanism. Block Diagram. Author's work.

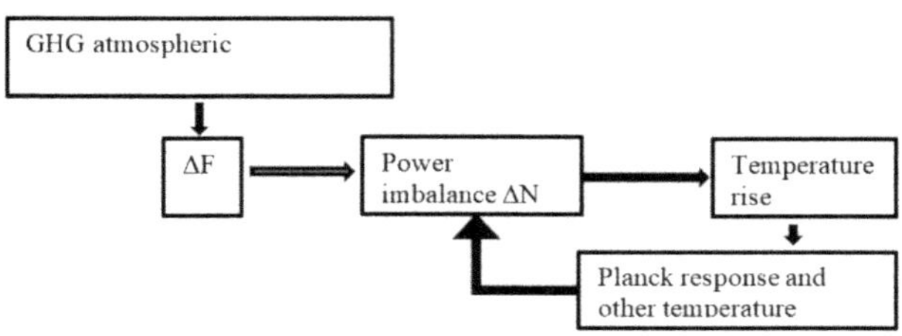

Figure 9.3 Effect of GHG emission to global energy balance. Block diagram. Author's work.

record temperatures both on land and sea. The anthropogenic greenhouse gases factor has set off alarms[13] threatening various aspects of life such as:

a. the survival of certain species[14]
b. human health[15]
c. "irreversible and existential impacts on vulnerable communities and countries across the globe."[16] So far the chapter explored the bad news related to greenhouse gases.

The good news consists of three items:

1. Greenhouse gases are not really news. Carbon dioxide and water vapor have existed in Earth's atmosphere from the first day of the planet;
2. From the earliest days of the planet greenhouse gases acted beneficially controlling the planet's temperature, allowing the appearance of flora, fauna, and human life. Figure illustrates that at equilibrium the concentration of greenhouse gases balance the feedback to warming. Hypothetically extreme reduction of greenhouse gases would reduce the surface temperature to undesirable level.
3. The greenhouse gases' effect is bad news; the good news is that the global warming is limited by a balancing effect (Figure 9.4). In other words the temperature may rise; however, at a point the global average temperature stabilizes. The "irreversible impacts on vulnerable communities" mentioned earlier are real; however, the magnitude of harm is limited.

The average global temperature that will be achieved at equilibrium is the key state variable in global warming. Both the heating due to added greenhouse gas and the

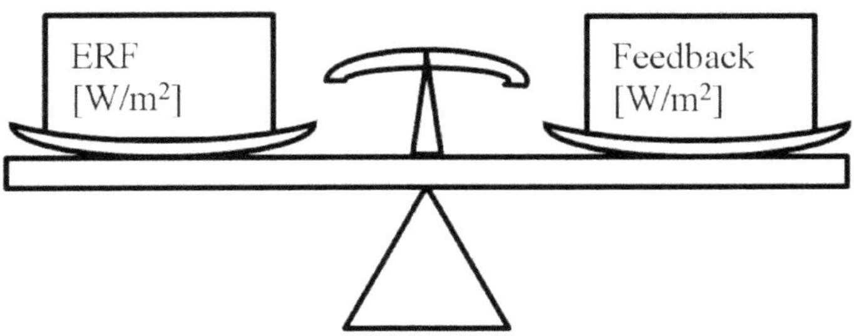

Figure 9.4 Greenhouse gases warm the planet; the warming energy rate is a variable; its symbol is ERF, and it is measured in W/m^2; the feedback response cools down the planet as the temperature rises. The cooling energy rate is also a variable measured in W/m^2. The cooling energy rate increases with the surface temperature. When the cooling energy rate reaches the value of the warming energy rate, an equilibrium is established; at equilibrium the power imbalance $\Delta N=0$ and the average temperature of the planet is steady. Author's work.

Table 9.1 Financial budget and greenhouse gases energy budget analogy; the feedback effects are temperature dependent; The effect a resonsible budget strategy also requires a deficit dependent spending, i.e., if the deficit rises the spending needs to decrease

	Financial Budget	**Greenhouse Gases Energy Budget**
IN	Annual Revenue	ΔF - Heating
OUT	Annual Spending	Feedback effects - Cooling
Difference	Deficit	Temperature

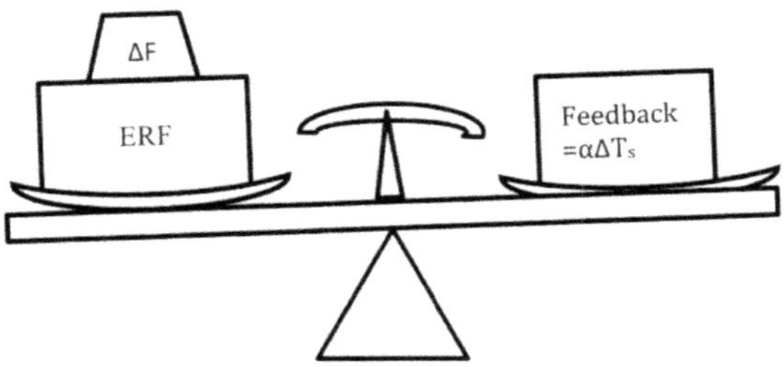

Figure 9.5 An increment of GHG will tip the equilibrium in favor of the ERF side. Author's work.

feedback response cooling are energy rates per unit area; therefore, the balance is similar to a financial budget balance (Table 9.1).

If the heating is increased (left side of the balance), then the balance will tip counter clockwise (Figure 9.5). The surface temperature T_s will rise (see the tipping of the balance in Figure 9.5).

The feedback effects are proportional to the increment of the surface temperature ΔTs; the ratio of proportionality is α; consequently the balancing power αΔTs will also increase (Figure 9.5) and the equilibrium of Figure 9.4 will be restored albeit at an increased surface temperature.

At equilibrium, *heating* balances *cooling* (Figure 9.4) or: $\Delta F = Feedbacks$. The IPCC-2023 report summarizes the sixth assessment of the panel.[17] Table 1 of the IPCC report predicts the temperature rise ΔT for several scenarios. For "an intermediate greenhouse gases emissions scenario (SSP2-4.5)" characterized by a $\Delta F = 4.5 W/m^2$ the report predicts an average global surface temperature rise of 3°C. This scenario "has CO2 emissions remaining around current levels until the middle of the century."[18] The same figure is provided as a best estimate of future warming by the detailed report.[19] A similar calculation has been carried out by Manowitz.[20] Manowitz assumed a forcing function $\Delta F=4W/m^2$; he arrived at 1.1°C. (Figure 9.5) Manowitz applied a greenhouse gas effect/surface temperature ratio $\alpha=-3.7W/(m^2 * {}^\circ K)$ derived by another contribution to Manowitz's workshop.[21] Therefore, Manowitz would arrive at $\Delta Ts = 1.21°C$ for $\alpha=-3.7W/(m^2 * {}^\circ K)$ if he also assumed $\Delta F=4.5W/m^2$ as did the IPCC summary.[22]

The IPCC sixth assessment team has used the same approach to estimate the ratio α.[23] However, their methodology arrives at α=-3.22 and a prediction of $\Delta Ts = 3.9°C$.

Appendix A details a rigorous numerical analysis indicating that the analysis of the IPCC sixth assessment team accounted twice for the greenhouse gas feedbacks. Once they reduced the Planck response as follows

1. They calculated the theoretical value the outward *irradiance*[24] *E* (see Figure) according to the Stefan Boltzmann law: $\left[\frac{W}{m^2}\right] = 5.678 \times 10^{-8} = 398$.
2. They determined the *irradiance* blocked by atmospheric greenhouse gases G (see Figure 9.6) from "current estimates"[25] to be $G\left[\frac{W}{m^2}\right] = 159$.
3. They obtained the ratio $\tilde{g} = \frac{G}{E} = \frac{159}{398} = .4$ (see IPCC report[26]). In other words 40% of the *outgoing (cooling) irradiance E* returns as *incoming (heating) irradiance G* (see Figure 9.6). This result also signifies that the net outgoing irradiance is 60%.
4. If the *total irradiance* $E\left[\frac{W}{m^2}\right] = \sigma T^4$ then the sensitivity of the *total irradiance* to temperature[27] is: $\frac{dE}{dT} = 4\sigma T^3$. For a surface temperature of 287°K corresponding to 57°F this becomes $\frac{dE}{dT} = 4 \times 5.678 \times 10^{-8} \times 287^3 = 5.36$
5. However, the net irradiance is 60% of the total irradiance; consequently the sensitivity of the net irradiance to temperature is $\frac{d\Phi}{dT} = (1 - \tilde{g})4\sigma T^3 = 0.6 \times 4\sigma T^3$ or 60% of the sensitivity of the total irradiance to temperature. This calculation is described in sect the IPCC report.[28] For a surface temperature of 287°K corresponding to 57°F one obtains $0.6 \times .6 \times 4 \times 5.678 \times 10^{-8} \times 287^3 = 3.22$. This result is inserted in the IPCC report[29] as Planck response (the negative sign signifies cooling). Table 9.2 replicates the values of the central estimate of Table 7.10 of the IPCC report.[30] This sensitivity is correct.
6. However, Table 9.2, or Table 7.10 of the IPCC report[31] shows that the AR6 team subtracted again the components of G the greenhouse gas reflection components—water vapor, surface albedo, and clouds—arrived at an irradiance sensitivity of $-1.16\frac{W}{m^2 \times °C}$ and that amounts to double accounting for the greenhouse gas effect:
   a. once they reduced the Stefan-Boltzmann constant[32] by a ratio of $g - 1 = 0.6$; they derived this from the calculation of point 3 above.
   b. once they subtracted the positive greenhouse gas feedbacks from the reduced constant (see Table 9.2).

The IPCC reports of the sixth assessment group needs to be revisited. I contacted Dr. Forster, the leader of Section 7; however I received no reaction.

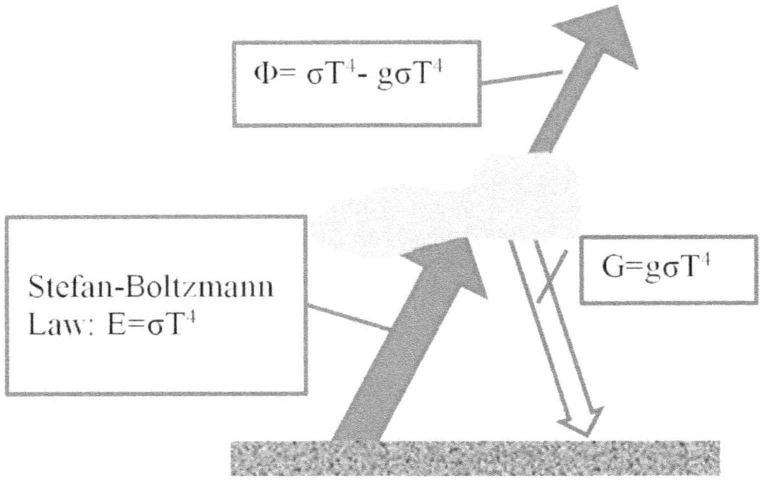

Figure 9.6 G denotes the GHG energy effect; E denotes Earth's outward radiation; Φ denotes the net energy flux leaving the top of the atmosphere. Author's work.

Table 9.2 IPCC AR6 Calculation of Climate Feedbacks—Data from the IPCC Report

Feedback Parameter α [W m^{-2} °C^{-1}]	**AR6 Assessed Ranges Central Estimate**
Planck [W m^{-2} °C^{-1}]	−3.22
WV+LR [W m^{-2} °C^{-1}]	1.30
Surface albedo [W m^{-2} °C^{-1}]	0.35
Clouds [W m^{-2} °C^{-1}]	0.42
Bio-geophysical and non-CO2 bio-geochemical [W m^{-2} °C^{-1}]	0.00
Residual of kernel estimates [W m^{-2} °C^{-1}]	−0.01
Net (i.e., relevant for ECS) [W m^{-2} °C^{-1}]	−1.16

Source: Table 7.10 of Forster P, Storelvmo T, Armour K, Collins W, Dufresne J-L, Frame D, Lunt D, Mauritsen T, Palmer M, Watanabe M: The Earth's energy budget, climate feedbacks, and climate sensitivity, IPCC report. Chapter 7. Cambridge, New York: Cambridge University Press; 2021: 923-1207.

Let us survey other predictions of the expected temperature at equilibrium. The Stefan-Boltzmann radiation is the most significant feedback coefficient, affecting the average surface temperature of the globe. This component of α is in consensus; it follows the proven Stefan-Boltzmann law, which is *scientific knowledge,* and all published works applied it correctly.

The second most significant contributor to α is α_{wv} the effect of tropospheric water vapor. A comprehensive research comprising about 20 models[33] focuses on this contributor. Figure of this chapter reproduces results of the investigation of Chung et al.[34] The values in brackets on the horizontal axis display α_{wv} results of the investigated studies. I calculated for each α_{wv} the corresponding surface temperature increase for a greenhouse gas warming of 4.5 W/m^2 (see the figures above them, displayed without

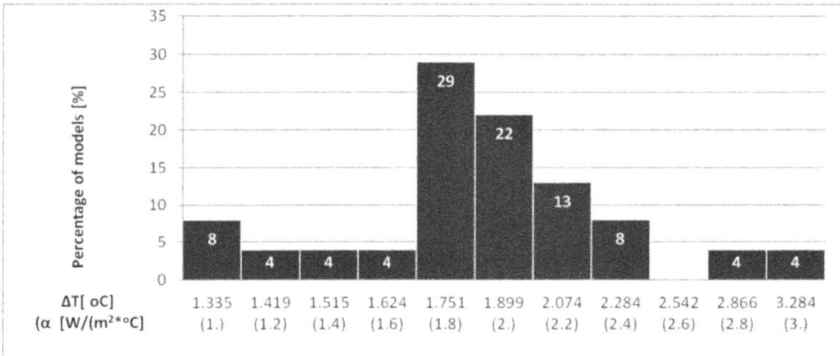

Figure 9.7 Histogram of predicted temperature rise ΔT, at equilibrium for various evaluated values of water vapor feedback coefficient, αwv. Author's work.

brackets). For example, the histogram (Figure 9.7) points out that 22% of the analyses arrived at a water vapor feedback coefficient, α_{wv} of 2 W/(m^{2*o}K]; the resulting global warming at equilibrium would be 1.9°C.

The histogram illustrates results of serious scientific work; however, none of the predicted temperature rise is science; not even the value of 1.751, obtained by most of the investigations is science. The confidence in each predicted temperature rise is low, because the wide range of predictions. Moreover, the use of the mean, median, or the variance of these results is not scientific either. Note that the IPCC report[35] corresponds to the upper bound of the wide range of surface temperature predictions; however, we discussed that the IPCC report is mistaken. This book is not about global warming; it is about stability of democratic regimes. Elected or unelected government officials should take notice that initiating major undertakings based on such results is not only unscientific but also risky. Such steps may strike at the foundations of the regime because actions have side effects and side effects lead to destabilizing vicious circles (see for example Figure 4.5).

Climate Change

Almost every box of the American democratic system (Figure 8.1) is involved with climate change; needless to say the three branches of the US government assume active role in legislating, regulating, and enforcing corrective actions regarding climate change. Every department of the executive branch employs dedicated administrators dealing with climate change. The EPA is probably the strongest contributor in this important endeavor.

> Understanding and addressing climate change is critical to EPA's mission of protecting human health and the environment. EPA tracks and reports greenhouse gas emissions, leverages sound science, and invests in America to combat climate change.[36]

Table 9.3 Climate Change–Related International Accords and Objectives

Year	Name	Objective
1987	Montreal Protocol	Halt ozone gas emission
1997	Kyoto Protocol	Limits on emissions developed countries
2009	Copenhagen Accord	Limit the global temperature rise to below 2°C
2015	Paris Agreement	Temperature rise below 2°C; aspirant to less than 1.5°C

The US government signed international accords mandating the three branches of government to act accordingly. Table 9.3 lists global conventions adopting mutual international agreements in order to stabilize greenhouse gases concentrations and limit their effects.

The previous section discussed the concept of anthropogenic global warming. The section showed that the theory regarding temperature rise makes sense; however, the wide range of numeric estimates indicates that predicting future global temperature increase is not yet proven science. The cause of climate change is commonly linked with global warming.[37] However, climate analysis is more complex than prediction of average global temperature change. Climate involves local temperatures, their variation with latitude, altitude, proximity to ocean, atmospheric pressure changes ocean currents, and consequential winds. The models are complex with many variables. Predicting future temperature is risky; predicting climate change is even more precarious.

The core writing team warns policymakers about "[e]vidence of observed changes in extremes such as heatwaves, heavy precipitation, droughts, and tropical cyclones."[38] Nevertheless, referring to tropical cyclones the information is subject to debate: "claims of linkages between global warming and hurricane impacts are premature."[39]

An original approach linking climate change to anthropogenic factors consists of correlating demographic variations in specific species living in particular climate ranges. For example, "[s]pecies' range boundaries have shifted polewards with a mean velocity of 6 km per decade, as well as upward in elevation."[40] Reasonably, anthropogenic-induced climate change is the primary suspect as far as the driver of such habitat relocations is concerned:

> However, the probability of successfully attributing climatic trends to greenhouse gases declines sharply at spatial scales smaller than 10^6 km^2 and at temporal scales shorter than 50 years.[41]

This argument is similar to the Fourier analysis examining cyclical temperature variations discussed earlier in section *Global Warming* above. Determining variations in time and space backed by scientific data is legitimate science. Establishing trends from these data is valid for a given range in time and space. Extrapolating these trends beyond the limits is not science. That does not mean that it is impossible to prove that greenhouse gases are drivers of global warming and climate change. It only means that the current methods of data processing are useless. The scientific community should keep trying other methods of proving the case for anthropogenic factors driving climate change. After all, scientific research has transposed several reasonable theories into proven knowledge.

Apparently, we are not yet on solid scientific ground as far as climate change is concerned. Theories and assumptions are a step of the scientific method. As long as knowledge consists of theory, it is not yet science. Theories are discussed, published, and debated. Publications are followed by rebuttals. Once a theory is proven it becomes science.

A scientific analysis[42] questioning the link between extreme climate events and global warming has been submitted, peer-reviewed, published, and subsequently retracted without the authors' consent.

First the article was placed "under dispute" based on personal opinions expressed by some scientists to a journalist of *The Guardian* newspaper.[43] Needless to say, personal opinions of scientists are not science, and *The Guardian* is not a guardian of science. The contesting arguments consisted of objections like the following:

> The choice of figures and sections headings focuses on results which can be used to make the case that extremes and/or their impacts are not increasing while ignoring other results which show that some extremes are increasing.[44]

The AFP article[45] summarized this approach as providing "cherry-picked" information. The article of Alimonti et al.[46] presents facts and demonstrates links and lack of links between facts. Even if one admitted that the article intentionally selected only information favorable "to make the case that extremes and/or their impacts are not increasing," the approach is justified. Cherry-picking is not sufficient to prove a hypothesis; however, it is sufficient to disprove one. If I claimed that my bank account was never overdrawn, the bank official can disprove my claim with one single "cherry-picked" monthly report. Consequently, the retraction of the article made a huge disservice to science, not only by disqualifying good peer-reviewed scientific analysis but mainly by casting doubt on the scientific value of many valuable papers making the case for anthropogenic climate change.

After all, this retraction reminds of another similar case. In the days of Pope Urban VIII, Galilei published his *Dialogue on the Two World Systems* (1632). The book[47] defended heliocentrism in a fictional conversation between three characters. The Inquisition found the book guilty of heresy. Galilei retracted the book. Nevertheless, according to rumors he did utter the famous words: "eppur si muove."

An overwhelming majority of scientists hold true that climate changes, that its cause is global warming, and its main contributor is human activity.[48] This argument does not prove that the theory is either true or not true. The number of researches grows with the value of grants funding them[49] and accepting grants significantly contribute to "strengthening researchers' career positions."[50] Typically climate change research grant applications are accepted as follows:

> In summer 2022, we accepted applications for projects focused on identifying, accelerating, and evaluating climate mitigation solutions and strategies that will

> contribute to achieving net-zero greenhouse gas emissions in Canada. Approved projects are underway.[51]

Reasonably, a grant application for research questioning the urgency of climate mitigation has a small chance of being accepted. Therefore the overwhelming majority of publications addressing the imminent threat of climate change may also be explained by the overwhelming majority of grants accepted for this research. On the other hand, this reasoning does not imply that one should not take climate change seriously.

Climate change is a serious subject, and it is seriously investigated. However, one should conclude that so far postulations regarding the linkage between climate change and anthropogenic global warming have not yet been scientifically proven. Table 9.3 proves that in spite of the weak scientific foundation, governments commit to binding accords using science as justification. The cost of compliance with international are estimated:

> An increase of at least 590% in annual climate finance is required to meet internationally agreed climate objectives by 2030 and to avoid the most dangerous impacts of climate change.[52]

The benefits are implied: it is about saving the planet. International and national governments take this mission seriously, and that is good news. In current political jargon there are "climate change deniers";[53] the opposition to climate change is less lucrative than anticipating environmental disaster. Nevertheless, this chapter does not endorse either of the climate camps; the message of this chapter is that both opinions are substantiated by immature science. Doing nothing about climate change is not sensible. However, signing binding commitments is equally unsafe. One should be less enthusiastic about international obligations because commitments require corrective action; such measures have side effects and lead to dangerous vicious circles of good intentions leading to bad results.

CO_2 Emission

The industrialized world has accelerated its utilization of fuel combustion motors in transport (on ground, in waterways, and in air), manufacturing, agriculture, and so on. The quality of life has significantly improved. However, improvements have side effects. One of the undesirable side effects of mechanization consists of increased CO_2 emissions. Figure 9.8 plots CO_2 emission data from published statistics.[54]

No doubt, emission of greenhouse gases is a major concern of anthropogenic *climate change.* Carbon dioxide (CO_2) is considered the prominent substance among greenhouse gases because it hangs on in the atmosphere for thousands of years. Opposed to that, water vapor condenses very fast, leaving the atmosphere as rain; methane's lifespan is about 10 years.[55]

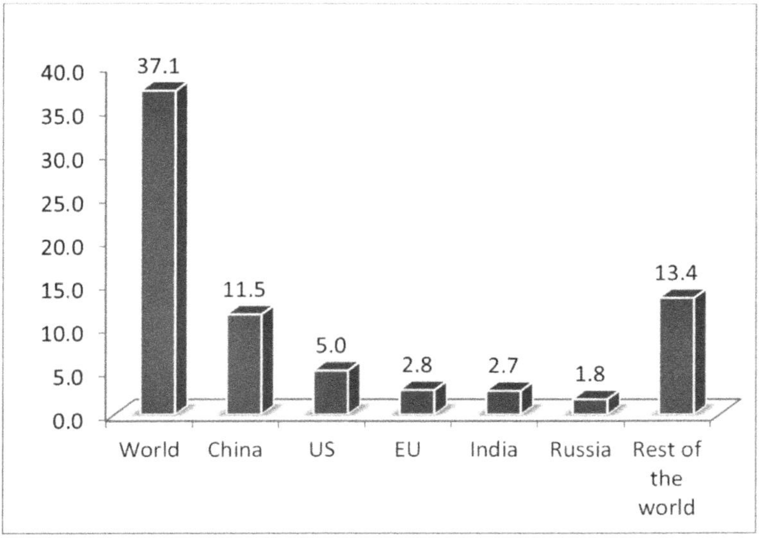

Figure 9.8 Major CO_2 emissions from fossil fuels [GT/year] in 2021. Author's work.

Increased CO_2 emission increases global warming, and very likely it affects climate change (see sections *Global Warming* and *Climate Change* in this chapter). The CO_2 concentrations in the atmosphere have produced intense activity in the political sphere of the planet. For example, in 2005 the 11th Conference of the Parties to the Kyoto protocol held in Montreal, Quebec, Canada, hosted more than 10,000 delegates representing the concerns of their respective governments in fighting greenhouse gas emissions. The purpose of these global conferences is clear:

> The ultimate objective of the United Nations Framework Convention on Climate Change (UNFCCC) is to stabilize atmospheric concentrations of greenhouse gases at a level that will prevent dangerous interference with the climate system.[56]

Undoubtedly, the political activity has been inspired by science. However, scientific investigations show not only uncertainty in the relation between CO_2 emission and CO_2 concentration[57] but also ambiguity in the expression "a level [of greenhouse gases concentration] that will prevent dangerous interference with the climate system."[58]

The weak connection between science and UNFCC is anticipated. For better or for worse, global politics frequently references scientific works. In this particular case postulating that CO_2 emissions increase warming and have a potential of changing climate is reasonable theory. However, representing one's government and one's governmental institution does not necessarily require distinguishing between reasonable and proven theory. Moreover, the priority of political delegates consists of promoting objectives of their respective governmental institution. This explains why delegates sign accords requiring safe levels of CO_2 emissions (Table 9.3), even though science has not yet established such safe levels.

The world total CO_2 emission in 2022 was of 3715 MT/year.[59] The share of road transport of global CO_2 emissions was 11.9%.[60] In other words the CO_2 emissions of road transportation consisted of 442 MT/year. Complying with requirements of global agreements constrains national governments to determine arbitrary safe levels because science has not yet determined them. For example in the United States,:

> On April 12, 2023, EPA announced new, more ambitious proposed standards to further reduce harmful air pollutant emissions from light-duty and medium-duty vehicles starting with model year 2027. The proposal builds upon EPA's final standards for federal greenhouse gases emissions standards for passenger cars and light trucks for model years 2023 through 2026 and leverages advances in clean car technology to unlock benefits to Americans ranging from reducing climate pollution, to improving public health, to saving drivers money through reduced fuel and maintenance costs. The proposed standards would phase in over model years 2027 through 2032.[61]

The previous example sets standards for road vehicles. Obviously the standards have good intentions. The following sections examine their effectiveness and their undesirable side effects.

Decarbonizing Transportation

If "we could electrify the whole road transport sector, and transition to a fully decarbonized electricity mix, we could feasibly reduce global emissions by 11.9%." This amounts to a decrease of 0.445 GT CO_2 emissions/year.

Sixty percent of total electric power generation in the United States is from fossil fuels, mostly from natural gas and coal.[62] The efficiency of these power generators is 36%;[63] it is about the same as internal combustion motors of ground transportation vehicles.[64] Therefore under current conditions if one electrified the whole transport sector one would reduce carbon emissions by 4.9%. Reasonably, this would reduce the CO_2 concentrations in the atmosphere; however, as explained earlier, current science does not predict by how much.

Nevertheless, governments vigorously focus on decarbonizing transportation. For example in the United States,:

> The domestic transportation sector presents an enormous opportunity to drastically reduce emissions that accelerate climate change and reduce harmful pollution.[65]

Governments have good intentions. They are democratically elected to serve the people. The problem is that governments do not have the capability to foresee the side effects of well-intentioned measures. One of the disciplines where side effects are foreseeable is economy. Economy 101 teaches that capitalist market economy is subject to the law of supply and demand. This law turns off pointless initiatives. Government decisions constrain the market; they tip the balance of the law of supply and demand favoring initiatives by financing investment, by taxation of adverse supply and by regulating unwanted demand.[66]

The economic side effects are usually foreseeable. Public investment in decarbonizing road transports allocates less investment in essential tasks of government: justice, defense, and public works.[67]

In North America, Western Europe, and Oceania climate investments were primarily funded by private sources.[68] As mentioned earlier, private financing takes place at favorable market conditions. However, noncommercial road transport has been financed due to government interference in the market "building on multiple years of government subsidy policies and falling technology costs."[69]

The legislative and executive branches of the US government are democratically elected. Undoubtedly, they have complete authority to allocate all necessary funds to combat future calamities. The EPA, for example, makes sure that "[n]ational efforts to reduce environmental risks are based on the best available scientific information."[70] This is good news; the bad news is that the best scientific information is not the same as proven science. The Energy Efficiency and Renewable Energy (EERE) "is the largest investor in clean energy technology development."[71] The investment objectives include decarbonizing transportation of all kinds:

> Decarbonizing transportation across all modes: air, sea, rail, and road: EERE will develop, demonstrate, and deploy technologies that can cost-effectively decarbonize all modes of transportation, including electrification of on-road vehicles, sustainable aviation fuel, and hydrogen fuel cells for long-haul heavy-duty truck.[72]

Chapter 2 showed how instability is caused by bad side effects of good intentions. Usually, executives cannot foresee hidden side effects. In this particular case the US government not only ignored negative outcomes but also concluded that decarbonizing transportation comes with a wide range of beneficial side effects like:

> improved transportation services; more mobility choices; improved air quality and health; greater energy security; better quality of life and accessibility; improved health outcomes; enhanced access to a variety of housing options, services, and amenities; well-paying jobs; and safer, more vibrant and resilient communities throughout the country.[73]

The next section looks through risks of such governmental endeavors.

Risk and Mitigation

This section scrutinizes the potential of undesirable side effects of mandatory replacement fossil fuel vehicles with electric ones. Chapter 2 discusses that such side effects are potential components of hidden feedback loops; as mentioned earlier such loops increase the likelihood of destabilizing the equilibrium of the regime.

Feasibility

An engineering project starts with a feasibility study. Here I propose to analyze the contribution of decarbonizing US vehicles to reducing greenhouse gas emissions. Two reasons come to mind why the United States is relevant:

a. The United States has the highest number of cars/capita which is 0.9 cars per capita.[74] This number is equaled only by New Zealand; reasonably, the United States is more relevant than New Zealand as far the global fight against climate change is concerned
b. The United States has the second largest greenhouse gas emission next to China (Figure 9.8). As opposed to China, the United States is a democracy; moreover, US statistics are available and reliable.

Table 9.4 estimates that decarbonizing every vehicle in the United States would reduce the US contribution to the yearly greenhouse gas emissions; the estimated range is 0.27 TG CO_2 to .92 TG CO_2. This value represents 5.4–18% of total US emissions (see Table 9.4) or 2.5–7% of total world greenhouse gas emissions

Batteries

The battery is an essential component of electric vehicles. The battery is responsible for the high initial *cost* of an electric vehicle.[75] The life expectancy of a vehicle is about

Table 9.4 Greenhouse gas emission reduction due to decarbonizing road transport

#	Description	Unit	Value		Explanation
1	Fuel economy	mpg	25.4[a]		
2	Emission CO^2	Kg/gallon	8.10[b]		
3	Total highway	miles	3.26×10^{12} [c]		
4	Total Gallons consumed	gallons	1.284×10^{11}		*Line* 3/ *Line* 1
6	Total emission reduction	GT CO_2	1.0405		*Line* 2 x *Line* 4/10^{12}
7	Emission increase caused by manufacturing batteries	GT CO_2	Low 0.115	High 0.771	See Table 9.5
8	Net emission reduction		High 0.925	Low 0.27	*Line* 6 — *Line* 7

a) US Government EPA: EPA Report: U.S. Cars Achieve Record High Fuel Economy and Low Emission Levels as Companies Fully Comply with Standards. In. Edited by EPA. Washington, DC: https://www.epa.gov/newsreleases/epa-report-us-cars-achieve-record-high-fuel-economy-and-low-emission-levels-companies; 2021.
b) US Government EIA: Carbon Dioxide Emissions Coefficients. In. Edited by EIA. Washington, DC: https://www.eia.gov/environment/emissions/co2_vol_mass.php; 2023.
c) US Government BTS: U.S. Vehicle-Miles. In: Table 1-35. Edited by Transportation Do. Washington, DC: Bureau of Transportation Statistics; 2022

fifteen years; however, the battery has a significantly shorter lifespan.[76] One needs more than one battery for an EV. The procedure of disposal of used batteries is by itself an ecological unknown (see the following paragraphs). The additional batteries and their disposal increase the cost of EV even more.

There are *ecological* side effects caused by the manufacture and disposal of batteries. For example:

1. Manufacture—Table 9.5 estimates the rise in greenhouse gas emissions that the current battery manufacturing process implies.
2. End-of-Life—current research examines methods of mitigating disposal risks. The most evident risks are:
   a. reactivity and ignitability hazards;[77] As a consequence:
      i. In the United States the disposal requires professional handlers to assure compliance with several regulations.[78]
      ii. In the EU the European Council mandates an Extended Producer Responsibility (EPR) for batteries; this means that producers or importers of batteries are responsible for "reducing overall resource use, in particular by reducing the generation of waste batteries and the adverse impacts linked to the management of waste batteries."[79]
      iii. In the UK rules mandate an Extended Producer Responsibility for Lithium-Ion Battery end-of-life management.[80]
   b. dangerous levels of ecotoxic heavy metals such as lead, nickel, and cobalt[81]

Current research deals mainly with two approaches to mitigate the risks involved with handling batteries after end-of-life:

a. Recycling
b. Second life

Table 9.5 Green house gas emissions caused by manufacturing batteries

Line	Description	Units	Lower bound	Upper bound	Calculation
1	Emissions per battery	KG CO_2/battery	2,400[a]	16,000[b]	
2	Number of vehicles in US	millions	289[c]	289	
3	Emissions of US vehicles	MT CO_2	694	4,624	*Line* 2 × *Line* 3
4	Lifespan of battery	years	6	6	
5	Yearly CO_2 emissions	GT CO_2	.116	.771	*Line* 3/*Line* 4

Source Compiled by the author using data from:

a) How much CO_2 is emitted by manufacturing batteries? [https://climate.mit.edu/ask-mit/how-much-co2-emitted-manufacturing-batteries].

b) Ibid.

c) US Vehicle Registration Statistics [https://hedgescompany.com/automotive-market-research-statistics/auto-mailing-lists-and-marketing/].

Free market demand does not yet drive battery *recycling*. "Recycling of LIB is currently low, mainly driven by legislation."[82] One of the costly materials of Li-ion batteries is lithium. However, the current technology of extracting lithium from used batteries is not yet cost effective.[83] The good news is that the US government is financially engaged in the research of recycling batteries (Table 9.6). The bad news is that the feasibility of the EV project essentially hinges on the battery research, development, manufacturing, logistic support, maintenance, and end-of-life management. Since all these are immature,[84] governments legislating mandatory transfer to battery dependent EV vehicle is not advisable.

In other words, there is a hasty optimism in executive orders like the one mandating that "by 2035, all new cars and passenger trucks sold in California be zero-emission vehicles."[85] The Lithium-ion Car Battery Recycling Advisory Group "of California has concluded its work for which it was established" in 2022.[86] The advisory group acknowledged the end-of-life management is still in basic research phase:

> The Lithium-ion Car Battery Recycling Advisory Group will meet at least quarterly and will consult with universities and research institutions that have conducted research in the area of battery recycling, with manufacturers of electric and hybrid vehicles, and with the recycling industry.[87]

Universities and research institutions are indeed engaged in basic research of mitigating ecological risks of extracting materials, manufacture, recycling and end-of-life treatment of EV batteries (Table 9.6). Basic research is phase one of innovative technological processes. The basic research is validated by applied research and development phases. Therefore, the California ban on gas-powered vehicles is premature. So are similar government directives. This example illustrates faulty management of engineering projects; however, I included this example in this book in order to illustrate how premature legislation has a potential of unintended side effects; Chapter 2 explains how such adverse unintended consequences play a destabilizing role.

Second Life of EV batteries is another mitigating measure currently researched. It consists of using the batteries after end-of-life in vehicle use. An EV battery must be replaced when it signals a drop of 20% from the rated power of the battery.[88]

Table 9.6 Grants—US Government—EV Batteries

Item	Grants	Objective
Materials	$3 billion	North American EV Battery Supply Chain
Manufacture	$3 billion	Building, retooling, extending manufacturing and recycling facilities
Recycling	$60 million	Research, development, and demonstration of recycling
Retail	$15 million	Cooperation
State/Local Gov.	$50 million	Cooperation
Reuse	$200 million	Recycling and second-life applications
Other	$750 million	Advanced Energy Manufacturing and Recycling Grant Program

This means that the battery can still provide power for electric power needs such as night compensation for off-grid solar power systems and RV and camper batteries. Technically speaking the proposal is feasible. However, so far, the examples of such use are by universities, research institutions, and various automakers testing the commercial feasibility of the idea.[89] Commercially speaking there is a cost in matching supply and demand when paying customers are involved. This cost is unknown. Nevertheless, the benefit of this plan may be estimated.

The life expectancy of a Li-ion battery for a primary use to power an EV vehicle is eight years.[90] I calculated the life history; assuming a decay of 2.8%/year in eight years the battery reaches 80% of its initial capacity and it must be replaced (Figure). In a second-life the battery is usable until it reaches 60% of its initial capacity.[91] An estimate of a similar decay of 2.8%/year during the second life of the battery is reasonable.[92] Figure 9.9 indicates an addition of ten more years until the end of second life of the battery.

Research estimates that by the year 2024, one would be sold cumulatively 45 million EV.[93] If the batteries were used for a primary life only, this will produce a total of 68.4 MT[94] of disposed batteries in 2032. Practicing secondary life batteries this same amount will be reached only ten years later, that is, in 2042. Figure evaluates the advantage of the second-life battery practice. It shows how many batteries per vehicle one would discard with or without second-life practice

For example in 25 years each driven vehicle would use up three batteries without second-life practice and about 1.5 batteries practicing second-life batteries. Figure 9.10

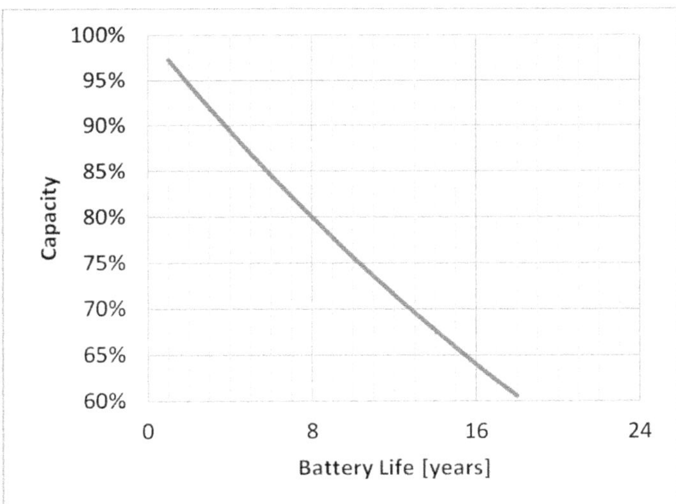

Figure 9.9 The battery weakening initial capacity is represented by a decay of 2.8%/ year; in eight years the battery reaches 80% of its initial capacity and is not usable in EV; another ten years the battery can function in a second-life application when at age eighteen it reaches its end of life. Author's work.

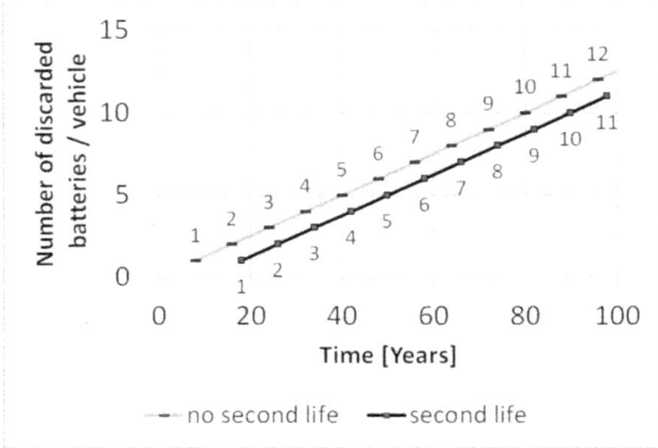

Figure 9.10 EV batteries. The benefit of second-life practice. Author's work.

Table 9.7 Charging duration of EV

Level	Outlet [V]	Duration [hours]	Miles added
1 - Home	120	8	40
2 – Home and Public	240	8	190
DC Fast		.5	50-170

also shows that as time goes by the advantage diminishes. In a hundred years the estimated benefit of second-life battery program is less than 10% in accumulated weight of disposed batteries.

Charging

One of the drawbacks of EV is related to charging the battery. The charging time depends on the battery, the amount of miles added to the vehicle, and the electric outlet (AC-120V, AC-240V, DC). Table 9.7 summarizes charging durations according to Union of Concerned Scientists a nonprofit organization founded by scientists and students at MIT.

Anotherst critical aspect of conversion to EV consists of the infrastructure required to build charging stations along highways, roads, and in public parking lots of communities, workplaces, and public establishments. Table 9.8 sums up the challenges projected by governments in the United States and the EU related to the endeavor of converting the current gas station network to electric charging.

The comparison between the United States and the EU is not straightforward. The US data are government budgetary figures submitted and approved by Congress either in the Infrastructure Investment and Jobs Act of 2021 or in the Inflation Reduction Act of 2022 (IRA). Reasonably these figures represent the share of the taxpayer in directly funding the project. The EU data, however, sum up the projected cost of the project unrelated to either public or private investment.

Table 9.8 United States and EU—EV Charging Station Infrastructure Plans for 2023–30

Description	US EV Charging Plan	EU EV Charging Plan
Number of charging points	500,000[a]	3,400,000[b]
Total Cost Estimate	$7.5 billion[c]	€240 billion[d] to €280 billion[e]
Ratio of public investment	100%	To be determined[f]
Number of registered vehicles in 2021	289 million[g]	250 million

Compiled by the author from the following sources:

[a] Granholm JM, Buttigieg P, Regan M, Fudge M: The U.S. National Blueprint for Transportation Decarbonization. In: *A Joint Strategy to Transform Transportatio.* Edited by Departments of Energy T, Housing, and EPA. Washington D.C.: US Government; 2022.

[b] Conzade J, Nägele F, Ramanathan S, Schaufuss P: Europe's EV opportunity—and the charging infrastructure needed to meet it. *McKinsey & Company* 2022.

[c] Harris K: FACT SHEET: The Biden-Harris Electric Vehicle Charging Action Plan. Washington D.C. US Government The White House; 2021.

[d] Conzade J, Nägele F, Ramanathan S, Schaufuss P: Europe's EV opportunity—and the charging infrastructure needed to meet it. *McKinsey & Company* 2022.

[e] European EV Charging Infrastructure Master Plan In. Brussels: ACEA - European Automobile Manufacturers' Association; 2022, 7.

[f] Ibid., 65.

[g] US Vehicle Registration Statistics [https://hedgescompany.com/automotive-market-research-statistics/auto-mailing-lists-and-marketing/].

The private vehicle owner funds the project; after all, he/she pays the public investment as taxpayer and the private investment as consumer. Since the number of vehicles in the United States is comparable to the one in the EU (Table 9.8), the EU figures should be considered as relevant for the cost to vehicle owners in both the United States and EU.

If in the United States the private sector will not contribute its share, then the US blueprint for decarbonizing road transport will not materialize. The decarbonization endeavor will not "make EVs accessible to all Americas for both local and long-distance trips."[95] The cost estimate of the EU has two figures: €240 billion and €280 billion. The latter figure includes corresponding investment in renewable energy sources; as explained earlier (subsection *Decarbonizing transportation*), if the electric power source consists of fossil fuels the greenhouse gas emission decline is negligible.

Electricity Production

Not surprisingly, an EV consumes electric power. Is there sufficient electric power supply for the conversion of all vehicles to EV? Table 9.9 calculates that the EV project requires an additional 2.32 million MWh yearly energy production in order to cover the US road decarbonization project. In 2022 the United States produced 4.2 million MWh electric energy,[96] of which .9 million MWh was produced from renewable source.[97] As a consequence, an effective road decarbonization requires increasing the renewable energy production 4.67-fold. However, one needs to consider the rate of supplying this energy, which is known as power.

Table 9.9 Calculation of Yearly Energy Consumption Required for the Conversion of All Vehicles to Electric Energy

Line	Description	Value	Explanation
1	Gasoline USA [Gallons/year]	1.36×10^{11}[a]	
2	Gasoline kWh/Gal	33[b]	
3	Energy [KWh]	4.50×10^{12}	Line1×Line2
4	Gasoline engine efficiency	0.36[c]	
5	EV efficiency	0.7[d]	
6	Electric Energy Required [Kwh]	2.32×10^{12}	Line3×Line5/Line4
7	Average duration of charging [h]	.5	Table 9.7
8	Electric Power Required KW	4.64×10^{12}	Lin6/Line 7

Compiled by author from the following sources:
[a] US Government EIA, "Gasoline Explained," Department of Energy (Washington DC: Independent Statistics and Analysis, 2023).
[b] The energy content of one gallon of gasoline is about 113,000 BTU, US Government - EPA, "Fuel Economy Impact of Rfg," in EPA 420-F-95-03, EPA (Washington D,C.: EPA Office of mobile source, 1995), ;in KWh it is 113,000 BTU//3,412BTU/Kwh=33.1 kWh.
[c] E.g., 36–38% in gasoline engines Wang, Zhijian, Shijin Shuai, Zhijie Li, and Wenbin Yu, "A Review of Energy Loss Reduction Technologies for Internal Combustion Engines to Improve Brake Thermal Efficiency," Figure 1.
[d] Julio A Sanguesa et al., "A Review on Electric Vehicles: Technologies and Challenges," Smart Cities 4, no. 1 (2021): 372–404, 373.

Line 8 of Table 9.9 assumes that all the US vehicles are charged simultaneously; it arrives at an electric power supply of about 4.64 million MW. Reasonably this energy will be supplied during 8 hours spread uniformly among vehicles. Thus the expected power should be about one third of the amount specified, that is, 1.55 million MW. The electric power supplied in 2022 in the United States was 1.16 million MW,[98] of which .332 million MW were produced by renewable source. Consequently, one needs to increase the electric power capacity by 155% to supply the demand of EV chargers and the renewable power by 466% in order to achieve the expected decarbonizing effect.

The increase of the electric power capacity by 155% is a separate engineering project; at first sight it seems feasible. The following sections of this chapter examine the side effects of converting all electric power production to renewables; after all the unintended side effects are the destabilizing terms of government endeavors.

> The exponential increase of the industrial use of electrical power and the communication technologies place the biosphere and mankind in conditions dramatically different than in the middle of the twentieth century.[99]

Reasonably, an increase of 155% of electric power involves an increase of 155% of electricity transmission lines. The ecological side effects of transmission lines include bird collision, avoiding crossing landscape portions, constraints on nest and rest sites, bird electrocution, diminishing suitable areas for reproduction of certain bird species, fire risk, noise effects, and soil degradation.[100] Researchers study technical complications and risks due to electromagnetic interference with electronic equipment.[101]

The following paragraphs address hazards that high-voltage electric transmission lines pose to humans. This work is not a complete review of health problems caused by electric transmission. It is intended to focus on researches warning of bad side effects of modern electric power transmission.

Studies of risk to exposure to electromagnetic fields in the proximity of high-voltage electric transmission lines are mostly statistical in nature. Statistical researches establish that among people who have been subjected to longer and stronger electromagnetic fields the incidence of a certain disease is higher than among people who were less exposed. This indicates that exposure to electromagnetic fields in the proximity of power lines causes the disease; however, it does not give details how exposure causes disease. Several studies reveal that "ELF exposure causes significant changes in cell survival, cell cycle, progression, DNA integrity, and proliferation."[102] "Science knows very little if anything about the effects of non-ionizing radiation."[103] Moreover, "it is unfortunate that the evidence regarding the majority of suggested exposures is limited and often contradictory."[104]

Nevertheless, among others, it was established that:

> Dermal fibroblasts that were exposed to 1 mT from one to five hours showed a reduction of their viability,[105] while the repetitive exposure to MF with ELF induced DNA double-strand breaks and apoptosis in lung fibroblasts.[106]

However, often the incidence of the disease in a population is either unknown or irrelevant; for example in investigating the risk of cancer among electric line maintenance workers, the incidence of cancer in the general population is irrelevant. The purpose of the examination is the risk associated with high exposure of power line electricians. In this case one compares electricians who were exposed to high level of electromagnetic fields (case group) to electric line workers who were not highly exposed (control group).

So far one can deduct that the three measures (SIR, OR, RR; see more in Chapter 1) indicate the risk of disease caused by electric lines. For example the OR of contracting acute non-lymphoid leukemia found for electric utility workers with high exposure is 1.91. The 95% confidence interval is 0.19–19.4 (Table 9.10). The leukemia odds of an electrician highly exposed to electromagnetic fields are about twice as much as the odds of an unexposed electrician. This is what the test found in the sample.

Table 9.11 lists examples of studies indicating that electric utility workers carry higher risk to contract cancers than the population at large. For example case-control tests of acute non-lymphoid leukemia consisted of four groups of electricians:

1. Electricians exposed to more than a time averaged magnetic field exceeding 4.7μT and contracted the disease; their number is N_{xl}
2. Electricians exposed to more than a time averaged magnetic field exceeding 4.7μT and contracted the disease; their number is N_{x0}
3. Electricians not exposed to more than a time averaged magnetic field exceeding 4.7μT however they contracted the disease; their number is N_{cl}
4. Electricians not exposed to more than a time averaged magnetic field exceeding 4.7μT and did not contract the disease; their number is N_{c0}

Table 9.10 Occupational Hazards, Electric Utilities Workers, Very High Exposure to Electric Lines

Disease	Identification	Significance		Exposure
		OR	95% CI	
Cancer	All cancers[a]	1.38	1.05–1.8	≥ 90th percentile
Leukemia	Chronic lymphoid[a]	2.98	0.2–41.7	
	Chronic lymphoid[b]	3.7	1.8–7.7	TWA* ≥ 4.7μT
	Non-Hodgkin's lymphoma[c]	1.8	0.62–5.25	≥ 90th percentile
	Acute non-lymphoid[d]	2.6	1.3–5.4	TWA* ≥ 4.7μT
	All type[e]	1.5	1.2–1.8	> 10 years
Brain cancer	All type[f]	1.9	0.48–7.58	≥ 90th percentile
	Brain tumors[g]	3.1	1–8.7	≥ 90th percentile
	Astrocytoma[h]	6.26	0.3–132	≥ 90th percentile
Breast cancer	Men[i]	6.0	1.7–21	All categories
Lung cancer	All type[j]	8.44	2.95–24	≥ 90th percentile

1. * TWA = Time Weighted Average.
2. The table has been compiled by the author from the following sources:

[a] Benedict Armstrong et al., "Association between Exposure to Pulsed Electromagnetic Fields and Cancer in Electric Utility Workers in Quebec, Canada, and France," *American Journal of Epidemiology* 140, no. 9 (1994)., exposure top 90th percentile.

[b] C. Portier, M.S. Wolfe, and NIEHS Working Group, *Assessment of Health Effects from Exposure to Power-Line Frequency Electric and Magnetic Fields: Niehs Working Group Report* (Research Triangle Park, NC: National Institute of Environmental Health Sciences, U.S. National Institute of Health, U.S. Department of Health and Human Services, Public Health Services, 1998), 112., time weighted average of exposure at least 4.7 μT

[c] Armstrong et al., "Association between Exposure to Pulsed Electromagnetic Fields and Cancer in Electric Utility Workers in Quebec, Canada, and France."

[d] Portier, Wolfe, and Group, *Assessment of Health Effects from Exposure to Power-Line Frequency Electric and Magnetic Fields: Niehs Working Group Report*, 112.

[e] Masayoshi Nakagawa, "A Study on Extremely Low-Frequency Electric and Magnetic Fields and Cancer: Discussion of Emf Safety Limits," *journal of Occupational Health* 39, no. 1 (1997); citing Tore Tynes, Aage Andersen, and FrØydis Langmark, "Incidence of Cancer in Norwegian Workers Potentially Exposed to Electromagnetic Fields," *American Journal of Epidemiology* 136, no. 1 (1992).

[f] Armstrong et al., "Association between Exposure to Pulsed Electromagnetic Fields and Cancer in Electric Utility Workers in Quebec, Canada, and France."

[g] Portier, Wolfe, and Group, *Assessment of Health Effects from Exposure to Power-Line Frequency Electric and Magnetic Fields: Niehs Working Group Report*, 117.; citing; Pascal Guenel et al., "Exposure to 50-Hz Electric Field and Incidence of Leukemia, Brain Tumors, and Other Cancers among French Electric Utility Workers," *American journal of epidemiology* 144, no. 12 (1996).

[h] Armstrong et al., "Association between Exposure to Pulsed Electromagnetic Fields and Cancer in Electric Utility Workers in Quebec, Canada, and France."

[i] Portier, Wolfe, and Group, *Assessment of Health Effects from Exposure to Power-Line Frequency Electric and Magnetic Fields: Niehs Working Group Report*, 119.citing ; Paul A Demers et al., "Occupational Exposure to Electromagnetic Fields and Breast Cancer in Men," *American Journal of Epidemiology* 134, no. 4 (1991).

[j] Armstrong et al., "Association between Exposure to Pulsed Electromagnetic Fields and Cancer in Electric Utility Workers in Quebec, Canada, and France," Table 7, adjusted for socio economic status and smoking.

Table 9.11 specifies an OR=2.6; this means that the test arrived at the ratio $\frac{\frac{N_{xl}}{N_{x0}}}{\frac{N_{cl}}{N_{c0}}}=2.6$. Table 9.11 also specifies a 95% CI of 1.3–5.4; this means the odds of an exposed electrician to contract the disease are more than 1.3 times and less than 5.5 times than the odds of an unexposed electrician with a confidence of 95%. A wide 95% confidence interval is less informative than a narrow 95%CI.[107]

Table 9.11 lists test results evaluating the risk of adults with high exposure to electric electromagnetic radiation of electric lines.

Table 9.12 lists the risk determined for children with high exposure to electric electromagnetic radiation of electric lines.

Lessons from an Ice Storm—Province of Quebec, 1988

This chapter reviewed some of the negative side effects of decarbonizing road transport. The grand EV project needs to evaluate these risks and propose mitigating measures. Chapter 2 discussed the mathematical demonstration of the theory that accumulation of such side effects can bring societies to sociopolitical collapse. This section discusses a true life trial of near-collapse of the city of Montreal, QC, Canada.

It started with a freezing rain on Sunday, January 4, 1998. The freezing rain developed into an ice storm; ice accumulation deposited on electric lines resulted in loads exceeding design loads of poles, of pylons, and of the electric wires. A total of 1,000 steel pylons and 16,000 wooden poles buckled under the load.[108] The supply of electricity crumbled; by January 10 "three million Quebecers—roughly half the province's population, are without power."[109] Forty-five deaths were caused in Canada and the United States by the storm and its effects.[110] No power in 1998 meant more

Table 9.11 Adults, High Exposure to Electromagnetic Radiation of Electricity Transmission Lines

Disease	Identification	Significance			Exposure
		SIR	OR	95% CI	
Brain tumor	All[a]		2.94	0.28–6.7	<50 m to high-voltage lines
	Glioma[a]		4.96	1.56–15.8	
Breast cancer[b]			1.58	1.30–1.92	≥.05 μT
Leukemia[c]		1.5		1.2–1.8	

Compiled by the author from the following sources:

[a] Maffei, "Magnetic Fields and Cancer: Epidemiology, Cellular Biology, and Theranostics"; citing Camille Carles et al., "Residential Proximity to Power Lines and Risk of Brain Tumor in the General Population," *Environmental research* 185 (2020).

[b] Jolanta Kliukiene, Tore Tynes, and Aage Andersen, "Residential and Occupational Exposures to 50-Hz Magnetic Fields and Breast Cancer in Women: A Population-Based Study," *American Journal of Epidemiology* 159, no. 9 (2004).

[c] Nakagawa, "A Study on Extremely Low-Frequency Electric and Magnetic Fields and Cancer: Discussion of Emf Safety Limits"; citing Tynes, Andersen, and Langmark, "Incidence of Cancer in Norwegian Workers Potentially Exposed to Electromagnetic Fields."

Table 9.12 Children, High Exposure to Electromagnetic Radiation of Electricity Transmission Lines

Disease	Significance		Exposure
	OR	95% CI	
Leukemia	1.72[a]	1.25–2.35[a]	≥ .4μT
	1.52[b]	.71–3.25[b]	≥ .4μT
	3.8[c]	1.4–9.3[c]	≥ .4μT
	1.45[d]	0.54–3.88[d]	-
Brain cancer	1.14[e]	.61–2.13[e]	≥ .4μT
Other cancer	1.8[f]	1.2–2.5[f]	-

Compiled by author using the following sources:

[a] GyeongAe Seomun, Juneyoung Lee, and Jinkyung Park, "Exposure to Extremely Low-Frequency Magnetic Fields and Childhood Cancer: A Systematic Review and Meta-Analysis," *PLoS One* 16, no. 5 (2021).

[b] L. Kheifets et al., "Residential Magnetic Fields Exposure and Childhood Leukemia: A Population-Based Case-Control Study in California," *Cancer Causes Control* 28, no. 10 (2017).

[c] Nakagawa, "A Study on Extremely Low-Frequency Electric and Magnetic Fields and Cancer: Discussion of Emf Safety Limits"; citing Maria Feychting and Michael Alhbom, "Magnetic Fields and Cancer in Children Residing near Swedish High-Voltage Power Lines," *American journal of epidemiology* 138, no. 7 (1993).

[d] Michael N Bates, "Extremely Low Frequency Electromagnetic Fields and Cancer: The Epidemiologic Evidence," *Environmental Health Perspectives* 95 (1991).

[e] Leeka Kheifets et al., "A Pooled Analysis of Extremely Low-Frequency Magnetic Fields and Childhood Brain Tumors," *American journal of epidemiology* 172, no. 7 (2010).

[f] Nakagawa, "A Study on Extremely Low-Frequency Electric and Magnetic Fields and Cancer: Discussion of Emf Safety Limits"; citing David A Savitz et al., "Case-Control Study of Childhood Cancer and Exposure to 60-Hz Magnetic Fields," *American journal of epidemiology* 128, no. 1 (1988).

than dark evenings; tons of food spoiled in defrosted freezers, no cooking, no heating, no refrigeration, no coffee, no radio, no TV, and no computer. Consumers inundated Hydro Québec with calls requesting prospects and updates. Hydro Québec set up a TV information service to provide answers. However, consumers could not read the information on TV because of the power failure. Individuals and trade experienced a significant degradation of cellphones, credit card handling, banking services, hospitals, emergency calls, and responses.

The disruption peaked on January 9:

> An example is the near-catastrophe which occurred on January 9, 1998 when at approximately 12:20 p.m., both of the water filtration plants that provide Montreal and the 15 surrounding municipalities with drinking water shut down simultaneously.[111]

If the drinking water supply had been compromised, the government would have been constrained to order evacuation. Evacuating a city located on an island with a few bridges leading out of the city predicts sociopolitical turmoil. Imagine the same evacuation when close to 100% of the vehicles are EVs with drained batteries.

Other lessons learned in Quebec of 1998 have been summarized by the Lecomte, Pang and Russel report.[112]

The following areas are identified as requiring review and possible specific recommendations:

- communications (cellular and telephone)
- vulnerability of water filtration plants and water systems
- availability of large, heavy-duty generators for chronic care facilities
- hospices, nursing homes, hospitals, and emergency operation centres
- both public and private
- development of alternative sources of energy to offset the staggering demands on normal sources at times of crisis
- sheltering accommodations, food and feeding
- medical, counseling, prescription services and security
- emergency fuel supplies—oil, gas (auto, diesel, propane) and wood
- building, health, fire, safety, and energy codes
- limited time pre-event actions; and
- event response activities (i.e., help lines and courtesy and emergency transportation).

A total conversion of all vehicles to electric power contradicts the following recommendations:

1. Development of alternative sources of energy
2. Emergency fuel supplies—oil, gas (auto, diesel, propane) and wood ; building infrastructure for all EC vehicles is a good thing; however, it undercuts the market's demand for maintaining the existing fossil fuel supply

The Canadian ice-storm event of 1998 illustrates how good intentions create unintended disruption threatening the stability of the sociopolitical order. Hydroelectric power is clean and renewable. In Quebec space heating, water heating, cooking is either fueled or controlled by electricity. Imagine that the power line repair vehicles are also powered by electricity! Fortunately power line maintenance was carried out with diesel trucks; there was a viable fossil fuel infrastructure to provide fuel to emergency generators in healthcare facilities, law enforcement, and security services. Ice-storms are rare events; however, many other factors can disrupt electric power supply: equipment failure, system overload, wildlife, trees, lightning,[113] hurricanes, high power demand, landslide, market manipulation, inadequate maintenance, fire in transformer station, damage to main line due to construction work, and hostile attacks.[114] Modern electric power systems are vulnerable because of interconnected networks. A large system of networks fails due to a positive feedback scenario discussed in Chapter 2. The failure of a single point in a network due to faulty equipment, for example, generates overload of the network; protective equipment switches the system off; however, this intended protection has unintended effect of overloading adjacent networks. A concise explanation is the following:

> a system failure consists of a sequence of cascading line tripping that originates from the faulty line and spreads sequentially from one location to another over an increasingly larger region of the network.[115]

The example of the 1998 ice storm illustrates the most sensitive impact of governments initiating, motivating, managing time tables, regulating, and funding large projects such as decarbonizing transport. Lucrative projects led by entrepreneurs are also prone to neglecting safety, health, and ecological constraints. This explains why government oversight is essential. For example in the United States, agencies like FAA, FDA, FCC, EPA, and the Federal Reserve Bank monitor the compliance with laws and regulations protecting safety, health, ecology, and financial responsibility. In equilibrium and stability study terms, the government agencies control, detect deviations, and initiate corrective actions. There is a technical conflict of interest when the project lead and its safety controller operate under the same umbrella. In stability terms, this dual function of government is destabilizing.

Conclusion

This chapter is intended to illustrate an example of a grand enterprise lead by governments. Decarbonizing road transport is required to meet CO_2 emission requirements of international treatises. These goals are understood to combat global warming predictions. These predictions are based on reasonable studies; nevertheless, the predictions are not scientifically validated by proof. The wide range of predicted surface temperatures reduces the significance of the predictions. Similarly the chapter discussed that effect of the global warming on climate change is reasonable; however, we still do not have a scientific proof of this effect. Scientists are probably correct assuming that current CO_2 concentration trends are damaging; however, science is still expected to establish the quantitative relationship between CO_2 concentration and rising temperatures. Governments encourage decarbonizing road transportation, and that is good. However, their active lead in decreeing time tables and enforcing compliance disregards the lack of knowledge regarding batteries, their charging demands and capabilities, electric power availability, and shortcomings associated with increased electric power supply. Equilibrium and stability science indicates that governments should dwell on risks and risk mitigation; industrial entrepreneurs should gallop to meet deadlines.

Notes

1 Taylor-Gooby and Benjamin Leruth, "Why British People Don't Trust the Government Any More – and What Can Be Done About It," *The Conversation* (2018).
2 E.g. Simon Blackburn, *Reason and Prediction* (Cambridge: Cambridge University Press, 1973), 2.
3 Daniel Yankelovich and Will Friedman, *Toward Wiser Public Judgment* (Nashville: Vanderbilt University Press, 2010).

4 E.g. Kamala Harris, "Fact Sheet: The Biden-Harris Electric Vehicle Charging Action Plan," ed. The White House (Washington, DC: US Government The White House, 2021).

5 Hedges Company, "How Many Cars Are There in the World in 2023," Hedges & Company, https://hedgescompany.com/blog/2021/06/how-many-cars-are-there-in-the-world/.

6 Isaac M. Held and Brian J. Soden, "Water Vapor Feedback and Global Warming," *Annual Review of Energy and the Environment* 25, no. 1 (2000): 441-75.

7 Joseph B. J. Fourier and A. Freeman, *The Analytical Theory of Heat* (Cambridge: Cambridge University Press, 1878).

8 E.g. equation (9) in Clarence R. Wylie J. R., *Advanced Engineering Mathematics* (New York: Mc-Graw-Hill, 1966), 183.

9 E.g. Donald Wuebbles et al., "Climate Science Special Report: Fourth National Climate Assessment (Nca4), Volume I," (Washington DC: U.S. Global Change Research Program 2017): 163.

10 ΔF stands for the GHG generated increment of for *effective radiative forcings* (ERF); ERF is the[top of atmosphere] TOA energy budget change resulting from the perturbation, excluding any radiative response related to a change in the [global surface temperature] GSAT" Piers Forster et al., "The Earth's Energy Budget, Climate Feedbacks, and Climate Sensitivity, IPCC Report" (Cambridge and New York: Cambridge University Press, 2021), 925, 29, 31.

11 J. Blunden and D. S. Arndt, "State of the Climate in 2019," *Bulletin of the American Meteorological Society* 101, no. 8 (2020): S1–S429.

12 Nathan J. L. Lenssen et al., "Improvements in the Gistemp Uncertainty Model," *Journal of Geophysical Research: Atmospheres* 124, no. 12 (2019): 6307–6326; Colin P. Morice et al., "Quantifying Uncertainties in Global and Regional Temperature Change Using an Ensemble of Observational Estimates: The Hadcrut4 Data Set," *Journal of Geophysical Research: Atmospheres* 117, no. D8 (2012): https://doi.org/10.1029/2011JD017187; Huai-Min Zhang et al., "Updated Temperature Data Give a Sharper View of Climate Trends," *Eos* 100 (2019), https://doi.org/10.1029/2019EO128229.

13 Christian Huggel et al., "The Existential Risk Space of Climate Change," *Climatic Change* 174, no. 1–2 (2022): 8–28.

14 Valérie Masson-Delmotte et al., *Global Warming of 1.5 C: Ipcc Special Report on Impacts of Global Warming of 1.5 C above Pre-Industrial Levels in Context of Strengthening Response to Climate Change, Sustainable Development, and Efforts to Eradicate Poverty* (Cambridge: Cambridge University Press, 2022).

15 Ochega A. Ataguba and John E. Ataguba, "Social Determinants of Health: The Role of Effective Communication in the Covid-19 Pandemic in Developing Countries," *Global Health Action* 13, no. 1 (2020): 1788263.

16 Reinhard Mechler et al., "Loss and Damage and Limits to Adaptation: Recent Ipcc Insights and Implications for Climate Science and Policy," *Sustainability Science* 15 (2020): 1245–51.

17 Core Writing Team, "Summary for Policymakers," in *Climate Change 2023: Synthesis Report. Contribution of Working Groups I, Ii and Iii to the Sixth Assessment Report of the Intergovernmental Panel on Climate Change-Ipcc*, ed. Hoesung Lee and José Romero (Geneva: UN - Intergovernmental Panel on Climate Change (IPCC), 2023).

18 Ibid., 9.
19 Forster et al., "The Earth's Energy Budget, Climate Feedbacks, and Climate Sensitivity, IPCC Report," 1024.
20 Bernard Manowitz, "Global Climate Feedbacks" (Upton: Brookhaven National Lab., 1990).
21 Ameet Raval and Veerabhadran Ramanathan, "Observational Determination of the Greenhouse Effect" (paper presented at the Global Climate Feedbacks; No. BNL-45321; CONF-9006134, Upton, 1990).
22 Core Writing Team, "Summary for Policymakers."
23 Section 7.4.2.1 of Forster et al., "The Earth's Energy Budget, Climate Feedbacks, and Climate Sensitivity, IPCC Report," 968.
24 Ian S. Robinson, *Measuring the Oceans from Space: The Principles and Methods of Satellite Oceanography* (Berlin, Heidelberg, and New York: Springer 2004), 152.
25 Section 7.4.2.1 of Forster et al., "The Earth's Energy Budget, Climate Feedbacks, and Climate Sensitivity, IPCC Report," 968.
26 Section 7.4.2.1 of ibid.
27 Sensitivity of irradiance to temperature represents the increment of irradiance/unit of temperature.
28 Section 7.4.2.1 of Forster et al., "The Earth's Energy Budget, Climate Feedbacks, and Climate Sensitivity, IPCC Report," 968.
29 Table 7.10 of ibid.
30 Table 7.10 of ibid.
31 Table 7.10 of ibid.
32 The Stefan-Boltzmann constant governs the energy radiated by a warm Earth into the extremely cold space.
33 Table 1 of Eui-Seok Chung et al., "Upper-Tropospheric Moistening in Response to Anthropogenic Warming," *Proceedings of the National Academy of Sciences* 111, no. 32 (2014): 11636-41.
34 Figure 4 of ibid.
35 Forster et al., "The Earth's Energy Budget, Climate Feedbacks, and Climate Sensitivity, IPCC Report."
36 US Government, "Climate Change," ed. EPA (Internet 2023), https://www.epa.gov/climate-change.
37 E.g. Core Writing Team, "Summary for Policymakers," 5.
38 Ibid.
39 Roger A. Pielke Jr. et al., "Hurricanes and Global Warming," *Bulletin of the American Meteorological Society* 86, no. 11 (2005): 1571–6.
40 Camille Parmesan et al., "Overstretching Attribution," *Nature Climate Change* 1, no. 1 (2011).
41 Ibid.
42 Gianluca Alimonti, "A Critical Assessment of Extreme Events Trends in Times of Global Warming," – *Brief History of the Troubled Life of the Article and Its Retraction* (2023) personal communication.
43 Gianluca Alimonti et al., "A Critical Assessment of Extreme Events Trends in Times of Global Warming," *The European Physical Journal Plus* 137, no. 1 (2022): https://doi.org/10.1140/epjp/s13360-021-02243-9.

44 Roland Lloyd Parry and Marlowe Hood, "Posts Downplaying Climate 'Emergency' Cite Paper with Cherry-Picked Evidence," *AFP*2022.
45 Ibid.
46 Alimonti, "A Critical Assessment of Extreme Events Trends in Times of Global Warming."
47 Galileo Galilei, *Dialogue Concerning the Two Chief World Systems (Original: 1632)* (Berkley: University of California Press, 1914).
48 Krista F. Myers et al., "Consensus Revisited: Quantifying Scientific Agreement on Climate Change and Climate Expertise among Earth Scientists 10 Years Later," *Environmental Research Letters* 16, no. 10 (2021).
49 Katrin Hussinger and João N. Carvalho, "The Long-Term Effect of Research Grants on the Scientific Output of University Professors," *Industry and Innovation* 29, no. 4 (2022): 463–87.
50 Carter Bloch, Ebbe Krogh Graversen, and Heidi Skovgaard Pedersen, "Competitive Research Grants and Their Impact on Career Performance," *Minerva* 52 (2014): 77-96.
51 Government of Canada, "Climate Action and Awareness Fund," ed. Environment and Natural Resources (Ottawa: ENR, 2023).
52 Barbara Buchner et al., "The Global Landscape of Climate Finance 2013" (Climate Policy Initiative, 2021).
53 This term is a derivative of "holocaust deniers"; to me using it is inappropriate because it dilutes the evil of denying the holocaust.
54 Hannah Ritchie, Max Roser, and Pablo Rosado, "Co_2 and Greenhouse Gas Emissions," OurWorldInData.org, https://ourworldindata.org/co2-and-greenhouse-gas-emissions; Global CO2 emissions from fossil fuels.
55 Paul Balcombe et al., "Methane Emissions: Choosing the Right Climate Metric and Time Horizon," *Environmental Science: Processes & Impacts* 20, no. 10 (2018): 1323–39 –Table 3.
56 Daniel Bodansky, "The United Nations Framework Convention on Climate Change: A Commentary," *Yale Journal of International Law* 18 (1993): 455.
57 E.g. F. M. Bréon et al., "An Attempt at Estimating Paris Area CO_2 Emissions from Atmospheric Concentration Measurements," *Atmospheric Chemistry and Physics* 15, no. 4 (2015): 1707–24.
58 Ken Caldeira, Atul K. Jain, and Martin I. Hoffert, "Climate Sensitivity Uncertainty and the Need for Energy without CO_2 Emission," *Science* 299, no. 5615 (2003): 2052–54.
59 Ritchie, Roser, and Rosado, "Co_2 and Greenhouse Gas Emissions"; Annual greenhouse gas emissions in CO2 equivalents.
60 Ibid.; Emissions by sector.
61 "Regulations for Greenhouse Gas Emissions from Passenger Cars and Trucks," ed. US Government/EPA (Internet 2023),htps://www.epa.gov/regulations-emissions-vehicles-and-engines/regulations-greenhouse-gas-emissions-passenger-cars-and#Overview:.
62 US Government EIA, "Electric Power Annual 2022," ed. Department of Energy (Washington, DC, 2022), https://www.eia.gov/electricity/Annual/pdf/epa.pdf.
63 "Combined Heat and Power (Chp) Partnership," in *US Government*, ed. EPA (Washington, DC, 2023), https://www.epa.gov/chp/chp-benefits.

64 E.g. 36–38% in gasoline engines Zhijian Wang et al., "A Review of Energy Loss Reduction Technologies for Internal Combustion Engines to Improve Brake Thermal Efficiency," *Energies* 14, no. 20 (2021): 6656 Figure 1.
65 Jennifer M. Granholm et al., "The U.S. National Blueprint for Transportation Decarbonization," in *A Joint Strategy to Transform Transportation*, ed. Transportation Departments of Energy, Housing, and EPA (Washington, DC: US Government, 2022).
66 "If investors believe governments will pass new regulations that favor climate-friendly renewable energy, they might worry about assets tied to fossil fuels, such as stocks of coal companies or bonds issued by oil-exporting countries," Gita Rao and Aaron Krol, "Investing and Climate Change," MIT, Climate Portal, https://climate.mit.edu/explainers/investing-and-climate-change.
67 According to Adam Smith, these are the three essential duties of government; see Philip A. Klein, *Beyond Dissent: Essays in Institutional Economics* (Armonk: M.E. Sharpe, 1994), 22.
68 Buchner et al., "The Global Landscape of Climate Finance 2013."
69 Ibid.
70 US Government EPA, "Mission Statement," ed. EPA (Washington DC, 2023), https://www.epa.gov/aboutepa/our-mission-and-what-we-do.
71 US Government EERE, "Funding Opportunities," ed. Energy (Washington DC, 2023), https://www.energy.gov/eere/funding/eere-funding-opportunities.
72 US Government, "Energy Efficiency and Renewable Energy" in *FY 2024 Congressional Justification*, ed. DOE (Washington DC: Department of Energy, 2003).
73 Granholm et al., "The U.S. National Blueprint for Transportation Decarbonization," Executive Summary.
74 Hedges Company, "How Many Cars Are There in the World in 2023."
75 Monsuru Olalekan Ramoni and Hong-Chao Zhang, "End-of-Life (Eol) Issues and Options for Electric Vehicle Batteries," *Clean Technologies and Environmental Policy* 15 (2013).
76 Ibid.
77 US Government EPA, "Lithium-Ion Battery Recycling Frequently Asked Questions," ed. EPA (Washington, DC, 2003), https://www.epa.gov/hw/lithium-ion-battery-recycling-frequently-asked-questions#hazwaste.
78 E.g. in the US: 40 CFR §273.15; 49 CFR §173.185; NFPA 855, Chapter 14; 2024 International Fire Code, Sections 321; CPUC Rule 21, CAISO/FERC.
79 European Union, "Regulation of the European Parliament and of the Council Concerning Batteries and Waste Batteries, Amending Directive 2008/98/Ec and Regulation (Eu) 2019/1020 and Repealing Directive 2006/66/Ec," in *2020/0353 (COD); PE-CONS 2/23; ENV 45; ENT 11; MI 32; CODEC 44* (Brussels: The European Parliament and the Council of The European Union, 2023).
80 Ministry of Environment, Forest and Climate Change: Battery Waste Management Rules 2022.
81 Carlos M. Costa et al., "Recycling and Environmental Issues of Lithium-Ion Batteries: Advances, Challenges and Opportunities," *Energy Storage Materials* 37 (2021): 433-65.
82 Ibid.
83 Ramoni and Zhang, "End-of-Life (Eol) Issues and Options for Electric Vehicle Batteries"; Costa et al., "Recycling and Environmental Issues of Lithium-Ion Batteries: Advances, Challenges and Opportunities."

84 E.g. Jason Porzio and Corinne D. Scown, "Life-Cycle Assessment Considerations for Batteries and Battery Materials," *Advanced Energy Materials* 11, no. 33 (2021): 2100771; Dominic A. Notter et al., "Contribution of Li-Ion Batteries to the Environmental Impact of Electric Vehicles," *Environmental Science & Technology* 44, no. 17 (2010): 6550-56; Ramoni and Zhang, "End-of-Life (Eol) Issues and Options for Electric Vehicle Batteries"; Yanyan Tang et al., "The Social-Economic-Environmental Impacts of Recycling Retired Ev Batteries under Reward-Penalty Mechanism," *Applied Energy* 251 (2019): 113313; Eklas Hossain et al., "A Comprehensive Review on Second-Life Batteries: Current State, Manufacturing Considerations, Applications, Impacts, Barriers & Potential Solutions, Business Strategies, and Policies," *Ieee Access* 7 (2019): 73215-52.

85 State of California, "Governor Newsom Announces California Will Phase out Gasoline-Powered Cars & Drastically Reduce Demand for Fossil Fuel in California's Fight against Climate Change," ed. Office of Governor (Sacramento, 2020), https://www.gov.ca.gov/2020/09/23/governor-newsom-announces-california-will-phase-out-gasoline-powered-cars-drastically-reduce-demand-for-fossil-fuel-in-californias-fight-against-climate-change/).

86 Lithium-ion Car Battery Recycling Advisory Group, "Final Policy Recommendations," in *Meetings*, ed. CalEPA (Sacramento, 2022), https://calepa.ca.gov/lithium-ion-car-battery-recycling-advisory-group/.

87 Ibid.

88 Lluc Canals Casals et al., "Evaluation of the End-of-Life of Electric Vehicle Batteries According to the State-of-Health," *World Electric Vehicle Journal* 10, no. 4 (2019), 10.3390/wevj10040063; Hossain et al., "A Comprehensive Review on Second-Life Batteries: Current State, Manufacturing Considerations, Applications, Impacts, Barriers & Potential Solutions, Business Strategies, and Policies"; Tang et al., "The Social-Economic-Environmental Impacts of Recycling Retired Ev Batteries under Reward-Penalty Mechanism"; Costa et al., "Recycling and Environmental Issues of Lithium-Ion Batteries: Advances, Challenges and Opportunities."

89 Hossain et al., "A Comprehensive Review on Second-Life Batteries: Current State, Manufacturing Considerations, Applications, Impacts, Barriers & Potential Solutions, Business Strategies, and Policies," 73218.

90 Ibid.

91 Mohammed Hussein Saleh Mohammed Haram et al., "Feasibility of Utilising Second Life Ev Batteries: Applications, Lifespan, Economics, Environmental Impact, Assessment, and Challenges," *Alexandria Engineering Journal* 60, no. 5 (2021): 4517-36.

92 The decay rate is varying by application, by frequency of charge, storage duration, temperature, and so on. See Hossain et al., "A Comprehensive Review on Second-Life Batteries: Current State, Manufacturing Considerations, Applications, Impacts, Barriers & Potential Solutions, Business Strategies, and Policies"; nevertheless, in average a similar rate of decay is sensible for a preliminary study.

93 Haram et al., "Feasibility of Utilising Second Life Ev Batteries: Applications, Lifespan, Economics, Environmental Impact, Assessment, and Challenges," Figure 2.

94 I assumed the weight of 450Kg/battery which corresponds to the weight of the Tesla Roadster battery.

95 Harris, "Fact Sheet: The Biden-Harris Electric Vehicle Charging Action Plan."

96 US Government EIA, "Electric Power Annual 2022," Table 3.1A.

97 Ibid., Table 3.1B.
98 Ibid., Table 4.1A.
99 M. Markov and Y. Grigoriev, "Protect Children from Emf," *Electromagnetic Biology and Medicine* 34, no. 3 (2015).
100 Larissa D. Biasotto and Andreas Kindel, "Power Lines and Impacts on Biodiversity: A Systematic Review," *Environmental Impact Assessment Review* 71 (2018): 110–19.
101 N. V. Buyakova et al., "Influence of Spatial Arrangement of Wires on Electromagnetic Ecology near High-Voltage Power Transmission Lines at Railway Station" (paper presented at the IOP Conference Series: Materials Science and Engineering, 2021).
102 Massimo E. Maffei, "Magnetic Fields and Cancer: Epidemiology, Cellular Biology, and Theranostics," *International Journal of Molecular Sciences* 23, no. 3 (2022): 1339–54; citing S. Lange, T. Viergutz, and M. Simko, "Modifications in Cell Cycle Kinetics and in Expression of G1 Phase-Regulating Proteins in Human Amniotic Cells after Exposure to Electromagnetic Fields and Ionizing Radiation," *Cell Proliferation* 37, no. 5 (2004): 337-49; and Adam Lacy-hulbert, James C. Metcalfe, and Robin Hesketh, "Biological Responses to Electromagnetic Fields 1," *The FASEB Journal* 12, no. 6 (1998): 395-420.
103 Markov and Grigoriev, "Protect Children from Emf."
104 Leeka Kheifets et al., "The Sensitivity of Children to Electromagnetic Fields," *Pediatrics* 116, no. 2 (2005): e303-13.
105 Handan Kayhan et al., "Effects of Extremely Low-Frequency Magnetic Field on Healthy Fibroblasts and Breast Cancer Cells," *Journal of Istanbul Faculty of Medicine* 83, no. 4 (2020):384-9. Cited by Maffei, "Magnetic Fields and Cancer: Epidemiology, Cellular Biology, and Theranostics."
106 Jiyeon Kim et al., "Repetitive Exposure to a 60-Hz Time-Varying Magnetic Field Induces DNA Double-Strand Breaks and Apoptosis in Human Cells," *Biochemical and Biophysical Research Communications* 400, no. 4 (2010). Cited by Maffei, "Magnetic Fields and Cancer: Epidemiology, Cellular Biology, and Theranostics."
107 A 100% confidence interval is between 0 and infinity. That is obvious, and one needs no test to establish it.
108 Claude Turcotte, "L'après- Crise Aura Coûté Deux Milliards," *Le Devoir* (2008).
109 Eugene L. Lecomte, Alan W. Pang, and James W. Russell, *Ice Storm '98* (Institute for Catastrophic Loss Reduction Toronto, Canada, 1998), 10.
110 Ibid., 1.
111 Ibid., 34.
112 Ibid., 28.
113 Vivian Sultan and Brian Hilton, "A Spatial Analytics Framework to Investigate Electric Power-Failure Events and Their Causes," *ISPRS International Journal of Geo-information* 9, no. 1 (2020): 64–76.
114 Wolfgang Kröger, "Securing the Operation of Socially Critical Systems from an Engineering Perspective: New Challenges, Enhanced Tools and Novel Concepts," *European Journal for Security Research* 2 (2017): 39-55.
115 Lamine Mili, Qun Qiu, and Arun G. Phadke, "Risk Assessment of Catastrophic Failures in Electric Power Systems," *International Journal of Critical Infrastructures* 1, no. 1 (2004):38-63.

Conclusion

Final Reflections

Hopefully, the reader of this book has been searching for answers to questions related to the resilience of democratic systems of government.

This book is odd because its author's profession and experience involved solving problems related to complex technological systems. In spite of that I offer answers to questions my typical reader has investigated, answered, and lectured.

Reasonably, the reader considers equilibrium and stability of aircraft an important subject as long as he/she is flying on an airplane; however, the moment the aircraft safely lands, questions like what is equilibrium or what is stability make place to other subjects of brain activity. Consider a researcher of resilience of democracy flying at 32,000 feet altitude. I would be surprised if he/she realized that his/her subject of interest is related to the short term worry about safety of flight. This assertion is sensible on the grounds that the similarity between safety of flight and resilience of democracy is buried in algebraic equations; I smuggled some of them into this book (see Chapter 2).

It is striking that those annoying algebraic relationships solve not only equilibrium and stability questions of various technological creations, like bridges, heating and cooling, and power lines, but also of biological systems. Therefore, it is not an accident that I extended the analogy to the question of resilience of democracy; after all, in order to make the case for the analogy, one needs to be familiar with abstract algebraic manipulations of idealized reflections of reality.

The book lists typical answers of scholars who know better than me how society in general and democracy in particular functions. The Introduction mentions justified measures proposed to strengthen democracy like strong legislature, judicial review, resisting autocratization, accountability, depolarization, and civic education. The book also lists works in history and archaeology focused on the collapse of strong empires and kingdoms of the past. It is remarkable that some scholars of the past linked the reasons of collapse not to absence or weakness of one or more government institutions but to the complexity of government system (see Chapter 4).

So far, I scanned some potential answers to questions related to the resilience of government in general and democracy in particular. However, quantitative answers require translating the questions to unequivocal language. What is resilience? What is complex system? "Questions don't have to make sense . . . but answers do."[1]

The book departs from conventional paradigms of viewing society as a unique occurrence of intelligent constructs of communal interactions, shared culture, institutions, and norms of behavior of rational human individuals. The next step consists of clarifying the notion of complex society. Governing involves, among others, actions intended to keep the society at a desired state of performance. The government has several functions and each function monitors several traits of public order. For example Table 3.1 lists examples of such governmental functions of the Roman Empire and connects its outcome to a measurable indicator. These indicators vary in time; their values at a given time describe the state of the society. Not surprisingly Table 3.1 calls these indicators *state variables.*

Chapter 1 mentions six different studies of equilibrium and stability carried out by six different teams of scholars in six different disciplines; all use the same idealized quantitative representation of their object of investigation. They determine state variables; subsequently they develop algebraic expressions. The resulting equations quantify how variations of one state variable affect several other state variables. In every field, scholars call equilibrium a state with no state variable changes. In every field, the system is called stable if a small perturbation of a system at equilibrium results in the return of the system to its initial state of equilibrium. In every field, the same mathematical criterion informs whether a system of algebraic expressions represents a stable system. Chapter 6 mentions that this method of assessing is known as the Routh–Hurwitz stability criterion.

I took a stab at using the same methodology to explain the cause of collapse of pre-industrial era Empires and Kingdoms. The results clearly support that growing social complexity measured as increasing the number of state variables is the chief factor of collapse. This was news. I published the investigation in a scientific journal.[2]

This book extends that finding to the industrial era in general and democratic states in particular. The practical application of this theory consists of distinguishing between stabilizing and destabilizing government structures and actions.

The following courses of action are found to be stabilizing

1. Constitutionalism—strong adherence to a set of rules that limit government to deviate from denying liberty, equality before the law, freedom of speech, freedom of business, freedom of religion, and so on.
2. Federalism—Do not govern what constituting states can govern.
3. Meritocracy, capitalism, and free competition—The book (Chapters 4, 6, 8) makes compelling arguments regarding the stabilizing power of capitalism in a democracy. Nevertheless, the literature provides counter arguments. I will not close the book before a brief rebuttal of arguments against two propelling components of capitalism: competition and meritocracy. A common method to combat a rational thought is to describe it as supported by "myths." Let me show some examples of perceptions characterized as myths and explain why they are in fact reality. The following examples list a phrase:
   a. Mcmpetition is an unavoidable fact of life."[3]

      Let me contradict the claim that this is a myth. Competition has been a fact of life from the beginning of civilization, and it was not born with capitalism as the Marxist dogma pretends. Chapter 5 discusses that ancient tyrannies (Mesopotamia, Egypt, Rome) rewarded skilled and talented individuals.

b. Myth: "Competition motivates us to do our best."[4]
   This is not a myth either. The negation of the argument sounds like "competition does not motivate us to do our best." I rest my case.
c. Myth: Competitive games give us joy.[5]
   The argument against joy in competition links competition with "isolation, hostility, and anxiety."[6] I admit to be primarily trained in the laws of physics. Anxiety is studied by psychologists. I will not pretend that I am competent to dismiss affirmations regarding factors of isolation, hostility, and anxiety. However, I have played tennis, bridge, and team sports. I would lie to you if I claimed that these games rule out anxiety. However, competition does produce joy. Anxiety and joy do not exclude each other. Ask someone who was just told that she needs no root canal intervention.
d. Myth: Competition builds character.[7]
   This is not a myth; it is a half-truth. Competition doesn't necessarily build character. Character of individuals is not a factor of equilibrium, stability, democracy, and constitutionalism.
e. Myth: "In America people get out the system what they put in it based exclusively or primarily on their individual merit."[8]
   This is not a myth if it is read in context. In the Islamic Republic of Iran men are evaluated according to their loyalty to Islam and to the Supreme leader; women share with men the right to remain silent. On the other hand, in America people are rewarded primarily on their individual merit.
f. Myth: America is a land of unlimited opportunity in which individuals can go as far as their individual talents and abilities can take them.[9]
   This is not a myth. In America if one strikes gold one is entitled to locate a mining claim on that gold deposit.[10] The gold is yours not only literally but also figuratively in examples like IBM, Ford Motors, Amazon, Walmart, Apple, Microsoft, and National Instruments.

4. Separation of powers
5. Judicial review
6. Keeping bureaucratic civil service on tracks specified by law under guidance of legislators

The book reveals the following stabilizing functions a government has:

- Combatting cartels and monopolies
- Defense and diplomatic relations
- Public works—roads airports railroads bridges ports
- Supporting justice administration
- Law enforcement
- Supervising the private sector in issues of public safety:
- Drugs
- Food
- Aviation

- Communications
- Environment
- Infectious disease
- National parks

The book explains that education is not necessarily stabilizing. Education is not harmful; however, many educated people spread evil (Chapter 6).

The book also points at destabilizing activities governments should avoid:

Initiate, guide, promote, and interfere in lucrative endeavors, for example, EV (Chapter 9).

Promote or suppress reasonable but not yet proven scientific theories (Chapter 9).

Accumulate federal decision power on the account of the power of constituent states and communities.

The worst course of action a government can take in order to avoid instability is consistently attempt to avoid instability.

Notes

1 Terry Pratchett, *Thief of Time: A Discworld Novel* (New York: HarperCollins, 2009), 25.
2 Joseph Livni, "Investigation of Collapse of Complex Socio-Political Systems Using Classical Stability Theory," *Physica A: Statistical Mechanics and Its Applications* (2019): 556-62.
3 Alfie Kohn, *No Contest: The Case Against Competition* (Boston and New York: Houghton Mifflin, 1992), 8.
4 Ibid.
5 Ibid.
6 Ibid.
7 Ibid., 8.
8 Stephen J. McNamee, "The Meritocracy Myth Revisited," *Sociation Today* 12, no. 2 (2014).
9 Ibid.
10 General Mining Act of 1872.

Appendix A

Global Warming: Predicting Surface Temperature Increment

At equilibrium, *heating* balances *cooling* (Figure 9.4) or $\Delta F = Feedbacks$. The feedbacks are temperature dependent. For a range of a few degrees (°C, or °F) the cooling response is directly proportional with the temperature rise ∇T. Thus at equilibrium the power imbalance is:

$$\Delta N = \Delta F + \alpha \nabla T = 0 \qquad \text{Equation A.1}$$

Equation A.1 is identical to equation 7.1 of the Foster IPCC (2021) report.[1] Consequently the temperature rise is $\Delta T = \frac{-\Delta F}{\alpha}$.

Section 7.4.2 of the Foster IPCC-2021 report[2] explains how the values of Table A.1 were calculated. Section 7.4.2.1 explains: Table A.1

> A crude estimate of αP can be made using the normalized greenhouse effect g̃, defined as the ratio between the greenhouse effect G and the upwelling LW flux at the surface.

The Foster report references the article of Raval and Ramanathan[3] to substantiate this approach. This source defines the greenhouse effect G as

$$G = E - \Phi \qquad \text{Equation A.2}$$

Table A.1 Calculation of α According to Table 7.10 of IPCC7-2021 of WA6 Assessment

Feedback	**Contribution to α[W/(m² * oK]**
DE/DT (Planck Response)	-3.25E+00
Cloud response	0.42
Albedo response	0.35
Bio-geophysical and non-CO_2 Bio-geochemical	-.01
Water Vapor response	1.3
Total α	-1.16E+00

Source: Table 7.10 of Piers Forster et al., "The Earth's Energy Budget, Climate Feedbacks, and Climate Sensitivity, IPCC Report," (Cambridge, New York: Cambridge University Press, 2021)

If E is the long-wave flux emitted by the surface at a certain location, and [Φ] is the flux leaving the top of the atmosphere (TOA) directly above that location, then the greenhouse effect G for that location can be defined as the ratio between the greenhouse effect G and the upwelling LW flux at the surface.

In other words, G[w/m²] is the rate of energy/unit area that returns to heat the planet because the GHG reflect the outward radiation, E[W/m²]. Only the energy rate Φ[W/m²] escapes into space (Figure 9.6). The total irradiation E is determined by the Stefan–Boltzmann relation (see Table A.2)

For an average temperature of Ts=289.5°K one obtains E=398 W/m². This is in agreement with Figure 7.2 of the Foster IPCC -2021 report.[4] Φ (Figure 10.5) is measured using in situ and satellite radiation measurements[5] and found to reach 239 W/m². Consequently one obtains: $G = E - F = 398 - 239 = 159$ W/m². This result is also in agreement with Foster IPCC -2021 report.[6] The net cooling of the Earth is (see Figure A.1):

$$\Phi = E - G \qquad \text{Equation A.3}$$

Raval and Ramanathan[7] insert the Stefan–Boltzmann relationship in Equation A.3:

$$\Phi = E - G = \sigma T_s^4 - G = \sigma T_s^4 \left(1 - \frac{G}{\sigma T_s^4}\right) \qquad \text{Equation A.4}$$

The article then defines a new magnitude:

$$g = \frac{G}{\sigma T_s^4} \qquad \text{Equation A.5}$$

The article coined the term *normalized trapping* for *g*.[8]

Table A.2 Stefan–Boltzmann Relation

Symbol	Magnitude	Units	Value
E	Total irradiation	w/m²	
σ	Stefan–Boltzmann constant	W/(m² °K⁴)	5.67×10^{-8}
T_s	Surface Temperature (GSAT)	°K	
Stefan–Boltzmann relation*			$E = \sigma T_s^4$
Sensitivity of total irradiation to temperature			$\frac{dE}{dT} = 4\sigma T^3$

Compiled by the author
*See for example Richard B. Alley, *Earth: The Operators' Manual* (New York and London: W. W. Norton, 2011

Accordingly, $\Phi = \sigma T_s^4 (1-g)$. The article then calculates $\frac{d\Phi}{dT_s}$ (the sensitivity of change of a the outward flux leaving the top of the atmosphere with respect to the surface temperature):

$$\frac{d\Phi}{dT_s} = \frac{dE}{dTs} - \frac{dG}{dTs} = 4\sigma T_s^3 - 4\sigma T_s^3 g^9 \qquad \text{Equation A.5}$$

or

$$\frac{d\Phi}{dT_s} = 4\sigma T_s^3 (1-g) \qquad \text{Equation A.6}$$

Raval and Ramanathan offer various ways to estimate for g.[10] One of them is described in Table A.3. It starts with rearranging Equation A.5:

$$\frac{dG}{dTs} = \frac{dE}{dTs} - \frac{d\Phi}{dT_s} = 4\sigma T_s^3 - \frac{d\Phi}{dT_s} \qquad \text{Equation A.7}$$

In Equation A.7 $\frac{d\Phi}{dT_s}$ is experimentally measured for a particular case (see parameters in Table A.3).

In the experimental case investigated by Raval and Ramanathan[11] ΔTs was measured. In a typical case ΔF, the anthropogenic increment of greenhouse gas forcing is either known or assumed; the objective is predicting ΔTs. Consequently, one uses Equation A.1. Therefore, the task consists of determining α (the sensitivity of the net

Table A.3 Estimating g from Measured Increment of Long-Wave Flux of Radiation to Space dF and the Increment of Surface Temperature dTs Causing It; the Procedure Follows Raval and Ramanathan

Magnitude	Value	Explanation
Ts	294.5°K	Surface Temperature, datum
Ts^3	25542059°K^3	
σ	5.67×10^{-8}	Stefan–Boltzmann constant
$4\sigma Ts^3$	5.79	
dΦ	6.3 W/m^2	Experimentally measure db
dTs	3oK	Experimentally measure dc
dΦ/dTs	$2.1\ W/(m^2 \times °K)$	
dG/dTs	$3.7\ W/(m^2 \times °K)$	Equation A.7
1-g	.64	$4\sigma T_s^3/(dG/dTs)$
g	.36	

Compiled by the author from the following sources:

[a] Ameet Raval and Veerabhadran Ramanathan, "Observational Determination of the Greenhouse Effect" (paper presented at the Global Climate Feedbacks; No. BNL-45321; CONF-9006134, Upton, NY, 1990), 12.

[b] Ibid.

[c] Ibid

Table A.4 Various Calculations of α

	Units	Approach a	Manowitz[a]	Approach b	IPCC Approach
DE/DT	W/(m²×°K)	−3.22		-5.04	−3.22
Cloud	W/(m²×°K)			0.42	0.42
albedo	W/(m²×°K)			0.35	0.35
bio-	W/(m²×°K)			−0.1	
WV	W/(m²×°K)			0.4[b]	1.3
α	W/(m²×°K)	−3.22	−3.7	−3.97	−1.16
Forcing	W/(m²×°K)	4.5	4.5[c]	4.5	4.5
ΔTs	°K	1.40	1.22	1.13	3.91

Compiled by the author using the following sources:

[a] Bernard Manowitz, "Global Climate Feedbacks," (Brookhaven National Lab., Upton, NY (USA), 1990), 1.

[b] "we have found it difficult to raise βH2O much above 0.4 for any plausible temperature change profiles" Isaac M Held and Brian J Soden, "Water Vapor Feedback and Global Warming," Annual review of energy and the environment 25, no. 1 (2000): 465.

[c] Manowitz used a forcing of 4 and obtained a ΔT=1.1oK; the result in the table is adjusted for a forcing of 4.5 (see Manowitz, "Global Climate Feedbacks," 1.

cooling response with surface temperature). There are several approaches to determine α. For example:

a. One can use Equation A.6 because Φ is the net outward radiation of Earth into space (Equation A.2 and Figure 9.5) and consequently $\frac{d\Phi}{dT_s}$ is the sensitivity of the net cooling effect with the surface temperature Ts.
b. One can calculate the sensitivity of net cooling radiation by observing that it consists of the difference between total radiation E and the returned radiation G (Equation A.4 and Figure 9.6). Therefore:

$$- = \frac{dE}{dTs} - \frac{dG}{dT_s} = 4\sigma T_s^3 - \sum_1^n \frac{dG_i}{dT_s} \qquad \text{Equation A.8}$$

In Equation A.8 G_i stands for the individual feedback effects like water vapor, lapse rate, clouds, albedo, bio-geophysical and non-CO2 bio-geochemical contributions.[12]

Table lists various calculations of α.

1. Column "Approach a" and Column "Manowitz" use the method described in a) above. The difference in the predicted surface temperature Ts is explained by different values of the measured greenhouse effect warming and the consequential normalized greenhouse effect *g*.
   a. Manowitz utilized the value of α=3.7 determined by Raval and Ramanathan; after all, Manowitz is the editor of the proceedings of the workshop and Raval and Ramanathan were contributors to it.
   b. The column "Approach a" derives *g* and α from a greenhouse effect of G=159 w/m² of the Forster IPCC-2021 report.[13]

2. Column "Approach b" follows the method described in b above. The individual feedback effects' sensitivities with the surface temperature are according to Table 7.10 of the IPCC report[14] except for the water vapor sensitivity which uses the upper bound of Held and Soden.[15]
3. Column "IPCC approach combines both approaches a and b. In other words it takes into account twice the individual heating greenhouse effects:
   a. once by reducing the Stefan–Boltzmann constant by 40%
   b. and once by adding each heating greenhouse factor individually.
   c. The physics of the problem (Equation A.4 and Figure 9.5) disagrees with double accounting of the greenhouse gas effects.

Notes

1 Piers Forster et al., "The Earth's Energy Budget, Climate Feedbacks, and Climate Sensitivity, IPCC Report" (Cambridge and New York: Cambridge University Press, 2021).
2 Ibid.
3 Ameet Raval and Veerabhadran Ramanathan, "Observational Determination of the Greenhouse Effect" (paper presented at the Global Climate Feedbacks; No. BNL-45321; CONF-9006134, Upton, NY, 1990).
4 see Figure 7.2 Forster et al., "The Earth's Energy Budget, Climate Feedbacks, and Climate Sensitivity, IPCC Report," 934.
5 Ibid., 935.
6 Ibid., 968.
7 Raval and Ramanathan, "Observational Determination of the Greenhouse Effect."
8 Ibid., 10.
9 Ibid., 12.
10 Ibid.
11 Ibid.
12 See Table 7.10 in Forster et al., "The Earth's Energy Budget, Climate Feedbacks, and Climate Sensitivity, IPCC Report," 978.
13 Ibid., 968. Section 7.4.2.1
14 See Table 7.10 in ibid., 978.
15 "we have found it difficult to raise $\beta H2O$ much above 0.4 for any plausible temperature change profiles" Isaac M. Held and Brian J. Soden, "Water Vapor Feedback and Global Warming," *Annual Review of Energy and the Environment* 25, no. 1 (2000): 465.

Appendix B

Global Warming: Predicting Time to Reach a Foreseen Surface Temperature

The IPCC summary report of 2023 of the Sixth Assessment team predicts an increase of 3°C of the surface temperature caused by the heating of greenhouse gas emissions at an intermediate level. At this level the specific power of heating is 4.5 W/m^2. [1]

The purpose of this appendix is to estimate how long will it take to reach the predicted average surface temperature.

The ocean will require most of the heating power because the high specific of the water. Therefore, the question is how long will it take to heat the ocean. However, the ocean will not reach the average temperature increase of 3°C. Table B.1 calculates that the Ocean surface temperature will increase only 81% of the average temperature increment.

The surface temperature is higher than the average temperature. Table B.2 estimates that average temperature rise of the ocean is ½ of the surface temperature rise. It is reasonable that the temperature at the bottom of the ocean will stay constant at about 4°C.

Table B.3 calculates, therefore, how long will it take to raise the average temperature of 1.37E+21 of water by 1.21°C at a specific heating power of 4.5 W/m^2. The estimate is of 136 years.

Table B.1 Global surface temperature increase in 2011–2020 over 1850–1900

Warming	Unit	Value
Average Increase	°C	1.09
Land Increase	°C	1.59
Ocean Increase	°C	0.88
Ratio Ocean/Average		0.81

Source: Core Writing Team, "Summary for Policymakers" in *Climate Change 2023: Synthesis Report. Contribution of Working Groups I, Ii and Iii to the Sixth Assessment Report of the Intergovernmental Panel on Climate Change-Ipcc*, ed. Hoesung Lee and José Romero (Geneva, Switzerland: UN - Intergovernmental Panel on Climate Change (IPCC), 2023), 4.

Table B.2 Estimate of Ocean Mean Temperature Increase When Land Surface Temperature Rises by 3°C

Symbol	Description	Units	Value	Explanation
ERF	GHG Heating Power	W/m^2	4.5[a]	
ΔTs	Surface Temperature	°C	3[b]	
Rao	Ratio Ocean/Average		0.88	Table B.1
ΔTos	Ocean Surface Temperature	°C	2.44	ΔTs×Rao
ΔTom	Ocean mean Temperature	°C	1.21	ΔTos×1/2

Compiled by the author from the following sources

[a] Core Writing Team, "Summary for Policymakers," in *Climate Change 2023: Synthesis Report. Contribution of Working Groups I, Ii and Iii to the Sixth Assessment Report of the Intergovernmental Panel on Climate Change-Ipcc*, ed. Hoesung Lee and José Romero (Geneva, Switzerland: UN - Intergovernmental Panel on Climate Change (IPCC), 2023), 10., Table 1, Row C6, Intermediate greenhouse emissions–

[b] Ibid., Table 1, Row C6, Intermediate greenhouse emissions

Table B.3 Estimating the Duration of Heating Up the Earth by 3°C Given a Specific Heating Power of 4.5 W/m^2

Symbol	Magnitude	Value	Units	Calculation
V	Ocean Volume	1.37E+18	m^3	Datum[a]
ρ	Water density	1000	Kg/m^3	Datum
m	Ocean mass	1.37E+21	Kg	m=ρ*V
c	Water specific heat	4188	J/(Kg*°C)	Datum[b]
En	Energy	6.94824E+24	J	m*c*ΔT
ΔF	GHG Specific Power	4.5	W/m^2	Datum[c]
Oa	Ocean Area	3.61E+14	m^2	Datum[d]
H	GHG Heating Power	1.62E+15	W	E×Ao
τ	time	4.28E+09	s	En/H
s→Y	Conversion to years	3.15E+07	s/Y	τ/(365×24×3600)
t	Time	136	Years	t/(s→Y)

[a] M. Pidwirny, *Chapter 14: The Oceans: Single Chapter from the Ebook Understanding Physical Geography* (Kelowna: Our Planet Earth Publishing, 2023).

[b] Royal Society, *Proceedings of the Royal Society of London: Containing Papers of a Mathematical and Physical Character. Series A* (London: Harrison and Son, 1909), 393.

[c] Core Writing Team, "Summary for Policymakers," in *Climate Change 2023: Synthesis Report. Contribution of Working Groups I, Ii and Iii to the Sixth Assessment Report of the Intergovernmental Panel on Climate Change-Ipcc*, ed. Hoesung Lee and José Romero (Geneva, Switzerland: UN - Intergovernmental Panel on Climate Change (IPCC), 2023), 10., Table 1, Row C6, Intermediate greenhouse emissions.

[d] Pidwirny, *Chapter 14: The Oceans: Single Chapter from the Ebook Understanding Physical Geography.*

Note

1 Core Writing Team, "Summary for Policymakers," in *Climate Change 2023: Synthesis Report. Contribution of Working Groups I, Ii and Iii to the Sixth Assessment Report of the Intergovernmental Panel on Climate Change-Ipcc*, ed. Hoesung Lee and José Romero (Geneva: UN - Intergovernmental Panel on Climate Change (IPCC), 2023), 10. Table 1, Row C6, Intermediate greenhouse emissions.

Appendix C

Temperatures

It is common practice to measure past time histories, analyze their behavior, and predict the expected magnitude in the future. One of the difficulties in predicting future behavior of a cyclical magnitude from current information consists of separating trends from long period cyclical components. The mathematical definition of a cyclical or periodic function is that the function repeats itself every cycle of duration τ or: $F(k\tau+t)=F\left[(k-1)\tau+t\right]$. Rigorously speaking this can only happen if t started at $-\infty$ and continues to ∞. The proof is that if the function started at finite time t_0 with the value $F(t_0)$ then $F(t_0)\neq F(t_0-\tau)$; consequently such a function is not cyclical. A similar proof shows that a cyclical function cannot end at a finite time.

Fourier demonstrated that a cyclical magnitude can be represented by a sum of trigonometric functions. For example cyclical variation of the temperature is represented by the following Fourier series:

$$T(t)=a_0+\sum_{n=1}^{\infty}\left(a_n\cos\frac{2n\pi t}{\tau}+b_n\sin\frac{2n\pi t}{\tau}\right) \qquad \text{Equation C.1}$$

The terms a_n and b_n are amplitudes of cyclical variations of the nth component. A component $\left(a_k\cos\frac{2k\pi t}{\tau}+b_k\sin\frac{2k\pi t}{\tau}\right)$ is called the kth harmonic of the function. The term $\frac{\tau}{k}$ is the period of the kth harmonic.

Theorem C-1 - The average of a periodical function is the average of its longest period. By definition of a periodic function this theorem is intuitive; however, its demonstration is straightforward:

The average over a period $t\in[0,\tau]\overline{T}_\tau$ over a period is $\overline{T}_\tau=\int_0^\tau T(t)dt$. The average over all values of $T(t)$ is obtained from the value over k periods from $-\infty$ to 0 and k periods from 0 to ∞: $\overline{T}(t)=\int_{-\infty}^{+\infty}F(t)dt=\lim_{k\to\infty}\frac{1}{2k}2k\overline{T}_\tau=\overline{T}_\tau$

Theorem C-2 –The average of periodical function of the form expressed by Equation C.1 is a_0

Demonstration:

The average of a periodic function is the average over its period (Theorem C-1). Therefore, the average of a Fourier series is:

$$\bar{T}=\frac{1}{\tau}\int_0^\tau T(t)\,dt=\frac{1}{\tau}\int_0^\tau a_0 dt+\frac{1}{\tau}\int_0^\tau\sum_{n=1}^{\infty}a_n\cos\frac{2n\pi t}{\tau}dt+\frac{1}{\tau}\int_0^\tau\sum_{n=1}^{\infty}b_n\sin\frac{2n\pi t}{\tau}dt$$

The term $\frac{1}{\tau}\int_0^\tau a_0 dt=\frac{1}{\tau}\left(a_0 t\Big|_0^\tau\right)=\frac{a_0\tau}{\tau}=a_0$

The cosine harmonics terms average to:

$$\frac{1}{\tau}\int_0^\tau\sum_{n=1}^{\infty}a_n\cos\frac{2n\pi t}{\tau}dt=\sum_0^{\infty}\int_0^{\frac{\tau}{n}}\cos\frac{2n\pi t}{\tau}dt=-\frac{\tau}{2n\pi}\left(\sin\frac{2n\pi}{\tau}\Big|_0^{\frac{\tau}{n}}\right)=$$

$$=\left[\sin(0)-\sin(2\pi)\right]=0 \text{ for any } n\neq 0$$

Similarly the term $\frac{1}{\tau}\int_0^\tau\sum_{n=1}^{\infty}b_n\sin\frac{2n\pi t}{\tau}dt=0$ for any n

Therefore $\bar{T}=a_0$

Theorem C-3 The average of a periodic function over finite time interval is $\bar{T}=a_0$ if the time interval consists of a n periods, where n is an integer. The demonstration of the theorem is identical to the demonstration of Theorem C-2.

Theorem C-4 The average of a periodic function over finite time interval is $\bar{T}\neq a_0$ if the time interval consists of a $n+x$ periods, where n is an integer and $x<1$.

The demonstration is as follows:

$$\bar{T}=\frac{1}{\tau}\int_0^\tau T(t)\,dt=\frac{1}{\tau}\int_0^{\tau+x\tau} a_0 dt+\frac{1}{\tau}\int_0^{\tau+x\tau}\sum_{n=1}^{\infty}a_n\cos\frac{2n\pi t}{\tau}dt+\frac{1}{\tau}\int_0^\tau\sum_{n=1}^{\infty}b_n\sin\frac{2n\pi t}{\tau}dt$$

The term $\frac{1}{\tau+x\tau}\int_0^{\tau+x\tau} a_0 dt=\frac{1}{\tau+x\tau}\left(a_0 t\Big|_0^{\tau+x\tau}\right)=\frac{a_0(\tau+x\tau)}{\tau+x\tau}=a_0$

The cosine harmonic terms average to:

$$\frac{1}{\tau}\int_0^{\tau+x\tau}\sum_{n=1}^{\infty}a_n\cos\frac{2n\pi t}{\tau}dt=\sum_0^{\infty}\int_0^{\frac{\tau}{n}}\cos\frac{2n\pi t}{\tau}dt=-\frac{\tau}{2n\pi}\left(\sin\frac{2n\pi}{\tau}\Big|_0^{\frac{\tau+x}{n}}\right)=$$

$$=\left[\sin(0)-\sin(2\pi+2\pi x)\right]=r_c\neq 0$$

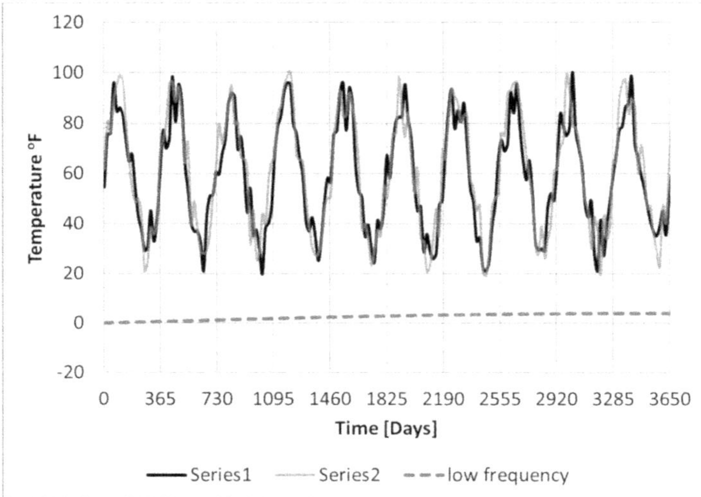

Figure C.1 Ten years span temperatures measurements—Series1 is periodic with an average temperature of 60°F. Series2 shows a higher average because it is superimposed on a harmonic (curve low frequency). This harmonic will not average to 0 because it is averaged during a time interval which is not a multiple of one period. This measurement is ambiguous because it means either that the temperature has a trend to rise or that it is a periodic function with a period significantly longer than 10 years. Author's work.

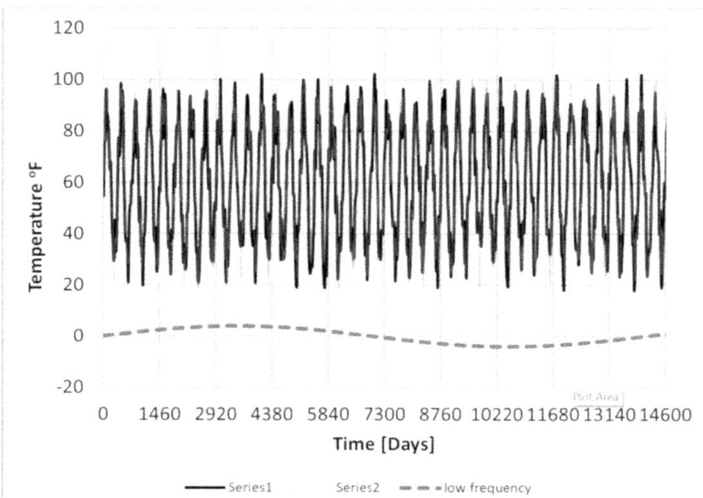

Figure C.2 Forty-year span temperature measurements. Author's work.

Similarly the sine harmonic terms average to a nonzero value r_s. Therefore, the average is $\bar{T} = a_0 + r_c + r_s \neq a_0$

The consequence of Theorem C-3 is that one can measure the average of a periodic function provided one knows its longest period.

For example the average temperature of Series1 (Figure C.1) is 60°F. However, if one measures the same for Series2 one should obtain close to 64°F. The reason for that is that the longest period of all components of Series1 is 365 days (1 year). The longest period of Series2 is 14,000 days (38.3 years). Measuring and averaging the data over 10 years (3,650) amounts to averaging over 0.26 of the fundamental period. In virtue of Theorem C-3 the average is incorrect. A close to correct average is obtained by measuring during an interval of 40 years (Figure C.2).

Bibliography

Abrutyn, Seth. “Pollution-Purification Rituals, Cultural Memory and the Evolution of Religion: How Collective Trauma Shaped Ancient Israel.” *AJCS* 3, no. 1 (February 2015): 123–55.

Acevedo, Carolina, and Jennifer P. Barfield. “Review: Reproductive Physiology of Bison and Application of Assisted Reproductive Technologies to Their Conservation.” *Animal* 17 (May 1, 2023): 100842.

Addo, Ping-Ann. “‘Is It Entrepreneurship, or Is It Survival?’: Gender, Community, and Innovation in Boston’s Black Immigrant Micro-Enterprise Spaces.” *Societies* 7, no. 3 (2017): 20.

Albanese, Jay S. “White Collar Crimes and Casino Gambling: Looking for Empirical Links to Forgery, Embezzlement, and Fraud.” *Crime, Law and Social Change* 49 (2008): 333–47.

Alexis, Muston. *L’israël Des Alpes: Première Histoire Complète Des Vaudois Du Piémont Et De Leurs Colonies.* Vol. I. Paris: Libr. de Marc Ducloux, 1851.

Algaze, Guillermo. *Ancient Mesopotamia at the Dawn of Civilization: The Evolution of an Urban Landscape.* Chicago and London: University of Chicago Press, 2009.

Alimonti, Gianluca. “A Critical Assessment of Extreme Events Trends in Times of Global Warming.” In *Brief History of the Troubled Life of the Article and Its Retraction*, 2023, personal communication.

Alimonti, Gianluca, Luigi Mariani, Franco Prodi, and Renato Angelo Ricci. “A Critical Assessment of Extreme Events Trends in Times of Global Warming.” *The European Physical Journal Plus* 137, no. 1 (2022): 1–20.

Alley, Richard B. *Earth: The Operators’ Manual.* New York and London: W. W. Norton, 2011.

Alston, Lee J., and Andrés A. Gallo. “Electoral Fraud, the Rise of Peron and Demise of Checks and Balances in Argentina.” *Explorations in Economic History* 47, no. 2 (2010): 179–97.

Alterio, Micaela, and Roberto Niembro. “Constitutional Culture and Democracy in Mexico: A Critical View of the 100-Year-Old Mexican Constitution.” In *A Constitutional Democracy in Crisis?* edited by Mark A. Graber, Sanford Levinson, and Mark Tushnet, 139–60. New York: Oxford University Press, 2018.

Alvarez-Palau, Eduard J., Alfonso Díez-Minguela, and Jordi Martí-Henneberg. “Railroad Integration and Uneven Development on the European Periphery, 1870–1910.” *Social Science History* 45, no. 2 (2021): 261–89.

Ames, Kenneth. “The Archaeology of Rank.” Chap. 28 In *Handbook of Archaeological Theories*, edited by R. Alexander Bentley, Herbert D. G. Maschner, and Christopher Chippindale, 487–513. Lanham: AltaMira Press, 2007.

Anholt, Rosanne, Caroline van Dullemen, Juliana Santos de Carvalho, Joris Rijbroek, Stijn Sieckelinck, and Marieke W. Slootman. “Understanding Societal Resilience: The Case for Engaged Scholarship.” In *Multisystemic Resilience: Adaptation and Transformation in Contexts of Change*, edited by Michael Ungar, 551–63. New York: Oxford University Press, 2021.

Anthony, David W. *The Horse, the Wheel, and Language: How Bronze-Age Riders from the Eurasian Steppes Shaped the Modern World.* Princeton: Princeton University Press, 2010.
Arduini, Carlo. *La Primogenita Di Galileo Galilei Rivelata Dalle Sue Lettere Edite Ed Inedite.* Florence: Felice Le Monnier, 1864.
Arendt, Hannah. *The Origins of Totalitarianism.* San Diego, New York, and London: Harcourt Brace Jovanovich, 1973.
Aristotle, Benjamin Jowett, and Henry William Carless Davis. *Politics.* Kindle edition. Mineola: Dover Publications, 2000.
Armstrong, Benedict, Gilles Theriault, Pascal Guenel, Jan Deadman, Marcel Goldberg, and Paul Heroux. "Association between Exposure to Pulsed Electromagnetic Fields and Cancer in Electric Utility Workers in Quebec, Canada, and France." *American Journal of Epidemiology* 140, no. 9 (1994): 805–20.
Arneson, Richard J. "Shame, Stigma, and Disgust in the Decent Society." *The Journal of Ethics* 11 (2007): 31–63.
Arthur, W. Brian. "Inductive Reasoning and Bounded Rationality." *The American Economic Review* 84, no. 2 (1994): 406–11.
Artz, Frederick B. *The Enlightenment in France.* Kent: Kent State University Press, 1968.
Ataguba, Ochega A., and John E. Ataguba. "Social Determinants of Health: The Role of Effective Communication in the Covid-19 Pandemic in Developing Countries." *Global Health Action* 13, no. 1 (December 31, 2020): 1788263.
Audisio, Gabriel. "Des Pauvres De Lyon Aux Vaudois Réformés." *Revue de l'histoire des religions* 217, no. 1 (2000): 155–66.
Audisio, Gabriel. *The Waldensian Dissent: Persecution and Survival C. 1170–C. 1570.* Translated by Claire Davison. Cambridge: Cambridge University Press, 1999.
Australian Bureau of Statistics. "National and State Information About Adult Prisoners and Community Based Corrections, Including Legal Status, Custody Type, Indigenous Status, Sex." Canberra: Corrective Services, Australia, 2023.
Ball, Philip. "The physical modelling of society: a historical perspective." Physica A: Statistical Mechanics and its Applications 314, no. 1-4 (2002): 1-14
Bădescu, Ilie. *Paul Anghel – the Genial Wallach. The Eight Worlds of the Romanian Literature.* Bucharest: Walachia Press, 2018.
Bădescu, Ilie, and Joseph Livni, eds. *A Civil Society with no Hierarchy.* Lanham: Lexington Books, 2023.
Bădescu, Ilie, Ozana Cucu-Oancea, and Gheorghe Şişeşte. *Dicţionar De Sociologie Rurală.* Bucharest: Editura Mica Valahie, 2005.
Bailey, Kristen. "The Causes of Recidivism in the Criminal Justice System and Why It Is Worth the Cost to Address Them." *Nashville Bar Journal* 6, no. 11 (2007): 6–9.
Baker, David P. *The Schooled Society: The Educational Transformation of Global Culture.* Stanford: Stanford University Press, 2014.
Balcombe, Paul, Jamie F. Speirs, Nigel P. Brandon, and Adam D. Hawkes. "Methane Emissions: Choosing the Right Climate Metric and Time Horizon." *Environmental Science: Processes & Impacts* 20, no. 10 (2018): 1323–39.
Balkin, Jack M. "The Roots of the Living Constitution." *Bulletin Review* 92 (2012): 1129.
Balogun, Oladele Abiodun. "A Philosophical Defence of Punishment in Traditional African Legal Culture: The Yoruba Example." *The Journal of Pan African Studies* 3, no. 3 (2009): 43–54.

Barry, Eloise. *Time*. 2022., https://time.com/6173229/countries-abortion-illegal-restrictions/
Bates, Michael N. "Extremely Low Frequency Electromagnetic Fields and Cancer: The Epidemiologic Evidence." *Environmental Health Perspectives* 95 (1991): 147–56.
Batinski, Michael C. *Jonathan Belcher, Colonial Governor.* Lexington: University Press of Kentucky, 1996.
Beccaria, Cesare. *Dei Delitti E Delle Pene.* Livorno: Marco Coltellini, 1764.
Beeghley, Leonard. *The Structure of Social Stratification in the United States, the, Coursesmart Etextbook.* London and New York: Routledge, 2015.
Bejski, Moshe. "The 'Righteous among the Nations' and Their Part in the Rescue of Jews." In *The Nazi Holocaust*, edited by Michael R. Marrus. Westport, Conn., 1989.
Benson, Robert L., G. Constable, Carol D. Lanham, and Charles H. Haskins. *Renaissance and Renewal in the Twelfth Century.* Toronto: University of Toronto Press, 1991.
Benton, Michael J., and Brent C. Emerson. "How Did Life Become So Diverse? The Dynamics of Diversification According to the Fossil Record and Molecular Phylogenetics." *Palaeontology* 50, no. 1 (2007): 23–40.
Bercovitch, Jacob. *Resolving International Conflicts: The Theory and Practice of Mediation.* Edited by Jacob Bercovitch. Boulder: Lynne Rienner Publishers, 1996.
Berg, Paul, and Maxine Singer. *Dealing with Genes: The Language of Heredity.* Mill Valley: University Science Books, 1992.
Biasotto, Larissa D., and Andreas Kindel. "Power Lines and Impacts on Biodiversity: A Systematic Review." *Environmental Impact Assessment Review* 71 (2018): 110–19.
Bideleux, Robert, and Ian Jeffries. *A History of Eastern Europe: Crisis and Change.* New York and London: Taylor & Francis, 2006.
Blackburn, Simon. *Reason and Prediction.* Cambridge: Cambridge University Press, 1973.
Bleeker, Claas J. "The Religion of Ancient Egypt." In *Historia Religionum, Volume 1 Religions of the Past*, edited by Claas J. Bleeker and G. Widengren. Leiden, New York, Copenhagen, and Köln: E.J. Brill, 1988.
Bloch, Carter, Ebbe Krogh Graversen, and Heidi Skovgaard Pedersen. "Competitive Research Grants and Their Impact on Career Performance." *Minerva* 52 (2014): 77–96.
Blunden, J., and D. S. Arndt. "State of the Climate in 2019." *Bulletin of the American Meteorological Society* 101, no. 8 (2020): S1–S429.
Boatwright, Maria T. *Hadrian and the Cities of the Roman Empire.* Princeton: Princeton University Press, 2000.
Bodansky, Daniel. "The United Nations Framework Convention on Climate Change: A Commentary." *Yale Journal of International Law* 18 (1993): 451.
Bodenmann, Reinhard. "Les Vaudois Et La Production Du Livre Évangélique Français (1525–1550)." *Revue Littératures| Université McGill* 24, no. 1 (2017): 25–30.
Bodin, Jean. *On Sovereignty.* Cambridge Texts in the History of Political Thought. Edited by Julian H. Franklin. Cambridge: Cambridge University Press, 1992.
Boese, Vanessa A., Amanda B. Edgell, Sebastian Hellmeier, Seraphine F. Maerz, and Staffan I. Lindberg. "How Democracies Prevail: Democratic Resilience as a Two-Stage Process." In *Resilience of Democracy*, edited by Anna Lührmann and Wolfgang Merkel, 17–39. Milton Park and Abingdon: Routledge, 2023.
Bonner, Stanley. *Education in Ancient Rome: From the Elder Cato to the Younger Pliny.* New York: Routledge, 2012.
Booth, John A., and Mitchell A. Seligson. "The Political Culture of Authoritarianism in Mexico: A Reexamination." *Latin American Research Review* 19, no. 1 (1984): 106–24.

Bottari, C., M. Coltelli, and C. Monaco. "Evidence of Late Roman Collapse at Catania (Sicily, Southern Italy): An Earthquake in the 4th Century Ad?." *Quaternary International* 357 (2015): 336–43.

Bowman, Alan. "Quantifying Egyptian Agriculture." In *Quantifying the Roman Economy. Methods and Problems, Oxford*, edited by Alan Bowman and Andrew Wilson, 177–204. Oxford: Oxford University Press, 2009.

Boyles, Michael. "Dei: What It Is & How to Champion It in the Workplace." Harvard Business School on Line. https://online.hbs.edu/blog/post/what-is-dei.

Braga, Anthony A., David M. Hureau, and Andrew V. Papachristos. "Deterring Gang-Involved Gun Violence: Measuring the Impact of Boston's Operation Ceasefire on Street Gang Behavior." *Journal of Quantitative Criminology* 30 (2014): 113–39.

Braga, Anthony A., and David L. Weisburd. "The Effects of Focused Deterrence Strategies on Crime: A Systematic Review and Meta-Analysis of the Empirical Evidence." *Journal of Research in Crime and Delinquency* 49, no. 3 (2012): 323–58.

Bragg, Melvyn, Tom Healey, Justin Champion, and Clare Jackson "The Divine Right of Kings." In *In Our Time*, edited by Melvyn Bragg, 45 min. London: BBC Radio 4, 2007.

Bréon, F. M., G. Broquet, V. Puygrenier, F. Chevallier, Irène Xueref-Remy, M. Ramonet, E. Dieudonné, et al. "An Attempt at Estimating Paris Area Co 2 Emissions from Atmospheric Concentration Measurements." *Atmospheric Chemistry and Physics* 15, no. 4 (2015): 1707–24.

Briggs, John DeQ. *America in Turmoil: Essays on Politics, the Economy, Society, and the Future*. Mount Pleasant: Bublish, Incorporated, 2023.

Britannica, The Editors of Encyclopedia. "S.V. Inflammation." In *Encyclopedia Britannica on Line*. Chicago: Encyclopaedia Britannica, Inc., 2024.

Broadhurst, Roderic G., and Ross A. Mailer. "The Recidivism of Prisoners Released for the First Time: Reconsidering the Effectiveness Question." *Australian & New Zealand Journal of Criminology* 23, no. 2 (1990): 88–104.

Bronner, Stephen E. *Reclaiming the Enlightenment: Toward a Politics of Radical Engagement*. New York: Columbia University Press, 2004.

Brunk, Gregory G. "Why Do Societies Collapse? A Theory Based on Self-Organized Criticality." *Journal of Theoretical Politics* 14, no. 2 (2002): 195–230.

Bryde, Brun-Otto. "Fundamental Rights as Guidelines and Inspiration: German Constitutionalism in International Perspective." *Wisconsin International Law Journal* 25 (2007): 189.

Buchner, Barbara, Baysa Naran, Pedro Fernandes, Rajashree Padmanabhi, Paul Rosane, Matthew Solomon, Sean Stout, Costanza Strinati, Rowena Tolentino, Githungo Wakaba, Yaxin Zhu, Chavi Meattle, and Sandra Guzmán. "The Global Landscape of Climate Finance 2013." Climate Policy Initiative, 2021.

Burnell, Peter J., and Peter Calvert. *The Resilience of Democracy: Persistent Practice, Durable Idea*. London and Portland: F. Cass, 1999.

Burns, John F. *Controversies between Royal Governors and Their Assemblies in the Northern American Colonies*. Boston: Wright and Potter Printing Company, 1923.

Buyakova, N. V., A. V. Kryukov, D. A. Seredkin, and K. V. Suslov. "Influence of Spatial Arrangement of Wires on Electromagnetic Ecology near High-Voltage Power Transmission Lines at Railway Station." Paper presented at the IOP Conference Series: Materials Science and Engineering, 2021.

Byrd, Randolph C. "Positive Therapeutic Effects of Intercessory Prayer in a Coronary Care Unit Population." *Southern Medical Journal* 81, no. 7 (1988): 826–9.

Calabresi, Steven G. "On Originalism in Constitutional Interpretation." National Constitution Center. https://constitutioncenter.org/the-constitution/white-papers/on-originalism-in-constitutional-interpretation.

Caldeira, Ken, Atul K. Jain, and Martin I. Hoffert. "Climate Sensitivity Uncertainty and the Need for Energy without Co2 Emission." *Science* 299, no. 5615 (2003): 2052–4.

Calder, Philip C. "Omega-3 Fatty Acids and Inflammatory Processes: From Molecules to Man." *Biochemical Society Transactions* 45, no. 5 (2017): 1105–15.

Canada, Government of. "Climate Action and Awareness Fund." Edited by Environment and Natural Resources. Ottawa: ENR, 2023.

Canada, Goverment of. *Water Temperature and Burns/Scalds*. Ottawa: Health Canada, 2011.

Canals Casals, Lluc, Marta Rodríguez, Cristina Corchero, and Rafael E. Carrillo. "Evaluation of the End-of-Life of Electric Vehicle Batteries According to the State-of-Health." *World Electric Vehicle Journal* 10, no. 4 (2019): 63.

Cantens, Thomas, Evans Jadotte, David Cal MacWilliam, and Javier Suarez. "Haiti: Strengthening Customs Administration in an Insecure Environment." Washingon, DC: World Bank Publications, 2024.

Carles, Camille, Yolande Esquirol, Maxime Turuban, Clément Piel, Lucile Migault, Camille Pouchieu, Ghislaine Bouvier, et al. "Residential Proximity to Power Lines and Risk of Brain Tumor in the General Population." *Environmental Research* 185 (2020): 109473.

Chaniotis, Angelos. "The Divinity of Hellenistic Rulers." *A Companion to the Hellenistic World*, 431–45. 2003.

Chase, Arlen F., and Diane Z. Chase. "Complex Societies in the Southern Maya Lowlands." In *The Oxford Handbook of Mesoamerican Archaeology*, edited by Deborah L. Nichols and Christopher A. Pool, 265. Oxford: Oxford University Press, 2012.

Chmielewski, Anna K. "The Global Increase in the Socioeconomic Achievement Gap, 1964 to 2015." *American Sociological Review* 84, no. 3 (2019): 517–44.

Chung, Eui-Seok, Brian Soden, B. J. Sohn, and Lei Shi. "Upper-Tropospheric Moistening in Response to Anthropogenic Warming." *Proceedings of the National Academy of Sciences* 111, no. 32 (2014): 11636–41.

Ciammariconi, Anna. "Chapter 9—Constitutional Justice in Argentina and Brazil." In *Comparative Latin American Constitutionalism*, edited by Silvia Bagni and Serena Baldin, 169–90. Triest: EUT Edizioni Universita di Trieste, 2023.

Clarke, James Alexander. "Fichte and Hegel on Recognition." *British Journal for the History of Philosophy* 17, no. 2 (2009): 365–85.

Clear, Todd R., and James Austin. "Mass Incarceration." *Reforming Criminal Justice: A Report of the Academy for Justice on Bridging the Gap between Scholarship and Reform* 4 (2017): 55–76.

Cline, Eric H. *1177 B.C.: The Year Civilization Collapsed.* Kindle edition. Princeton: Princeton University Press, 2015.

Cochrane, Glynn. *Max Weber's Vision for Bureaucracy: A Casualty of World War I.* Cham, Switzerland: Springer International Publishing, 2017.

Colb, Sherry F. "Freedom from Incarceration: Why Is This Right Different from All Other Rights." *New York University Law Review* 69 (1994): 781.

Cole, David. "Turning the Corner on Mass Incarceration." *Ohio State Journal of Criminal Law* 9 (2011): 27.

"Combined Heat and Power (Chp) Partnership." In *US Government*, edited by EPA. Washington, DC, 2023. https://www.epa.gov/chp/chp-benefits.

Comen, Evan, Michael B. Sauter, Samuel Stebbins, and Thomas C. Frohlich. "Universities Getting the Most Money from the Federal Government." 24/7 Wall ST. https://247wallst.com/special-report/2017/03/22/universities-getting-the-most-money-from-the-federal-government/.

Conzade, Julian, Florian Nägele, Swarna Ramanathan, and Patrick Schaufuss. "Europe's Ev Opportunity—and the Charging Infrastructure Needed to Meet It." *McKinsey & Company*, 2022.

Coogan, Tim P. *The Famine Plot: England's Role in Ireland's Greatest Tragedy.* New York: St. Martin's Publishing Group, 2012.

Core Writing Team. "Summary for Policymakers." In *Climate Change 2023: Synthesis Report. Contribution of Working Groups I, Ii and Iii to the Sixth Assessment Report of the Intergovernmental Panel on Climate Change—Ipcc*, edited by Hoesung Lee and José Romero. Geneva: UN—Intergovernmental Panel on Climate Change (IPCC), 2023.

Costa, Carlos M., João C. Barbosa, Renato Gonçalves, Helder Castro, F. J. Del Campo, and Senentxu Lanceros-Méndez. "Recycling and Environmental Issues of Lithium-Ion Batteries: Advances, Challenges and Opportunities." *Energy Storage Materials* 37 (2021): 433–65.

Couderc-Barraud, Hélène. *La Violence, L'ordre Et La Paix: Résoudre Les Conflits En Gascogne Du Xie Au Début Du Xiiie Siècle.* Toulouse: Presses universitaires du Mirail, 2008.

Council of Europe. "Guidelines for Constitutional Referendums at National Level." In *CDL-INF (2001) 10*, edited by Council of Europe. Strasbourg Venice Commission at its 47th Plenary Meeting 2001.

Crawford, Iris, Yang Shao-Horn, and David Keith. "How Much Co2 Is Emitted by Manufacturing Batteries?" MIT, Climate Poertal. https://climate.mit.edu/ask-mit/how-much-co2-emitted-manufacturing-batteries.

Dadras, Soodeh, Ryan M. Gerdes, and Rajnikant Sharma. "Vehicular Platooning in an Adversarial Environment." Paper presented at the Proceedings of the 10th ACM Symposium on Information, Computer and Communications Security, 2015.

Dahlstedt, Magnus, and Maria Olson. *Education, Democracy, Citizenship—Utbildning, Demokrati, Medborgarskap.* Malmö: Gleerups Utbildning AB, 2013.

Dart, Bradley. "Tyranny of the Majority." 2008. https://www.researchgate.net/publication/3601473.

Davidson, Audrey B., and Robert B. Ekelund Jr. "The Medieval Church and Rents from Marriage Market Regulations." *Journal of Economic Behavior & Organization* 32, no. 2 (1997): 215–45.

De Blois, Lukas. "Army and General in the Late Roman Republic." In *A Companion to the Roman Army*, edited by Paul Erdkamp, 164–80. Malden, Oxford, and Australia: Blackwell, 2007.

De Freitas, Shaun A. "Samuel Rutherford on Law and Covenant: The Impact of Theologico-Political Federalism on Constitutional Theory." University of the Free State, 2003.

de Lagrèze, Gustave Bascle. *Histoire Du Droit Dans Les Pyrénées—Comté De Bigorre.* Paris: Imprimerie Impériale, 1867.

Demers, Paul A., David B. Thomas, Karin A. Rosenblatt, L. Margarita Jimenez, Anne McTiernan, Helge Stalsberg, Annette Stemhagen, et al. "Occupational Exposure to Electromagnetic Fields and Breast Cancer in Men." *American Journal of Epidemiology* 134, no. 4 (1991): 340–7.

Demougin, S. "Considérations Sur L'avancement Dans Les Carrières Procuratoriennes Équestres." In *Administration, Prosopography and Appointment Policies in the Roman Empire*, edited by Lukas De Blois, 24–34. Leiden: Brill, 2001.

Derfler, Leslie. *The Dreyfus Affair*. Westport and London: Greenwood Press, 2002.

Dershowitz, Alan M. *The Genesis of Justice*. New York: Warner Books, 2000.

Deutscher, Isaac. "Roots of Bureaucracy." *Canadian-American Slavic Studies* 3, no. 3 (1969): 453–72.

Dianda, Bas. *A History of the Seventies: The Political, Cultural, Social and Economic Developments That Shaped the Modern World*. Wilmington: Vernon Press, 2019.

Dickson-Gilmore, Jane. "Resurrecting the Peace: Traditionalist Approaches to Separate Justice in Kahnawake Mohawk Nation." In *Law & Anthropology*, edited by René Kuppe and Richard Potz, 83–106. The Hague: Martinus Nijhoff Publishers, 1996.

Diehl, Michael W. *Some Thoughts on the Study of Hierarchies*. Hierarchies in Action: Cui Bono. Carbondale: Southern Illinois University 2000: 11–30.

Dillon, John F. *The Law of Municipal Corporations*. New York: James Cockcroft, 1873.

Do Valle, Vanice Regina Lírio. "Dialogical Constitutionalism Manifestations in the Brazilian Judicial Review." *Revista de Investigações Constitucionais* 1 (2014): 59–90.

Dorislaus, Isaac. "Inaugural Lecture, Drss6311." University of Cambridge: Cambridge Alumni Database, 1627.

Drake, Brandon L. "The Influence of Climatic Change on the Late Bronze Age Collapse and the Greek Dark Ages." *Journal of Archaeological Science* 39, no. 6 (2012): 1862–70.

Duby, Georges. *The Early Growth of the European Economy*. Ithaca: Cornell University Press, 1978.

Duistermaat, Johannes J., and Johan A. C. Kolk. *Distributions: Theory and Applications*. New York, Dordrecht, Heidelberg, and London: Birkhäuser, 2010.

Dunn, Susan. *Sister Revolutions: French Lightning, American Light*. New York: Farrar, Straus and Giroux, 2000.

Durand, John D. "Mortality Estimates from Roman Tombstone Inscriptions." *American Journal of Sociology* 65, no. 4 (January 1960): 365–73.

Durose, Matthew R., and Leonardo Antenangeli. "Recidivism of Prisoners Released in 34 States in 2012: A 5-Year Follow-up Period (2012–2017)." Washington, DC: Bureau of Justice Statistics, 2021.

Dwight, Winthrop E. "An Episode in the Affaire Dreyfus." *The Yale Law Journal* 8, no. 6 (1899): 272–9.

Eccles, Ronald. "Mechanisms of Symptoms of Common Cold and Flu." *Common Cold* (2009): 23–45.

Edelstein-Keshet, Leah. *Mathematical Models in Biology*. New York: Random House, 1988.

Encyclopaedia Britannica, s.v. "Hugo Preuss," last modified October 24, 2024, https://www.britannica.com/biography/Hugo-Preuss

The Editors of Encyclopaedia Britannica. "Text of the Constitution of the United State." In *Encyclopedia Britannica*. 2023. https://www.britannica.com/topic/Constitution-of-the-United-States-2231775.

Eisenstadt, Shmuel Noah. "Bureaucracy and Bureaucratization." *Current Sociology* 7, no. 2 (1958): 99–124.

Ekman, Joakim, and Erik Amnå. "Political Participation and Civic Engagement: Towards a New Typology." *Human Affairs* 22 (2012): 283–300.

Elazar, Daniel J. *Covenant & Commonwealth: From Christian Separation through the Protestant Reformation.* New Brunswick: Transaction Publishers, 1995.
Elazar, Daniel J. *Covenant & Constitutionalism: The Great Frontier and the Matrix of Federal Democracy.* New Brunswick: Transaction Publishers, 1997.
Elazar, Daniel J. *Covenant and Polity in Biblical Israel: Volume 1, Biblical Foundations and Jewish Expressions: Covenant Tradition in Politics.* London and New York: Routledge, 2018.
Elazar, Daniel J., J. Kincaid, J. W. Baker, J. D. Bratt, H. Fisch, D. S. Lutz, W. S. Reid, et al. *The Covenant Connection: From Federal Theology to Modern Federalism.* Lanham: Lexington Books, 2000.
Emerson, Everett H. "Calvin and Covenant Theology." *Church History* 25, no. 2 (1956): 136–44.
Epstein, Joshua M. *Nonlinear Dynamics, Mathematical Biology, and Social Science: Wise Use of Alternative Therapies.* Boca Raton: CRC Press, 2018.
"European Ev Charging Infrastructure Master Plan." Brussels: ACEA—European Automobile Manufacturers' Association, 2022.
European Union. "Regulation of the European Parliament and of the Council Concerning Batteries and Waste Batteries, Amending Directive 2008/98/Ec and Regulation (Eu) 2019/1020 and Repealing Directive 2006/66/Ec." In *2020/0353 (COD); PE-CONS 2/23; ENV 45; ENT 11; MI 32; CODEC 44.* Brussels: The European Parliament and the Council of The European Union, 2023.
Evans, Charles M., and Angela E. Evans. "Plague–a Disease of Children and Servants? A Study of the Parish Records of St Peter Upon Cornhill, London from 1580 to 1605." *Continuity and Change* 34, no. 2 (2019): 183–208.
Faust, Avraham. *Israel's Ethnogenesis: Settlement, Interaction, Expansion and Resistance.* London: Equinox Pub., 2006.
Feibleman, J. K. *Justice, Law and Culture.* Springer Netherlands, 2012.
Feichtinger, Gustav, Christian V. Forst, and Carlo Piccardi. "A Nonlinear Dynamical Model for the Dynastic Cycle." *Chaos, Solitons & Fractals* 7, no. 2 (1996): 257–71.
Feinman, Gary M. "The Emergence of Social Complexity." In *Cooperation and Collective Action: Archaeological Perspectives*, edited by David M. Carballo, 35–56. Boulder: University Press of Colorado, 2012.
Feldenkirchen, Wilfried. *Werner Von Siemens: Inventor and International Entrepreneur.* Columbus: Ohio State University Press, 1994.
Feldman, Stephen M. *Free Expression and Democracy in America: A History.* Chicago University of Chicago Press, 2009.
Ferman, Marty A. *A Wing Design Method for Aerospace Students and Home Builders: Strength, Weight, Flutter, Divergence, Buckling, Deflection, and Twist.* Bloomington: Trafford Pub., 2011.
Feychting, Maria, and Michael Alhbom. "Magnetic Fields and Cancer in Children Residing near Swedish High-Voltage Power Lines." *American Journal of Epidemiology* 138, no. 7 (1993): 467–81.
Finkel, Steven E., and Junghyun Lim. "The Supply and Demand Model of Civic Education: Evidence from a Field Experiment in the Democratic Republic of Congo." In *Resilience of Democracy*, edited by Anna Lührmann and Wolfgang Merkel, 102–23. Milton Park and Abingdon: Routledge, 2023.
Follain, Antoine, and Jean-Michel Matz. *L'argent Des Villages Du Xiiie Au Xviiie Siècle: Comptabilités Paroissiales Et Communales, Fiscalité Locale: Actes Du Colloque D'angers, 30–31 Oct. 1998.* Rennes: Presses universitaires de Rennes, 1999.

Forster, Piers, Trude Storelvmo, Kyle Armour, William Collins, Jean-Louis Dufresne, David Frame, Dan Lunt, et al. "The Earth's Energy Budget, Climate Feedbacks, and Climate Sensitivity, IPCC Report." 923–1207. Cambridge and New York: Cambridge University Press, 2021.

Fourier, Joseph B. J., and A. Freeman. *The Analytical Theory of Heat.* Cambridge: Cambridge University Press, 1878.

Freeman, Richard B. "The Economics of Crime." *Handbook of Labor Economics* 3 (1999): 3529–71.

Friedman, Thomas L. *The World Is Flat: A Brief History of the Twenty-First Century.* New York: Farrar, Straus and Giroux, 2005.

Fulton, John. *Free Government in England and America: Containing the Great Charter, the Petition of Right, the Bill of Rights, the Federal Constitution.* S.M. Johnson is the Pseudonym of John Fulton. New York: Carleton, Publisher, 1864.

Galilei, Galileo. *Dialogue Concerning the Two Chief World Systems (Original: 1632).* Berkeley: University of California Press, 1914.

Garro, Alejandro M. "Judicial Review of Constitutionality in Argentina: Background Notes and Constitutional Provisions." *Duquesne Law Review* 45 (2006): 409–21.

Gentile, Giovanni. *Origins and Doctrine of Fascism: With Selections from Other Works.* New York: Taylor & Francis, 2017.

Geras, Norman. "Richard Rorty and the Righteous among the Nations." *Journal of Applied Philosophy* 12, no. 2 (1995): 151–73.

Gibbon, Edward. *The History of the Decline and Fall of the Roman Empire.* Boston: Little, Brown, 1854.

Gibbs, Penelope. "The Myth That Tough Sanctions Deter Crime – Revealed by the Sentencing Council." Transform Justice. https://www.transformjustice.org.uk/news-insight/the-myth-that-tough-sanctions-deter-crime-revealed-by-the-sentencing-council/.

Gilly, William Stephen. *Narrative of an Excursion to the Mountains of Piemont, and Researches among the Vaudois, or Waldenses, Protestant Inhabitants of the Cottian Alps: With an Appendix Containing Copies of Ancient Manuscripts and Other Interesting Documents.* London: C. and J. Rivington, 1824.

Gilly, William Stephen. *Waldensian Researches During a Second Visit to the Vaudois of Piemont.* London: Rivington, 1831.

Gimbel, Steven. *Exploring the Scientific Method: Cases and Questions.* Chicago: University of Chicago Press, 2011.

Goede, Miguel. "The Future of Democracy: The End of Democracy as We Know It." *Kybernetes* 48, no. 10 (2019): 2237–65.

Gonner, Edward C. K. "The Economic History." In *Germany in the Nineteenth Century: Five Lectures,* edited by John H. Rose, Charles H. Herford, Edward C. K. Gonner, and Michael Sadler. Manchester: Manchester University Press, 1912.

Göran, Ohlin P. "The Positive and the Preventive Check: A Study of the Rate of Growth of Pre-Industrial Populations." PhD Thesis, Cambridge, MA, Harvard, 1955.

Granholm, Jennifer M., Pete Buttigieg, Michael Regan, and Marcia Fudge. "The U.S. National Blueprint for Transportation Decarbonization." In *A Joint Strategy to Transform Transportatio,* edited by Transportation Departments of Energy, Housing, and EPA. Washington, DC: US Government, 2022.

Green, Alex E. S. "Socio-Physics: Should We Take It Seriously?." *Quarterly Journal of the Florida Academy of Sciences* 34, no. 3/4 (1971): 161–71.

Greene, Jay P., Albert Cheng, and Ian Kingsbury. "Education and Anti-Semitism." EDRE Working Paper Series No. 2021–02. University of Arkansas, 2021. https://scholarworks.uark.edu/edrepub/121.

Gross, Oren. "Hitler's Willing Law Professors." In *The Betrayal of the Humanities: The University during the Third Reich*, edited by Bernard M. Levinson and Robert P. Ericksen. Bloomington: Indiana University Press, 2022.

"Gross Domestic Product, Fourth Quarter and Year 2023 (Second Estimate)." Edited by Department of Commerce. Suitland: Bureau of Econopmic Analysis (BEA), 2024.

Group, Lithium-ion Car Battery Recycling Advisory. "Final Policy Recommendations." In *Meetings*, edited by CalEPA. Sacramento, 2022. https://calepa.ca.gov/lithium-ion-car-battery-recycling-advisory-group/.

Guenel, Pascal, Javier Nicolau, Ellen Imbernon, Anne Chevalier, and Marcel Goldberg. "Exposure to 50-Hz Electric Field and Incidence of Leukemia, Brain Tumors, and Other Cancers among French Electric Utility Workers." *American Journal of Epidemiology* 144, no. 12 (1996): 1107–21.

Guiney, Thomas, and Henry Yeomans. "Explaining Penal Momentum: Path Dependence, Prison Population Forecasting and the Persistence of High Incarceration Rates in England and Wales." *The Howard Journal of Crime and Justice* 62, no. 1 (2023): 29–45.

Haefeli, Evan. *New Netherland and the Dutch Origins of American Religious Liberty.* Philadelphia: University of Pennsylvania Press, Incorporated, 2013.

Hamerow, Theodore S. *Social Foundations of German Unification, 1858–1871, Volume II: Struggles and Accomplishments.* Princeton: Princeton University Press, 2015.

Hamilton, Alexander. "The Federalist # 32 'Founders on Line.'" https://founders.archives.gov/documents/Hamilton/01-04-02-0189.

Hamilton, Alexander. *The Papers of Alexander Hamilton.* Edited by Harold C. Syrett. New York: Columbia University Press, 1962.

Hamilton, Alexander, James Madison, and John Jay. *The Federalist Papers.* New York: Bantam Books, 1982.

Hamilton, Walter H. "Constitutionalism." In *Encyclopedia of the Social Sciences*, edited by Edwin R. A. Seligman and Alvin Johnson. New York: Macmillan, 1931.

Hanstad, Tim, and Jennifer Brown. "Land Reform Law and Implementation in West Bengal: Lessons and Recommendations." Seattle: Landesa, Rural Development Institute, 2001.

Haram, Mohammed Hussein Saleh Mohammed, Jia Woon Lee, Gobbi Ramasamy, Eng Eng Ngu, Siva Priya Thiagarajah, and Yuen How Lee. "Feasibility of Utilising Second Life Ev Batteries: Applications, Lifespan, Economics, Environmental Impact, Assessment, and Challenges." *Alexandria Engineering Journal* 60, no. 5 (2021): 4517–36.

Harari, Yuval N. *Sapiens: A Brief History of Humankind.* New York: HarperCollins, 2015.

Harris, Kamala. "Fact Sheet: The Biden-Harris Electric Vehicle Charging Action Plan." Edited by The White House. Washington, DC: US Government The White House, 2021.

Hartmann, Bernd J. "The Arrival of Judicial Review in Germany under the Weimar Constitution of 1919." *Brigham Young University Journal of Public Law* 18 (2003): 107.

Hartung, Frank E. "Methodological Assumption in a Social-Psychological Theory of Criminality." *Journal of Criminal Law Criminology and Police Science* 45 (1954): 652.

Hawkins, Cameron. "Contract, Coercion, and the Boundaries of the Roman Artisanal Firm." In *Work, Labour, and Professions in the Roman World*, edited by Koenraad Verboven and Christian Laes, 36–61. Leiden: Brill, 2017.

Hayek, Fridrich A. *The Constitution of Liberty*. Chicago: University of Chicago Press, 1978.

Hayes, Brett K., Evan Heit, and Haruka Swendsen. "Inductive Reasoning." *Wiley Interdisciplinary Reviews: Cognitive Science* 1, no. 2 (2010): 278–92.

Hedges Company. "How Many Cars Are There in the World in 2023." Hedges & Company, https://hedgescompany.com/blog/2021/06/how-many-cars-are-there-in-the-world/.

Hedges Company. "Us Vehicle Registration Statistics." Hedges & Company, https://hedgescompany.com/automotive-market-research-statistics/auto-mailing-lists-and-marketing/.

Hegel, Georg W. F. *The Difference between Fichte's and Schelling's Systems*. Edited by H. S. Harris and W. Cerf. Albany: SUNY Press, 1984.

Heit, Evan. "Properties of Inductive Reasoning." *Psychonomic Bulletin & Review* 7 (2000): 569–92.

Heit, Evan, and Caren M. Rotello. "Relations between Inductive Reasoning and Deductive Reasoning." *Journal of Experimental Psychology: Learning, Memory, and Cognition* 36, no. 3 (2010): 805.

Held, Isaac M., and Brian J. Soden. "Water Vapor Feedback and Global Warming." *Annual Review of Energy and the Environment* 25, no. 1 (2000): 441–75.

Herford, Charles H. "The Intellectual and Literary History." In *Germany in the Nineteenth Century: Five Lectures*, edited by John H. Rose, Charles H. Herford, Edward C. K. Gonner, and Michael Sadler. Manchester: Manchester University Press, 1912.

Heywood, Andrew. "Conservatism—a Defence for the Privileged and Prosperous?." *Politics Review* 25, no. 1 (2015).

Hoberman, John M. "The Transformation of East German Sport." *Journal of Sport History* 17, no. 1 (1990): 62–8.

Holling, Crawford S. "Understanding the Complexity of Economic, Ecological, and Social Systems." *Ecosystems* 4, no. 5 (2001): 390–405.

Horowitz, Irving Louis. "Daniel J. Elazar and the Covenant Tradition in Politics." *Publius: The Journal of Federalism* 31, no. 1 (Winter 2001): 1–7.

Hossain, Eklas, Darren Murtaugh, Jaisen Mody, Hossain Mansur Resalat Faruque, Md Samiul Haque Sunny, and Naeem Mohammad. "A Comprehensive Review on Second-Life Batteries: Current State, Manufacturing Considerations, Applications, Impacts, Barriers & Potential Solutions, Business Strategies, and Policies." *Ieee Access* 7 (2019): 73215–52.

Houston, Stephen, and David Stuart. "Of Gods, Glyphs and Kings: Divinity and Rulership among the Classic Maya." *Antiquity* 70, no. 268 (1996): 289–312.

Huggel, Christian, Laurens M. Bouwer, Sirkku Juhola, Reinhard Mechler, Veruska Muccione, Ben Orlove, and Ivo Wallimann-Helmer. "The Existential Risk Space of Climate Change." *Climatic Change* 174, no. 1–2 (2022): 8–28.

Hull, Kathleen. *Same-Sex Marriage: The Cultural Politics of Love and Law*. Cambridge: Cambridge University Press, 2006.

Hurwitz, Adolf. "Ueber Die Bedingungen, Unter Welchen Eine Gleichung Nur Wurzeln Mit Negativen Reellen Theilen Besitzt." *Mathematische Annalen* 46, no. 2 (June 1, 1895): 273–84.

Hussinger, Katrin, and João N. Carvalho. "The Long-Term Effect of Research Grants on the Scientific Output of University Professors." *Industry and Innovation* 29, no. 4 (2022): 463–87.

Illescas, Santiago Redondo, Julio Sánchez-Meca, and Vicente Garrido Genovés. "Treatment of Offenders and Recidivism: Assessment of the Effectiveness of Programmes Applied in Europe." *Psychology in Spain* 5, no. 1 (2001): 47–62.

Irvine, Michael A., Jane A. Buxton, Michael Otterstatter, Robert Balshaw, Reka Gustafson, Mark Tyndall, Perry Kendall, et al. "Distribution of Take-Home Opioid Antagonist Kits During a Synthetic Opioid Epidemic in British Columbia, Canada: A Modelling Study." *The Lancet Public Health* 3, no. 5 (2018/05/01/ 2018): e218–e25.

Israel, Jonathan. *A Revolution of the Mind: Radical Enlightenment and the Intellectual Origins of Modern Democracy*. Princeton: Princeton University Press, 2010.

Ivanova, Veneta Todorova. "Occult Communism: Culture, Science and Spirituality in Late Socialist Bulgaria." Urbana: University of Illinois at Urbana-Champaign, 2017.

James, Harold. *Krupp: A History of the Legendary German Firm*. Princeton: Princeton University Press, 2012.

Jarvis, Paul. "Commodus' Court: Conspiracy and Consequences." *Ancient History Bulletin* 37, no.1-2 (2023): 53–79.

Johnson, Vincent Robert. "The Declaration of the Rights of Man and of Citizens of 1789, the Reign of Terror, and the Revolutionary Tribunal of Paris." *Boston College International and Comparative Law Review* 13 (1990): 1.

Jones, Mark, and Peter Johnstone. *History of Criminal Justice*. Waltham: Elsevier, 2012.

Junger, Marianne, Robert West, and Reinier Timman. "Crime and Risky Behavior in Traffic: An Example of Cross-Situational Consistency." *Journal of Research in Crime and Delinquency* 38, no. 4 (2001): 439–59.

Kallis, Aristotle. "Nazi Propaganda and 'Coordination': The Haphazard Path to Totalitarianism." *European Review of History: Revue européenne d'histoire* 13, no. 1 (2006): 115–39.

Kant, Immanuel, and J. M. D. Meiklejohn. *Critique of Pure Reason*. New York: Colonial Press, 1899.

Karsten, Rafael. *A Totalitarian State of the Past: The Civilization of the Inca Empire in Ancient Peru*. Port Washington and London: Kennikat Press, 1969.

Kassinger, Ruth. *Gold: From Greek Myth to Computer Chips*. Brookfield: Twenty-First Century Books, 2003.

Katz, Eric. "The Nazi Engineers: Reflections on Technological Ethics in Hell." *Science and Engineering Ethics* 17 (2011): 571–82.

Kayhan, Handan, Babek Erdebilli, Sevim GÖNEN, Meriç Arda EŞMEKAYA, Ersen Ertekin, and Ayşe Gülnihal Canseven. "Effects of Extremely Low-Frequency Magnetic Field on Healthy Fibroblasts and Breast Cancer Cells." *Journal of Istanbul Faculty of Medicine* 83, no. 4 (2020): 384–9.

Keeling, Matt J., and Pejman Rohani. *Modeling Infectious Diseases in Humans and Animals*. Princeton and Oxford: Princeton University Press, 2011.

Kennedy, Ellen. *Constitutional Failure: Carl Schmitt in Weimar*. Durham and London: Duke University Press, 2004.

Kennedy, Michael Peter. "Bifurcation and Chaos." In *The Circuits and Filters Handbook, Second Edition*, edited by Wai K. Chen, 1093–162. Boca Raton: Taylor & Francis, 2002.

Kermack, William O., and Anderson G. McKendrick. "A Contribution to the Mathematical Theory of Epidemics." Paper presented at the Proceedings of the Royal Society of London A: Mathematical, Physical and Engineering Sciences, 1927.

Kertzer, David I. *The Kidnapping of Edgardo Mortara*. New York: Vintage, 2008.

Kheifets, Leeka, A. Ahlbom, C. M. Crespi, M. Feychting, C. Johansen, J. Monroe, M. F. G. Murphy, et al. "A Pooled Analysis of Extremely Low-Frequency Magnetic Fields and Childhood Brain Tumors." *American Journal of Epidemiology* 172, no. 7 (2010): 752–61.

Kheifets, Leeka, C. M. Crespi, C. Hooper, M. Cockburn, A. T. Amoon, and X. P. Vergara. "Residential Magnetic Fields Exposure and Childhood Leukemia: A Population-Based Case-Control Study in California." [In eng]. *Cancer Causes Control* 28, no. 10 (October 2017): 1117–23.

Kheifets, Leeka, Michael Repacholi, Rick Saunders, and Emilie Van Deventer. "The Sensitivity of Children to Electromagnetic Fields." *Pediatrics* 116, no. 2 (2005): e303–e13.

Kiehl, Kent A., and Morris B. Hoffman. "The Criminal Psychopath: History, Neuroscience, Treatment, and Economics." *Jurimetrics* 51 (2011): 355.

Kim, Jiyeon, Chang Seung Ha, Hae June Lee, and Kiwon Song. "Repetitive Exposure to a 60-Hz Time-Varying Magnetic Field Induces DNA Double-Strand Breaks and Apoptosis in Human Cells." *Biochemical and Biophysical Research Communications* 400, no. 4 (2010): 739–44.

Kirby, Mayson. *History of Civilizations*. Waltham Abbey: EDTECH, 2018.

Klarman, Michael J. "Fidelity, Indeterminacy, and the Problem of Constitutional Evil." *Fordham Law Review* 65 (1997): 1739.

Klarman, Michael J. *The Framers' Coup: The Making of the United States Constitution*. Oxford and New York: Oxford University Press, 2016.

Klarman, Michael J. "Rethinking the History of American Freedom (Review Essay of Eric Foner, the Story of American Freedom (1998))." *William & Mary Law Review* 42 (2000): 265.

Klein, Philip A. *Beyond Dissent: Essays in Institutional Economics*. Armonk: M.E. Sharpe, 1994.

Kliukiene, Jolanta, Tore Tynes, and Aage Andersen. "Residential and Occupational Exposures to 50-Hz Magnetic Fields and Breast Cancer in Women: A Population-Based Study." *American Journal of Epidemiology* 159, no. 9 (2004): 852–61.

Kocher, Matthew Adam, Adria K. Lawrence, and Nuno P. Monteiro. "Nationalism, Collaboration, and Resistance: France under Nazi Occupation." *International Security* 43, no. 2 (2018): 117–50.

Kohn, Alfie. *No Contest: The Case against Competition*. Boston and New York: Houghton Mifflin, 1992.

Kounadis, Anthony N. "Nonlinear Dynamic Buckling and Stability of Autonomous Dissipative Discrete Systems—Potential Systems." In *Nonlinear Stability of Structures: Theory and Computational Techniques*, edited by Anthony N. Kounadis and Wilfried B. Krätzig. Vienna: Springer 2014.

Kraemer, Casper J. "Bureaucracy and Petty Graft in Ancient Egypt." *The Classical Weekly* 20 (1927): 163–8.

Kramer, Samuel N. *The Sumerians: Their History, Culture, and Character*. Chicago: University of Chicago Press, 2010.

Kröger, Wolfgang. "Securing the Operation of Socially Critical Systems from an Engineering Perspective: New Challenges, Enhanced Tools and Novel Concepts." *European Journal for Security Research* 2 (2017): 39–55.

Kroner, Richard. "The Year 1800 in the Development of German Idealism." *The Review of Metaphysics* 1 (1948): 1–31.

Lacy-hulbert, Adam, James C. Metcalfe, and Robin Hesketh. "Biological Responses to Electromagnetic Fields 1." *The FASEB Journal* 12, no. 6 (1998): 395–420.

Laebens, Melis G., and Anna Lührmann. "What Halts Democratic Erosion? The Changing Role of Accountability." In *Resilience of Democracy*, edited by Anna Lührmann and Wolfgang Merkel, 40–60. Milton Park and Abingdon: Routledge, 2023.

Landau, David. "Constitution-Making Gone Wrong." *Alabama Law Review* 64 (2012): 923.

Lange, S., T. Viergutz, and M. Simko. "Modifications in Cell Cycle Kinetics and in Expression of G1 Phase-Regulating Proteins in Human Amniotic Cells after Exposure to Electromagnetic Fields and Ionizing Radiation." *Cell Proliferation* 37, no. 5 (2004): 337–49.

Langewiesche, Dieter. "Revolution in Germany." In *Europe in 1848*, edited by Dieter Dowe, Heinz-Gerhardt Haupt, Dieter Langewiesche, and Jonathan Sperber. New York and Oxford: Berghahn Books, 2008.

Leckey, Robert. "Following Same-Sex Marriage: Redefining Marriage and the Impact for Polygamy." *Les ateliers de l'éthique* 2, no. 1 (2007): 30–34. https://ssrn.com/abstract=2066100.

Lecomte, Eugene L., Alan W. Pang, and James W. Russell. *Ice Storm '98*. Institute for Catastrophic Loss Reduction Toronto, Canada, 1998.

Lee, Stephen J. *Hitler and Nazi Germany*. London: Taylor & Francis, 2013.

Lee, Stephen J. *The Weimar Republic*. London: Taylor & Francis, 2013.

Lee, W. Robert, and Jörg P. Vögele. "The Benefits of Federalism? The Development of Public Health Policy and Health Care Systems in Nineteenth-Century Germany and Their Impact on Mortality Reduction." Paper presented at the Annales de démographie historique, 2001.

Léger, Jean. *Histoire Generale Des Eglises Evangeliques Des Vallees De Piemont Ou Vaudoises*. Leiden: Jean le Carpentier, 1669.

Leipold, Andrew D. "Is Mass Incarceration Inevitable." *American Criminal Law Review* 56 (2019): 1579.

Lenssen, Nathan J. L., Gavin A. Schmidt, James E. Hansen, Matthew J. Menne, Avraham Persin, Reto Ruedy, and Daniel Zyss. "Improvements in the Gistemp Uncertainty Model." *Journal of Geophysical Research: Atmospheres* 124, no. 12 (2019): 6307–26.

Lethen, H., and D. Reneau. *Cool Conduct: The Culture of Distance in Weimar Germany*. Berkley, Los Angeles, and London: University of California Press, 2002.

Levinson, Bernard M. "Gerhard Von Rad's Struggle against the Nazification of the Old Testament." In *The Betrayal of the Humanities: The University during the Third Reich*, edited by Bernard M. Levinson and Robert P. Erickse. Bloomington: Indiana University Press, 2022.

Levinson, Bernard M., and Robert P. Ericksen, eds. *The Betrayal of the Humanities: The University during the Third Reich*. Bloomington: Indiana University Press, 2022.

Levinson, Bernard M., and Jeffrey Stackert. "Between the Covenant Code and Esarhaddon's Succession Treaty: Deuteronomy 13 and the Composition of Deuteronomy." *Journal of Ancient Judaism* 3, no. 2 (2012): 123–40.

Levitt, Steven D. "Juvenile Crime and Punishment." *Journal of Political Economy* 106, no. 6 (1998): 1156–85.

Lewis, Christopher. "The Paradox of Recidivism." *Emory Law Journal* 70 (2020): 1209.

Liang, Hsi-Huey. *The Berlin Police Force in the Weimar Republic.* Berkley, Los Angeles, and London: University of California Press, 2023.

Lippman, Matthew. "They Shoot Lawyers Don't They: Law in the Third Reich and the Global Threat to the Independence of the Judiciary." *California Western International Law Journal* 23 (1992): 257.

Lithwick, Dara. *A Pas De Deux: The Division of Federal and Provincial Legislative Powers in Sections 91 and 92 of the Constitution Act, 1867.* Ottawa: Library of Parliament, 2015.

Livni, Joseph. *The Biblical Roots of American Constitutionalism—from 'I Am the Lord' to 'We the People.'* Lanham: Lexington Books, 2021.

Livni, Joseph. "Christianity and the Romanian Communities Named Obşte." [In Romanian]. *Romanian Journal of Sociological Studies* 1 (January 2016): 61–71.

Livni, Joseph. "Investigation of Collapse of Complex Socio-Political Systems Using Classical Stability Theory." *Physica A: Statistical Mechanics and Its Applications* 524 (2019): 553–62.

Livni, Joseph. "Nomadism and the Sociological Seed of Pre-Monarchic Israel." Chap. 1 In *A Civil Society with No Hierarchy*, edited by Ilie Bădescu and Joseph Livni, 25–66. Lanham: Lexington Books, 2023.

Livni, Joseph, and Ilie Bădescu. "The Battle of the Covenantal Society against Elitism. An Overlooked Chapter in the History of Social Inequality." *Romanian Journal of Sociological Studies*, New Series, no. 1 (2020): 3–36.

Locatelli, Carlo. *Vita Di S. Ambrogio.* Milano: S. Majocchi, 1874.

Lohne, Jardar, Frode Drevland, Tina Åsgård, Tore Hoven, Ola Lædre, and Truls Ryum. "Homines Oeconomici or Moral Saints? On the Purpose of Educating Civil Engineers." Paper presented at the Proceedings of the 9th Nordic Conference on Construction Economics and Organization, 2017.

Long, Hannah T. S. "The Inequability of Incarceration." *Columbia Journal of Law and Social Problems* 31 (1997): 321.

Lotka, Alfred J. *Analytical Theory of Biological Populations.* New York: Plenum Press, 1998.

Lotka, Alfred J. "Contribution to the Theory of Periodic Reactions." *The Journal of Physical Chemistry* 14, no. 3 (1910): 271–4.

Lotka, Alfred J. *Elements of Physical Biology.* Baltimore: Williams & Wilkins, 1925.

Lührmann, Anna, and Wolfgang Merkel. *Resilience of Democracy: Responses to Illiberal and Authoritarian Challenges.* Milton Park and Abingdon: Routledge, 2023.

Lutz, Donald S. *Colonial Origins of the American Constitution: A Documentary History.* Indianapolis: Liberty Fund, 1998.

Lutz, Donald S. *The Origins of American Constitutionalism.* Baton Rouge: Louisiana State University Press, 1988.

Lutz, Henry F. "Kingship in Babylonia, Assyria, and Egypt." *American Anthropologist* 26, no. 4 (1924): 435–53.

Maffei, Massimo E. "Magnetic Fields and Cancer: Epidemiology, Cellular Biology, and Theranostics." *International Journal of Molecular Sciences* 23, no. 3 (2022): 1339–54.

Mancini, Anna. *Maat Revealed, Philosophy of Justice in Ancient Egypt*. Buenos Aires: Buenos Books America, 2004.

Măndiță, Mădălina. "The Covenant as Ideal Type, a Sociological Study of a Covenanted Community Model." In *A Civil Society with no Hierarchy*, edited by Ilie Bădescu and Joseph Livni. Lanham: Lexington Books, 2023.

Manowitz, Bernard. "Global Climate Feedbacks." Upton: Brookhaven National Lab., 1990.

Marchand, Suzanne L. "The 'Orient' and 'Us.'" In *The Betrayal of the Humanities: The University during the Third Reich*, edited by Bernard M. Levinson and Robert P. Ericksen, Bloomington: Indiana University Press, 2022.

Marie, Olivier. "Education Is Key to Deconstruct Racial Narratives." Edited by UN. Paris: UNESCO, 2023.

Markov, M., and Y. Grigoriev. "Protect Children from Emf." *Electromagnetic Biology and Medicine* 34, no. 3 (2015): 251–6.

Martos, Marcella, and Meredith Turnbough. "Protein Parts." Arizona State University School of Life Sciences Ask a Biologist. https://askabiologist.asu.edu/venom/building-blocks-protein.

Marx, Karl, and Fridrich Engels. *The Communist Manifesto*. Redwood City: SoftBook Press, 2020.

Masson-Delmotte, Valérie, Panmao Zhai, Hans-Otto Pörtner, Debra Roberts, Jim Skea, and Priyadarshi R. Shukla. *Global Warming of 1.5 C: Ipcc Special Report on Impacts of Global Warming of 1.5 C above Pre-Industrial Levels in Context of Strengthening Response to Climate Change, Sustainable Development, and Efforts to Eradicate Poverty*. Cambridge: Cambridge University Press, 2022.

Mazzacano, Peter. "From Covenant to Compact to Contract: The Legal Transplantation of Puritan Jurisprudence to America." In *A Civil Society with No Hierarchy*, edited by Ilie Bădescu and Joseph Livni. Lanham: Lexington Books, 2023.

McCallum, Dennis. "The Waldensian Movement from Waldo to the Reformation." American Waldesian Society, History: Founded in the Middle Ages, Waldenses, Global Anabaptist Mennonite Encyclopedia, 2014.

McCoy, Charles S., and Wayne J. Baker. *Fountainhead of Federalism: Heinrich Bullinger and the Covenantal Tradition*. Louisville: Westminster John Knox Press, 1991.

McDonald, Maryon. "Accountability, Anthropology and the European Commission." In *Audit Cultures*, edited by Marilyn Strathern, 118–44. London and New York: Routledge, 2003.

McIlwain, Charles Howard. *Constitutionalism: Ancient and Modern*. Clark: Lawbook Exchange, 2005.

McKean, Lise, and Charles Ransford. *Current Strategies for Reducing Recidivism*. Center for Impact Research Chicago, 2004.

McKechnie, William S. *Magna Carta: A Commentary on the Great Charter of King John*. New York: Burt Franklin, 1914.

McNamee, Stephen J. "The Meritocracy Myth Revisited." *Sociation Today* 12, no. 2 (2014).

Mechler, Reinhard, Chandni Singh, Kristie Ebi, Riyante Djalante, Adelle Thomas, Rachel James, Petra Tschakert, et al. "Loss and Damage and Limits to Adaptation: Recent Ipcc Insights and Implications for Climate Science and Policy." *Sustainability Science* 15 (2020): 1245–51.

Mili, Lamine, Qun Qiu, and Arun G. Phadke. "Risk Assessment of Catastrophic Failures in Electric Power Systems." *International Journal of Critical Infrastructures* 1, no. 1 (2004): 38–63.

Millar, Charlotte-Rose. "Iii. 9 Church and Parish Records." In *Early Modern Emotions*, edited by Susan Brrohall, 153–5. London and New York: Routledge, 2016.

Mingarelli, Bernardo. "Collapse of the Hunnic Empire: Jordanes, Ardaric and the Battle of Nedao." Ottawa: Université d'Ottawa/University of Ottawa, 2018.

Mipham, Jamgon, and José I. Cabezon. *The Just King: The Tibetan Buddhist Classic on Leading an Ethical Life*. Boulder: Shambhala, 2017.

Mitterrand, François. *Le Coup D'état Permanent*. Vol. 296. Paris: Plon Paris, 1964.

Montada, Leo, and Jürgen Maes. "Introduction." In *Handbook of Social Justice Theory and Research*, edited by Clara Sabbagh and Manfred Schmitt, 237–56. Heidelberg, Dordrecht, and London: Springer, 2016.

Montesquieu, Charles de Secondat baron de. *The Spirit of Laws*. London and New York: Colonial Press, 1900.

Moreau, Claudia, Rose-Marie Rebillard, Stefan Wolking, Jacques L. Michaud, Frederique Tremblay, Alexandre Girard, Joanie Bouchard, et al. "Polygenic Risk Scores of Several Subtypes of Epilepsies in a Founder Population." *bioRxiv* (2019): 728816.

Morice, Colin P., John J. Kennedy, Nick A. Rayner, and Phil D. Jones. "Quantifying Uncertainties in Global and Regional Temperature Change Using an Ensemble of Observational Estimates: The Hadcrut4 Data Set." *Journal of Geophysical Research: Atmospheres* 117, no. D8 (2012).

Myers, Krista F., Peter T. Doran, John Cook, John E. Kotcher, and Teresa A. Myers. "Consensus Revisited: Quantifying Scientific Agreement on Climate Change and Climate Expertise among Earth Scientists 10 Years Later." *Environmental Research Letters* 16, no. 10 (2021): 104030.

Nakagawa, Masayoshi. "A Study on Extremely Low-Frequency Electric and Magnetic Fields and Cancer: Discussion of Emf Safety Limits." *Journal of Occupational Health* 39, no. 1 (1997): 18–28.

Neugebauer, Otto. *The Exact Sciences in Antiquity*. Second edition. New York: Dover Publications, 1969.

Nixon, St. John C. *The Invention of the Automobile—(Karl Benz and Gottlieb Daimler)*. Ancarano: Edizioni Savine, 2016.

Notter, Dominic A., Marcel Gauch, Rolf Widmer, Patrick Wäger, Anna Stamp, Rainer Zah, and Hans-Jörg Althaus. "Contribution of Li-Ion Batteries to the Environmental Impact of Electric Vehicles." *Environmental Science & Technology* 44, no. 17 (2010/09/01 2010): 6550–6.

Novak, David. *Covenantal Rights, a Study in Jewish Political Theory*. Princeton: Princeton University Press, 2000.

Nuño, Juan C., Miguel A. Herrero, and Mario Primicerio. "A Triangle Model of Criminality." *Physica A: Statistical Mechanics and Its Applications* 387, no. 12 (2008): 2926–36.

Nussbaum, Martha C. *Hiding from Humanity: Disgust, Shame, and the Law.* Princeton: Princeton University Press, 2009.

Nyirkos, Tamás. *The Tyranny of the Majority: History, Concepts, and Challenges.* New York: Taylor & Francis, 2018.

OECD. *Pensions at a Glance 2019 Oecd and G20 Indicators.* Paris: OECD Publishing, 2019.

Oliner, Samuel P., and Pearl Oliner. *Altruistic Personality: Rescuers of Jews in Nazi Europe.* New York: Touchstone, 1992.

Olliaro, Piero, Els Torreele, and Michel Vaillant. "Covid-19 Vaccine Efficacy and Effectiveness—the Elephant (Not) in the Room." *The Lancet Microbe* 2, no. 7 (2021): e279–e80.

Oppenheim, A. Leo. "On an Operational Device in Mesopotamian Bureaucracy." *Journal of Near Eastern Studies* 18, no. 2 (1959): 121–8.

Osmond, Candace. "Muddy the Waters - Idiom, Meaning, and Origin." The Grammarist. https://grammarist.com/idiom/muddy-the-waters/.

Outram, Dorinda. *Panorama of the Enlightenment.* Los Angeles: J. Paul Getty Museum, 2006.

Paravy, Pierrette. *De La Chrétienté Romaine À La Réforme En Dauphiné. Évêques, Fidèles Et Déviants (Vers 1340–Vers 1350).* [in Français] Collection De L'école Française De Rome. Vol. 1. Rome: École française de Rome, 1993.

Parker, Andrew J. "Revealing Rembrandt." *Frontiers in Neuroscience* 8 (2014): 76.

Parmesan, Camille, Carlos Duarte, Elvira Poloczanska, Anthony J. Richardson, and Michael C. Singer. "Overstretching Attribution." *Nature Climate Change* 1, no. 1 (2011): 2–4.

Parry, Roland Lloyd, and Marlowe Hood. "Posts Downplaying Climate 'Emergency' Cite Paper with Cherry-Picked Evidence." *AFP*, 2022.

Pearson, Roger. *Voltaire Almighty: A Life in Pursuit of Freedom.* London: Bloomsbury Publishing, 2010.

Pérez, Orlando J. "Democratic Legitimacy and Public Insecurity: Crime and Democracy in El Salvador and Guatemala." *Political Science Quarterly* 118 (2003): 627.

Perlstein, Michael. "NOPD Says 71 Arrested in Recent Weeks; Murders, Shootings Down through June." *4WWL*, 2018.

Peukert, Detlev. *The Weimar Republic.* New York: Farrar, Straus and Giroux, 1993.

Peyran, Jean Rodolphe. *An Historical Defence of the Waldenses or Vaudois.* London: C & J Rivington, 1826.

Pfister, Ulrich, Jan-Otmar Spoerer Hesse, Mark, and Nikolaus Wol. *An Economic History of the First German Unification.* London and New York: Routledge, 2023.

Philbrick, Nathanel. *Mayflower: A Story of Courage, Community, and War.* Kindle edition. New York: Penguin Publishing Group, 2006.

Pidwirny, M. *Chapter 14: The Oceans: Single Chapter from the Ebook Understanding Physical Geography.* Kelowna, BC: Our Planet Earth Publishing, 2023.

Pielke Jr., Roger A., Chris Landsea, Max Mayfield, J. Layer, and Richard Pasch. "Hurricanes and Global Warming." *Bulletin of the American Meteorological Society* 86, no. 11 (2005): 1571–6.

Pokorny, Julius. "Indogermanisches Etymologisches Wörterbuch." Bern: Francke, 1959.

Popov, Vladimir. "The State in the New Russia (1992–2004): From Collapse to Gradual Revival?." *PONARS Policy Memos* 324 (2004).

Porta, Miguel S. *A Dictionary of Epidemiology*. Oxford: Oxford University Press, 2016.
Portier, C., M. S. Wolfe, and NIEHS Working Group. *Assessment of Health Effects from Exposure to Power-Line Frequency Electric and Magnetic Fields: Niehs Working Group Report*. Research Triangle Park: National Institute of Environmental Health Sciences, U.S. National Institute of Health, U.S. Department of Health and Human Services, Public Health Services, 1998.
Porzio, Jason, and Corinne D. Scown. "Life-Cycle Assessment Considerations for Batteries and Battery Materials." *Advanced Energy Materials* 11, no. 33 (2021): 2100771.
Pouzet, Philippe. "Les Origines Lyonnaises De La Secte Des Vaudois." *Revue d'histoire de l'Église de France* 22, no. 94 (1936): 5–37.
Pratchett, Terry. *Thief of Time: A Discworld Novel*. New York: HarperCollins, 2009.
Preuß, Hugo. "Über Organpersönlichkeit: Eine Begriffskritische Studie." *Jahrbuch für Gesetzgebung, Verwaltung und Volkswirtschaft im Deutschen Reich* 26 (1902): 1–54.
Pross, Christian. "Breaking through the Postwar Coverup of Nazi Doctors in Germany." *Journal of Medical Ethics* 17, no. Suppl (1991): 13.
"Proyecto De Reformas Con Y Para El Poder Judicial De La Federación." Edited by Poder Judicial de la Federacion. Mexico City: Government of Mexico, 2020.
Pryor, Frederic L. "The Red and the Green: The Rise and Fall of Collectivized Agriculture in Marxist Regimes." 2014. https://works.swarthmore.edu/fac-economics/91.
Przeworski, A. *Democracy and the Market: Political and Economic Reforms in Eastern Europe and Latin America*. Cambridge: Cambridge University Press, 1991.
Rajagopalan, Shruti. "Incompatible Institutions: Socialism Versus Constitutionalism in India." *Constitutional Political Economy* 26 (2015): 328–55.
Ramoni, Monsuru Olalekan, and Hong-Chao Zhang. "End-of-Life (Eol) Issues and Options for Electric Vehicle Batteries." *Clean Technologies and Environmental Policy* 15 (2013): 881–91.
Rao, Gita, and Aaron Krol. "Investing and Climate Change." MIT, Climate Portal. https://climate.mit.edu/explainers/investing-and-climate-change.
Raval, Ameet, and Veerabhadran Ramanathan. "Observational Determination of the Greenhouse Effect." Paper presented at the Global Climate Feedbacks; No. BNL-45321; CONF-9006134, Upton, 1990.
Ravetz, Jerome R. *Scientific Knowledge and Its Social Problems*. Milton Park: Taylor & Francis, 2020.
Rawls, John. *A Theory of Justice: Original Edition*. Cambridge, MA: Harvard University Press, 2005.
Rayner, Gordon. "Leveson Inquiry: British Press Freedom Is a Model for the World, Editor Tells Inquiry." *The Telegraph*, 2011.
Reay-Jones, Francis P. F. "Pest Status and Management of Corn Earworm (Lepidoptera: Noctuidae) in Field Corn in the United States." *Journal of Integrated Pest Management* 10, no. 1 (2019): 19.
Redslob, Robert. *Le Régime Parlementaire: Étude Sur Les Institutions D'angleterre, De Belgique, De Hongrie, De Suède, De France, De Tchécoslovaquie, De L'empire Allemand, De Prusse, De Bavière Et D'autriche*. Paris: M. Giard, 1924.
"Regulations for Greenhouse Gas Emissions from Passenger Cars and Trucks." Edited by US Government/EPA. Internet 2023. htps://www.epa.gov/regulations-emissions-vehicles-and-engines/regulations-greenhouse-gas-emissions-passenger-cars-and#Overview.

Rennard, Barbara O., Ronald F. Ertl, Gail L. Gossman, Richard A. Robbins, and Stephen I. Rennard. “Chicken Soup Inhibits Neutrophil Chemotaxis in Vitro.” *Chest* 118, no. 4 (2000): 1150–7.

“Research and Development: U.S. Trends and International Comparisons.” Edited by National Science Foundation. Alexandria: National Science Board, 2022.

Riddle, Stewart, and Michael W. Apple. “Education and Democracy in Dangerous Times.” In *Re-Imagining Education for Democracy*, edited by Stewart Riddle and Michael W Apple, 1–10. London: Routledge, 2019.

Ritchie, Hannah, Max Roser, and Pablo Rosado. “Co_2 and Greenhouse Gas Emissions.” OurWorldInData.org. https://ourworldindata.org/co2-and-greenhouse-gas-emissions.

Robinson, Ian S. *Measuring the Oceans from Space: The Principles and Methods of Satellite Oceanography*. Berlin, Heidelberg, and New York: Springer 2004.

Roodenburg, Herman. *Social Control in Europe: 1500–1800*. Columbus: Ohio State University Press, 2004.

Rosenzweig, Michael L. “Loss of Speciation Rate Will Impoverish Future Diversity.” *Proceedings of the National Academy of Sciences* 98, no. 10 (2001): 5404–10.

Rosner, Fred. *The Medical Legacy of Moses Maimonides*. Hoboken: KTAV Publishing House, 1998.

Ross, Jennifer C., and Sharon R. Steadman. *Ancient Complex Societies*. New York and London: Taylor & Francis, 2017.

Rossi, Carla. “The Role of Dynamic Modelling in Drug Abuse Epidemiology.” *Bulletin on Narcotics* LIV, no. 1 and 2 (2002): 33–44.

Rossner, Meredith, and Helen Taylor. “The Transformative Potential of Restorative Justice: What the Mainstream Can Learn from the Margins.” *Annual Review of Criminology* 7 (2024): 357–81.

Rousseau, Jean-Jacques, Quintin Hoare, and Christofer Bertram. *Of the Social Contract and Other Political Writings*. London: Penguin Books Limited, 2012.

Rousselier, Nicolas. “France and the Fifth Republic.” In *Constitutional Democracy in Crisis?*, edited by Mark A. Graber, Sanford Levinson, and Mark Tushnet, 215–25. New York: Oxford University Press, 2018.

Rovelli, Carlo. “Aristotle’s Physics: A Physicist’s Look.” *Journal of the American Philosophical Association* 1, no. 1 (2015): 23–40.

Rutherford, Samuel. *Lex, Rex, or, the Law and the Prince*. Penn Laird: Sprinkle Publications, 1982.

Sabbagh, Clara, and Manfred Schmitt. “Introduction.” In *Handbook of Social Justice Theory and Research*, edited by Clara Sabbagh and Manfred Schmitt, 237–56. Heidelberg, Dordrecht, and London: Springer, 2016.

Sabetti, Filippo. “Covenant Language in Canada.” Paper presented at the Workshop on Covenant and Politics, Center for the Study of Federalism, Temple University, 1980.

Sabine, George H., and Thomas L. Thorson. *A History of Political Theory*. Oxford: Oxford and IBH Publishing, 2018.

Sadler, Michael. “The History of Education.” In *Germany in the Nineteenth Century: Five Lectures*, edited by John H. Rose, Charles H. Herford, Edward C. K. Gonner, and Michael Sadler. Manchester: Manchester University Press, 1912.

Sagan, Carl. *Dragons of Eden: Speculations on the Evolution of Human Intelligence*. New York: Ballantine Books, 2012.

Sagan, Carl, and Ann Druyan. *The Varieties of Scientific Experience: A Personal View of the Search for God.* Kindle edition. London: Penguin, 2006.
Sakamoto, Arthur, Kimberly A. Goyette, and ChangHwan Kim. "Socioeconomic Attainments of Asian Americans." *Annual Review of Sociology* 35 (2009): 255–76.
Sallustius, Crispus C. and Charles Anthon, *Jugurthine War.* New York: Harper, 1840.
Salzman, Michele Renee. *The Making of a Christian Aristocracy: Social and Religious Change in the Western Roman Empire.* Kindle edition. Cambridge, MA: Harvard University Press, 2002.
Samson, Steven Alan. "Covenant Origins of the American Polity." *Faculty Publications and Presentations. 5.* Liberty University, 1994.
Sanguesa, Julio A., Vicente Torres-Sanz, Piedad Garrido, Francisco J. Martinez, and Johann M. Marquez-Barja. "A Review on Electric Vehicles: Technologies and Challenges." *Smart Cities* 4, no. 1 (2021): 372–404.
Sant, Edda. "Democratic Education: A Theoretical Review (2006–2017)." *Review of Educational Research* 89, no. 5 (2019): 655–96.
Santini, L. *De Pierre Valdo À L'eglise Vaudoise.* Geneva: Labor et Fides, 1974.
Savitz, David A., Howard Wachtel, Frank A. Barnes, Esther M. John, and Jiri G. Tvrdik. "Case-Control Study of Childhood Cancer and Exposure to 60-Hz Magnetic Fields." *American Journal of Epidemiology* 128, no. 1 (1988): 21–38.
Scheidel, Walter. *Debating Roman Demography.* Leiden: Brill, 2001.
Schmitt, Carl, and Ellen Kennedy. *The Crisis of Parliamentary Democracy.* Edited by Carl Schmitt. Cambridge, MA and London: MIT Press, 1988.
Schott, Richard L. "The Origins of Bureaucracy: An Anthropological Perspective." *International Journal of Public Administration* 23, no. 1 (January 01, 2000): 53–78.
Schrag, Joel, and Suzanne Scotchmer. "The Self-Reinforcing Nature of Crime." *International Review of Law and Economics* 17, no. 3 (1997): 325–35.
Schuelke-Leech, Beth-Anne. "The Place of Wicked Problems in Engineering Problem Solving: A Proposed Taxonomy." Paper presented at the 2020 IEEE International Symposium on Technology and Society (ISTAS), 2020.
Schulte, Peter, Laia Alegret, Ignacio Arenillas, José A. Arz, Penny J. Barton, Paul R. Bown, Timothy J. Bralower, et al. "The Chicxulub Asteroid Impact and Mass Extinction at the Cretaceous-Paleogene Boundary." *Science* 327, no. 5970 (2010): 1214–18.
Schultz, David A. *Encyclopedia of the United States Constitution.* New York: Infobase Publishing, 2010.
Schwitzgebel, Eric. "Human Nature and Moral Education in Mencius, Xunzi, Hobbes, and Rousseau." *History of Philosophy Quarterly* 24, no. 2 (2007): 147–68.
Seomun, GyeongAe, Juneyoung Lee, and Jinkyung Park. "Exposure to Extremely Low-Frequency Magnetic Fields and Childhood Cancer: A Systematic Review and Meta-Analysis." *PLoS One* 16, no. 5 (2021): e0251628.
Şerban, Adela. "Brief Theoretical Perspective on Traditional Society." In *A Civil Society with no Hierarchy: The Covenantal Societal Model*, edited by Ilie Bădescu and Joseph Livni, 207–25. Lanham: Lexington Books, 2023.
Shahaed, Heba, Sai Surabi Thirugnanasampanthar, and Dale Guenter. "Make or Break: Succeeding in Transition from Incarceration." *PLoS One* 19, no. 1 (2024): e0296947.
Shirer, William L. *Rise and Fall of the Third Reich: A History of Nazi Germany.* New York: Simon & Schuster, 1990.

Siemens, Daniel. "Explaining Crime: Berlin Newspapers and the Construction of the Criminal in Weimar Germany." *Journal of European Studies* 39, no. 3 (2009): 336–52.

Šmahel, František. "Crypto-Et Semi-Vaudois Dans La Bohême Hussite." *Revue de l'histoire des religions* 217 (2000): 101–20.

Smelser, Ronald M. "Hitler and the Dnsap. Between Democracy and Gleichschaltung." *Bohemia* 20, no. 1 (1979): 137–55.

Smith, William. *Dictionary of Greek and Roman Antiquities.* London: C.C. Little and J. Brown, 1853.

Society, Royal. *Proceedings of the Royal Society of London: Containing Papers of a Mathematical and Physical Character. Series A.* London: Harrison and Son, 1909.

Somer, Murat, Jennifer L. McCoy, and Russell E. Luke. "Pernicious Polarization, Autocratization and Opposition Strategies." In *Resilience of Democracy*, edited by Anna Lührmann and Wolfgang Merkel, 61–80. Milton Park and Abingdon: Routledge, 2023.

Spencer, Herbert. *Essays, Scientific, Political, and Speculative.* New York: D. Appleton, 1892.

Spiro, H. John. "Constitution." In *Encyclopaedia Britannica*. Chicago: Encyclopædia Britannica, Inc., 2024 https://www.britannica.com/topic/constitution-politics-and-law.

Squire, Peverill. *The Rise of the Representative: Lawmakers and Constituents in Colonial America.* Ann Arbor: University of Michigan Press, 2017.

Srinivasulu, Karli. "Caste, Class and Social Articulation in Andhra Pradesh: Mapping Differential Regional Trajectories." Hyderabad: Osmania University, 2002.

Sripati, Vijayashri. "Constitutionalism in India and South Africa: A Comparative Study from a Human Rights Perspective." University of Alberta, 2006.

Stahl, Henri H. *Traditional Romanian Village Communities.* Cambridge: Cambridge University Press, 1980.

Starr-LeBeau, Gretchen, and Kimberly Lynn. "Inquisitions." In *Judging Faith, Punishing Sin*, edited by C. H. Parker and G. Starr-LeBeau. Cambridge: Cambridge University Press, 2017.

State of California. "Governor Newsom Announces California Will Phase out Gasoline-Powered Cars & Drastically Reduce Demand for Fossil Fuel in California's Fight against Climate Change." Edited by Office of Governor. Sacramento, 2020. https://www.gov.ca.gov/2020/09/23/governor-newsom-announces-california-will-phase-out-gasoline-powered-cars-drastically-reduce-demand-for-fossil-fuel-in-californias-fight-against-climate-change/.

Steinberg, Dave S. *Cooling Techniques for Electronic Equipment.* Hoboken: Wiley, 1991.

Steinberg, Dave S. *Vibration Analysis for Electronic Equipment.* Hoboken: Wiley-Interscence, 2000.

Stirk, Peter. "Hugo Preuss, German Political Thought and the Weimar Constitution." *History of Political Thought* 23, no. 3 (2002): 497–516.

Strum, Arthur. "What Enlightenment Is." *New German Critique*, no. 79 (2000): 106–36.

Sullivan, Larry E. *The Sage Glossary of the Social and Behavioral Sciences.* Los Angeles, London, New Delhi, Singapore, and Wasington, DC: SAGE Publications, 2009.

Sultan, Vivian, and Brian Hilton. "A Spatial Analytics Framework to Investigate Electric Power-Failure Events and Their Causes." *ISPRS International Journal of Geo-information* 9, no. 1 (2020): 54.

Swedberg, Richard. *Max Weber and the Idea of Economic Sociology*. Princeton: Princeton University Press, 2018.

Tainter, Joseph A. *The Collapse of Complex Societies*. Cambridge: Cambridge University Press, 1990.

Tainter, Joseph A. "Social Complexity and Sustainability." *Ecological Complexity* 3, no. 2 (2006): 91–103.

Tang, Yanyan, Qi Zhang, Yaoming Li, Hailong Li, Xunzhang Pan, and Benjamin Mclellan. "The Social-Economic-Environmental Impacts of Recycling Retired Ev Batteries under Reward-Penalty Mechanism." *Applied Energy* 251 (2019): 113313.

Taylor, Bayard. *A School History of Germany: From the Earliest Period to the Establishment of the German Empire in 1871*. New York: D. Appleton & Company, 1874.

Taylor-Gooby, and Benjamin Leruth. "Why British People Don't Trust the Government Any More – and What Can Be Done About It." *The Conversation*, 2018.

Teague, Elizabeth. "Russia's Constitutional Reforms of 2020." *Russian Politics* 5, no. 3 (2020): 301–28.

Tec, Nechama. *When Light Pierced the Darkness: Christian Rescue of Jews in Nazi-Occupied Poland*. Oxford: Oxford University Press, 1987.

Teeman, Colby. "Does Chicken Soup Really Help When You're Sick?." *The Conversation*. https://theconversation.com/does-chicken-soup-really-help-when-youre-sick-a-nutrition-specialist-explains-whats-behind-the-beloved-comfort-food-213847.

Tocqueville, Alexis de. *Democracy in America*. Translated by Henry Reeve. Kindle edition. Vol. 1. Project Gutenberg, 2006. https://www.gutenberg.org/ebooks/815.

Town of Winchester. "Boards and Committees." Winchester, 2024. https://www.winchester.us/251/Boards-and-Committees.

Trinterud, Leonard J. "The Origins of Puritanism." *Church History* 20, no. 1 (1951): 37–57.

True, Hans. "Nonlinear Vehicle Dynamics." In *Road and Off-Road Vehicle System Dynamics Handbook*, edited by G. Mastinu and M. Ploechl, 69–120. Boca Raton: CRC Press, 2014.

Turchin, Peter. *Complex Population Dynamics: A Theoretical/Empirical Synthesis (Mpb-35)*. Princeton: Princeton University Press, 2013.

Turcotte, Claude. "L'après—Crise Aura Coûté Deux Milliards." *Le Devoir*, 2008.

Turner, Bryan S. *Max Weber: From History to Modernity*. London and New York: Taylor & Francis, 2002.

Tynes, Tore, Aage Andersen, and FrØydis Langmark. "Incidence of Cancer in Norwegian Workers Potentially Exposed to Electromagnetic Fields." *American Journal of Epidemiology* 136, no. 1 (1992): 81–8.

US Government. "Climate Change." Edited by EPA. https://www.epa.gov/climate-change: Internet 2023.

US Government. "Energy Efficiency and Renewable Energy." In *FY 2024 Congressional Justification*, edited by DOE. Washington, DC: Department of Energy, 2003.

US Government BTS. "U.S. Vehicle-Miles." In *Table 1–35*, edited by Department of Transportation. Washington, DC: Bureau of Transportation Statistics, 2022.

US Government EERE. "Funding Opportunities." Edited by Energy. Washington, DC, 2023. https://www.energy.gov/eere/funding/eere-funding-opportunities.

US Government EIA. "Carbon Dioxide Emissions Coefficients." Edited by EIA. Washington, DC, 2023. https://www.eia.gov/environment/emissions/co2_vol_mass.php.

US Government EIA. "Electric Power Annual 2022." Edited by Department of Energy. Washington, DC, 2022. https://www.eia.gov/electricity/Annual/pdf/epa.pdf.

US Government EIA. "Gasoline Explained." Edited by Department of Energy. Washington, DC: Independent Statistics and Analysis, 2023.

US Government EPA. "Epa Report: U.S. Cars Achieve Record High Fuel Economy and Low Emission Levels as Companies Fully Comply with Standards." Edited by EPA. Washington, DC, 2021. https://www.epa.gov/newsreleases/epa-report-us-cars-achieve-record-high-fuel-economy-and-low-emission-levels-companies.

US Government EPA. "Fuel Economy Impact of Rfg." In *EPA 420-F-95-03*, edited by EPA. Washington, DC: EPA Office of mobile source, 1995.

US Government EPA. "Lithium-Ion Battery Recycling Frequently Asked Questions." Edited by EPA. Washington, DC, 2023. https://www.epa.gov/hw/lithium-ion-battery-recycling-frequently-asked-questions#hazwaste.

US Government EPA. "Mission Statement." Edited by EPA. Washington, DC, 2023. https://www.epa.gov/aboutepa/our-mission-and-what-we-do.

US Government FAA. "Federal Aviation Regulations; Sec. 25.233—Directional Stability and Control." In *Part 25*, edited by FAA. Washington, DC: Federal Aviation Administration, 1992.

US Government NTSB. "Aircraft Accident Report Ntsb/Aar-92/06." Washington, DC: NTSB-National Transportation Safety Board, 1992.

US Government NTSB. "Aircraft Accident Report Ntsb/Aar-99/01." Washington, DC: NTSB-National Transportation Safety Board, 1999.

van Cutsem, Thierry, and Costas Vournas. *Voltage Stability of Electric Power Systems*. New York: Springer, 2007.

Van der Horst, Peter W. *Ancient Jewish Epitaphs*. Louvain: Peeters Publishers, 1991.

Van Deth, Jan W. "Studying Political Participation: Towards a Theory of Everything." Paper presented at the Joint Sessions of Workshops of the European Consortium for Political Research, Grenoble, 2001.

Viscusi, W. Kip. "The Risks and Rewards of Criminal Activity: A Comprehensive Test of Criminal Deterrence." *Journal of Labor Economics* 4, no. 3, Part 1 (1986): 317–40.

Vlassopoulos, Kostas. "Free Spaces: Identity, Experience and Democracy in Classical Athens." *The Classical Quarterly* 57, no. 1 (2007): 33–52.

Vögele, Jörg, and Wolfgang Woelk. "Public Health and the Development of Infant Mortality in Germany, 1875–1930." *The History of the Family* 7, no. 4 (2002): 585–99.

Volterra, Vito. "Variations and Fluctuations of the Number of Individuals in Animal Species Living Together." *ICES Journal of Marine Science* Vol. 3, no. 1 (1928): 3–51.

Wang, Zhijian, Shijin Shuai, Zhijie Li, and Wenbin Yu. "A Review of Energy Loss Reduction Technologies for Internal Combustion Engines to Improve Brake Thermal Efficiency." *Energies* 14, no. 20 (2021): 6656.

Wardle, Lynn D. "The Constitution as Covenant." *Brigham Young University Studies* 27, no. 3 (1987): 11–28.

Weber, Max, and Talcott Parsons. *The Theory of Social and Economic Organization.* New York: Simon & Schuster, 2009.
Weil, Frederick D. "The Variable Effects of Education on Liberal Attitudes: A Comparative-Historical Analysis of Anti-Semitism Using Public Opinion Survey Data." *American Sociological Review* 50, no. 4 (1985): 458–74.
Weiner, Douglas R. "The Roots of 'Michurinism': Transformist Biology and Acclimatization as Currents in the Russian Life Sciences." *Annals of Science* 42, no. 3 (1985): 243–60.
Weirich, Paul. "Rousseau on Proportional Majority Rule." *Philosophy and Phenomenological Research* 47, no. 1 (1986): 111–26.
Wenzel, Michael, and Tyler G. Okimoto. "Retributive Justice." In *Handbook of Social Justice Theory and Research*, edited by Clara Sabbagh and Manfred Schmitt, 237–56. Heidelberg, Dordrecht, and London: Springer, 2016.
Wesseling, Henk. "History: Science or Art?." *European Review* 6, no. 3 (1998): 265–7.
West, Franklin C. *A Crisis of the Weimar Republic: A Study of the German Referendum of 20 June 1926.* Philadelphia: American Philosophical Society, 1985.
Whiteway, Augustine Robert. "The Pyrenean Neighbour; or, the Vicinal System in the Western Pyrenees." *Archaeological Journal* 58, no. 1 (1901): 182–98.
Wildt, Michael. *An Uncompromising Generation: The Nazi Leadership of the Reich Security Main Office.* Madison: University of Wisconsin Press, 2009.
Wilkinson, Benjamin G. *Our Authorized Bible Vindicated.* Fort Oglethorpe: Teach Services, 2014.
Williams, Joan C. "The Constitutional Vulnerability of American Local Government: The Politics of City Status in American Law." *Wisconsin Law Review* (1986): 83.
Williamson, David G. *Bismarck and Germany: 1862–1890.* London and New York: Taylor & Francis, 2013.
Willyams, Jealn Loisa. *A Short History of the Waldensian Church in the Walleys of Piedmont.* London: James Nisbet et co., 1855.
Winter, Irene. "Touched by the Gods: Visual Evidence for the Divine Status of Rulers in the Ancient near East." Paper presented at the Oriental Institute Seminars 4, Chicago, 2008.
Winthrop, John. *Winthrop Papers*, edited by Robert Charles Winthrop Jr., Vol. 3. Boston: Massachusetts Historical Society, 1947.
Wood, Allan T. "What Is Renewal, Why Now?." In *Education and the Making of a Democratic People*, edited by J. I. Goodlad, R. Soder, and B. McDaniel, 29–47. Milton Park: Taylor & Francis, 2015.
Wright, Thomas. *The History of France: From the Earliest Period Fo the Present Time.* London and New York: London Print and Publishing Company, 1858.
Wuebbles, Donald J., David W. Fahey, and Kathy A. Hibbard, eds. *Climate Science Special Report: Fourth National Climate Assessment*, Volume I. U.S. Global Change Research Program, 2017. https://doi.org/10.7930/J0J964J6.
Wylie J.R., Clarence R. *Advanced Engineering Mathematics.* New York: Mc-Graw-Hill, 1966.
Yang, Xue. "The Confucianization of Law and the Lenient Punishments in China." *International Journal of Criminal Justice Sciences* 10, no. 1 (2015): 32–47.
Yankelovich, Daniel, and Will Friedman. *Toward Wiser Public Judgment.* Nashville: Vanderbilt University Press, 2010.

York, Historical Records Survey. New. *Guide to Vital Statistics Records of Churches in New York State (Exclusive of New York City).* WPA, 1942.
Zhang, Huai-Min, Jay H. Lawrimore, Boyin Huang, Matthew J. Menne, Xungang Yin, Ahira Sánchez-Lugo, Byron E. Gleason, et al. "Updated Temperature Data Give a Sharper View of Climate Trends." *Eos* 100 (2019). https://doi.org/10.1029/2019EO128229.
Zhao, Haiyun, Zhilan Feng, and Carlos Castillo-Chavez. "The Dynamics of Poverty and Crime." MTBI-02-08M (2002): 225–35.
Zipernovszky, Hanna. "Parish Records as a Source for Comparitive Pedagogical Research." *Scriptum* (2002): 46–55.
Zoekauer, Ludovico. "Sui Framenti I Piu Antichi Del Constituto Di Pistoia." In *Rivista Italiana Per Le Scienze Giuridiche*, edited by G. Fusinato and F. Schupfer, 72–81. Roma: E. Loescher & Company, 1892.

Index

About the Author

For thirty-four years (1979–2013) **Joseph Livni** was busy creating and applying mathematical modeling of aircraft physics. The models certified that aircraft systems like fuel, hydraulic, electrical, and flight control will withstand severe vibrations during flight. Other models served to demonstrate aero-elastic stability and structural integrity during hard landing and during emergency landing on ground and water. For aircraft in service Joseph generated and utilized models to diagnose and fix failures of systems due to excessive vibration.

After retirement Joseph turned to use his experience in mathematical modeling to investigate controversial topics in biological and social phenomena; in academic terms he changed direction from aerospace engineering to biophysics and socio-physics. He is the author or coauthor/co-editor of ten articles, two monographs, and one edited collection.

www.ingramcontent.com/pod-product-compliance
Ingram Content Group UK Ltd.
Pitfield, Milton Keynes, MK11 3LW, UK
UKHW020216290926
15470UKWH00001B/217

9 781666 965216